Classical Period Wind Band and Wind Ensemble Repertoire

Books by David Whitwell

Philosophic Foundations of Education
Foundations of Music Education
Music Education of the Future
The Sousa Oral History Project
The Art of Musical Conducting
The Longy Club: 1900–1917
A Concise History of the Wind Band
Wagner on Bands
Berlioz on Bands
Chopin: A Self-Portrait
La Téléphonie and the Universal Musical Language
Extraordinary Women
Aesthetics of Music in Ancient Civilizations
Aesthetics of Music in the Middle Ages
Aesthetics of Music in the Early Renaissance

The History and Literature of the Wind Band and Wind Ensemble Series

Volume 1 The Wind Band and Wind Ensemble Before 1500
Volume 2 The Renaissance Wind Band and Wind Ensemble
Volume 3 The Baroque Wind Band and Wind Ensemble
Volume 4 The Wind Band and Wind Ensemble of the Classical Period (1750–1800)
Volume 5 The Nineteenth-Century Wind Band and Wind Ensemble
Volume 6 A Catalog of Multi-Part Repertoire for Wind Instruments or for Undesignated Instrumentation before 1600
Volume 7 Baroque Wind Band and Wind Ensemble Repertoire
Volume 8 Classical Period Wind Band and Wind Ensemble Repertoire
Volume 9 Nineteenth-Century Wind Band and Wind Ensemble Repertoire
Volume 10 A Supplementary Catalog of Wind Band and Wind Ensemble Repertoire
Volume 11 A Catalog of Wind Repertoire before the Twentieth Century for One to Five Players
Volume 12 A Second Supplementary Catalog of Early Wind Band and Wind Ensemble Repertoire
Volume 13 Name Index, Volumes 1–12, The History and Literature of the Wind Band and Wind Ensemble

www.whitwellbooks.com

David Whitwell

Classical Period Wind Band and Wind Ensemble Repertoire

THE HISTORY AND LITERATURE OF THE WIND BAND AND WIND ENSEMBLE, VOLUME 8

EDITED BY CRAIG DABELSTEIN

WHITWELL PUBLISHING • AUSTIN, TEXAS, USA

Whitwell Publishing, Austin 78701
www.whitwellbooks.com

© 1984, 2012 by David Whitwell
All rights reserved. First edition 1984.
Second edition 2012

Printed in the United States of America

PAPERBACK
ISBN-13: 978-1-936512-44-7
ISBN-10: 1936512440

All images used in this book are in the public domain except where otherwise noted.

Composed in Bembo Book

Contents

Foreword		vii
Instrumentation code		ix
Text abbreviations		ix
Secondary Sources		x
Library Abbreviations		xi
Acknowledgments		xvii

Part I		Opera, Ballet, Symphonic, and Keyboard Literature Arranged for Harmoniemusik	1
Part II		Wind Ensemble and Wind Band Literature of the Classical Period	161
	1	Austria–Bohemia	163
	2	Belgium	248
	3	Denmark	249
	4	England	250
	5	France	267
	6	Germany	294
	7	The Netherlands	360
	6	Italy	362
	8	Poland	369
	9	Spain	370
	6	Switzerland	371
		Index	375
		About The Author	399

Foreword

THIS VOLUME IS THE EIGHTH, and a companion to the fourth volume, in the series, *The History and Literature of the Wind Band and Wind Ensemble*, comprised of the following volumes:

1. The Wind Band and Wind Ensemble before 1500
2. The Renaissance Wind Band and Wind Ensemble
3. The Baroque Wind Band and Wind Ensemble
4. The Classical Period Wind Band and Wind Ensemble
5. The Nineteenth-Century Wind Band and Wind Ensemble
6. A Catalog of Multi-Part Repertoire for Wind Instruments or for Undesignated Instrumentation before 1600
7. Baroque Wind Band and Wind Ensemble Repertoire
8. Classical Period Wind Band and Wind Ensemble Repertoire
9. Nineteenth-Century Wind Band and Wind Ensemble Repertoire
10. A Supplementary Catalog of Early Band and Wind Ensemble Repertoire
11. A Catalog of Wind Repertoire before the Twentieth Century for One to Five Players
12. A Second Supplementary Catalog of Early Wind Band and Wind Ensemble Repertoire
13. Name Index, Volumes 1–12, The History and Literature of the Wind Band and Wind Ensemble

The first section of the following volume presents sources for opera and ballet transcriptions for *Harmoniemusik*, all of which were originally made between ca. 1780 and ca. 1835. While this material extends somewhat beyond the Classical Period, I have decided to present it together here as the music and the medium are entirely of this period in spirit.

By '*Harmoniemusik*' I mean six-, eight- or nine-part wind band music in which one always finds the nucleus of two bassoons, two horns and either, or both, pairs of oboes or clarinets. During the nineteenth century the term is sometimes used to mean military band and while there are many military band arrangements of operas, etc., these are not included in this section. Similarly, sources for six- or eight-part wind ensembles with percussion have not been listed as they too are presumed to be of the military sphere.

The second section is limited to original wind ensemble and wind band music of the Classical Period, ca. 1750–1800.

David Whitwell
Austin, Texas

Instrumentation Code

As an abbreviation for wind instrumentation I use a code of 0000-0000, representing: flute, oboe, clarinet, bassoon - trumpet, horn, trombone, tuba.

Thus:
3000-	means a work for three flutes
-204	means a work for two trumpets and four trombones
1-1; 2 cornetts	means bassoon, trumpet, and two cornetts.

Text Abbreviations

MS	Manuscript
EP	Early print
MP	Modern print
PN	Plate number

Secondary Sources

In some cases I have given information on works which I myself have not found in libraries; in these cases the source for my information is represented by abbreviations given in [brackets], the full titles for which are given here.

AMZ	*Allgemeine Musikalische Zeitung* (Leipzig)
DTO	*Denkmäler der Tonkunst in Österreich* (Guido Adler, ed., 1894)
EDM	*Das Erbe deutscher Musik* (1935)
Eitner	Robert Eitner, *Biographish-bibliographisches Quellen-Lexikon* (1900–1904)
F	François-Joseph Fétis, *Biographie universelle* (1978–1880)
G1, G2	Ernst Ludwig Gerber, *Historisch biographisches Lexikon der Tonkünstler* (Leipzig, 1790–1792); and *Neues historisch biographisches Lexikon der Tonkünstler* (Leipzig, 1812–1814)
Grove	*The New Grove Dictionary of Music and Musicians* (Stanley Sadie, ed., 1980)
HA	Bruce Haynes, *Catalog of Chamber Music for Oboe* (1980)
Hellyer	Roger Hellyer, 'Harmoniemusic' (Dissertation, Oxford, 1973)
HI	Hummel's 'Inventory of 1806 of the Esterházy kapelle at Eisenstdt'
J	'Thematische Verzeichniss by Jos Jerkowitz Schasslowitz den 1 July 1832' (now in BRD:Mbs [Mus .Ms .6330])
M	Willem Middelhoven, 'Het et Blaasensemble Omstreeks 1800,' *Mens & Melodie* (Utrecht, 1976)
MAB	*Musica Antiqua Bohemica* (Prague)
MGG	*Die Musik in Geschichte und Gegenwart* (Friedrich Blume, ed., 1949-1968)
MH	Miroslav Hosek, *Oben Bibliographie* (Wilhelmshaven, 1975)
S	John Sainsbury, *A Dictionary of Musicians* (London, 1825)
SJK	S. James Kurtz, 'A Study and Catalog of Ensemble Music ... ca. 1700 to ca. 1825' (Dissertation, University of Iowa, 1971)
V	Gottfried Veit, *Die Blasmusik* (Innsbruck, 1972)

Library Abbreviations for this Catalog

Where the location of a work is known, the library is given in abbreviation according to the following international R.I.S.M. system. Shelf-marks, or call-numbers, are given immediately after the library abbreviations and contained by (parentheses). I have given many works which are no longer believed to exist for the purpose of expanding the reader's perspective of the wind music of this period.

In the interval since this catalog was first published in 1983 there has been a reunification of Germany with the result that the old R.I.S.M. library symbols have been changed and indeed in many cases the music has been moved to the Staatsbibliothek in Berlin. In this catalog, however, we retain the old R.I.S.M. symbols and shelf-mark because even in those cases where the music has been moved to a new location the old information is necessary for the new library to identify these specific manuscripts for those who may want copies today.

A: Austria

Ee	Eisenstadt, Esterházy-Archiv (secular music now in H:Bn)
Eh	Eisenstadt, Haydn-Museum
Gk	Graz, Hochschule für Musik
GÖ	Göttweig, Benediktinerstift Göttweig, Musikarchiv
KR	Kremsmünster, Benediktiner-Stift Kremsmünster, Musikarchiv
M	Melk an der Donau, Benediktiner-Stift Melk
Sca	Salzburg, Museum Carolino Augusteum, Bibliothek
Sm	Salzburg, Mozarteum
Ssp	Salzburg, St. Peter, Musikarchiv
Wgm	Wien, Gesellschaft der Musikfreunde in Wien
Wn	Wien, Österreichische Nationalbibliothek, Musiksammlung
Wn-h	Österreichische Nationalbibliothek, Sammlung Anthony van Hoboken
Wsp	Wien, St. Peter, Musikarchiv
Wst	Wien, Stadtbibliothek, Musiksammlung

B: Belgium

Bc	Bruxelles, Conservatoire Royal de Musique, Bibliothèque
Br	Bruxelles, Bibliothèque Royale Albert Ier
Lc	Liège, Conservatoire Royal de Musique, Bibliothèque

BRD: West Germany (Bundesrepublik Deutschland)

As	Augsburg, Staats- und Stadtbibliothek
AB	Amorbach, Fürstlich Leiningische Bibliothek
AM	Amberg, Staatliche Provinzialbibliothek
B	Berlin, Staatsbibliothek, Musiksammlung
Bhm	Berlin, Staatliche Hochschule für Musik
Bu	Berlin, Universitätsbibliothek der Freien Universität
Buc	Bückeburg, Fürstl. Institut für Musikwissenschaft
BAR	Bartenstein, Füirst zu Hohenlohe-Bartensteinsches Archiv
BFb	Burgsteinfurt, Fürstlich Bentheimsche Bibliothek (now in MÜu)
BNu	Bonn, Universitätsbibliothek
BÜu	[a few titles were sent me under this code by a correspondent who died before he could identify the library; library is the same as that given for BFb]
DO	Donaueschingen, Fürstlich Fürstenbergische Hofbibliothek
DS	Darmstadt, Hessische Landes- und Hochschulbibliothek
F	Frankfurt/Main, Stadt- und Universitätsbibliothek
Hs	Hamburg, Staats- und Universitätsbibliothek, Musikabteil ung
HEms	Heidelberg, Musikwissenschaftliches Seminar der Universität
HL	Haltenbergstetten, Schloss uber Niederstetten, Fürst zu Hohenlohe-Jagstberg'sche Bibliothek
HR	Harburg, Fürstlich Öttingen-Wallerstein'sche Bibliothek, Schloss Harburg
KA	Karlsruhe, Badische Landesbibliothek, Musikabteilung
KNh	Köln, Staatliche Hochschule für Musik
LB	Langenburg, Fürstlich Hohenlohe-Langenburg'sche Bibliothek
LÜh	Lübeck, Bibliothek der Hansestadt Lübeck
Mbs	München, Bayerische Staatsbibliothek, Musiksammlung
Mmb	München, Stldtische Musikbibliothek
MGmi	Marburg, Betriebseinbeit Musikwissenschaft im Fachbereich Geschichtswis senschaften der Philipps-Universität Marburg
MÜu	Münster, Universitätsbibliothek
MZsch	Mainz, Musikverlag Schott
NEhz	Neuenstein, Kreis Öhringen, Hohenlohe- Zentralarchiv
OF	Offenbach, Verlagsarchiv André
Rp	Regensburg, Bischöfliche Zentralbibliothek
Rtt	Regensburg, Fürstlich Thurn und Taxissche Hofbibliothek
RH	(sometimes, Rheda) Rheda, Fürst zu Bentheim- Tecklenburgische Bibliothek
Sl	Stuttgart, Württembergische Landesbibliothek
Tes	Tübingen, Evangelisches Stift, Bibliothek
Tu	Tübingen, Universitätsbibliothek der Eberhard-Karls-Universität
TSCH	Tübingen, Musikwissenschafliches Institut der Eberdhard-Karls-Universitäts (now contains this collection)

LIBRARY ABBREVIATIONS XIII

W	Wolfenbüttel, Herzog-August-Bibliothek, Musikabteilung
WERl	Wertheim, Fürstlich Löwenstein'sche Bibliothek
WEY	Weyarn, Pfarrkirche, Bibliothek
WS	Wasserburg, Chorarchiv St. Jakob, Pfarramt
ZL	Zeil, Fürstlich Waldburg-Zeil'sches Archiv

CH: SWITZERLAND

E	Einsiedeln, Kloster Einsiedeln, Musikbibliothek
EN	Engelberg, Stift Engelberg, Musikbibliothek
Fcu	Fribourg, Bibliothèque cantonale et universitaire
Gc(GLiceo)	Genève, Bibliothèque du Conservatoire de Musique
Gpu	Genève. Bibliothèque publique et universitaire de Genève
Lz	Luzern; Zentralbibliothek
N	Neuchâtel, Bibliothèque publique de la Ville de Neuchâtel
Zz	Zürich, Zentralbibliothek

CS: CZECHOSLOVAKIA

Bm	Brno, Moravsé'muzeum, Ústav dejin hudby
BA	Bakov, Boleslav
BMähr	Mähr Museum
BRnm	Bratislava, Slovenské narodné múzeum, hodobné oddelenie
K	Ceský Krumlov, Státní arbív Trebon
KRa	Kromeríz, Státní zámek a zahrady
Ksm	Kromeríz, Archiv Collegiate Church of St. Maurice (now in KRa)
MH	Mnichovo Hradiste, Mestské muzeum
OLu	Olomouc, Státní vedeckiá knihovna
Pk	Prag, Konservatol v Praze, hudebni archfv
Pnm	Prag, Národni muzeum, hudební oddelení
Pu	Prag, Státní knihovna CSR, Universitní knihovna, hudební oddllení

DDR: EAST GERMANY (DEUTSCHE DEMOKRATISCHE REPUBLIK)

AG	Augustusburg, Erzgebirge Pfarrarchiv
Bds	Deutsche Staatsbibliothek, Musikabteilung
Dlb	Dresden, Sächsische Landesbibliothek, Musikabteilung
Dmb	Dresden Musikbibliothek
GOL	Goldbach bei Gotha, Pfarrarchiv
HAu	Halle, Universitäts- und Landesbibliothek Sachsen-Anhalt, Musiksammlung
HER	Herrnhut, Archiv der Brüder-Unität

Lem   Leipzig, Musikbibliothek der Stadt Leipzig
LEt   Leipzig, Thomasschule, Bibliothek
MEIr   Meiningen, Staatliche Museenmit Reger-Archiv, Abteilung Musikgeschichte
MERZ   Merseburg, Deutsches Zentral-Archiv, Historische Abteilung
RUl   Rudolstadt, Staatsarchiv
SWl   Schwerin, Wissenschaftliche Allgemeinbibliothek
WRgs   Weimar, Goethe-Schiller-Archiv
WRtl   Weiman, Thüringische Landesbibliothek
Z   Zwickau, Ratsschulbibliothek
ZI   Zittau, Stadt- und Kreisbibliothek

DK: Denmark

A   Arhus, Statsbiblioteket i Arhus
Kk   Kobenhavn, Det kongelige Bibliotek
Dmk   Kobenhavn, Det kongelige danske Musikkonservatorium
Sa   Soro, Soro Akademis Bibliotek

E: Spain

Mn   Madrid, Biblioteca nacional

ERIE: Ireland

Da   Dublin, Royal Irish Academy
Dn   Dublin, National Library and Museum of Ireland

F: France

BO   Bordeaux, Bibliothèque municipale
Pa   Paris, Bibliothèque de l'Arsenal
Pn   Paris, Bibliothèque nationale
Po   Paris, Bibliothèque-Musée de l'Opéra
TO   Tours, Bibliothèque municipale

GB: Great Britain

Cfm   Cambridge, Fitzwilliam Museum
Ckc   Cambridge, Rowe Music Library, King's College
Cu   Cambridge, University Library
DU   Dundee, Public Libraries

Gm	Glasgow, Mitchell Library
Gu	Glasgow University Library
Lbbc	London, British Broadcasting Corporation, Music Library
Lbm	London, The British Museum
Lcm	London, Royal College of Music
Lcs	London, Vaughan Williams Memorial Library
Lgc	London, Gresham College (Guildhall Library)
Lrs	London, Royal Society of Musicians
Ob	Oxford, Bodleian Library

H: Hungary

Bn	Budapest, Országos Széchény Könyvtár
BuNM	Budapest, Kiadjda a Magyar Nemzeti Muzeum
KE	Keszthely, Helikon Kastélymúzeum
P	Pécs (Fünfkirchen), Székesegyházi Kottatár

I: Italy

Bc	Bologna, Civico Museo Bibliografico-Musicale
Bl	Bologna, Conservatorio di Musica G. B. Martini
Bsf	Bologna, Archivio del Convento di San Francesco
Fc	Firenze, Biblioteca del Conservatorio di Musica
Gi(l)	Genova, Biblioteca dell'Istituto Musicale
Mc	Milano, Biblioteca del Conservatorio
MOe	Modena, Biblioteca Estense
Nc	Napoli, Biblioteca del Conservatorio di Musica
Ppriv	Pisa, Collezione private pisane di musiche
PS	Pistoia, Archivio capitolare della Cattedrale
Vcr	Venezia, Pia Casa di Ricovero
Vmc	Venezia, Museo Civica Correr (now in the Biblioteca del Conservatorio)
Vsmc	Venezia S. Maria della Consolazione detta 'della Fava'

NL: The Netherlands

At	Amsterdam, Toonkunst-Bibliotheek
CV	Moergestel, private collection, Cees Verheijen
DHgm	Den Haag, Gemeente Museum
M	Amsterdam, private collection, Willem Middelhoven
Ura/mZ	Zeist, Archief van de Evangelische Broedergemeente

PL: Poland

GDj	Danzig, Kirchenbibliothek St. Johann
LA	Lancut, Biblioteka, muzyczna zamku w Lancucie
Wbu	Warszawa, Biblioteka Uniwersytecka
WRu	Wroclaw, Biblioteka Uniwersytecka

S: Sweden

J	Jönköping, Per Brahgymnasiet Biblioteket
L	Lund, Universitetsbiblioteket
Uu	Uppsala, Universitetsbiblioteket

SF: Finland

A	Abo, Sibeliusmuseum

US: The United States of America

Bp	Boston, Boston Public Library
BE	Berkeley, University of California, Music Library
BETm	Bethlehem, Archives of the Moravian Church
Cn	Chicago, Newberry Library
DW	Los Angeles, private collection, David Whitwell (now Whitwell Archiv, Bundesakademie für Musik, Trossingen, Germany)
NYp	New York, New York Public Library
PHf	Philadelphia, Philadelphia Free Library
R	Rochester, Sibley Music Library, Eastman School of Music
Wc	Washington, D.C., Library of Congress
WS	Winston-Salem, Moravian Music Foundation

USSR: Russia

Lk	St. Petersburg, Biblioteka Gosudarstvennoj konservatorii
Lsc	St. Petersburg, Gosudarstvennaja publicnaja biblioteka

YU: Yugoslavia

Zha	Zabreb, Hrvatski glazbeni zavod

Acknowledgments

The reader is indebted for the second edition of this book to Mr. Craig Dabelstein of Brisbane, Australia. Without his contribution to design and all things involved as an editor this book would never again have been available.

> David Whitwell
> Austin, 2012

PART I

OPERA, BALLET, SYMPHONIC AND KEYBOARD LITERATURE ARRANGED FOR HARMONIEMUSIK

Arrangements for Harmoniemusik

Alessandri, Felice (1742–1798)

Il Vecchio geloso (opera, 1781)
    Il Vecchio
    Arranger unknown
    222-02
    MS I:Fc (D.V.496)

Anfossi, Pasquale (1727–1797)

Isabella e Rodrigo (ballet?)
    Isabella e Rodrigo
    Arranged by Schacht, ca. 1780
    21-02
    MS BRD:Rtt (Anfossi 7)

Aspelmayr, Franz (1728–1786)

Ballet, original unknown
    Ballo
    Arranger unknown
    201-02
    MS CS:Pnm (XLII.D.13)

Auber, Daniel François Espirit (1782–1871)

La Bergère Châtelaine (opera, 1820)
    Ouverture de la Bergère châtelaine
    Arranger unknown
    Harmoniemusik
    EP (Paris, Erard)

    Airs de la Bergère chatelaine
    Arranger unknown
    Harmoniemusik
    EP (Paris, Ebend) [Liv. 1–3]

Emma (opera, 1821)
    Ouverture de Emma
    Arranger unknown
    Harmoniemusik
    EP (Paris, Ebend)

Airs d'Emma
Arranger unknown
Harmoniemusik
EP (Paris, A. Petit) [Liv. 1–3]

La Neige (opera, 1823)
Ouverture et Airs de la Neige
Arranger unknown
Harmoniemusik
EP (Paris, Frère) [Liv. 1, 2]

La Neige
Arranged by Widder
1022-02
EP (Berlin, Schlesinger)
This is a collection of eight works which includes arias from Auber's *La Maçon* and *Semiramide* by Rossini.

La Maçon (opera, 1825)
Ouverture zur Opera: Der Maurer
Arranger unknown
1022-02
EP (Offenbach, André)

La Maçon
Arranged by Widder
1022-02
EP (Berlin, Schlesinger)
This is a collection of eight works which includes arias from Auber's *La Neige* and *Semiramide* by Rossini.

La Muette de Portici (opera, 1828)
La Musette de Portici
Arranged by Sedlak, 11 movements
222-22
MS A:Wn (Sm. 3795)

Die Stumme von Portici
Arranged by Sedlak, 11 movements
222-221
MS CS:Bm (A.35.146/147)

La Muette de Portici
Arranged by Weller
Eight- or twelve-part *Harmoniemusik*
EP (Berlin, Schlesinger) [Liv. 1, 2]

Piccen a. d. Oper: Die Stumme
Arranger unknown
1021-02
EP (Offenbach, André)

Ouverture zu Die Stumme
Arranger unknown
Harmoniemusik
EP (Paris, Ebend)

Ouverture de la Muette de Portici
Arranged by Weller
Harmoniemusik
EP (Berlin, Schlesinger)

Le Philtre (opera, 1831)
Ouverture de l'Opèra: Le Philtre
Arranger unknown
Nine- or fourteen-part *Harmoniemusik*
EP (Paris, Ebend)

Le Serment (opera, 1832)
Ouverture de l'Opèra: Le Serment ou les Faux-Monnoyeurs
Arranged by Berr
Eight-part *Harmoniemusik*
EP (Paris, Ebend)

Le Duc d'Olonne (opera, 1842)
Der Olnum
Arranged by Sedlak (MS. by Perschl), 3 movements
222-22
MS A:Wn (Sm. 3796)

Der Klausner (original unknown)
Der Klausner
Arranger unknown, dated 1829, 5 movements
222-22; contrabassoon
MS CS:Bm (A.35.856)

Beethoven, Ludwig van (1770–1827)

Egmont Music, op. 84
Ouverture d'Egmont
Arranged Starke
Nine part *Harmoniemusik*
MS (autograph score for 'Harmonie und türkische Musik') DDR:Bds (Mus.Ms.Auto.Fr.Starke 1)
EP (Vienna, Steiner; reprinted by Haslinger)

Fidelio (opera, 1805)
> *Fidelio*
> Arranged Sedlak, 11 movements
> 222-02
> EP (Vienna, Artaria, Nr. 2363, [1814])
> A:Wn (MS 10812, MS 40105) [two copies]
> A:Wst (M.12355/c)
> US:DW (10)
> An announcement by Beethoven in the *Wiener Zeitung* (July 1, 1814) reads that he, 'herewith declares that he has given the score of his opera *Fidelio* to the aforesaid publisher (Artaria) for publication under his supervision in a complete piano score, quartets, or arrangements for Harmonie …'

Quintet, op. 16
> *Quintet for fortepiano*
> Arranged by Triebensee
> 222-02
> MS A:Wn (Sm. 3739, Jg. I, Oevre 2, Nr. 2)

Septet, op. 20
> *Septetto*
> Arranged by Bernhard Crusell
> 1032-121, serpent
> EP (Leipzig, Peters, Nr. 1856, 1856a, [1825]), Partie 1, 2, BRD:Bhm (6983, 6984) [score and parts]
>
> *Septet*
> Arranged by Druschetzky
> 222-02, contrabassoon
> EP (Vienna, Magasin de l'imprimerie chimique; reprinted by Steiner, 'Nr. 32', Plate number 1886, [ca. 1812]; reprinted by Haslinger [after 1826]) US:DW
>
> *Septet*
> Arranged by Carl Czerny (1805)
> 22-02
> MS DDR:Bds (Artaria Sammlung)
>
> *Septetto*
> Arranger unknown
> Nine-part *Harmoniemusik*
> EP (Paris, Ebend)
>
> *Sestetto*
> Arranger unknown
> 22-02
> EP (Leipzig, Breitkopf & Härtel)

Septetto
Arranger unknown (1833)
222-02, contrabassoon
MS CS:Bm (A.35.149)

Septet
Arranger unknown (ca. 1810)
1022-02
MS BRD:Rtt (Beethoven 1)

Sonata (pathétique)
   Harmonie
   Arranger unknown
   222-02, contrabassoon
   EP (Vienna, Chemische Druckerei; reprinted Steiner; reprinted Haslinger) US:DW

   Sonate Pathétique
   Arranger unknown (ca. 1830)
   222-02
   MS CS:Bm (A.37.330)

   Sonate pathétique
   Arranger unknown
   Nine-part *Harmoniemusik*
   EP (Paris, Ebend)

First Symphony
   Symphony
   Arranged by Hutschenrieyter, Sen.
   2022-12
   MS NL:CV [photocopy]

Seventh Symphony
   7te grande Sinfonie
   Arranger unknown
   Nine-part *Harmoniemusik*
   EP (Paris, Ebend)

   [*Seventh Symphony*]
   Arranger unknown
   222-02, contrabassoon
   EP (Vienna, Steiner, Nr. 2563) BRD:Essen (private collection); US:DW (183)

Eighth Symphony
   8te grande Sinfonie
   Arranger unknown
   Nine-part *Harmoniemusik*
   EP (Paris, Ebend)

[*Eighth Symphony*]
Arranger unknown
222-02, contrabassoon
EP (Vienna, Steiner, Nr. 2573)

Trauer Marsch (original unknown)
Trauer Marsch
Arranger unknown
222-02
MS A:Wn (Sm.5793)

Harmonie (original unknown)
Harmonie
Arranger unknown
Nine- or twelve-part *Harmoniemusik*
EP (Paris, Gambaro)

Wellingtons Sieg oder die Schlacht bei Vittoria
Wellingtons Sieg oder die Schlacht bei Vittoria Arranger unknown
Nine-part *Harmoniemusik*
EP (Vienna, Haslinger)

Bellini, Vincenzo (1801–1835)

Bianca e Gernando (opera, 1826)
'All'udir del padre afflitto,' from *Bianca e Fernando*
Arranged by Benedetto Carulli
2032-22
MS I:Bsf (M.B.IV-10)

La Straniera (opera, 1829)
La *Staniera*
Arranged by Sedlak? (MS by Perschl), 11 movements
222-22
MS A:Wn (Sm. 3801)

I Capuleti e i Montecchi (opera, 1830)
I Capuleti e i Montecchi
Arranged Sedlak?, 6 movements
222-02
MS A:Wn (Sm. 3798)

'Cavatina,' from *I Capuleti e i Montecchi*
Arranger unknown
222-221
MS (1832) CS:Bm (A.36.857)

'Duetto,' from *I Capuleti e i Montecchi*
Arranger unknown
222-22
MS (after 1830) CS:Bm (A.37.325)

La Sonnambula (opera, 1831)
    La Sonnambula
    Arranged by Sedlak? (MS by Perschl)
    222-221
    MS (1837) A:Wn (Sm. 3800)

Norma (opera, 1831)
    Norma
    Arranged by Sedlak? (MS by Perschl)
    222-22
    MS A:Wn (Sm. 3799)

Breatrice di Tenda (opera, 1833)
    Breatrice di Tenda
    Arranged by Sedlak? (MS by Perschl), one long movement
    222-22
    MS A:Wn (Sm. 3797)

I Puritani di Scozia (opera, 1835)
    I Puritani di Scozia
    Arranger unknown, 3 long movements
    222-02
    MS A:Wn (Sm. 4459)

    I Puritani di Scozia
    Arranged by Sedlak, 'Part I,' 13 movements
    222-02, contrabassoon
    MS CS:Bm (A.35.151)

    'Cavatina,' from *I Puritani di Scozia*
    Arranged by Sedlak
    222-22
    MS CS:Bm (A.35.152)

Berton, Henri Montan (1767–1844)

Montano et Stéphanie (opera, 1799)
    Airs choisis de Montano et Stéphanie
    Arranged by Fuchs, 7 movements
    2022-02 (the 2 flutes given as optional)
    EP (Paris, Imbault, Nr. 796; BRD:AB, Bhm (6932); CH:Gpu; F:Pn (Vm.27.592); US:Wc

Le grand Deuil (opera, 1801)
    Ouverture du Grand Deuil
    Arranged by Vanderhagen
    Harmoniemusik
    EP (Paris) F:Pn (Vm.27.4175)

Airs du Grand Deuil
Arranged by Vanderhagen
Harmoniemusik
EP (Paris) F:Pn (Vm.27.4174)

Ouverture du grand Deuil
Arranger unknown
Eight- or eleven-part *Harmoniemusik*
EP (Paris, Ebend)

Airs du grand Deuil
Arranger unknown
Eight- or eleven-part *Harmoniemusik*
EP (Paris, Pleyel)

Aline, Reine de Golconde (opera, 1803)
Aline
Arranger unknown, 14 movements
222-02, contrabassoon
MS CS:KRa (IV.B.3)

'Allegro,' from *Alline*
Arranged by Triebensee
222-02
MS A:Wn (Sm. 3794, Nr. 1)

Alina
Arranger unknown
222-02
MS I:Fc (D.V.500)

Aline Reine de Goloconde
Arranger unknown
22-02
MS PL:LA (2299)

Ouverture d'Aline
Arranger unknown
Six- or seven-part *Harmoniemusik*
EP (Paris, Ebend)

Airs d'Aline
Arranger unknown
Six- or seven-part *Harmoniemusik*
EP (Paris, Sieber)

Féodor (opera?)
Ouverture de Féodor
Arranger Unknown
Eight- or nine-part *Harmoniemusik*
EP (Paris, A. Petit)

Francoise de Foix (opera, 1809)
>   *Ouverture et Airs de Francoise de Foix*
>   Arranger unknown
>   Eight-part *Harmoniemusik*
>   EP (Paris, Dufaut et Dubois)

Bianchi, Francesco (1752–1810)

La Villanella rapita (opera, 1783)
>   *Première suite d'airs d'opéra buffa*
>   Arranged by Fuchs
>   2022-02
>   EP (Paris, Imbault, Hr. 535) US:Cn
>   Undetermined number of movements together with arias by Cimarosa, Palma, and anonymous.

>   *La Villanella, nouvelle suite Nr. 12*
>   Arranged by M. J. Gebauer
>   222-02, serpent
>   EP (Paris, Boyer) BRD:BÜu (B-Ia-59), MÜu
>   *La Villanella rapita*
>   Arranger unknown
>   222-02
>   MS PL:LA (2451)

Bierey, Gottlob Benedikt (1772–1840) and Weigl, Josef (1766–1846)

>   *Harmonie*
>   Arranger unknown
>   222-02
>   MS BRD:HR (III.4.1/2.20.358)
>   A manuscript note reads, 'Das Blumenmädchen von Bierey.'

Bocchoroni, ?

Hamlet (original unknown)
>   *Hamlet*
>   Arranged by Ruzni
>   222-22
>   MS CS:Bm (A.36.850)

Boieldieu, Francois Adrien (1775–1834)

Ma Tante Aurore (opera, 1803)
>   *Ouverture de Ma tante Aurore*
>   Arranged by J. Koslowsky, 'amateur'
>   222-02
>   MS PL:LA (2452)

Jean de Paris (opera, 1812)
> *Jean de Paris*, Act I
> Arranged by Triebensee, 10 movements
> 222-02
> MS A:Wn (Sm. 3739, Jg. III, Oevre 3)
>
> *Jean de Paris*, Act II
> Arranged by Triebensee, 7 movements
> 222-02
> MS A:Wn (Sm. 3739, Jg. III, Oevre 4, Nr. 1–7)
>
> *Johann in Paris*
> Arranged by Sedlak
> 222-02
> MS A:Wgm (VIII 41157) [10 movements], Wn (Sm. 3802) [14 movements]
>
> *Jean de Paris*
> Arranger unknown, 10 movements
> 222-22
> MS CS:Bm (A.35.253)
>
> *Johan von Paris*
> Arranger unknown, 10 movements
> 22-02
> EP (Vienna, Chemischen Druckerey, *Journal für Sechstimmige Harmonie. Nr. VI*, reprinted by Steiner) CS:KRa (IV.B.182)
>
> *Johan von Paris*
> Arranger unknown, 10 movements
> 22-02
> MS CS:KRa (IV.B.4)

La Dame blanche (opera, 1825)
> *Piecen aus Dame blanche*
> Arranger unknown
> 1021-02
> EP (Offenbach, André)

Bresciani, Pietro

L'Arbore di Diana (ballet?)
> *Overture, L'Arbore di Diana*
> Arranged by Nickolaus Scholl
> 1222-12
> MS I:MOe (Mus.F.1410)

Diane ed Endymione (ballet)
    Parthia
    Arranger unknown
    201-02
    MS CS:K (Nr. 238.K.II) [missing horn 2]

Bruni, Antonio Bartolommeo (1751–1821)

La Recontre en voyage (opera)
    Première Suite d'airs d'opéra comiques
    Arranged by Fuchs
    2022-02
    EP (Paris, Imbault, ca. 1799) F:Pn (Vm.7.6965, Vm.27.1603, and Vm.27.1591) [three copies]; US:Cn
    Undetermined number of movements together with arias by Dalayrac and Tarchi.

    Ouverture, La Rencontre
    Arranged by Fuchs
    Harmoniemusik
    EP (Paris) F:Pn (Vm.27.1598)

Toberne (opera, 1795)
    Toberne
    Arranged by M.J. Gebauer
    2022–02
    EP (Paris, Gaveaux) BRD:AB [missing bsn. 1, fl. 2]

Spinette et Marini (opera?)
    Spinette et Marini
    Arranged by Fuchs
    42-12
    EP (Paris, Nadermann, Nr. 163) F:Pn (Vm.27.1601); BRD:Tu

Calenberg, ? [perhaps Gallenberg, Wenzel Robert, 1783–1839]

Hamlet (original unknown)
    Overture to Hamlet
    Arranged by Gambaro
    Harmoniemusik
    EP (Paris) F:Pn (Vm.27.1624)

di Capua, Marcello [Marcello Bernardini] (b. ca. 1740–41)

Furberia et Pontiglio (opera ?)
    Furberia et Pontiglio
    Arranger unknown
    2022-02
    EP (Paris, Imbault, Nr. 535) US:Cn

Carafa, Michele (1787–1872)

Gabriella di Vergy (opera, 1816)
    Gabrielle di Vergi
    Arranger unknown, 10 movements
    222-22
    MS CS:Bm (A.35.156) [incomplete copy]

    Overture to Gabrielle di Vergi
    Arranger unknown
    222-22
    MS CS:Bm (A.35.155) [incomplete copy]

Le Solitaire (opera, 1822)
    Ouverture du Solitaire
    Arranger unknown
    Harmoniemusik
    EP (Paris, Langlois)

Catel, Charles-Simon (1773–1830)

Sémiramis (opera, 1802)
    Semiramis
    Arranger unknown
    222-02
    MS I:Fc (D.V.502)

    Semiramis
    Arranger unknown
    Eight-part *Harmoniemusik*
    EP (Paris, Ebend) [Liv. 1, 2]

    Airs des Africains de Semiramis
    Arranger unknown
    Harmoniemusik
    EP (Paris, Ebend)

l'Officier enlevé (opera?)
    Ouverture de l'Officier enlevé
    Arranger unknown
    Harmoniemusik
    EP (Paris, A. Petit)

Wallace (opera, 1817)
    Ouverture de Wallace
    Arranger unknown
    Eight-part *Harmoniemusik*
    EP (Paris, Ebend)

Airs de Wallace
Arranger unknown
Harmoniemusik
EP (Paris, Ebend) [Liv. 1–3]

Zirphile et Fleur de Myrte (opera?)
Ouverture et Airs de Zirphile et Fleur de Myrte
Arranged by Schaffner
Harmoniemusik
EP (Paris, Ebend) [Liv. 1–3]

Catrufo, Giuseppe (1771–1851)

Félicie (opera, 1815)
Ouverture de Felicie
Arranger unknown
Harmoniemusik
EP (Paris, Pacini)

Airs de Felicie
Arranger unknown
Harmoniemusik
EP (Paris, Pacini) [Liv. 1, 2]

Champein, Stanislas (1753–1830)

La Mélomanie (opera, 1781)
Ouverture de Melomanie
Arranger unknown
Eight- to twelve-part *Harmoniemusik*
EP (Paris, Sieber)

Airs de Melomanie
Arranger unknown
Six-part *Harmoniemusik*
EP (Paris, Sieber)

Nouvelle Suite (original unidentified)
Nouvelle Suite
Arranged by Gebauer
Nine-part *Harmoniemusik*
MS BRD:BÜu (C-Ha-50)

Cherubini, Luigi (1760–1842)

Lodoiska (opera, 1791)
> *Overtura aus der Opera Lodoiska*
> Arranger unknown
> 22-02
> MS PL:LA (2300)

> *Overture, Lodiska*
> Arranger unknown
> 42-12
> MS DDR:Dlb (Mus. 4011-F-510), DDR:ZI (Sigl.Exner)

> *Ludouiska*
> Arranged by Havel, 9 movements
> 22-02
> MS CS:KRa (IV.B.9)

> *Lodoiska*
> Arranger unknown, 11 movements
> 22-02
> MS CS:KRa (IV.B.7)

> *Ouverture de Lodiska*
> Arranger unknown
> *Harmoniemusik*
> EP (Paris, Nadermann)

Élisa (opera, 1794)
> *Elise oder der Bernhardsberg*
> Arranged by Triebensee, in two Acts
> *Harmoniemusik*
> MS(?) (Vienna, Triebensee)
> Advertized in AMZ, January, 1804.

Médée (opera, 1797)
> *Medea*
> Arranged by Sedlak
> 22-02
> MS PL:LA (2301)

L'Hôtellerie Portugaise (opera, 1798)
> *Osteria Portughese*
> Arranger unknown
> 222-02
> MS I:Fc (D.V.493)

> *Ouverture de l'Hôtellerie portugaise*
> Arranger unknown
> Twelve-part *Harmoniemusik*
> EP (Paris, Frey)

La Prisonnière (opera, 1799)
> *La Prisonnière*
> Arranger unknown (perhaps Wendt), 8 movements
> 222-02
> MS A:Wn (Sm. 3804)
>
> *Die Gefangene*
> Arranged by Triebensee, 9 movements
> 222-02, contrabassoon
> MS CS:K (Nr. 52.K.I.)
>
> *Ouverture de la Prisonnière*
> Arranger unknown
> Twelve-part *Harmoniemusik*
> EP (Paris, Frey)

Les deux Journées (opera, 1800)
> *Due Giornati*
> Arranger unknown
> 222-02
> MS I:Fc (D.V.492)
>
> *Airs des 2 Journees*
> Arranged by Javault
> *Harmoniemusik*
> EP (Paris, G. Gaveaux) [Liv. 1, 2]
>
> *Ouverture des 2 Journees*
> Arranged by Javault
> *Harmoniemusik*
> EP (Paris; Ebend)
>
> *Pieces d'Harmonie des 2 Journees*
> Arranged by Gopfert
> 1121-12, serpent
> EP (Offenbach, André)

Anacréon (opera, 1803)
> *Anacreon*
> Arranger unknown
> 222-02
> MS I:Fc (D.V.498)
>
> *Grossen Tornz Aria von Anacreon*
> Arranged by Triebensee
> 222-02
> MS A:Wn (Sm. 3739, Jg. I, Oevre 1, Nr. 10)

Faniska (opera, 1806)
    Faniska
    Arranger unknown
    222-02
    MS I:Fc (D.V.502)

    Faniska
    Arranged by Sedlak
    222-02
    MS A:Wgm (VIII 43277)

    Faniska
    Arranger unknown
    Harmoniemusik
    MS A:Ee

    Fauiska
    Arranger unknown, 10 movements
    22-02
    MS CS:KRa (IV.B.8)

La Punition (opera?)
    Ouverture de la Punition
    Arranger unknown
    Eleven-part *Harmoniemusik*
    EP (Paris, Janet et C.)

Konig Saul von Israel (opera?)
    Konig Saul von Israel
    Arranger unknown, 5 movements
    22-02
    MS CS:KRa (IV.B.6)

Cimarosa, Domenico (1749–1801)

Giannina e Bernadone (opera, 1781)
    Gianina e Bernardone
    Arranged by Fuchs
    2022-02
    EP (Paris, Imbault, Nr. 535) US:Cn
    Undetermined number of movements together with arias by Pabna, Bianchi, and Anonymous.

L'Impresario in Angustie (opera, 1786)
    Il Impressarrie in Augustie
    Arranged by Fuchs
    2022-02
    EP (Paris, Imbault, Nr. 535)
    Undetermined number of movements together with arias by Palma, Bianchi, and Anonymous.

Impressario in Angustie
Arranged by Fuchs
22-02
EP (Paris, Imbault, Nr. 106) BRD:MÜu

Overture to Impressario
Arranger unknown
Six-part *Harmoniemusik*
MS BRD:BÜu (C-Im-30)

Il Matrimonio segreto (opera, 1792)

Il Matrimonio Segreto
Arranger unknown (probably Wendt), 11 movements
202-02, 2 English horns
MS CS:K (Nr. 24.K.I.)

Matrimonio segreto
Arranger unknown
MS I:Fc (D.V.501)

Il matrimonio Secreto
Arranger unknown, 11 movements
22-02
MS CS:KRa (IV.B.98)

Il Matrimonio segreto
Arranger unknown (perhaps Wendt), 13 movements
222-02
MS A:Wn (Sm. 3807)

Matrimonio segreto
Arranger unknown
Harmoniemusik
MS A:Ee

Il Matriomonio Secreto
Arranger unknown
222-02
MS [listed in Traeg's Catalog, Vienna, 1799]

Il Matrimonio Segreto
Arranger unknown
22–02
MS [listed in Traeg's Catalog, Vienna, 1799]

Il Matrimonio segreto, Airs et Ouverture in harmonie complete
Arranger unknown, 4 Suites, 24 movements
1042-12, serpent
EP (Paris, Gaveaux) NL:At [First suite only]; BRD:AB

Morceaux choisis
Arranged by Fuchs
2022-02
EP (Paris, Imbault, Nr. 750) F:Pn (Vm.27.1589 and Vm.7.6980)

Airs de l'Opéra: il Matrimonio segretto
Arranger unknown
Six- and eight-part *Harmoniemusik*
EP (Paris, G. & S. Gaveaux, Janet et C.) NL:At

Ouverture et Airs de l'Opéra il Matrimonio segretto
Arranger unknown
Harmoniemusik
EP (Paris, P. Petit) [Liv. 1, 2]

Ouverture et Airs de l'Opéra il Matrimonio segretto
Arranged by Fuchs
Eight-part *Harmoniemusik*
EP (Paris, Janet et C.) F:Pn

Ouverture et Airs de l'Opéra il Matrimonio segretto
Arranger unknown
Six- and eight-part *Harmoniemusik*
EP (Paris, Sieber)

Ouverture, Matrimonio segreto
Arranged by Fuchs
Harmoniemusik
EP (Paris) F:Pn (Vm.27.1599)

Le Astuzie femminili (opera, 1794)
   Airs from Asturie feminili
   Arranged by Vanderhagen
   Harmoniemusik
   EP (Paris) F:Pn (Vm.27.4171)

   L'Astuzie feminile
   Arranger unknown
   Six-part *Harmoniemusik*
   EP (Paris, Janet)

Gli Orazi ed i Curiazi (opera, 1796)
   Air aus Orazi e Curiazi
   Arranger unknown
   222-02
   MS CS:Pnm (XX.F.54)

Overture, Orasie i curiazi
Arranger unknown
222-02
MS CS:Kra (IV.B.183)

Oragi e Curizzi
Arranger unknown
222-02
MS I:Fc (D.V.485)

Orazy & Curiazy
Arranger unknown
Harmoniemusik
MS A:Ee

Amor rende Sagace (opera?)
   Amor rende Sagace
   Arranger unknown
   Harmoniemusik
   MS A:Ee

Matrimonio per Raggiro (opera?)
   Airs del Matrimonio per Raggiro
   Arranger unknown
   Harmoniemusik
   EP (Paris, Frey)

i Nemici generosi (opera)
   Ouverture de l'Opéra: i Nemici generosi
   Arranger unknown
   Eight-part *Harmoniemusik*
   EP (Paris, Janet et C.)

i Zingari in Fiera (opera)
   Airs de l'Opéra: i Zingari in Fiera
   Arranger unknown
   Eight-part *Harmoniemusik*
   EP (Paris, Ebend)

   Marceaux choisis de I Zingari in Fiera
   Arranged by Fuchs
   2022-02
   EP (Paris, Imbault, Nr. 418) BRD:AB

   Morceaux choisis de I Zingari in Fiera
   Arranger unknown
   2022-02
   EP (Leipzig, Breitkopf & Härtel)
   Advertized in AMZ, December, 1804.

Bohémiens en foire (unidentified)
> *Marceau choisis des Bohémiens en foire*
> Arranged by Fuchs
> *Harmoniemusik*
> EP (Paris) F:Pn (Vm 27.1590)

1re Suite d'Airs d'l'Opéra (unidentified)
Arranged by Fuchs
Harmoniemusik
EP (Paris) F:Pn (Vm.27.1591)

3e Suite d'Airs del'opéra buffa (unidentified)
Arranged by Vanderhagen
22-02
EP (Paris) F:Pn (Vm.27.4177)

Clerico, Francesco [a choreographer in Venice who composed music for two ballets]

Der Tod des Hercules (ballet, ca. 1790)
> *Der Tod des Hercules*
> Arranger unknown (probably Triebensee), 12 movements
> 222-02
> MS A:Wn (Sm. 3885)

Cleopatras Tod (ballet)
> *Cleopatras Tod*
> Arranger unknown, 13 movements
> 222-02
> MS CS:KRa (IV.B.10)

Cramer, Johann (1771–1858)

March, from the clavier Divertimento
Arranged by Triebensee
222-02
MS A:Wn (Sm. 3739, Jg. I, Oevre 2, Nr. 4)

Dalayrac, Nicolas (1753–1809)

Nina (opera, 1786)
> *Nina*
> Arranged by Ehrenfried
> 220-02, string bass
> MS BRD:HR (III.4.1/2.20.351/352)

> *Nina*
> Arranged by Ignaz Beecke (1733–1803), 8 movements
> 2222-02, string bass
> MS BRD:Rtt (Beecke 12)

    Nina
    Arranger unknown
    222-02
    MS BRD:DO [may be lost]

Azemia (opera, 1786)
    Suite d'Azemia
    Arranged by Fuchs
    Harmoniemusik
    MS BRD:BÜu (D-AR-15)

    Airs d'Azemia, ou Les sauvages
    Arranged by Fuchs
    42-02, serpent; or 22-02
    EP (Paris, Sieber, Nr. 1247, as 'Suite Nr. 94') BRD:AM, MÜu

    Ouverture d'Azemia
    Arranger unknown
    Seven- or nine-part *Harmoniemusik*
    EP (Paris, Ebend)

    Overture aus Die Wilden
    Arranger unknown
    222-02, contrabassoon
    MS DDR:RUl (RH-D1)

Les deux petits Savoyards (opera, 1789)
    Beiden Savoyarden
    Arranger unknown
    222-02
    MS I:Fc (D.V.500)

    Die beiden Savojarden
    Arranged by Sedlak
    22 02
    MS PL:LA (2302)

Camille (opera, 1791)
    Camille, ou Le souterrain
    Arranger unknown (probably Fuchs)
    22-02; or 42-02
    EP (Paris, Sieber, Nr. 1333, as 'Suite Nr. 62') S:Uu [clarinets 2, 3, 4 and horn 2 missing]

Gulnare (opera, 1798)
    Airs de Gulnare oul'esclave
    Arranged by Fuchs
    Eight-part *Harmoniemusik*
    EP (Paris, Janet et C.) F:Pn (Vm.27.1183); BRD:MÜu

Ouverture de Gulnare
Arranged by Fuchs
Nine-part *Harmoniemusik*
EP (Paris, Imbault, Nr. 64) F:Pn [two copies]

Maison à vendre (opera, 1800)
Ouverture and Airs from Maison à vendre
Arranged by Fr. Blasius
Harmoniemusik
EP (Paris, Imbault, Nr. 178) F:Pn; BRD:AM

La jeune Prude (opera, 1804)
Airs de la jeune Prude
Arranged by Vanderhagan
Eight-part *Harmoniemusik*
EP (Paris, Pleyel, Nr. 657 and 687) H:KE

Ouverture de la jeune Prude
Arranged by Vanderhagan
Eight- and ten-part *Harmoniemusik*
EP (Paris, Ebend) H:KE

Gulistan (opera, 1805)
Giulistan
Arranger unknown
222-02
MS I:Fc (D.V.499)

Gulistan
Arranger unknown, 12 movements
222-02
MS CS:KRa (IV.B.1)

Airs de Gulistan
Arranger unknown
Harmoniemusik
EP (Paris, Ebend) [Suites 1, 2]

Ouverture de Gulistan
Arranger unknown
Harmoniemusik
EP (Paris, Ebend)

Michelange (opera)
Michelange
Arranged by Vanderhagen
2022-12, serpent
MS DDR:HER (Mus.N.1=2)

la Tour de Neustadt (opera)
> *Airs de la Tour de Neustadt*
> Arranger unknown
> *Harmoniemusik*
> EP (Paris, Erard) BRD:AM

> *Ouverture de la Tour de Neustadt*
> Arranged by M.J. Gebauer
> *Harmoniemusik*
> EP (Paris, Ebend)

Poëte et le Musicien
> *Airs du Poëte et le Musicien*
> Arranger unknown
> *Harmoniemusik*
> EP (Paris, Dufaut et Dubois)

> *Ouverture de Poëte et le Musicien*
> Arranger unknown
> Eight-part *Harmoniemusik*
> EP (Paris, Ebend)

> *Marsch aus Der Dichter und Tonsetzer*
> Arranger unknown
> 222-22, piano
> MS CS:Bm (A.35.267)

> *Overture aus Der Dichter und Tonsetzer*
> Arranged by Sedlak
> 222-22
> MS CS:Bm (A.35.159)

> *Ouverture du Prologue du Poëte et le Musicien*
> Arranger unknown
> Eight-part *Harmoniemusik*
> EP (Paris, Ebend)

Die Nacht im Walde (opera?)
> *Die Nacht im Walde*
> Arranged by Schmitt
> 2222-221, string bass
> MS BRD:AB (S.31)

Corsaire (opera?)
> *Corsaire*
> Arranged by M.J. Gebauer
> 222-02, serpent
> EP (Paris, Boyer, as 'Novelle Suite, Nr. 11') BRD:MÜu

Sargines (opera?)
> *Sargines*
> Arranged by M.J. Gebauer
> 42-02
> EP (Paris, Sieber, Nr. 1248, as 'Suite Nr. 95') BRD:F

la Boucle de Cheveux (opera)
> *Airs de la Boucle de Cheveux*
> Arranger unknown
> *Harmoniemusik*
> EP (Paris, Erard) BRD:AM

> *Ouverture de la Boucle de Cheveux*
> Arranger unknown
> *Harmoniemusik*
> EP (Paris, Ebend) BRD:AM

une Heure de Marriage (opera, 1804)
> *Airs d'une Heure de Marriage*
> Arranger unknown
> Eight-part *Harmoniemusik*
> EP (Paris, Pleyel) F:Pn

> *Ouverture de une Heure de Marriage*
> Arranger unknown
> Eight- and eleven-part *Harmoniemusik*
> EP (Paris, Ebend)

Jean et Genevieve (opera)
> *Airs de Jean et Genevieve*
> Arranger unknown
> *Harmoniemusik*
> EP (Paris, Nadermann)

Picaros et Diègo (opera)
> *Airs de Picaros et Diègo*
> Arranger unknown
> Eight-part *Harmoniemusik*
> EP (Paris, Pleyel)

> *Ouverture de Picaros et Diègo*
> Arranger unknown
> Eight- and eleven-part *Harmoniemusik*
> EP (Paris, Pleyel)

Suite (unidentified)
> Arranged by Gebauer
> Nine-part *Harmoniemusik*
> MS(?) BRD:BÜu (D-AR-25)

Danzi, Franz (1763–1826)

Chorus aus Freudenfest
Arranged by Sartorius
22-02, contrabassoon
MS BRD:DS (Mus. 215)

Daroudeau, ?

Ouverture du Rosier
Arranger unknown
Harmoniemusik
EP (Paris, Gambaro)

Delaborde, ?

Ouverture de Cinquantine
Arranged by Fuchs
22-62
EP (Paris, Nadermann) F:Pn (Vm.7.6975; Vm.7.1029; and Vm.27.1597)

Della Maria, Pierre-Antoine Dominique (1769–1800)

L'Opéra-comique (opera, 1798)
    Airs de l'Opéra comique
    Arranger unknown
    Harmoniemusik
    EP (Paris, H. Lemoine) BRD:MÜu

    Ouverture de l'Opéra comique
    Arranger unknown
    Harmoniemusik
    EP (Paris, Ebend)

    [L'Opéra comique]
    Arranged by Nicolas Jörg
    22-02
    EP (Mainz, Schott, Nr. 231) BRD:MZsch

Le Prisonnier (opera, 1798)
    Airs du Prisonnier
    Arranger unknown
    Eight-part *Harmoniemusik*
    EP (Paris, Janet et C.)

    Ouverture du Prisonnier
    Arranger unknown
    Eight-part *Harmoniemusik*
    EP (Paris, Ebend)

L'Oncle Valet (opera, 1798)
    Airs de l'Oncle Valet
    Arranger unknown
    Eight-part *Harmoniemusik*
    EP (Paris, Sieber)

    Ouverture de l'Oncle Valet
    Arranger unknown
    Nine-part *Harmoniemusik*
    EP (Paris, Ebend)

vieux Chateau (opera?)
    Ouverture du vieux Chateau
    Arranger unknown
    Harmoniemusik
    EP (Paris, B. Lemoine)

    Ouverture du vieux Chateau
    Arranged by Gebauer
    Harmoniemusik
    EP (Paris, Pacini)

    Airs de vieux Chateau
    Arranged by Gebauer
    Harmoniemusik
    EP (Paris, Pacini)

Ouverture (to an unidentified opera)
    Arranged by M.J. Gebauer
    1022-121, serpent
    EP (Paris, Lemoine) F:Pn (Vm.27.1743)

Dezède, Nicolas (1740?–1792)

Blaise et Babet (opera, 1783)
    Desaides [Blaise et Babet]
    Arranger unknown
    222-02
    MS I:Fc (D.V.490)

    Ouverture de Blaise et Babet
    Arranger unknown
    Eight- and twelve-part *Harmoniemusik*
    EP (Paris, Sieber)

La fête de la Cinquantaine (Opera, 1796)
    Airs de la Cinquantaine
    Arranger unknown
    Harmoniemusik
    EP (Paris, Nadermann) [Suite 1, 2]

Ouverture de la Cinquantaine
Arranger unknown
Harmoniemusik
EP (Paris, Ebend)

Deshayes, Prosper-Didier

Le faux serment Nouvelle suite d'harmonie ... ouverture et airs ...
Arranged by Ozi
22-02
EP (Paris, Boyer) S:Uu [missing clarinet 2, bassoon 2]

Zelia or *Le Mari a deux femmes* (opera, 1791)
Ouverture de Zelia or *Le Mari a deux femmes*
Arranger unknown
Nine-part *Harmoniemusik*
EP (Paris, Sieber)

Devienne, Francois (1759–1803)

Les Visitandines (opera, 1792)
Les visitandines, oder Die Herrhuterinnen
Arranged by Stumpf
22-02
EP (Hamburg, J. A. Böhme) BRD:Hs; S:Skma
Advertized in the *Weiner Zeitung*, October 28, 1801.

Ouverture, Les visitandines
Arranged by Fuchs
42-02; or 22-02
EP (Paris, Sieber, Nr. 1328) S:Uu [missing clarinets 2, 3, 4 and horn 2]

Ouverture de Visitandines
Arranger unknown
Six- and seven-part *Harmoniemusik*
EP (Paris, Ebend)

Airs des Visitandines
Arranged by Fuchs
42-02; or 22-02
EP (Paris, Sieber, Nr. 1310, as 'Suite Nr. 97') BRD:AB [missing clarinet 4]

Le valet de deux maîtres (opera, 1799)
Airs du Valet de 2 Maitres
Arranger unknown
Harmoniemusik
EP (Paris, Beaucé)

Ouverture du Valet de 2 Maitres
    Arranger unknown
    Harmoniemusik
    EP (Paris, Beaucé)

Diabelli, Antonio (1781–1858)

Tambourin solo, from *Madmoiselle Neuman*
    Arranged by Triebensee
    222-02
    MS A:Wn (Sm. 3739, Jg. I, Oevre 1, Nr. 4)

Dittersdorf, Karl Ditters von (1739–1799)

Betrug durch Aberglauben (opera, 1786)
    Arranger unknown
    222-02
    MS (Advertized in Traeg's Catalog, Vienna, 1799)

Doctor und Apotheker (opera, 1786)
    Dokter u. Apothecker
    Arranger unknown
    22-02
    MS (Advertized in Traeg's Catalog, Vienna, 1799)

    Doktor und Apothecker
    Arranger unknown
    222-02
    MS (Advertized in Traeg's Catalog, Vienna, 1799)

    Der Doctor und Apotheker
    Arranged by Wendt [Went], 6 movements
    202-02, 2 English horns
    MS CS:K (Nr. 17.K.I.)

    Doctor und Apotheker
    Arranger unknown, in two parts
    Eight-part *Harmoniemusik*
    MS BRD:DO [may be lost]

    Der Apotheker and der Doktor
    Arranged by Wendt, 9 movements
    222-02
    MS NL:Ura/mZ (M.A.Zcm.17)
    The ninth movement is from Mozart's *Figaro*.

Hironimus Knicker (opera, 1789)
    Hironimus Knicker
    Arranger unknown
    Eight-part *Harmoniemusik*
    MS BRD:DO [may be lost]

> *Hironimus Knicker*
> Arranger unknown
> 222-02
> MS NL:M

Dobihal, Josef (clarinetist, military band conductor, mentioned in Beethoven's conversation book for 1813–1814)

> *Farso*
> Arranger unknown, 12 movements
> 222-02, contrabassoon
> MS CS:KRa (IV.B.17)

Donizetti, Gaetano (1797–1848)

> *Anna Bolena* (opera, 1830)
>> *Aria aus Anna Bollena*
>> Arranger unknown
>> 222-22
>> MS CS:Bm (A. 35.160)
>
> *L'Elisir d'Amore* (opera, 1832)
>> Arranged by Sedlak (MS by Perschl), 6 movements
>> 222-22
>> MS A:Wn (Sm. 3808)
>
> *Torquato Tasso* (opera, 1833)
>> *Torquato Tasso*
>> Arranged by Sedlak? (first five movements, MS by Perschl; sixth movement MS by Sedlak), 6 movements
>> 222-22
>> MS A:Wn (Sm. 3810)
>
>> *Cavatina aus Torquato Tasso*
>> Arranger unknown
>> 222-02
>> MS A:Wn [lost]
>
> *Marino Faliero* (opera, 1835)
>> Arranged by Sedlak? (MS by Perschl), 3 movements
>> 222-02
>> MS A:Wn (Sm. 3967)
>
> *Lucia di Lammermoor* (opera, 1835)
>> Arranged by Sedlak?, 2 movements
>> 222-22
>> MS A:Wn (Sm. 3809)

Duport, Jean Louis (1749–1819)

Der blöde Ritter (ballet)
    Der bloede Ritter
    Arranged by Triebensee
    222-02
    MS A:Wn (Sm. 3739, Jg. III, Oevre 6) [12 movements, final act]; A:Wn (Sm. 3795, Nr. 18–22) [5 movements]

    Der blönde Ritter
    Arranger unknown, 10 movements
    22-02
    MS CS:KRa (IV.B.23)

    Der blöde Ritter
    Arranger unknown
    Nine-part *Harmoniemusik*
    EP (Vienna, Haslinger)

Figaro (ballet)
    Figaro
    Arranged by Triebensee, 6 movements
    222-02
    MS A:Wn (Sm. 3739, Jg . I, Oevre 8, Nr. 5–10)

Zephir (ballet)
    Arranged by Triebensee, 12 movements
    222-02
    MS A:Wn (Sm. 3739, Jg. III, Oevre 5)

    Zephier
    Arranger unknown, 10 movements
    22-02
    MS CS:KRa (IV.B.22)

    Zephir
    Arranger unknown
    222-02
    EP (Vienna, Haslinger) CS:Bm (A.18.709)

    Zephir
    Arranger unknown
    Six-part *Harmoniemusik*
    EP (Vienna, Haslinger)

Duttilieu, Pierre (1754–1797)

Die Macht des schönen Geschlechts (ballet)
    Die Macht des schönen Geschlechts
    Arranged by Wendt [Went], 13 movements
    202-02, 2 English horns
    MS CS:K (Nr. 174.K.II)

die Macht des schönen Geschlechts
Arranger unknown
222-02
MS (Advertized in Traeg's Catalog, Vienna, 1799)

Die Macht des Schönen Geschlechts
Arranger unknown
22-02
MS (Advertized in Traeg's Catalog, Vienna, 1799)

Ernst, Franz Anton (d. 1805?)

les airs de l'opéra Tarrare
Arranger unknown
22-02
EP (Berlin and Amsterdam, Hummel, *grand magazin de musique*, Nr. 805) DDR:Dlb; SF:A

Federici, Francesco (d. 1830)

Andante from Zaira (opera, 1803)
Arranged by Triebensee
222-02
MS A:Wn (Sm. 3794, Nr. 9)

Ferrari, Giacomo (1759–1842)

La Villenella rapita (opera)
  Airs de la Villenella rapita
  Arranger unknown
  Six- and eight-part *Harmoniemusik*
  EP (Paris, Sieber)

  Ouverture de la villenella rapita
  Arranger unknown
  Eight- and ten-part *Harmoniemusik*
  EP (Paris, Sieber)

Fioravanti, Valentino (1764–1837)

Le Cantarici villane (opera, 1799)
  Airs des Cantatrice villane
  Arranger unknown
  2022-02
  EP (Paris, Imbault, Nr. 943) BRD:Rtt; F:Pn (Vm.27.4172) [two copies]

La Capricciosa pentita (opera, 1802)
    La Capriciosa
    Arranger unknown
    222-02
    MS I:Fc (D.V.498)

    La Capriciosa Revedute
    Arranger unknown, 12 movements
    22-02
    MS CS:KRa (IV.B.143)

Fiorillo, Ignazio (1715–1787)

Il Venditore d'aceto
    Arranger unknown
    222-02
    MS BRD:DO [may be lost]

Fischer, ?

Vincent (opera)
    Arie aus Vincent
    Arranged by Triebensee
    222-02
    MS A:Wn (Sm. 3739, Jg. I, Oevre 1, Nr. 9)

Foignet, Charles Gabriel (1750–1823)

Ouverture de Mont Alphéa
    Arranged by Fuchs
    42-12
    EP (Paris, Nadermann, Nr. 166) F:Pn (Vm.27.1600 and Vm.7.6971) [two copies]; BRD:Tu

Gallenberg, Robert (1783–1839)

Alfred der Grosse (ballet, 1820)
    Alfred der Grosse
    Arranged by Sedlak (his '24th work')
    222-22
    MS A:Wn (Sm. 3862)

    Alfred Marsch
    Arranger unknown
    222-02
    MS CS:Bm (A.35.257) [incomplete]

Marsch aus Alfred der Grosse
Arranged by Sedlak? (MS by Perschl)
222-02
MS A:Wn (Sm. 3863)

Jeanne d'Arc (ballet, 1821)
Arranger unknown
222-22, contrabassoon
EP (Vienna, Mechetti)
Advertized in the *Wiener Zeitung*, February 21, 1821.

Ottavio Pinelli (ballet, 1830)
Arranged by Sedlak
222-22
MS A:Wn (Sm. 3864)

Gaveaux, Pierre (1761–1825)

L'Amour filial (opera, 1792)
L'Amour filial
Arranged by Devienne
2022-02
EP (Paris, as '2nd Suite d'harmonie') BRD:DS

Ouverture et Airs du l'Amour filial
Arranger unknown
Harmoniemusik
EP (Paris, P. Petit)

Le petit Matelot (opera, 1796)
Ouverture et Airs du petit Matelot
Arranger unknown
Harmoniemusik
EP (Paris, Ebend)

Le diable en vacances, ou La suite du diable couleur de rose (opera, 1805)
Ouverture et Airs du Diable Couleur de Rose
Arranger unknown
Harmoniemusik
EP (Paris, Ebend)

Ouverture du Diable en Vacance
Arranger unknown
Harmoniemusik
EP (Paris, P. Petit)

Airs de Diable en Vacance
Arranger unknown
Harmoniemusik
EP (Paris, Ebend)

Le Diable Auteur (opera?)
>Ouverture et Airs du Diable Auteur
Arranged by M. J. Gebauer
Harmoniemusik
EP (Paris, Gaveaux Frere, Nr. 211, 217) BRD:AB

Le traité nul (opera, 1797)
>Ouverture et Airs du Traité nul
Arranger unknown
Harmoniemusik
EP (Paris, Ebend)

Sophie et Moncars, ou L'intrigue portuguaise (opera, 1797)
>Ouverture et Airs du Sophie et Moncars
Arranger unknown
Harmoniemusik
EP (Paris, Ebend)

Monsieur Deschalumeaux (opera, 1806)
>Ouverture de Mr. Deschalumeaux
Arranger unknown
Harmoniemusik
EP (Paris, S. Gaveaux)

>*Airs de Mr. Deschalumeaux*
Arranger unknown
Harmoniemusik
EP (Paris, Ebend)

Gerl (Görl), Franz Xaver (1764–1827)

Der dumme Gärtner aus dem Gebirge (opera, 1789)
>*der dume Gärtner*
Arranger unknown
222-02
MS (Advertized in Traeg's Catalog, Vienna, 1799)

Gianella, Louis (1778–1817)

Acis et Galathée (ballet, 1805)
>*Acis u. Galathea*
Arranged by Triebensee
Blas-Instr.
MS (cited in MGG)

>*Acis et Galatee*
Arranger unknown
Harmoniemusik
EP (Paris, Leduc, as 'Journal Liv. 12')

Gluck, Christoph Willibald (1714–1787)

La Rencontre imprevue [*Les pèlerins de la Mecque*] (opera, 1764)
> *Pellegrino di Mecca*
> Arranger unknown
> 222-02
> MS I:Fc (D.V.480)
>
> *2 Arien aus Pilgrime von Mecka*
> Arranger unknown
> 212-02; or 222-02
> MS (Advertized in Traeg's Catalog, Vienna, 1799)
>
> *Aria (and) Chorus aus Pilgrime von Mecka*
> Arranger unknown
> 232-02
> MS (Advertized in Traeg's Catalog, Vienna, 1799)
>
> [Gluk] *2 Arias aus Pilgrime von Messa*
> Arranger unknown
> 222-; and 1122-
> MS (Advertized in Traeg's Catalog, Vienna, 1799)
>
> [Rouck] *2 Arias aus Die Pilger nach Mecca*
> Arranger unknown (probably Wendt)
> 202-02, 2 English horns
> MS CS:K (Nr. 31.K.I. and Nr.32.K.I.)
>
> [Klik] *Aria aus Die Pilgram nach Mecha*
> Arranger unknown (probably Wendt)
> 202-02, 2 English horns
> MS CS:K (Nr. 35.K.I.)
>
> *Die Pilgrime von Mecca*
> Arranged by Wendt
> 222-02
> MS (Advertized in the *Weiner Zeitung*, 1784)

Alceste (opera, 1767)
> [Kluk] *Aria aus d'Alceste*
> Arranger unknown (probably Wendt)
> 202-02, 2 English horns
> MS CS:K (Nr. 36.K.I)

Iphigénie en Aulide (opera, 1774)
> *Ouverture d'Iphigenie en Aulide*
> Arranger unknown
> *Harmoniemusik*
> EP (Paris, Sieber; and Schlesinger)

Armide (opera, 1777)
    Armida
    Arranger unknown
    222-02
    MS I:Fc (D.V.509)

    March and Echo Aria from Armide
    Arranged by Triebensee
    222-02
    MS A:Wn (Sm. 3739, Jg. I, Oevre 7, Nr. 5, 6); BRD:Mbs (Mus.Ms.2583); CS:KRa (IV.B.146)
    [as *Miscellannes de Musique*, op. 7 for 222-12, contrabassoon]

Iphigénie en Tauride (opera, 1779)
    Iphigenia in Tauride
    Arranged by Triebensee
    Harmoniemusik
    MS A:Ee

    Iphigenie en Tauride
    Arranger unknown
    222-02
    MS A:Wn [lost]

    Iphigenia in Tauris
    Arranger unknown
    222-02
    MS I:Fc (D.V.509)

    Airs d'Iphigenie en Tauride
    Arranger unknown
    Eight- or eleven-part *Harmoniemusik*
    EP (Paris, Sieber)

das kleine Wasser (opera, original unidentified)
    [Klik] *das kleine Wasser*
    Arranger unknown (probably Wendt)
    202-02, 2 English horns
    MS CS:K (Nr. 33.K.I.)

Mochomet (opera, original unidentified)
    [Klik] *Mochomet*
    Arranger unknown (probably Wendt)
    202-02, 2 English horns
    MS CS:K (Nr. 34.K.I.)

Gesang (original unidentified)
    Arranger unknown
    2222-02, contrabassoon
    MS BRD:BÜu (G-lu-6/2)

Gossec, François Joseph (1734–1829)

Le triomphe de la république, ou Le camp de Grandpré (Divertissement, 1793)
    Ouverture et Airs du Triomphe de la Republic
    Arranged by Fuchs
    42-12
    EP (Paris, Nadermann, Nr. 152, 158) F:Pn (Vm.27.876)

Grétry, André Ernest Modeste (1741–1813)

Silvain (opera, 1770)
Lucile (opera, 1769)
    7 Ariettes du Silvain et une de Lucile
    Arranged by Röser
    22-02
    MS DDR:Dlb

Zémire et Azor (opera, 1771)
    Zemire et Azor
    Arranger unknown
    222-02
    MS I:Fc (D.V.490)

    Zemire et Asor
    Arranger unknown, 6 movements
    22-02
    MS CS:Pnm (XLI.B.110)

    Semire & Azor
    Arranger unknown
    222-02
    MS (Advertized in Traeg's Catalog, Vienna, 1799)

    Trio aus Zermire et Azor
    Arranger unknown
    22-02
    MS DDR:WRtl (Mus. II.C=5)

    Terzett aus Zemire und Azor
    Arranged by Triebensee
    222-02
    MS A:Wn (Sm. 3739, Nr. 8)

La Caravane du Caire (opera, 1783)
    Airs de la Caravanne
    Arranger unknown
    Six-part *Harmoniemusik*
    EP (Paris, Sieber)

Ouverture de la Caravanne
Arranger unknown
Eight- or twelve-part *Harmoniemusik*
EP (Paris, Ebend)

Richard Coeur-de-Lion (opera, 1784)
Richard Coeur de Lion
Arranged by M. Habert, 8 movements
222-02
MS (score) BRD:DS (Mus. 486)

Three Partitas based on Richard Coeur de Lion
Arranged by Ehrenfried
Nr. 1, 3: 220-02, string bass; Nr. 2: 221-02, string bass
MS BRD:HR (111.4.1/2.353–355)

Airs de Richard Coeur de Lion
Arranger unknown
Six-part *Harmoniemusik*
EP (Paris, Ebend)

Panurge dans l'Isle des Lanternes (opera, 1785)
Panurge
Arranged by Vanderhagen
22-02
EP (Paris, Le Duc) S:Uu [missing clarinet 2 and horn 2]

Ouverture de Panurge
Arranger unknown
Eight- or twelve-part *Harmoniemusik*
EP (Paris, Ebend)

Raoul Barbe Bleue (opera, 1789)
Raul der Blaubart
Arranger unknown
22-02
MS PL:LA (2303)

Raul der Blaubart
Arranged by Anton Fischer
222-02
MS I:Fc (D.V.502) [Cataloged under 'Fischer']

Raul der Blaubart
Arranger unknown, 14 movements
22-02
MS CS:KRa (IV.B.34)

Raul der Blaubart
Arranger unknown
22-02
MS CS:Pnm (XLI.A.88)

Le rival confident (opera, 1788)
Arranger unknown
22-02
EP (Paris, Imbault, Nr. 89) S:Uu [missing clarinet 2 and horn 2]

Twelve opera arias (original unidentified)
Arranger unknown
1120-02
MS NL:Ura/mZ

Guglielmi, Pietro (1728–1804)

La Pastorella nobile (opera, 1788)
   Ouverture de Pastorella Nobile
Arranger unknown
22-02
EP (Paris, Imbault) BRD:MÜu

Pastorella Nobile
Arranger unknown
222-02
MS I:Fc (D.V.486)

La Pastorella Nobile
Arranged by Wendt [Went], 10 movements
202-02, 2 English horns
MS CS:K (Nr. 11.K.I)

La Pastorella nobile
Arranger unknown
222-02
MS A:Wn [lost]

Pastorella nobile
Arranger unknown
Harmoniemusik
MS A:Ee

Le Pastorella Nobile
Arranger unknown
222-02
MS (Advertized in Traeg's Catalog, Vienna, 1799)

La bella Pescatrice (opera, 1789)
    Bella Pescatrice
    Arranger unknown
    222-02
    MS I:Fc (D.V.491)

    La bella Pescatrice
    Arranged by Wendt [Went], 11 movements
    202-02, 2 English horns
    MS CS:K (Nr. 10.K.I.)

    La Bella Pescatrice
    Arranger unknown
    Harmoniemusik
    MS A:Ee

    La bella Pescatrice
    Arranger unknown
    222-02
    MS A:Wn [lost]

    La bella Piscatrice
    Arranger unknown
    222-02
    MS (Advertized in Traeg's Catalog, Vienna, 1799)

    La bella Piscatrice
    Arranger unknown
    22-02
    MS (Advertized in Traeg's Catalog, Vienna, 1799)

Overture (source unidentified)
    Arranger unknown
    Six-part *Harmoniemusik*
    MS BRD:BÜu (G-Ug-41)

Gyrowetz, Adalbert (1763–1850)

Agnes Sorel (opera, 1806)
    Agnes Sorel
    Arranger unknown
    222-02
    MS I:Fc (D.V.503)

    [Girowetz] *Agnes Sorel*
    Arranged by Sedlak, 13 movements
    22-02
    MS CS:Pnm (XLI.B.106), CS:Pnm (XXVII.B.231)

Agnes Sorel
Arranger unknown, in Two Acts
Harmoniemusik
MS A:Ee

Agnes Sorel
Arranger unknown, 11 movements
22-02
MS CS:KRa (IV.B.32)

Agnes Sorel
Arranged by Triebensee, 3 movements
222-02
MS A:Wn (Sm. 3791, Nr. 1–3)

Der Augenarzt (opera, 1811)

Der Augenartz
Arranged by Starke
Nine-part *Harmoniemusik*
EP (Vienna, Mechetti, Nr. 78) CS:Bm
Advertized in the *Wiener Zeitung*, April 25, 1812.

[Girovetz] *Der Augenarzt*
Arranger unknown, 6 movements
22-02
MS CS:KRa (IV.B.31)

[Jirovec] *Augenarzt*
Arranged by Starke
222-22
MS CS:Bm (A.35.167) [incomplete]

Federica ed Adolfo (opera, 1812)

Federica ed Addolfo
Arranged by Triebensee, 14 movements from Act I and 7 movements from Act II
222-02
MS A:Wn (Sm. 3739, Jg. III, Oevre 1; and Jg. III, Oevre 2)

Die Hochzeit der Thetis und des Peleus (ballet, 1816)

Hochzeit der Thetis
Arranged by Sedlak
222-02
MS A:Wn (Sm. 3865)

die Hochzeit der Thetis
Arranger unknown, 6 movements
222-22
MS CS:Bm (A.35.170)

Die Pagen des Herzoge von Vendome (ballet, 1808)
> *Die Pagen des Herzoge von Vendome*
> Arranged by Sedlak
> 222-02
> MS A:Wn (Sm. 3851)

> [Jirovec] *Die Pagen des Herzogs von Vendom*
> Arranged by Starke, 6 movements
> 222-02, contrabassoon
> MS CS:Bm (A.35.171)

Miriam (original unidentified)
> Arranger unknown
> 222-02
> MS I:Fc (D.V.503)

[Jirovec] *Die Zwey Tanten* (original unidentified)
> Arranger unknown, 4 movements
> 222-22, contrabassoon
> MS CS:Bm (A.35.169)

Die beiden Eremiten (1816, original unidentified)
> Arranger unknown
> 222-02
> MS A:Wn [lost]

(unidentified opera)
> Arranged by Triebensee, 2 movements
> 222-02
> MS A:Wn (Sm. 3795, Nr. 16–17)

Händel, Georg Friedrich (1685–1759)

Saul
> Arranger unknown
> Six or seven-part *Harmoniemusik*
> EP (Paris, Sieber)

Haydn, Joseph (1732–1809)

Gatt erhalte den Kaiser
> Arranger unknown
> SATB, 222-02
> MS H:BuNM (Ms.Mus.1578/9)

The Creation (Oratorio)
> *Creazione*
> Arranger unknown
> 222-02
> MS I:Fc (D.V.506)

Die Schöpfung
Arranger unknown, 10 movements
22-02
MS CS:KRa (IV.B.35)

Die Schöffung
Arranger unknown
222-02
MS I:Fc (D.V.507)

La Creation
Arranger unknown
2042-221, serpent
EP (Paris, Pleyel, Nr. 414, 415, as two suites of 5 movements each) CH:Zz [first suite only]; CH:Gpu

Die Schöpfung
Arranged by Druschetzky, complete
222-02
MS A:Wgm (VIII 40509); US:DW (348, 355)

The Seasons (Oratorio)

Jahrszeiten
Arranged by Druschetzky, complete
1222-02
MS A:Wgm (VIII 47734); US:DW (349)

The Seasons
Arranger unknown
222-02
MS I:Fc (D.V.507)

Symphony (I, 51)
Arranged by M.J. Gebauer
1032-121, serpent
EP (Paris, Sieber, Nr. 1364 [1813]) BRD:F

Symphony (I, 55)
Arranger unknown
222-02
MS PL:LA (2453)

Symphony (I, 70)
Arranger unknown
222-02
MS PL:LA (2454)

Symphony (I, 73)
> *Sinfonia par Mr. Hayden*
> Arranger unknown
> 222-02
> MS PL:LA (2455)

> *Symphony*
> Arranged by M. J. Gebauer, movements I, IV
> Six- and eight-part *Harmoniemusik*
> EP (Paris, Pirro) I:Bc

Symphony (I, 75)
> Arranger unknown
> 222-02
> MS PL:LA (2456)

Symphony (I, 85, 'La Reine')
> Arranged by Charles Bochsa
> 2022-121, serpent
> EP (Paris, Duhan, Nr. 1; reprinted Dufaut et Dubois) F:Pn (Vm.27.2073, Nr. 1), F:Pn (Vm.7.10542)

Symphony (I, 91)
> Arranged by Bochsa
> 2022-121, serpent
> EP (Paris, Dunan, Nr. 3) F:Pn (Vm.25.33 and Vm.7.10544)

Symphony (I, 102)
> Arranged by Bochsa
> 2022-121, serpent
> EP (Paris, Dunan, Nr. 2) F:Pn (Vm.7.10543 and Vm.27.2073, Nr. 2)

Symphony ('Oxford')
> Arranged by Triebensee
> 222-12, contrabassoon
> MS A:Wn (Sm. 3739, Jg. II, Oevre 11, Nr. 1–4)

Andante mit den Paukenschlag
> Arranger unknown
> 222-02
> MS (Advertized in Traeg's Catalog, Vienna, 1799)

(Unidentified Symphonies)
> *Adagio, Menuetto, Presto*
> Arranged by Triebensee
> 222-02
> MS A:Wn (Sm. 3739, Jg. I, Oevre 3, Nr. 2–4)

> *Presto*
> Arranged by Triebensee
> 222-02
> MS A:Wn (Sm. 3739, Jg. I, Oevre 2, Nr. 10)

Sinfonie
    Arranged by F. R. Gebauer
    Harmoniemusik
    EP (Paris, Sieber)

Sinfonia in E♭
    Arranger unknown
    1222-12
    MS I:Bc

Harmonie tirée des ouvres d'Haydn
    Arranged by Gambaro
    Harmoniemusik
    EP (Paris) F:Pn (Vm.27.1622)

Morceaux choisis dans les oeuvres du célèbre Haydn
    Arranged by Vanderhagen
    2022-02
    EP (Paris, Pleyel, Nr. 967) CH:Gpu

Haydn, Michael (1737–1806)

Sinfonia par Hayden
    Arranger unknown
    222-02
    MS PL:LA (2457)

Hérold, Louis Joseph Ferdinand (1791–1833)

La Clochette (opera, 1817)
    Ouverture et Pas redouble du Clochette
    Arranger unknown
    Harmoniemusik
    EP (Paris, Gambaro)

Zampa (opera, 1831)
    Arranged by Sedlak?, 15 movements
    222-02
    MS A:Wn (Sm. 3811)

Le Pré aux Clercs (opera, 1832)
    Ouverture de l'Opéra: Le Pré aux Clercs
    Arranger unknown
    Harmoniemusik
    EP (Paris, Ebend)

Le dernier jour de Missolonghi (incidental music, 1828)
    Ouverture de Missolunghi
    Arranged by Berr
    Harmoniemusik
    EP (Mainz, Schott) BRD:MZsch

Zweikampf oder Schreiber Wiese bey Paris (original unidentified)
> Arranged by Sedlak?, 3 movements
> 222-22
> MS A:Wn (Sm. 3812)

Himmel, Friedrich Heinrich (1765–1814)

Fanchon, das Leiermädchen (opera, 1804)
> *Fanchon*
> Arranged by J. C. Düring
> 2222-02
> MS BRD:F (Mus.Ms.1788)

> *Fanibon*
> Arranger unknown
> 222-02
> MS I:Fc (D.V.491)

> *Fauchon*
> Arranger unknown (probably Triebensee) 10 movements
> 222-02
> MS CS:KRa (IV.B.40)

> *Fanchon*
> Arranged by Triebensee, 10 movements
> 222-02
> MS A:Wn (Sm. 3739, Jg. I, Oevre 11, Nr. 1–10)

> *Airs de Fanchon*
> Arranger unknown
> Eight- or ten-part *Harmoniemusik*
> EP (Paris, Sieber)

> *Ouverture de Fanchon*
> Arranger unknown
> Eight- or twelve-part *Harmoniemusik*
> EP (Paris, Sieber)

Hoffmeister, Franz Anton (1754–1812)

Der Königssohn aus Ithaka (opera, 1795)
> *Der Könige-Sohn*
> Arranged by Satorus
> 22-02, contrabassoon
> MS BRD:DS (Mus. 248)

Aria aus Donaus Weibschen (original unidentified)
> Arranger unknown
> 22-02
> MS CS:KRa (IV.B.41)

Hummel, Johann Nepomuk (1778–1837)

Die Eselshaut, oder Die blaue Insel (opera, 1814)
   Die Esels Haus
   Arranged by Starke?, 7 movements
   1222-22
   MS CS:KRa (IV.B.142)

   Die Eselshaut
   Arranged by Sedlak
   222-02
   EP (Vienna, Steiner [1814]) US:Wc

Helena und Paris (ballet)
   One movement, arranged by Triebensee
   222-02
   MS A:Wn (Sm. 3739, Jg. I, Oevre 7, Nr. 8)

Isouard, Niccolò (1775–1818)

Michel-Ange (opera, 1802)
   Ouverture aus Michael Angelo
   Arranged by Sedlak
   222-22
   MS CS:Bm (A.37.334)

   Airs de Michel Ange
   Arranger unknown
   Eight-part *Harmoniemusik*
   EP (Paris, Ebend)

   Ouverture de Michel Ange
   Arranger unknown
   Nine-part *Harmoniemusik*
   EP (Paris, Ebend)

   Ouverture de Michel Ange
   Arranged by Vanderhagen
   2022-121, serpent
   EP (Paris, Magasin de Musique) CS:Bm (A.36.885)

   Airs de Michel Ange
   Arranger unknown
   Eight-part *Harmoniemusik*
   EP (Paris, Frey)

   aus Michael Angelo
   Arranger unknown
   222-22
   MS CS:Bm (A.37.344)

Les Confidences (opera, 1803)
    Les confidences
    Arranged by Vanderhagen
    2022-121, serpent
    EP (Paris, Magasin de Musique [ca. 1803]) CS:Bm (A.36.884)

Le Médecin Turc (opera, 1803)
    Ouverture du Médecin Turc
    Arranger unknown
    2022-021, serpent
    EP (Zürich, Nägeli, Nr. 262) H:KE

    Airs du Médecin turc
    Arranger unknown
    Nine-part *Harmoniemusik*
    EP (Paris, Frey)

    Ouverture du Médecin turc
    Arranger unknown
    Harmoniemusik
    EP (Paris, Ebend)

L'Intrigue aux Fenêtres (opera, 1805)
    Airs de l'Intrigue aux Fenêtres
    Arranger unknown
    Harmoniemusik
    EP (Paris, Frey)

    Ouverture de l'Intrigue aux Fenêtres
    Arranger unknown
    Harmoniemusik
    EP (Paris, Ebend)

Un Jour à Paris (opera, 1808)
    Airs d'un Jour à Paris
    Arranger unknown
    Harmoniemusik
    EP (Paris, Ebend) [Suite 1, 2]

Cendrillon (opera, 1810)
    Aschenbröd
    Arranger unknown, 13 movements
    222-02, contrabassoon
    MS CS:Bm (A.35.168) [as 'V Journal für Harmonie']

    Aschenbrödel
    Arranged by Triebensee, 17 movements
    222-02
    MS A:Wn (Sm. 3739, Jg. II, Oevre 9; Jg. II, Oevre 10, Nr. 1–6)

Aschenbrödel
Arranger unknown, 4 movements
22-02
EP (Vienna, K. K. Druckerey) CS:KRa (IV.B.57)

Aschenbrödel
Arranger unknown
222-02
MS I:Fc (D.V.511)

Aschenbrödl
Arranger unknown, 13 movements
222-02, contrabassoon
EP (Vienna, Haslinger) CS:Bm (A.35.168)
Haslinger also advertized a version for six-part *Harmoniemusik*.

Ouverture de Cendrillon
Arranger unknown
Six-part *Harmoniemusik*
EP (Paris, Ebend)

Cendrillon
Arranger unknown
22-02
EP (Vienna, Steiner)

Airs de Cendrillon
Arranger unknown
Harmoniemusik
EP (Paris, Troupenas) [Suites 1–3]

Ouverture de Cendrillon
Arranger unknown
Harmoniemusik
EP (Paris, Troupenas)

Airs de Cendrillon
Arranger unknown
Harmoniemusik
EP (Paris, Ebend) [Suites 1–3]

Le Billet de Loterie (opera, 1811)
  Airs du Billet de Lotterie
  Arranger unknown
  Harmoniemusik
  EP (Paris, Ebend)

  Ouverture du Billet de Lotterie
  Arranger unknown
  Harmoniemusik
  EP (Paris, Ebend)

Le Magicien sans Magie (opera, 1811)
    Airs du Magicien sans Magie
    Arranger unknown
    Harmoniemusik
    EP (Paris, Ebend)

    Ouverture du Magicien sans Magie
    Arranger unknown
    Harmoniemusik
    EP (Paris, Ebend)

Lully et Quinault (opera, 1812)
    Airs de Lulli et Quinault
    Arranger unknown
    Harmoniemusik
    EP (Paris, Troupenas)

    Ouverture de Lulli et Quinault
    Arranger unknown
    Harmoniemusik
    EP (Paris, Ebend)

Le Prince de Catane (opera, 1813)
    Airs du Prince de Catane
    Arranger unknown
    Harmoniemusik
    EP (Paris, Troupenas) [Suites 1, 2]

Joconde (opera, 1814)
    Joconde
    Arranged by Sedlak, 12 movements
    222-02
    MS A:Wgm (VIII 41156); CS:KRa (IV.B.184)

    Airs de Joconde
    Arranger unknown
    Harmoniemusik
    EP (Paris, Ebend) [Suites 1–3]

    Ouverture de Joconde
    Arranger unknown
    Harmoniemusik
    EP (Paris, Ebend)

Jeannot et Colin (opera, 1814)
    Airs de Jeannot et Colin
    Arranger unknown
    Harmoniemusik
    EP (Paris, Troupenas) [Liv. 1, 2]

    Ouverture de Jeannot et Colin
    Arranger unknown
    Harmoniemusik
    EP (Paris, Ebend)

Aladin (opera, 1822)
    Airs d'Aladin
    Arranger unknown
    Harmoniemusik
    EP (Paris, Troupenas) [Liv. 1, 2]

    Ouverture d'Aladin
    Arranger unknown
    Harmoniemusik
    EP (Paris, Ebend)

L'impromptude campagne (opera, 1797)
    Airs de l'Impromptu
    Arranger unknown
    Eight- and twelve-part *Harmoniemusik*
    EP (Paris, Pleyel)

Léonce (opera, 1805)
    Airs de Léonce
    Arranger unknown
    Harmoniemusik
    EP (Paris, Frey)

    Ouverture de Léonce
    Arranger unknown
    Harmoniemusik
    EP (Paris, Ebend)

Josepf und der Kleinen Dieblin (original unidentified)
    Arranged by Sedlak, 24 movements
    222-02
    MS A:Wn (Sm. 3852)

Kanne, ?

Orpheus (opera)
    Arranged by Triebensce, 1 movement
    222-02
    MS A:Wn (Sm. 3739, Jg. I, Oevre 7, Nr. 9)

Kauer, Ferdinand (1751–1831)

Das Donauweibchen (opera, 1798)
> *Ouverture aus Donau-Weibchen*
> Arranged Schmitt?
> 2222-22, serpent
> MS BRD:AB (S.9)

> *Das Donau-Weibchen*
> Arranged by Satorus
> 22-02, contrabassoon
> MS BRD:DS (Mus.Ms.243)

Kinsky, Josef, Prince of Bohemia (b. 1781, one of the three financial supporters of Beethoven)

Das ländliche Fest im Wäldchen bei Kis-Bér (opera?)
> *Das landliche Fest im Waldchen bei Kis-Ber*
> Arranged by Triebensee, 5 movements
> 222-02
> MS A:Wn (Sm. 3791, Nr. 4–8)

> *Das Ländliche Fest in Wäldchen*
> Arranger unknown
> 222-22
> MS BRD:TSCH (Z.25)

Kozeluch, Leopold (1752–1818)

La ritrovata Figlia d'Ottone II (ballet?)
> *Le Ritrovata Figlia*
> Arranged by Wendt
> 222-02
> MS A:Wn (Sm. 3866)

> *La ritrovata Figlia*
> Arranged by Satorus
> 22-02, contrabassoon
> MS BRD:DS (Mus.Ms.804)

> *La ritro vatasiglio di Ottone II*
> Arranger unknown
> 222-02
> MS (Advertized in Traeg's Catalog, Vienna, 1799)

Die wieder gefundene Tochter Otto III (ballet)
> *Die wieder gefundene Tochter Otto III*
> Arranger unknown
> 22-02
> MS (Advertized in Traeg's Catalog, Vienna, 1799)

Die gefundene Tochter Kaiser Otto II
Arranged by Krommer
Harmoniemusik
MS BRD:DO [may be lost]

Eroico Die Wiedergassundene Tochter Kaiser Otta des III
Arranger unknown (probably Wendt), 17 movements
202-02, 2 English horns
MS CS:K (Nr. 180.K.II)

Die wiedergefundene Tochter
Arranger unknown
Harmoniemusik
MS A:Ee

Kreutzer, Rodolphe (1766–1831)

Paul et Virginie (opera, 1791)
    Airs du Paul et Virginie et de Francois I
    Arranger unknown
    Harmoniemusik
    EP (Paris, Frey)

    Ouverture de Paul et Virginie
    Arranged by Fucbs
    42-1, serpent; or 22-02
    EP (Paris, Sieber) S:Uu [clarinet I, bassoons I, II, and horn I only]

Lodoiska (opera, 1791)
    Lodoisca
    Arranged by Richter
    Harmoniemusik
    MS BRD:DO [may be lost]

Antonius und Cleopatra (ballet)
    Marcia aus Antonius und Cleopatra
    Arranged by Triebensee
    222-02
    MS A:Wn (Sm. 3791, Nr. 12)

    Airs du Cleopatre
    Arranger unknown
    Harmoniemusik
    EP (Paris, Frey)

Krommer, Franz (1759–1831)

Symphony
Arranged by Triebensee, 4 movements
222-02
MS A:Wn (Sm. 3739, Jg. I, Oevre 7, Nr. 1–4); BRD:Mbs (Mus. 2583); CS:KRa (IV.B.146)
[for 222-12, contrabassoon]

Kunzen, Friedrich (1761–1817)

Das Fest der Winzer (opera)
Arranged by Simoni, 22 movements
2000-02, basso
MS CS:K (Nr. 7.K.I)

Kürzinger, Paul (ca. 1755–ca. 1820)

Robert und Caliste (ballet)
Arranged by Sussmayr, 1 movement
22-02
MS GB:Lbm (Add.32181, ff. 156–160)

Leidersdorf, Franz

Fest Overture bei Gelegenheit der Feyerlichen Krönung Ibrer Majestät Carolina Kaiserin von Osterreich zur Königin von Ungarn (1837)
Arranged by Oscar Kolbe
222-02
MS H:BuNM (Ms.Mus.1498)

Lemoyne, Jean Baptiste (1751–1796)

Ouverture (original unidentified)
Arranger unknown
22-02
EP (Paris, Imbault, Nr. 105) S:Uu

Les Prétendus (opera, 1789)
  Airs des Prétendus
  Arranger unknown
  Six- or eight-part *Harmoniemusik*
  EP (Paris, Sieber)

  Ouverture de Prtendus
  Arranger unknown
  Six-part *Harmoniemusik*
  EP (Paris, Janet et C.)

Ouverture de Prétendus
Arranger unknown
Six-, eight-, or ten-part *Harmoniemusik*
EP (Paris, Sieber)

Lesueur, Jean François (1760–1837)

La Caverne (opera, 1793)

Ouverture de la Caverne
Arranged by Fuchs
42-12
EP (Paris, Nadermann) F:Pn (Vm.27.2586 and Vm.7.6974) [two copies]

Ouverture de la Caverne
Arranger unknown
Nine-part *Harmoniemusik*
EP (Paris, Ebend)

Airs de la Caverne
Arranger unknown
Harmoniemusik
EP (Paris, Nadermann)

Ossian (opera, 1804)

Ouverture d'Ossian ou les Bardes
Arranger unknown
Six-part *Harmoniemusik*
EP (Paris, Janet Et C.)

Airs d'Ossian
Arranger unknown
Six-part *Harmoniemusik*
EP (Paris, Ebend)

le Songe d'Ossian dans les Bardes
Arranger unknown
Eight-part *Harmoniemusik*
EP (Paris, Janet et C.)

Ouverture, Ossian ou les Bardes
Arranger unknown
22-02
EP (Paris, Imbault, Nr. 190) F:Pn (Vm.27.2585)

[Notturno] Songe d'Ossian
Arranger unknown
1202-02, serpent
EP (Paris, Imbault) F:Pn (Vm.27.3358); BRD:AB

Morceaux choises des Les Bardes
Arranged by Fuchs
22-02
EP (Paris, Imbault) F:Pn (Vm.27.1588) [1, 2]

March, 'Der Kaledonier', aus Der Barden
Arranged by Triebensee
222-02
MS A:Wn (Sm. 3739, Jg. I, Oevre 2, Nr. 9)

Paul et Virginie, ou Le triomphe de la vertu (opera)
   Ouverture de Paul et Virginia
   Arranged by Fuchs
   42-22
   EP (Paris, Nadermann) F:Pn (Vm.27.2587 and Vm.7.6974) [two copies]; US:Cn

Suitte d'harmonie
Arranged by Vanderhagen
22-02
EP (Paris, Sieber) BRD:AB

Lindpainter, Peter Joseph von (1791–1856)

Joko (ballet)
   Arranged by C. H. Meyer
   Harmoniemusik
   EP (Leipzig, Peters)

Liverati, Giovanni (1772–?)

David, oder Goliaths Tod (oratorio, 1811)
   David, oder Goliaths Tod
   Arranged by Sedlak
   222-02
   MS A:Wgm (VIII 38236)

   David
   Arranged by Sedlak, 7 movements
   22-02
   MS CS:Pnm (XLI.B.107); CS:KRa (IV.B.81)

   David
   Arranger unknown
   Nine-part *Harmoniemusik*
   EP (Vienna, Haslinger)

Lortzing, Gustav Albert (1801–1851)

Czaar und Zimmermann (opera, 1837)
    Ouverture aus Czaar und Zimmermann
    Arranged by Wallentin
    222-22, contrabassoon
    MS CS:Bm (A.37.339)

Malherbe, l'aîné

Trois marches dont la première est à grand orchestre execute à La Haye le vingt neuf février 1788
    Arranger unknown
    2 clarinets or 2 oboes with 2-02
    EP (Den Haag-Amsterdam, Hummel)

Marcello di Capua (1730–1799)

Ouverture, Furberia et Pontiglio
    Arranger unknown
    Eight-part *Harmoniemusik*
    EP (Paris, Janet et C.)

Prinzessin Marie Esterházy

Ländler
    Arranged by Triebensee
    222-02
    MS A:Wn (Sm. 3739, Jg. II, Oevre 12, Nr. 10)

Marschner, Heinrich August (1795–1861)

Stücke aus Der Templer und die Jüdin (opera, 1829)
    Arranged by Barth
    Harmoniemusik
    EP (Leipzig, Hoffmeister)

Martin y Soler, Vicente (1754–1806)

Una Cosa rara (opera, 1786)
    Una Cosa Rara
    Arranger unknown
    222-02
    MS I:Fc (D.V.478)

    Una cosa rara
    Arranger unknown
    222-02
    MS A:Wn [lost]

Cosa Rara
Arranger unknown
Harmoniemusik
MS BRD:DO [may be lost]

Ouvertura. Opera Cosa Rara
Arranger unknown
222-02
MS PL:LA (2461)

Una cosa rara
Arranged by Sartorus
22-02, contrabassoon
MS BRD:DS (Mus. 800)

Una Cosa rara
Arranged by Wendt [Went], 16 movements
202-02, 2 English horns
MS CS:K (Nr. 22.K.I.)

Una Cosa Rara
Arranger unknown
Harmoniemusik
MS A:Ee

Cosa rara
Arranger unknown
222-02
MS (Advertized in Traeg's Catalog, Vienna, 1799)

Airs d'una Cosa rara
Arranger unknown
Harmoniemusik
EP (Paris, Ebend)

Ouverture d'una Cosa rara
Arranger unknown
Harmoniemusik
EP (Paris, Nadermann)

L'Abore di Diana (opera, 1787)
L'arbore di Diana
Arranger unknown
Harmoniemusik
MS A:Ee

L'Arbore di Diana
Arranged by Wendt
Harmoniemusik
MS A:Wn (Sm. 3816); BRD:DO (Ms. 1282)

Arbore di Diana
Arranger unknown
222-02
MS I:Fc (D.V.478)

Arbore di Diana et Axur (Salieri)
Arranger unknown
22-02
MS CS:Pnm (XLII.D.86)

L'Arbore di Diana
Arranged by Wendt, 24 movements
202-02, 2 English horns
MS CS:K (Nr. 23.K.I)

L'Arbore di Diana
Arranged by Sartorus
222-22
MS BRD:DS (Mus. 797)

L'Arbore di Diana
Arranger unknown
222-02
MS (Advertized in Traeg's Catalog, Vienna, 1799)

La scola de' maritati (opera, 1791)
    polaca della Capriccioza Coretta
    Arranged by Fuchs
    Harmoniemusik
    EP (Paris, Imbault, Nr. 794); BRD:AB [flute 2 and clarinet 2 only]; Printed together with arias by Rossini and Paisiello.

    La Capriciosa corretta
    Arranged by Stumpf
    22-02
    EP (Offenbach, André, Nr. 13 of 20 Recueils, each of six movements); A:KR, Wn; CH:Zz; CS:Pnm (XLI.B.136) [incomplete]; DDR:SWl; US:Wc, WS [incomplete]

    Pieces d'Harmonie de la Capricciosa corretta
    Arranged by Stumpf
    22-02
    EP (Paris, Imbault) BRD:AB

    Ouverture et Airs de la Capricciosa corretta
    Arranger unknown
    Eight-part *Harmoniemusik*
    EP (Paris, Sieber)

Andramaca (opera, 1780)
> *Duet & recitative d'Andromaca*
> Arranger unknown
> 202-02
> MS (sc) DK:Sa (R.128)

Die geberserte Eigensinnige (original unidentified)
> Arranged by Sartorus
> 22-02: contrabassoon
> MS BRD:DS (Mus. 798)

Martini, Jean Paul (1741–1816)

Henri IV (opera, 1774)
> *Ouverture de Henri IV*
> Arranger unknown
> Eight- or twelve-part *Harmoniemusik*
> EP (Paris, Sieber)

Maurer, Louis (1789–1878)

Pas de Deux and Pantomime Arlequin, from Alznu (ballet)
> Arranged by Triebensee
> 222-02
> MS A:Wn (Sm. 3739, Jg. I, Oevre 1, Nr. 6)

Mayr, Johann Simon (1763–1845)

Lodoiska (opera, 1796)
> *Lodoiska*
> Arranger unknown
> 222-02
> MS I:Fc (D.V.505)

> *La Lodioiska*
> Arranger unknown
> 222-02
> EP (Vienna, K.K .Hof Theatermusik Verlag [ca. 1800])

> *Lodoiska*
> Arranger unknown
> 222-02
> MS A:Wn [lost]

> *Lodoiska*
> Arranger unknown
> *Harmoniemusik*
> MS A:Ee

Ginevra di Scozia (opera, 1801)
    Ginevra di Scozia
    Arranger unknown
    222-02
    MS I:Fc (D.V.494)

    Ginevra di Scozia
    Arranger unknown
    22-02
    MS PL:LA (2304)

    Stücke aus Ginevra
    Arranged by J. Buchal
    21-02
    MS PL:LA (2283)

    Ginevra
    Arranger unknown, in Two Acts
    Harmoniemusik
    MS A:Ee

Alonso e Cora (opera, 1803)
    Alonzo e Cora
    Arranger unknown
    222-02
    MS I:Fc (D.V.497)

    Allonsa e Cora
    Arranged by Sedlak, 8 movements
    22-02
    MS CS:KRa (IV.B.85)

Adelasia e Aleramo (opera, 1806)
    Adelaria e Aleramo
    Arranger unknown
    222-02
    MS I:Fc (D.V.501)

    Adelasia et Aleranio
    Arranger unknown, 14 movements
    222-02, contrabassoon
    MS CS:KRa (IV.B.86)

    Arie aus Adelasia
    Arranged by Triebensee
    222-02
    MS A:Wn (Sm. 3739, Jg. I, Oevre 3, Nr. 7)

Duetto aus Adelasia
Arranged by Triebensee
222-02
MS A:Wn (Sm. 3739, Jg. I, Oevre 7, Nr. 7); BRD:Mbs (Mus. 2583); CS:KRa (IV.B.146)

Ercole (opera?)
Arranger unknown
222-02
MS I:Fc (D.V.492)

Scene aus Solitari (opera?)
Arranged by Leo. Ratti
1021-02, serpent
MS I:Ppriv

Méhul, Etienne Nicolas (1763–1817)

Euphrosine (opera, 1790)
   Suite ...
Arranged by Fuchs
22-02
EP (Paris, Sieber) S:Uu [missing clarinet 2, horn 2]

Cora (opera, 1791)
   Alonso e Cora
Arranger unknown, 8 movements
222-22, contrabassoon
MS CS:Bm (A.36.869)

Le jeune Henry (opera, 1797)
   Ouverture in C
Arranger unknown
222-02
MS PL:LA (2462)

   Ouverture du jeune Henry
Arranger unknown
2022-041, serpent
EP (Paris, magazin de musique) BRD:AB

   Ouverture du jeune Henry
Arranger unknown
Harmoniemusik
EP (Paris, Schlesinger)

Adrien (opera, 1799)
   Ouverture d'Adrien
Arranger unknown
2022-02
EP (Paris, Pleyel, Nr. 387) BRD:Rp

Ariodant (opera, 1799)
    Marceaux choisis d'Ariodant
    Arranged by Fuchs
    2022-02
    EP (Paris, Imbault, Nr. 748); BRD:AB [missing flute 1]; F:Pn (Vm.27.2899 and Vm.7.6981) [two copies]

    Airs d'Ariodant
    Arranger unknown
    Eight-part *Harmoniemusik*
    EP (Paris, Janet et C.)

L'Irato (opera, 1801)
    Ouverture et airs d'Irato
    Arranged by Ozi
    22-02
    EP (Paris, Pleyel, Nr. 454)

Une Folie (opera, 1802)
    Une Folie
    Arranged by Sedlak
    22-02
    MS PL:LA (2305)

    Airs d'une Folie
    Arranger unknown
    Eight-part *Harmoniemusik*
    EP (Paris, Pleyel) [Liv. 1, 2]

    Ouverture d'une Folie
    Arranger unknown
    Nine-part *Harmoniemusik*
    EP (Paris, Ebend)

Le Trésor supposé (opera, 1802)
    Der Schatzgrüber
    Arranger unknown
    222-02
    MS I:Fc (D.V.499)

    Der Schatzgräber
    Arranged by Triebensee ['Trubense'], 9 movements
    222-02, contrabassoon
    MS CS:K (Nr. 51.K.I.); CS:KRa (IV.B.94)

    Ouverture du Tresor suppose
    Arranger unknown
    Harmoniemusik
    EP (Paris, Langlois)

Héléna (opera, 1803)
> [*Helene*]
> Arranger unknown, 7 movements
> 222-02
> MS CS:KRa (IV.B.92)
>
> *Ouverture d'Hélène*
> Arranger unknown
> Eleven-part *Harmoniemusik*
> EP (Paris, Langlois)
>
> *Ouverture d'Hélène*
> Arranger unknown
> Ten-part *Harmoniemusik*
> EP (Paris, Ebend)

Les deux Aveugles de Tolede (opera, 1806)
> *Airs des 2 Aveugles des Tolede*
> Arranger unknown
> *Harmoniemusik*
> EP (Paris, Langlois) [Suite 1, 2]
>
> *Ouverture des 2 Aveugles des Tolede*
> Arranger unknown
> *Harmoniemusik*
> EP (Paris, Ebend)

Joseph (opera, 1807)
> *Overture aus Joseph und seine Bruder*
> Arranged by Sedlak
> 222-02, contrabassoon
> MS CS:KRa (IV.B.185)
>
> *Josephine und Seiner Bruder*
> Arranger unknown
> 222-02
> MS I:Fc (D.V.511)
>
> *Joseph*
> Arranged by J. Weigl
> 222-22, contrabassoon
> MS CS:Bm (A.37.341)
>
> *Airs de Joseph*
> Arranger unknown
> *Harmoniemusik*
> EP (Paris, Ebend)

  Ouverture de Joseph
  Arranger unknown
  Harmoniemusik
  EP (Paris, Ebend)

La Journée aux Aventures (opera, 1816)
  Airs de la Journee aux Aventures
  Arranger unknown
  Harmoniemusik
  EP (Paris, P. Petit) [Liv. 1, 2]

  Ouverture de la Journée aux Aventures
  Arranger unknown
  Harmoniemusik
  EP (Paris, Ebend)

  Rondeau de la Journée aux Aventures
  Arranger unknown
  -421
  EP (Paris, Ebend)

  Rondeau de la Journée aux Aventures arr. en Pas redouble
  Arranged by Gambaro
  Harmoniemusik
  EP (Paris, Ebend)

Bion (original unidentified)
  Ouverture de Bion
  Arranger unknown
  Ten- and fourteen-part *Harmoniemusik*
  EP (Paris, Pleyel)

Stratonice (original unidentified)
  Airs de Stratonice
  Arranger unknown
  Six- and eight-part *Harmoniemusik*
  EP (Paris, Sieber)

  Ouverture de Stratonice
  Arranger unknown
  Seven- and nine-part *Harmoniemusik*
  EP (Paris, Ebend)

Der Bauer (opera, original unidentified)
  Der Bauer
  Arranger unknown, 9 movements
  222-02
  MS CS:KRa (IV.B.93)

Overture aus Der Bauer
Arranged by Triebensee
222-02
MS A:Wn (Sm. 3739, Jg. I, Oevre 8, Nr. 1); BRD:Mbs (Mus. 2584)

Der Temperamente (opera, original unidentified)
Arranged by Triebensee, 1 movement
222-02
MS A:Wn (Sm. 3739, Jg. I, Oevre 2, Nr. 7)

Beiden Füchse (original unidentified)
Arranger unknown
222-02
MS I:Fc (D.V.499)

Mendelssohn, Felix (1809–1847)

Overture zum Sommernachtstraum
Arranged by C. B. Meyer
Eight-part *Harmoniemusik*
EP (Leipzig, Breitkopf & Härtel)

Mercadante, Saverio (1795–1870)

Elisa e Claudio (opera, 1821)
Elisa und Claudio
Arranged by Sedlak
222-22, contrabassoon
MS CS:Bm (A.35.188) [Part I, 12 movements]; CS:Bm (A.35.188) [Part II, 6 movements]

Elisa und Claudio
Arranged by Starke
222-22, contrabassoon
MS CS:Bm (A.35.185)

Elisa und Claudio
Arranger unknown (1824)
222-22, contrabassoon
MS CS:Bm (A.35.186) [Part I, 7 movements]

Il Posto abbandonato (opera)
Il Posto Abbandanato
Arranger unknown
222-12, contrabassoon
MS CS:Bm (A.35.189) [incomplete]

Duet aus Il Posto abbandonato
Arranger unknown
222-22, contrabassoon
MS CS:Bm (A.19.412)

Anacreonte in Samo (opera?)
>Arranged by Sedlak?, 1 long movement
>222-221
>MS A:Wn (Sm. 3819)

Donna Caritea (opera?)
>Arranger unknown, 4 movements
>222-22, contrabassoon
>MS CS:Bm (A.35.184)

Meyer, ?

Theresa et Claudio
>Arranged by Richter
>222-02
>MS BRD:DO [may be lost]

Meyerbeer, Giacomo (1791–1864)

Margherita d'Anjou (opera, 1820)
>*Ouverture de Marguerie d'Anjou*
>Arranged by Berr
>Nine-part *Harmoniemusik*
>EP (Mainz, Schott) BRD:MZsch

Il Crociato in Egitto (opera, 1824)
>*Die Kriezfahrt in Egypten*
>Arranger unknown, 6 movements
>222-221
>MS CS:Bm (A.35.190)

Robert-le-Diable (opera, 1831)
>*4 Favorit-Stücke aus der Oper: Robert der Teufel*
>Arranged by Neithardt
>*Harmoniemusik*
>EP (Berlin, Schlesinger)

>*Robert Walzer*
>Arranger unknown, 5 movements
>32-221, contrabassoon
>MS CS:Bm (A.37.340) [missing trumpet 2]

Les Huguenots (opera, 1836)
>*Les Huguenots*
>Arranged by Sedlak? (MS by Perschl), 6 movements
>222-22
>MS A:Wn (Sm. 3820)

Hugnenotten
Arranger unknown
1221-421, contrabassoon
MS CS:Bm (A.20.930)

Moniuszko, Stanislaw (1819–1872)

Halka (opera, 1854)
    Canzone aus Halka
    Arranger unknown
    122-1
    EP (Oertel)

Monsigny, Pierre (1729–1817)

1r suitte des amusements militaires contenant un choix d'ariettes tirées des opéra comique ...
Arranged by Vanderhagen
22-02
EP (Paris, de La Chevardière) S:Uu [missing clarinet 2 and horn 2]

Morlacchi, Francesco (1784–1841)

Tebaldo e Isolina (opera, 1822)
    Overture aus Tebaldo
    Arranger unknown
    222-22, contrabassoon
    MS CS:Bm (A.35.191)

Möser, ?

Die Berg-Schotten (quadrille)
    Allegro, contradanz, 2 trios and coda
    Arranged by Triebensee
    222-02
    MS A:Wn (Sm. 3795, Nr . 15)

    Contradanse
    Arranged by Triebensee
    222-02
    MS A:Wn (Sm. 3739, Jg. I, Oevre 7, Nr. 10); BRD:Mbs (Mus. 2583); CS:KRa (IV.B.146)

Mozart, Wolfgang (1756–1791)

Idomeneo (opera, 1781)
    Idomeneo
    Arranger unknown
    222-02
    MS I:Fc (D.V.492)

Die Entführung aus dem Serail (opera, 1782)
    Die Entführung
    Arranged by Wendt
    222-02
    MS I:Fc (P.370)

    Die Entführung aus dem Serail
    Arranger unknown (probably Wendt)
    202-02, 2 English horns
    MS CS:K (Nr. 38.K.I.)
    MP (ed. Schmid, 1955)

    Die Entführung aus dem Serail
    Arranger unknown
    222-02
    MS BRD: DO (Mus.Ms. 1392)

    Entführung
    Arranger unknown
    222-02
    MS A:Ee

    Die Entführung aus dem Serail
    Arranged by Mozart
    222-02(?)
    MS (lost?)
    Mentioned in a letter to his father, July 20, 1782.

    Entführung
    Arranger unknown
    41-2
    MS BRD:Rtt (Mozart 17/I, Nr. 7–9)

    die Entführung aus dem Serail
    Arranger unknown
    222-02
    MS (Advertized in Traeg's Catalog, Vienna, 1799)

Der Schauspieldirektor (opera, 1786)
    Schauspieldirektor
    Arranger unknown
    41-2
    MS BRD:Rtt (Mozart 17/I, Nr. 6)

Le Nozze di Figaro (opera, 1786)
    Figaro
    Arranger unknown
    Harmoniemusik
    MS A:Ee

Le nozze di Figaro
Arranged by Wendt [Went]
202-02, 2 English horns
MS CS:K (Nr. 39a.K.I. and Nr. 39b.K.I.)

Figaro
Arranger unknown
202-02, basset horn
MS DDR:Bds (Mus.Ms.15150/4)

Le Nozze di Figaro
Arranged by Rosiniack
Eight-part *Harmoniemusik*
MS BRD:DO [may be lost]

Mariage de Figaro
Arranger unknown
222-02
MS I:Fc (D.V.484)

Le Nozze di Figaro
Arranged by Wendt
222-02
MS I:Fc (P.329); US:DW (128)
This copy was formerly owned by the Royal Prussian Library.

Die Hochzeit des Figaro
Arranged by Nowotny
222-22, contrabassoon
MS CS:Bm (A.37.343)

Die Hochzeit des Figaro
Arranged by Wendt
Harmoniemusik
MS DDR:Bds (Konig.Hausbibl. Nr. 345)
An eight-part arrangement by Wendt was advertized in the *Wiener Zeitung* for August, 27, 1791.

Figaro
Arranged by Sartorus
22-02, contrabassoon
MS BRD:DS (Mus.Ms.818)

Le nozze di Figaro
Arranged by Kajetan Vogel
Six- and eight-part *Harmoniemusik*
EP (Vienna, Balzer) CS:Pnm [incomplete version of the six-part print, according to Grove XX, 55]
Advertized in the *Wiener Zeitung*, June 6, 1787.

Airs du Mariage de Figaro
Arranged by Vanderhagen
2022-02
EP (Paris, Sieber) [in 3 volumes] CH:Gpu [Vols. 2, 3 complete]

Ouverture de l'opera: Le nozze di Figaro
Arranged by Hammerl
2022-12, serpent
EP (Hamburg, Böhme, Nr. 'M.1') CH:Lz

Ouverture de Figaro
Arranger unknown
Eight- and eleven-part *Harmoniemusik*
EP (Paris, Janet et C.)

Marsch aus Figaro
Arranger unknown
212-1
MS DDR:Bds (Hausbibl. Nr. 115)

3 Märsche aus Figaro
Arranger unknown
202-22
MS DDR:Bds (Hausbibl. Nr. 116)

Rundtanz aus Figaro
Arranged by Purebl
222-02
EP (Vienna, K.K.priv.chem.Druckerei, Nr. 960) CS:Pnm (XLI.B.123)

Figaro
Arranged by Nowotny, 1 movement
222-22, contrabassoon
MS CS:Bm (A.37.343)

Overture aus Figaro
Arranger unknown
222-02
MS CS:KRa (IV.B.93) [the tenth movement, under Méhul, *Der Bauer*]

Figaro
Arranged by Wendt
222-02
MS NL:Ura/mZ (M.A.Zcm 17) [the ninth movement, under Dittersdorf, *Der Apotheker und der Doktor*]

Don Giovanni (opera, 1787)
  Don Giovanni
  Arranger unknown
  222-02
  MS (Advertized in Traeg's Catalog, Vienna, 1799)

Don Giovanni
Arranged by Triebensee
Harmoniemusik
MS A:Ee (Mus. 1091)

Don Giovanni
Arranger unknown
22-02
MS CS:Pnm (XLI.B.154)

Don Juan Suita
Arranger unknown
22-02
MS CS:Pnm (XLI.B.150)

Don Juan
Arranger unknown, 1 movement
221-221
MS CS:Bm (A.36.866)

Don Juan
Arranged by Nowatny
212-13, contrabassoon
MS CS:Bm (A.37.342)

Don Juan
Arranged by Triebensee, 13 movements
222-02
MS CS:Bm (A.35.129)

Don Juan
Arranged by Osswald, 1 movement
222-22, contrabassoon
MS CS:Bm (A.40.158)

Don Juan
Arranger unknown, 1 movement
212-22, contrabassoon
MS CS:Bm (A.40.159)

Don Juan
Arranger unknown
222-02
MS DDR:Bds (Mus.Ms. 15151/4)

Don Juan
Arranger unknown, 15 movements
22-02
EP (no town, as *Journal für Sechstimige Harmonie*, Nr. 97) CS:KRa (IV.B.97)

Don Giovanni
Arranged by Wendt [Went]
202-02, 2 English horns
MS CS:K (Nr. 37.K.I)

Overture aus Don Juan
Arranger unknown
Ten-part *Harmoniemusik*
MS CS:Pnm (VII.B.1) [in *Opernstücke für 10 Blas Inst.*]

Don Giovanni
Arranged by Rosiniack
Harmoniemusik
MS BRD:DO [may be lost]

Don Joan
Arranger unknown
22-02
MS PL:LA (2307)

Don Giovanni
Arranged by Stumpf
2222-02, basse
MS NL:M

Don Giovanni
Arranged by Triebensee
222-02
MS CS:Pnm (Archiv Lobovic X.Gf.69)

Don Giovanni
Arranged by Schacht, 13 movements
22-02, 2 violas(?), string bass
MS BRD:Rtt (Mozart 17/III)

Don Giovanni
Arranged by Ehrenfried
222-02
MS I:Fc (Mus. 477A)

Airs de Don Juan
Arranged by Fuchs
2022-02
EP (Paris, Sieber, Nr. 367) CH:Gpu

Ouverture de Don Juan
Arranged by Vanderhagen
2022-121
EP (Paris, Pleyel, Nr. 956) CH:Gpu

Airs de Don Juan
Arranger unknown
Eight-part *Harmoniemusik*
EP (Paris, Dufant et Dubois)

Cosi fan tutte (opera, 1790)

Cosi fan Tutti
Arranger unknown
Harmoniemusik
(Advertized in Traeg's Catalog, Vienna, 1799)

Cosi
Arranged by Vojácek, 1 movement
222-22
MS CS:Bm (A.20.281)

Cosi fan Tutti
Arranged by Wendt [Went], 18 movements
202-02, 2 English horns
MS CS:K (Nr. 41.K.I)
Köchel incorrectly gives the location of this manuscript as CS:Pnm.

Cosi fan Tutte
Arranger unknown
222-02
MS CS:Pnm (XX.F.21)

Cosi fan tutti
Arranged by Legrand
1122-02
MS BRD:Rtt (Mozart 25/III)

Cosi fan tutte
Arranged by Wendt
Harmoniemusik
MS I:Fc (D.V.482)

Ouverture, Cosi
Arranged by Stumpf
2222-12, contrabassoon [trumpet appearing only on the title-page]
MS (score, modern copy) US:DW (398)

Cosi fan tutte
Arranger unknown
222-02
MS I:Fc (P.317)

Cosi fan tutte
Arranger unknown
222-02
MS KRa (R.I.26/1, 4)

Overture aus Cosi fan tutte
Arranger unknown
222-22, contrabassoon
MS CS:Bm (A.20.281)

Cosi
Arranger unknown
41-2
MS BRD:Rtt (Mozart, 17/I)

Douze nouvelles suites d'harmonie
Arranged by Stumpff; here further arranged as *marches et pas redoublés* by J. Gebauer
222–02
EP (Paris, Sieber, père, Nr. 1581) [as *suite 115, 8ème livraison*] BRD:F

Douze nouvelles suites d'harmonie
Arranged by J. Gebauer
222-02
EP (Paris, Sieber, père) [as *suite 116, 9e livraison*] BRD:F

La Clemenza di Tito (opera, 1791)

Marcia, aus La Clemenza di Tito
Arranger unknown
Harmoniemusik
MS (Advertized in Traeg's Catalog, Vienna, 1799)

La Clemenza di Tito
Arranged by Fuchs
2022-02
MS CH:Zz (AMG XIII)

La Clemenza di Tito
Arranger unknown
222-02
MS A:Ee (Nr. 1058)

La Clemenza di Tito
Arranged by Seyfried, 1 movement
SATB, 222-02
MS A:Wsp (Celle B.87)

La Clemenza di Tito
Arranged by Triebensee?
222-02
MS CS:Pnm (Archiv Lobovic X.Ha.60, X.62)

3 arias aus Tito
Arranger unknown
22-02
MS CS:Pnm (XLI.B.156, 157, 158)

La Clemenza di Tito
Arranger unknown
222-02
MS CS:KRa (R.I.24.A/9)

La Clemenza di Tito
Arranger unknown, 9 movements
222-02, contrabassoon
MS CS:Bm (A.35.192)

Clemenza di Tito
Arranger unknown
22-02
MS PL:LA (2306)

La Clemenza di Tito
Arranged by Krechtler
222-02
MS I:MOe (Mus.D.262)

Titus
Arranged by Sartorus
22-02, contrabassoon
MS BRD:DS (Mus.Ms.815)

Overture aus Clemenza di Tito
Arranged by Schmitt
2232-24, serpent, timpani
MS BRD:AB (N.1/4)

Clemenza di Tito
Arranged by Stumpf
222-02
MS BRD:DO (Mus. 1398)

Clemenza di Tito
Arranger unknown
Twelve-part *Harmoniemusik*
MS BRD:DO [may be lost]

Marcia, aus La Clemenza di Tito
Arranger unknown
222-02
MS (Advertized in Traeg's Catalog, Vienna, 1799)

La Clemenza di Tito
Arranged by Triebensee
222-02, contrabassoon
EP (Vienna, Steiner) I:Fc (P.358)

Ouverture de la clémence de Titus
Arranged by Fuchs
Six-part *Harmoniemusik*
EP (Paris, Decombe) CH:Gpu

Airs de la clémence de Titus
Arranged by Fuchs
Six-part *Harmoniemusik*
EP (Paris, Decombe) CH:Gpu; I:Fc (B.2763)

La clemenza di Tito
Arranged by Stumpf
2022-12, string bass
EP (Augsburg, Gombart, Nr . 369, 449) [Liv. 1, 2]; BRD:AB [Liv. 1]; BRD:HR [Liv. 1, 2]; BRD:Mbs [Liv. 1]; BRD:NEhz [Liv. 1, 2]; GB:Lbm [Liv. 1]

Ouverture
Arranged by Hammerl
2022-12, serpent
EP (Hamburg, Böhme) CH:Lz

Airs de La clémence de Titus
Arranged by Fuchs
Eight-part *Harmoniemusik*
EP (Paris, Decombe) [as *2. suite*]

Ouverture de Titus
Arranger unknown
Ten-part *Harmoniemusik*
EP (Paris, Ebend)

Ouverture de Titus
Arranger unknown
Eight-part *Harmoniemusik*
EP (Paris, Janet et C.)

Ouverture et Airs de Titus
Arranger unknown
Eight-part *Harmoniemusik*
EP (Paris, Janet et C.) [Liv. 1–4]

Die Zauberflöte (opera, 1791)
Zauberflöte
Arranger unknown
222-02
MS (Advertized in Traeg's Catalog, Vienna, 1799)

Zauberflöte
Arranger unknown
222-02
MS A:Ee

Die Zauberflöte
Arranged by Stumpf
Harmoniemusik
MS CS:Pnm

Overture, Die Zauberflöte
Arranger unknown
22-02
MS CS:Bm (A.15816)

Zauberflöte
Arranged by Oswald, 7 movements
222-22, contrabassoon
MS CS:Bm (A.35.193)

Zauberflöte
Arranger unknown, Part II, 6 movements
Harmoniemusik
MS CS:Bm (A.40.160)

Zauberflöte
Arranger unknown, 8 movements
222-02
MS CS:KRa (IV.B.99)

Die Zauberflöte
Arranged by Wendt [Went]
202-02, 2 English horns
MS CS:K (Nr. 40.K.I.)

Zauberflöte
Arranger unknown
222-02
MS I:Fc (D.V.489, 490)

Die Zauberflöte
Arranged by Haydenreich
222-02
EP (Vienna, Arranger) I:Fc (P.334, 333)
Haydenreich advertized this arrangement in the *Wiener Zeitung* on January 14, 1792: 'As many friends of music have expressed the wish to possess a wind arrangement of that well-known opera, *die Zauberflöte*, the last work of the great Mozart, the undersigned flatters himself that he gives no unpleasant tidings when he announces …'

Partita in F
Arranged by Johann N. Hiebesch
1212-03, string bass
MS BRD:HR (III.4.1/2.20.608)

Zauberflötte
Arranged by Feldmayer, 11 movements
2o1-02, viola (?)
MS BRD:DO (Mus.Ms.418); BRD:HR (III.4.1/2.40.474) [autograph score]

Zauberflöte
Arranged by Sartorus
22-02, contrabassoon
MS BRD:DS (Mus.Ms.819)

Die Zauberflöte
Arranged by Rosiniack
222-02
MS BRD:DO (Ms. 1396)

Harmonie aus der Zauberflöte
Arranger unknown
21-02
MS DDR:Bds (Mus.Ms.15154/30)

la Flute enchantée
Arranger unknown
222-02
MS PL:LA (2464)

Die Zauberflöte
Arranger unknown
22-02
MS PL:LA (2308)

Terzetto
Arranger unknown
222-02
MS PL:LA (2463)

Die Zauberflöte
Arranged by Göpfert
Harmoniemusik
MS [lost]
Göpfert mentions this arrangement in a letter of February 25, 1817, to Prince Oettingen-Wallerstein: 'As I have been studying music some 20 years with the greatest zeal, also for 1 1/2 years I was associated with the immortal Mozart studying advanced theory. I feel a great partiality for *Harmoniemusik blasende Instrumente*; for this reason my great teacher, Mozart, handed over the scores of his complete works, with the instruction that I set them in this manner.'

Die Zauberflöte
Arranged by Stumpf
22-02
EP (Offenbach, André) [First three of 20 Recueils, each of six movements] A:KR, Wn; DDR:SWl, Dlb (Mus.3972-F-133, 134, 135); CH:Zz; US:Wc; CS:Pnm (XLI.B.136) [three unidentified Recueils], CS:Pnm (XLI.B.135b, 137) [Recueils 2, 3]; BRD:OF [Recueil 1, 2;

Recueil 1, second edition; Recueil 3, second edition], BRD:RH [Recueil 3, incomplete], BRD:F [Recueil 1, second edition], BRD:WERl [Recueil 1, 3, second edition], BRD:B [Recueil 2, second edition; Recueil 3, second edition], BRD:AB [Recueil 3]; F:Pn (Recueil 1–3, reprinted by Paris: Imbault, Nr. 623, 624, 625)

Nr. 122. Suite d'harmonie de La flûte enchantée
Arranged by Stumpf
2022-02
EP (Paris, Sieber, père, Nr. 1665) [Liv.2] BRD:WERl

Douze airs choisies de La flute enchantée
Arranger unknown
222-02
EP (Paris, Pleyel, Nr. 82) A:Wn; CH:Gpu; CS:Pnm (XLII.A.3); US:DW (416)

Airs des Mystères d'Isis
Arranger unknown
Eight-part *Harmoniemusik*
EP (Paris, Sieber) [Liv. 1, 2]

Mozartscher Opern
    Arranged by Fleischmann
    Eight-part *Harmoniemusik*
    EP (Offenbach, André) [cited by MGG]

Six pièces d'harmonie, Nr. I
    Arranged by Göpfert
    2022-12, serpent
    EP (Bonn, Simrock; Paris, Simrock, Nr. 456) CR:E; BRD:B
    Based on K.530, 529, Anh. 246, 596, 392, 518: Anh. B zu 530, 529, Anh. 246 (Anh. C 8.06), 596, 392 (340a), 518.

Six pièces d'harmonie, Nr. II
    Arranged by Göpfert
    2022-12, serpent
    EP (Bonn, Simrock, Nr. 457) CR:E; BRD:B; DDR:LEm
    Based on K.468, 531, 391, 597, 433: Anh. B zu 468, 531, 391 (340b) 597, 519, 433 (416c).

Six pièces d'harmonie
    Arranged by Göpfert
    2022-12, serpent
    EP (Bonn, Simrock; Paris, Simrock, Nrs. 456–457) DDR:LEm
    Based on K.391, 468, 519, 531, 597 433: Anh. B zu 391 (340b), 468, 519, 531, 597, 433 (416c).

Pièces d'harmonie
    Arranged by Göpfert
    122-12
    EP (Offenbach, André, Nr. 1798) A:Wgm; BRD:OF
    Based on K. 523, 476, 524, 307, 539: Anh. B zu 523, 476, 524, 307 (284d), 539.

VI Marches pour harmonie
    Arranged by Göpfert
    Harmoniemusik
    EP (Bonn, Simrock; Paris, Simrock, Nr. 420) DDR:LEm
    Based on K.320a (335) [Nr. 2, 4]; 383e (408/1 [Nr. 1]; 383F (408/3) [Nr. 3]; *Idomeneo* [Nr. 6]; and *Tito* [Nr. 5]

Trois Pièces d'Harmonie
    Arranger unknown
    222-02
    EP (Leipzig, Breitkopf & Härtel [1800]) [Liv.1–7] CS:Bm (A.19.490) [Liv. 1, 2 only]

Harmonie (Nr. 1)
    Arranged by Göpfert
    222-12, contrabassoon
    EP (Bonn, Simrock) CS:Bm (A.18.828)

Pieces d'Harmonie
    Arranged by Göpfert
    222-12
    EP (unknown) BRD:B (DMS.86.548)

Harmoniemusik (3 Quartets)
    Arranged by Hermstedt
    Harmoniemusik
    EP (Leipzig, Peters)

Grande Serenade tirée des oeuvres de Mozart
    Arranged by Stumpf
    22-02
    EP (Hamburg) BRD:DS
    MS (Advertized in Traeg's Catalog, Vienna, 1799)

Douze nouvelles suites d'harmonie
    Arranged by J. Gebauer
    Eight-part *Harmoniemusik*
    EP (Paris, Sieber, père) [as *suite 109, 2md livraison*] BRD:F

Quintet (K.386c/407)
    Quintet
    Arranged by Rajhrad
    22-02
    MS CS:Bm (A.12792)

    Quintet
    Arranged by Haydenreich
    Eight-part *Harmoniemusik*
    MS A:Ee (Nr. 1113)

Quintet
    Arranger unknown
    22-02
    MS (sc) BRD:B (Mus.Ms.15351) [as, *Pièce d'Harmonie, Livre IV, Nr. 7*]

Sonate (K.300i/331)
    Arranger unknown
    Harmoniemusik
    EP (Bonn, Simrock, Nr. 421)

Sinfonie en harmonie (K.297/300a)
    Arranged by Göpfert
    222-12, serpent
    MS DDR:HER (Mus.N.1:6) [missing bassoons]
    EP (Bonn, Simrock, Nr. 415; reprinted in Leipzig, Breitkopf & Härtel [advertized in AMZ, 1805]; BRD:HR, Rtt; CS:Bm (A.18.828)

Symphony (K.425)
    Andante aus Sinfonie v. Mozart
    Arranged by Triebensee
    222-02
    MS A:Wn (Sm. 3739, Jg. I, Oevre 2, Nr. 8)

    Symphony
    Arranger unknown
    2022-02
    MS BRD:Rtt (Mozart 17/II) [missing flute 1]

Symphony (K.543)
    Adagio und Allegro Molto
    Arranged by Triebensee
    222-02
    MS A:Wn (Sm. 3739, Jg. I, Oevre 1, Nr. 1)

Müller, Wenzel (1767–1835)

Das Sonnenfest der Braminen (opera, 1790)
    Das Sonnenfest der Braminen
    Arranged by Triebensee
    222-02
    MS A:Wgm (VIII 40726)

    Sonnenfest der Brummen
    Arranger unknown
    222-02
    MS I:Fe (D.V.489)

    das Sonnenfest der Braminen
    Arranger unknown
    222-02
    MS (Advertized in Traeg's Catalog, Vienna, 1799)

Kaspar der Fagottist, oder die Zauberzither (opera, 1791)
> *Finale, Die Zauberzitter*
> Arranger unknown
> 22-02
> MS CS:KRa (IV.B.95)

> *Der Fagotist*
> Arranger unknown
> *Harmoniemusik*
> KS BRD:DO [may be lost]

> *Der Fagottist*
> Arranger unknown
> *Harmoniemusik*
> MS A:Ee

> *Der Fagottist*
> Arranger unknown
> 222-02
> KS I:Fc (D.V.489)

> *Der Fagottist*
> Arranged by Sartorus
> 22-02
> MS BRD:DS Mus.Ms.830)

> *Cavatina aus Der Fagottist*
> Arranged Schmitt
> 2222-021, serpent
> MS BRD:AB (S.57)

> *Der Fagotist*
> Arranger unknown
> 22-02
> MS (Advertized in Traeg's Catalog, Vienna, 1799)

> *Der Fagottist*
> Arranger unknown
> 222-02
> MS (Advertized in Traeg's Catalog, Vienna, 1799)

Das Neusonntagskind (opera, 1793)
> *dem Sonntagskind*
> Arranged by Schmitt
> 2222-02, serpent
> MS BRD:AB (S.45)

> *Das Neu Sontags*
> Arranger unknown
> 222-02
> MS I:Fc (D.V.487)

das Neue Sontags Kind
Arranger unknown, 9 movements
22-02
MS CS:KRa (IV.B.100)

Das neue Sonntagskind
Arranger unknown
Six-part *Harmoniemusik*
MS BRD:DO [may be lost]

Das Namenstags Kind
Arranger unknown
Harmoniemusik
MS A:Ee

das neue Sonntagskind
Arranger unknown
222-02
MS (Advertized in Traeg's Catalog, Vienna, 1799)

Die Schwestern von Prag (opera, 1794)
   Zwei Schwestern von Prag
   Arranger unknown
   222-02
   MS I:Fc (D.V.487)

   Die 2 Schwestern von Prag
   Arranger unknown
   Harmoniemusik
   MS A:Ee

   Aria aus Zwey Schwester von Prag
   Arranged by Wanerzovsky
   22-02
   MS CS:KRa (IV.B.96)

Die Jungfrauen (opera)
   Die Jungfrauen
   Arranger unknown
   222-02
   MS I:Fc (D.V.496)

   Die 12 schlafenden Jungfrauen
   Arranger unknown
   Harmoniemusik
   MS A:Ee

Tiroller Vastel
   Arranger unknown, 6 movements
   22-02
   MS CS:KRa (IV.B.101)

Betrüg durch Aberglänben
  Arranger unknown
  222-02
  MS I:Fc (D.V.488)

Pizzichi
  Arranged by Sartorius
  Harmoniemusik
  MS BRD:DS

Der Alte Uiberall u. N.
  Arranger unknown
  Harmoniemusik
  MS A:Ee

Nasolini, Sebastiano (1768–ca. 1806)

Sesostri
  Arranger unknown
  222-02
  MS I:Fc (D.V.504)

Naumann, Johann Gottlieb (1741–1801)

Cora och Alonzo (opera, 1782)
  Cora
  Arranger unknown
  222-02
  MS I:Fc (D.V.509)

Protesilao (opera, 1789)
  Overture aus Protesilao
  Arranged by Schmitt
  2222-22, 2 basset horns, string bass
  MS BRD:AB (S.7a)

Dama Soldato (opera?, 1791)
  (6) Märsche aus Dama Soldato
  Arranger unknown
  222-22, contrabassoon
  MS DDR:Bds (Hausbibl. M.M.172)

Niccolini, Giuseppe (1763–1842)

Traiano in Dacia (opera, 1807)
  Traiano in Dacia
  Arranged by Triebensee, Act I, 10 movements
  222-02
  MS A:Wgm (VIII 40733); A:Wn (Sm. 3739, Jg. II, Oevre 5)

Traiano in Dacia
Arranged by Triebensee, Act II, 10 movements
222-02
MS A:Wgm (VIII 47729); A:Wn (Sm. 3739, Jg. II, Oevre 6, Nr. 1–10)

Tragan in Dacia
Arranger unknown
220-02, contrabassoon
MS CS:KRa (IV.B.187) [missing bassoons]

Tragan di Dacia
Arranged by Triebensee ['Tribusee'], 8 movements
22-12
MS CS:KRa (IV.B.145)

Trajano in Dacia
Arranged by Sedlak, 10 movements
222-22, contrabassoon
MS CS:Bm (A.35.196)

Coriolano (opera, 1808)
Coriolano
Arranger unknown, 5 movements
222-02, contrabassoon
MS CS:Bm (A.35.195)

Quinto Fabir (original unknown)
Ouverture, Quinto Fabir
Arranger unknown
222-02
MS CS:KRa (IV.B.186)

Der Türkisch Artzt (original unknown)
Overture aus Der Türkisch Artzt
Arranged by Triebensee
222-02
MS A:Wn (Sm. 3739, Jg. I, Oevre 3, Nr. 1)

Pacini, Giovanni (1796–1867)

L'ultimo Giorno di Pompei (opera, 1825)
L'ultimo giorno di Pompei
Arranged by Sedlak, Part I, 8 movements
Harmoniemusik
MS CS:Bm (A .19 .613a) .

L'u1timo giorno di Pompei
Arranged by Sedlak, Part II, 6 movements
Harmoniemusik
MS CS:Bm (A.19.613b)

Paer, Ferdinando (1771–1839)

 L'Intrigo amoroso (opera, 1795)
  Intrigo Amoroso
  Arranger unknown
  222-02
  MS I:Fc (D.V.495)

  L'Intrigo amoroso
  Arranged by Sedlak?
  222-02
  MS A:Wn (Sm. 3825)

  L'Intrigo amoroso
  Arranger unknown
  MS A:Ee

 Il Principe di Taranto (opera, 1797)
  Il Principe di Taranto
  Arranger unknown
  222-02
  MS BRD:DO [may be lost]

  Il Principe di Taranto
  Arranged by Sedlak?, 10 movements
  222-02
  MS A:Wn (Sm. 3827)

 La Virttù al Cimento (opera, 1798)
  Airs de Griselda
  Arranged by Fuchs
  22-02
  EP (Paris, Imbault) F:Pn (Vm.27.3292)

  Ouverture de Griselda
  Arranged by Fuchs
  22-02
  EP (Paris, Imbault, Nr. 188) F:Pn (Vm.27.3295)

  Pièces d'harmonie
  Arranged by C. Ahl
  EP (Offenbach, André, Nr. 2226) [Recueil, 1, 2] A:KR; DDR:SWl; A:Wn; CH:Zz; CS:KRa (IV.B.191); US:Wc

  Airs de Griselda
  Arranger unknown
  Six-part *Harmoniemusik*
  EP (Paris, Janet et C.)

Ouverture de Griselda
Arranger unknown
Harmoniemusik
EP (Paris, Ebend)

Camilla (opera, 1799)
Camilla
Arranged by Stumpf
Six-part *Harmoniemusik*
MS BRD:DO [may be lost]

Camilla
Arranged by Wendt, 11 movements
222-02
MS A:Wn (Sm. 3824); CS:Pnm (XLI.B.146)

Camilla
Arranger unknown, 7 movements
222-02, contrabassoon
MS CS:Bm (A.35.202)

La Camilla
Arranger unknown
Harmoniemusik
MS A:Ee

La Camilla
Arranged by Wendt [Went]
22-02
MS PL:LA 92310)

La Camilla
Arranged by Stumpf
22-02
EP (Offenbach, André) [Recueil 14–15] A:KR, A:Wn; DDR:SWl; CH:Zz; US:Wc; CS:Pnm (XLI.B.136) [three unidentified recueils of 20]

Airs de Camilla
Arranger unknown
Eight-part *Harmoniemusik*
EP (Paris, Sieber)

Il Morto vivo (opera, 1799)
Allegro vivace aus E Morto Vivo
Arranged by Triebensee
222-02
MS A:Wn (Sm. 3795, Nr. 1)

Il Morto vivo
Arranged by Stumpf
22-02
EP (Offenbach, André) [Recueil 16–17] A:KR, A:Wn; DDR:SWl; CH:Zz; US:Wc; CS:Pnm (XLI.B.136) [three unidentified recueils of 20]

Achille (opera, 1801)

Achilla
Arranger unknown, 15 movements
21-02
MS KRa (IV.B.108)

Achilles
Arranger unknown, 15 movements
22-02
MS CS:Pnm (XLI.B.148)

Achilles
Arranger unknown
202-02
MS CS:Pnm (XLII.C.158)

Achille
Arranged by Sedlak, 15 movements
222-02
MS A:Wn (Sm. 3823)

Achilles
Arranged by Buchnal
21-02
MS PL:LA (2285)

Achille
Arranger unknown
22-02
MS PL:LA (2309)

Achille
Arranger unknown
Harmoniemusik
MS A:Ee

Ouverture d'Achille
Arranged by Fuchs
Harmoniemusik
EP (Paris?) F:Pn (Vm.27.1596 and Vm.3297) [two copies]

Ouverture d'Achille
Arranger unknown
Six- or eleven-part *Harmoniemusik*
EP (Paris, Janet et C.)

Sargino (opera, 1803)
    Sargino
    Arranger unknown
    222-02
    MS I:Fc (D.V.500)

    Sargino
    Arranged by Triebensee?
    222-02
    MS A:Wn (Sm. 3829)

    Sargines
    Arranger unknown, 13 movements
    22-02
    MS CS:Pnm (XLI.B.147)

    Sargino
    Arranged by Sedlak
    222-02
    MS A:Wn (Sm. 3828)

    Duet aus Sargines
    Arranged by Triebensee
    222-02
    MS A:Wgm (VIII 43275, Nr. 5)

Léonora (opera, 1804)
    Pièces d'Harmonie de Léonore
    Arranged by Barth
    1022-02
    EP (Leipzig, Hofmeister)

Sofonisba (opera, 1805)
    Ouverture and Duet from Sofoniska
    Arranged by Triebensee
    222-02
    MS A:Wn (Sm. 3739, Jg. I, Oevre 2, Nr. 1; and Jg. I, Oevre 1, Nr. 5)

    March aus Sofoniska
    Arranged by Triebensee
    222-02
    MS A:Wgm (VIII 43275, Nr. 6)

Una in bene et en male (opera, 1805)
    Ouverture d'Una in bene et una in male
    Arranged by Fuchs
    2022-02
    EP (Paris, Imbault) F:Pn (Vm.27.3298)

Airs d'Una in bene et una in male
Arranged by Fuchs
2022-02
EP (Paris, Imbault) F:Pn (Vm.27.3293, 1/2)

Airs d'Una in bene et una in male
Arranger unknown
Harmoniemusik
EP (Paris, Janet et C.) [Suites 1, 2]

Ouverture d'Una in bene et una in male
Arranger unknown
Nine-part *Harmoniemusik*
EP (Paris, Ebend)

Agnese di Fitz-Henry (opera, 1809)
   L'Agnese
   Arranged by Gambaro, in Two Acts
   2042-121, serpent
   EP (Paris) F:Pn (Vm.27.1619) [here, 'Suite 1,' 4 movements from Act I]

   Agnese
   Arranged by Lachnith
   Harmoniemusik
   EP (Paris, Carli) [Suites 1, 2]

Numa Pompilio (opera, 1809)
   Numa Pompilio
   Arranged by Wendt?, 23 movements
   222-02
   MS A:Wn (Sm. 3826); CS:KRa (IV.B.109)

   Numa Pompilio
   Arranger unknown
   222-02
   MS I:Fc (D.V.505)

   Numa Pompilion
   Arranger unknown, 5 movements
   222-12
   MS CS:Bm (A.40.163)

   Ouverture de Numa Pompilio
   Arranger unknown
   Nine-part *Harmoniemusik*
   EP (Paris, Janet et C.)

Der lustige Schuster (opera?, 1809)
>   *Der lustige Schuster*
>   Arranged by Stumpf
>   22-02
>   EP (Offenbach, André) [Recueil 18] A:KR, A:Wn; DDR:SWl; CH:Zz; US:Wc; CS:Pnm (XLI.B.136) [three unidentified recueils of 20]

Le Maître de Chapelle (opera, 1821)
>   *Airs du Matire de Chapelle*
>   Arranger unknown
>   *Harmoniemusik*
>   EP (Paris, A. Petit) [Liv. 1, 2]
>
>   *Ouverture de Maitre de Chapelle*
>   Arranger unknown
>   *Harmoniemusik*
>   EP (Paris, Ebend)

Die Wanderuten Komedianten (original unidentified)
>   Arranger unknown, 10 movements
>   22-02
>   MS CS:KRa (IV.B.107)

Tarsino (original unidentified)
>   Arranger unknown, 10 movements
>   222-02
>   MS CS:KRa (IV.B.106)

Oratorio del Passione
>   Arranger unknown
>   222-02
>   MS I:Fc (D.V.506)

Cantate per Il Natale
>   Arranger unknown
>   222-02
>   MS I:Fc (D.V.506)

Pièces d'Harmonie (original unidentified)
>   Arranged by Barth
>   22-02
>   EP (Leipzig, Hofmeister) CS:Pnm (XXI.C.178)

6 Pièces d'Harmonie (original unidentified)
>   Arranger unknown
>   22-02
>   EP (Offenbach, André) I:Nc (48.2.25)

Duetto [source unknown]
>   Arranger unknown
>   222-22
>   MS CS:Bm (A.20.880)

6 Walser
> *6 Walser*
> Arranged by Vanderhagen
> 1032-121, serpent
> EP (Paris, Imbault, Nr. 957) F:Pn (Vm.27.3300)
>
> [*6 Walses*]
> Arranger unknown
> Six- or ten-part *Harmoniemusik*
> EP (Paris, Janet et C.)

Paisiello, Giovanni (1740–1816)

Le finte Contesse (opera, 1766; later: *Il marchese Tulipano*)
> *Ouverture du Marquis de Tulipano*
> Arranger unknown
> Six- or eight-part *Harmoniemusik*
> EP (Paris, Sieber)

La Frascatana (opera, 1774)
> *La Frascatana*
> Arranged by Satorus
> 22-02
> MS BRD:DS (Mus.Ms.849)
>
> *La Frascatana*
> Arranger unknown
> 222-02
> MS I:Fc (D.V.482)
>
> *La Frascatana*
> Arranger unknown (probably Wendt), 9 movements
> 202-02, 2 English horns
> MS CS:K (Nr. 26.K.I.)
>
> *La Frascatana*
> Arranger unknown
> 222-02
> MS A:Wn [lost]
>
> *Frascetana*
> Arranger unknown
> 222-02
> MS (Advertized in Traeg's Catalog, Vienna, 1799)
>
> *Frascetaena*
> Arranger unknown
> 22-02
> MS (Advertized in Traeg's Catalog, Vienna, 1799)

La Frascetana
Arranger unknown (probably Wendt)
202-02, 2 English horns
MS (Advertized in Traeg's Catalog, Vienna, 1799)

Le due Contesse (opera, 1776)
Due Contese
Arranger unknown
222-02
MS I:Fc (D.V.483)

La Nitteti (opera, 1777)
Nitteti
Arranger unknown
222-02
MS PL:LA (2466)

Gli Astrologi immaginari (opera, 1779; later *I filosofi immaginari*)
Le Philosophe imaginaire
Arranged by Wendt, 10 movements
222-02
MS A:Wn (Sm. 1961)

Filosofi
Arranger unknown, 5 movements
Harmoniemusik
MS DDR:Bds (Hausbibl. 347)

die eingebildeten Philosophen
Arranger unknown
222-02
MS (Advertized in Traeg's Catalog, Vienna, 1799)

die eingebildeten Philosophen
Arranger unknown
22-02
MS (Advertized in Traeg's Catalog, Vienna, 1799)

La finta Amante (opera, 1780)
Finta Amante
Arranger unknown
222-02
MS I:Fc (D.V.508)

La Fint Amante
Arranged by Wendt [Vent], 7 movements
202-02, 2 English horns
MS CS:K (Nr. 21.K.I.)

La finta Amante
Arranger unknown
222-02
MS A:Wn [lost]

La Serva Padrona (opera, 1781)
    La Serva Padrona
    Arranger unknown
    222-02
    MS I:Fc (D.V.477)

Il Barbiere di Siviglia (opera, 1782)
    Il Barbiere
    Arranger unknown
    222-02
    MS I:Fc (D.V.479)

    Il Barbiere di Seviglia
    Arranger unknown
    222-02
    MS A:Wn [lost]

    Barbiere di Seviglia
    Arranger unknown
    Harmoniemusik
    MS A:Ee

La Passione di Gesù Cristo (oratorio, 1783)
    La Passione
    Arranger unknown
    222-02
    MS I:Fc (D.V.507)

Il Re Teodoro in Venezia (opera, 1784)
    Re Teodoro di Venezia
    Arranger unknown
    222-02
    MS I:Fc (D.V.479)

    Theodore in Venezia
    Arranged by Rosiniack
    Harmoniemusik
    MS BRD:DO [may be lost]

    Theodore in Venezia
    Arranger unknown
    Six-part *Harmoniemusik*
    MS BRD:DO [may be lost]

Il Re Teodore in Venezia
Arranged by Wendt [Went], 14 movements
202-02, 2 English horns
MS CS:K (Nr. 30.K.I.)

Quintet aus Ré Theodoro
Arranged by Kreith?
1-02, 2 flute d'amore
EP (Vienna, Eder, Nr. 267) A:Wgm (VIII 30603)

March aus Il Re Theodoro in Venezia
Arranger unknown
2201-02
MS CS:KRa (IV.B.103)

Re Theodore
Arranger unknown
Harmoniemusik
MS A:Ee

Theodore in Venezia
Arranger unknown
22-02
MS (Advertized in Traeg's Catalog, Vienna, 1799)

Theodore in Venezia
Arranger unknown
222-02
MS (Advertized in Traeg's Catalog, Vienna, 1799)

Le Gare generose (opera, 1786)
   Le Gare Generose
   Arranger unknown
   222-02
   MS I:Fc (D.V.486)

   Le Gare generose
   Arranger unknown
   222-02
   MS A:Wn [lost]

   Le Gare Generosa
   Arranger unknown
   222-02
   MS (Advertized in Traeg's Catalog, Vienna, 1799)

L'Olimpiade (opera, 1786)
   Arranged by Witt
   2222-02, string bass
   MS BRD:HR (III.4.1/2.20.421)

L'Amor contrastato (opera, 1788; known as *La Molinara*)

> *La Molinara*
> Arranger unknown
> *Harmoniemusik*
> MS BRD:DS

> *La Molinara*
> Arranger unknown
> 222-02
> MS I:Fc (D.V.486)

> *L'amor Morinara*
> Arranger unknown, 11 movements
> 22-02
> MS CS:KRa (IV.B.104)

> *La Molinara*
> Arranged by Wendt [Went], 12 movements
> 202-02, 2 English horns
> MS CS:K (Nr. 27.K.I.)

> *L'Amor contrastato*
> Arranger unknown
> 222-02
> MS A:Wn [lost]

> *La Molinara*
> Arranger unknown
> *Harmoniemusik*
> MS A:Ee

> *La Molinara*
> Arranger unknown
> 22-02
> MS (Advertized in Traeg's Catalog, Vienna, 1799)

> *La Molinoro*
> Arranger unknown
> 222-02
> MS (Advertized in Traeg's Catalog, Vienna, 1799)

> *La Molinara*
> Arranged by Stumpf, 6 movements
> 22-02
> EP (Offenbach, André) [Recueil 7] A:KR, A:Wn; BRD:W [missing part of clarinet 2]; DDR:SWl; CH:Zz; US:Wc; CS:Pnm (XLI.B.136) [three unidentified recueils of 20]

> *La Molinara*
> Arranged by Wendt
> 22-02
> EP (Bonn, Simrock, Nr. 559) CH:N; BRD: Bbm, HR; S:Skma

Pièces d'harmonie
Arranged by Stumpf
EP Offenbach, André, Nr. 976) BRD:AB [incomplete], BRD:OF, BRD:W
EP (Offenbach, André, reprinted as Nr. 2698) BRD:OF

Nina (opera, 1789)
   Nina
   Arranger unknown
   222-02
   MS A:Wn [lost]

   La Nina
   Arranged by Luigi Gianella
   1202-02
   MS (score) I:Vmc (Busta 59-72N.72)

   Potpouri de Nina et Noces de Dorine
   Arranged by Fuchs
   42-02
   EP (Paris, Nadermann) F:Pn (Vm.27.1602)

Didone abbandonata (opera, 1794)
   Duetto nel'opera Didone Abbandonata
   Arranger unknown
   222-02
   MS PL:LA (2465)

Proserpine (opera, 1803)
   Airs d'Prosperpine
   Arranged by Fuchs
   22-02
   EP (Paris, Imbault) [Suites 1, 2]
   F:Pn (Vm.7.6953 and Vm.27.3304) [multiple copies]

   Ouverture d'Proserpine
   Arranged by Fuchs
   1022-02, serpent
   EP (Paris, Imbault) F:Pn (Vm.27.3305)

Noces de Dorine (opera?)
   Arranged by Fuchs
   2022-02
   EP (Paris, Imbault, Nr. 794) BRD:AB [here, flute 2 and clarinet 2 only]

La Cantadina di Spinto (opera?)
   La Cantadina di Spinto
   Arranger unknown
   222-02
   MS I:Fc (D.V.482)

La Contadina
Arranged by Wendt [Went], 8 movements
202-02, 2 English horns
MS CS:K (Nr. 28.K.I)

(Unidentified opera)
Arranger unknown
Six-part *Harmoniemusik*
MS BRD:BÜu (P-Ai-39)

Palma, Silvestro (1762–1834)

La Pietra simpatica (opera, 1795)
La Pietra Simpatica
Arranger unknown
222-02
MS I:Fc (D.V.481)

La Pietra simpatica
Arranged by Sedlak and Wendt (eight movements appear to be in Sedlak's hand, with all titles and a ninth movement in Wendt's hand)
222-02
MS A:Wn (Sm. 3830)

La Pietra Simpatica
Arranger unknown
Harmoniemusik
EP (Vienna, Hoftheater)
Advertized in the *Wiener Zeitung*, 1796.

Airs de Pietra simpatica, together with works by Cimarosa, Bianchi, and anonymous
Arranged by Fuchs
2022-02
EP (Paris, Imbault, Nr. 535)

La Pietra Simpatica
Arranger unknown
222-02
MS (Advertized in Traeg's Catalog, Vienna, 1799)

Pavesi, Stefano (1779–1850)

Ser Marcantonio (opera, 1810)
Marc Antonio
Arranged by Sedlak
222-02
MS A:Wn (Sm. 3831)

Persuis, Louis (1769–1819)

Estelle (opera, 1793)
> *Ouverture d'Estelle*
> Arranged by Fuchs
> 42-12
> EP (Paris, Nadermann) F:Pn (Vm.7.6970 and Vm.27.3357) [two copies]

Nina (ballet, 1813)
> *Nina*
> Arranged by Sedlak ('Nr. 113'), Act I, 12 movements
> 222-02
> MS CS:KRa (IV.B.110), CS:Bm (A.35.203)

> *Nina*
> Arranged by Sedlak, Act II, 8 movements
> 222-02
> MS CS:KRa (IV.B.111)

> *Nina*
> Arranger unknown
> Nine-part *Harmoniemusik*
> EP (Vienna, Haslinger)

Philidor, François André Danican (1726–1795)

Ernelinde Princesse de Norvège (opera, 1767)
> *Ariettes et airs de danse d'Ermelinde*
> Arranged by Röser
> *Harmoniemusik*
> MS DDR:Dlb

12e suitte des amusements militaires contenant une choix d'ariettes …
> Arranged by Vanderhagen
> 22-02
> EP (Paris, de La Chevardière) S:Uu [missing clarinet 2 and horn 2]

Piccinni, Nicola (1728–1800)

Alessandro nell'Indie (opera, 1774)
> *Alexander von Indien*
> Arranger unknown, 2 movements
> 232-221, contrabassoon
> MS CS:Bm (A.35.201)

Didon (opera, 1783)
> *Didone*
> Arranger unknown
> 222-02
> MS I:Fc (D.V.480)

Didon
Arranger unknown
222-02
MS (two versions advertized in Traeg's Catalog, Vienna, 1799)

Amazilia (opera?)
Amazilia
Arranged by Sedlak, 5 movements
222-22, contrabassoon
MS CS:Bm (A.40.101)

Aria, 'Lasciami respirar' (original unidentified)
Arranger unknown
222-02
MS PL:LA (2467)

Pizzini, ?

Das Mädchen von Frascati (original unidentified)
Arranged by Rosiniack
Harmoniemusik
MS BRD:DO [may be lost]

Pleyel, Ignaz (1757–1831)

3 Quartets
Arranged by F. Michel
222-02
MS PL:LA (2468) [Op. 1, Nr. 4], PL:LA (2469) [Op. 6, Nr. 3], PL:LA (2470) [Op. 6, Nr. 4]

Quintet in E♭
Arranged by F. Michel
222-02
MS PL:LA (2471)

Sonata (for clavier)
Arranged by Triebensee
222-02
MS A:Wn (Sm. 3739, Jg. I, Oevre 1, Nr. 2)

Pièces d'harmonie
Arranged by Mr. Bisch
22-02
EP (Offenbach, André, Nr. 470) DDR:HER [here, clarinet 1 only]; S:SKma [here, clarinet 1 only]

Suite de morceaux
Arranged by Mr. Bisch
Six-part *Harmoniemusik*
EP (Paris, Imbault, Nr. 262) S:Uu [missing clarinet 2 and horn 2]

Reissiger, Karl Gottlieb (1798–1859)

Die Felsenmühle zu Estalières (opera, 1831)
    Overture aus die Felsenmühle
    Arranger unknown
    222-221, contrabassoon
    MS CS:Bm (A.36.886)

Ricci, Luigi (1805–1859)

Il nuovo Figaro (opera, 1832)
    Il nuovo Figaro
    Arranged by Sedlak? (MS by Perschl), 4 movements
    222-221
    MS A:Wn (Sm. 3834)

Il desertore per amore (opera, 1836)
    Il desertore per amore
    Arranged by Sedlak [finished by Perschl]
    222-02
    MS A:Wn

    Cavatina aus Il desertore per amore
    Arranger unknown
    222-20
    MS A:Wn [lost]

Riegel, Henri-Jean (1772–1852)

Les Deux Meuniers (opera, 1799)
    Ouverture pastorale des 2 Meuniers
    Arranger unknown
    Harmoniemusik
    EP (Paris, Erard)

Righini, Vincenzo (1756–1812)

L'Incontro Inaspettato (opera, 1785)
    L'Incontro Inaspettato
    Arranged by Triebensee?, 12 movements
    222-02
    MS A:Wn (Sm. 3832)

    L'incontro Inaspettato
    Arranged by Wendt [Went], 13 movements
    202-02, 2 English horns
    MS CS:K (Nr.9.K.I)

Contratto Inaspetta
Arranger unknown
222-02
MS I:Fc (D.V.480)

Contra in aspettato
Arranger unknown
22-02
MS (Advertized in Traeg's Catalog, Vienna, 1799)

Contra in aspettalo
Arranger unknown
222-02
MS (Advertized in Traeg's Catalog, Vienna, 1799)

Enea nel Lazio (opera, 1793)
   Trio aus Enea nel Latzia
   Arranged by Schmitt
   2222-22, 2 basset horns, string bass
   MS BRD:AB (S.7b)

Armida (opera, 1797)
   Arranged by Ehrenfried
   222-02, string bass
   MS BRD:HR (III.4.1/2.20.357)

Gerusalemme liberata (opera, 1803)
   Two choruses from Gerusalemme liberata
   Arranger unknown
   Harmoniemusik
   MS DDR:SWl (Righini, 6)

Pièces d'harmonie
   Arranged by F. Tausch
   22-02
   MS CS:Bm (A.35.207)

Romberg, Andreas (1767–1821)

Simphonie
   Arranged by Walch
   1132-22, corno basso
   MS DDR:RUl (RH.R25)

Rossini, Gioacchino (1792–1868)

L'Inganno felice (opera, 1812)
    L'Inganno Felice
    Arranged by Starke, 16 movements
    222-22, contrabassoon
    MS CS:Bm (A.36.890)

    L'Inganno felice
    Arranged by Legrand
    1022-02
    EP (Leipzig, Breitkopf & Härtel)

    Ouverture de L'Inganno felice
    Arranged by Blasius
    Harmoniemusik
    EP (Paris, Ebend)

    Airs de L'Inganno felice
    Arranged by Fuchs
    2022-02
    EP (Paris, Imbault, Nr. 794) BRD:AB [here flute 2 and clarinet 2 only]

Ciro in Babilonia (opera, 1812)
    Cirus in Babilon
    Arranged by Sedlak, Part I, 12 movements
    222-22, contrabassoon
    MS CS:Bm (A.35.212) A:Wn [lost]

La Scala di Seta (opera, 1812)
    La Scala di Seta
    Arranger unknown, 3 movements
    222-221, contrabassoon
    MS CS:Bm (A.35.221)

Tancredi (opera, 1813)
    Tancred
    Arranger unknown, 12 movements
    222-22, contrabassoon
    MS CS:Bm (A.35.224)

    Tancredi
    Aranger unknown, 12 movements
    222-12
    MS CS:KRa (IV.B.189)

    Tancredi
    Arranged by Legrand
    1122-02
    EP (Paris, P. Petit) BRD:HR (III.4.1/2.20.928)

Tancredi
Arranged by Sedlak
222-02
MS A:Wn (Sm. 3841)

Airs de Tancredi
Arranged by Grégoire
Eight- or ten-part *Harmoniemusik*
EP (Paris, Ebend)

Airs de Tancredi
Arranged by Gambaro
Seven- or fourteen-part *Harmoniemusik*
EP (Paris, Dufant et Dubois)

Ouverture de Tancredi
Arranged by Fuchs
Harmoniemusik
EP (Paris, Carli)

Ouverture de Tancredi
Arranged by Rummel
Harmoniemusik
EP (Mainz, Schott; reprinted Paris, Richault) BRD:MZsch

Tancredi
Arranger unknown
1222-02
EP (Leipzig, Breitkopf & Härtel)

Tancredi
Arranger unknown
Eight-part *Harmoniemusik*
EP (Vienna, Hoftheater)
Advertized in *Theaterzettel*, January, 16, 1817.

L'Italiana in Algeri (opera, 1813)
  Overture, Italiana in Algeria
  Arranger unknown
  22-12
  MS CS:Pnm (XLI.B.121)

  L'Italiana in Algeri
  Arranged by Sedlak, 12 movements
  222-22, contrabassoon
  MS CS:Bm (A.35.217); A:Wn (Sm. 3838)

  Italiner in Algier
  Arranger unknown, 3 movements
  2021-221
  MS BRD:TSCH (Gg 306) [missing clarinet 2]

Le Italiana in Algieri
Arranged by Legrand
1122-02
EP (Leipzig, Breitkopf & Härtel; reprinted Paris, P. Petit) BRD:HR (III.4.1/2.20.928)

L'Italiana in Algeri
Arranger unknown
1222-02
EP (Leipzig, Breitkopf & Härtel)

Ouverture de l'Italiana in Algeri
Arranged by Fuchs
Harmoniemusik
EP (Paris, Carli)

Il Turco in Italia (opera, 1814)
Der Turk in Italien
Arranged by Starke, 24 movements
222-22, contrabassoon
MS CS:Bm (A.36.892)

il Turco in Italia
Arranged by Grégoire
Eight- or ten-part *Harmoniemusik*
EP (Paris, Ebend) [Liv. 1, 2]

Elisabetta, Regina d'Inghilterra (opera, 1815)
Elisabetta, Regina d'Inghilterra
Arranged by Sedlak (his '26th and 27th work'), 24 movements
222-02
MS A:Wn (Sm. 3837)

Elisabeth Konigin v. England
Arranger unknown. Part I, 10 movements; Part II, 9 movements
222-22, contrabassoon
MS CS:Bm (A.35.214 and A.35.215)

Torvaldo e Dorliska (opera, 1815)
Ouverture de Torvaldo e Dorliska
Arranged by Fuchs
Harmoniemusik
EP (Paris, Carli)

Almaviva (opera, 1816)
Duetto aus Salvaggia
Arranger unknown
222-221
MS CS:Bm (A.36.891) [incomplete]

Der Barbier von Sevilla
Arranged by Sedlak
22-02
MS CS:Pnm (XLI.B.120); PL:LA (2311)

Il barbiere di Seviglia
Arranger unknown, 7 movements
222-22, contrabassoon
MS CS:Bm (A.35.210)

Il barbiere di Seviglia
Arranger unknown, 9 movements
222-02, contrabassoon
MS CS:Bm (A.36.888)

Barbier von Sevilla
Arranged by Ruzni, Part II, 8 movements
222-22, contrabassoon
MS CS:Bm (A.35.209)

Ouverture, Der Barbier von Sevilla
Arranged by Osswald
222-221, contrabassoon
MS CS:Bm (A.37.346)

Il barbiere di Siviglia
Arranged by Sedlak (his '22nd' work)
222-02
MS A:Wn (Sm. 3835)

Le Barbier de Seville
Arranged by Fuchs, Nr. 1, 6 movements; Nr. 2, 13 movements
2022-02
EP (Paris, Carli) F:Pn (Vm.27.3665) [Nr. 1, 2]

Ouverture du Barbier de Seville
Arranged by Fuchs
1042-021, serpent
EP (Paris, Carli; reprinted Ebend) F:Pn (Vm.27.3691)

Airs du Barbier de Seville
Arranged by Gambaro
Harmoniemusik
EP (Paris, Janet et C.) [Liv. 1–3]

Ouverture du Barbier de Seville
Arranged by Gambaro
Harmoniemusik
EP (Paris, Janet et C.)

Otello (opera, 1816)
    Romance aus Othello
    Arranger unknown
    222-22, contrabassoon
    MS CS:Bm (A.36.875)

    Othello Mohr in Venedig
    Arranged by Starke, 5 movements
    222-22, contrabassoon
    MS CS:Bm (A.35.218)

    Otello
    Arranger unknown
    222-02
    MS A:Wn [lost]

    Otello
    Arranger unknown
    Ten- and eleven-part *Harmoniemusik*
    EP (Paris, Ebend)

    Otello
    Arranged by Gambaro
    Seven- or ten-part *Harmoniemusik*
    EP (Paris, Gambaro) [Liv. 1–3]

    Otello
    Arranged by Küffner
    Harmoniemusik
    EP (Paris, Richault)

    Ouverture d'Otello
    Arranged by Grégoire
    Harmoniemusik
    EP (Paris, Carli)

La Cenerentola (opera, 1817)
    Ouverture de Cenerentola
    Arranged by Fuchs
    Harmoniemusik
    EP (Paris, Carli)

La Gazza Ladra (opera, 1817)
    La Gazza Ladra
    Arranger unknown
    222-02
    MS A:Wn [lost]

    La Gazza ladra
    Arranged by Legrand
    1022-02
    EP (Leipzig, Breitkopf & Härtel)

la Gazza ladra
Arranged by Grégoire
Ten-part *Harmoniemusik*
EP (Paris, Ebend) [Liv. 1–4]

la Gazza ladra
Arranged by Gambaro
Seven- or twelve-part *Harmoniemusik*
EP (Paris, Gambaro) [Liv. 1–3]

Ouverture d'la Gazza ladra
Arranged by Fuchs
Harmoniemusik
EP (Paris, Carli)

Armida (opera, 1817)
   Armida
   Arranged by Starke, Act II, 7 movements
   222-22, contrabassoon
   MS CS:Bm (A.35.208)

   Ouverture d'Armida
   Arranged by Fuchs
   Harmoniemusik
   EP (Paris, Carli)

Mosè in Egitto (opera, 1818)
   Moyses in Egypten
   Arranger unknown, 12 movements
   222-22, contrabassoon
   MS CS:Bm (A.37.347)

   Moses in Aegypten
   Arranger unknown, 2 movements
   2022-221
   MS BRD:TSCH (Gg.306) [missing clarinet 2]

   Praghiera aus Mose in Egitto
   Arranger unknown
   222-02
   MS A:Wn [lost]

   Mose in Egitto
   Arranged by Grégoire
   Ten- or thirteen-part *Harmoniemusik*
   EP (Paris, Carli) [Liv. 1–3]

Ricciardo e Zoraide (opera, 1818)
> *Richard und Zoraide*
> Arranged by Sedlak, Part 1, 11 movements; Part II, 14 movements
> 222-22, contrabassoon
> MS CS:Bm (A.35.220 and A.36.876)

> *Ricciardo e Zoraide*
> Arranger unknown
> 222-02
> MS A:Wn [lost]

Eduardo e Cristina (opera, 1819)
> *Ouverture d'Edoardo e Cristina*
> Arranged by Fuchs
> *Harmoniemusik*
> EP (Paris, Ebend)

La Donna del Lago (opera, 1819)
> *La donna dell'lago*
> Arranger unknown, 10 movements
> 222-22, contrabassoon
> MS CS:Bm (A.36.874)

> *la Donna del Lago*
> Arranged by Grégoire
> Ten- or eleven-part *Harmoniemusik*
> EP (Paris, Ebend) [Liv. 1–3]

Bianca e Falliero (opera, 1819)
> *Quartet aus Bianca d. Faliero*
> Arranged by Skacel
> 222-02, contrabassoon
> MS CS:Bm (35.211)

Zelmira (opera, 1822)
> *Zelmira*
> Arranged by Sedlak, Part I, 12 movements; Part II, 13 movements
> 222-22, contrabassoon
> MS CS:Bm (A.37.348 and A.35.226)

> *Zelmira*
> Arranged by Sedlak ('39th and 40th' work), Part I, II
> Six-part *Harmoniemusik*
> MS PL:LA (2312)

> *Zelmira*
> Arranged by Sedlak, 20 movements
> 222-02
> MS A:Wn (Sm. 3844)

Zelmira
Arranged by Starke
222-22, contrabassoon
MS CS:Pnm (XLI.B.122)

Zeimira
Arranged by Starke
222-02
EP (Vienna, Artaria [1822])

Semiramide (opera, 1823)

Semiramis
Arranged by Sedlak, 20 movements (his '52nd' work)
222-02
MS A:Wgm

Semiramis
Arranger unknown, Part II, 13 movements
222-22
MS CS:Bm (A.40.166)

Duet aus Semirannis
Arranger unknown
222-22, contrabassoon
MS CS:Bm (A.40.165)

8 Pièces de Neige et le Macon (Auber) et Semiramide
Arranged by Widder
1022-02
EP (Berlin, Schlesinger)

Le Siège de Corinthe (opera, 1826)

Le Siège de Corintba
Arranged by Sedlak, Part I, 14 movements; Part II, 6 movements
222-02
MS A:Wn (Sm. 3836); CS:Bm (A.35.222 and A.35.223)

Le Siège de Corinth
Arranger unknown
222-02
EP (Vienna, Haslinger and Artaria [1826])

Le Comte Ory (opera, 1828)
Arranger unknown, Part I, 5 movements; Part II, 7 movements
222-22, contrabassoon
MS CS:Bm (A.36.873 and A.35.216)

Guillaume Tell (opera, 1829)
    Wilhelm Tell
    Arranged by Sedlak, Part I, 8 movements; Part II, 7 movements
    222-221, contrabassoon
    MS CS:Bm (A.36.664 and A.35.225)

    Wilhelm Tell
    Arranged by Sedlak, Part I, 12 movements
    222-22, contrabassoon
    MS CS:Bm (A.37.348)

    Guillaume Tell
    Arranger unknown
    222-02
    MS A:Wn [lost]

Pietro il Grando (opera)
    Cavatina aus Pietro il Grando
    Arranger unknown
    222-22, contrabassoon
    MS CS:Bm (A.35.219)

    Cavatina aus Pietro il Grand
    Arranger unknown
    1032-12, serpent
    MS CS:BA (189/59-613)

Blaubart (ballet)
    Arranged by Sedlak, 12 movements
    222-22, contrabassoon
    MS CS:Bm (A.36.871) [incomplete]

Die diebische Elster (original unidentified)
    Arranged by Starke, Part II, 12 movements
    222-22, contrabassoon
    MS CS:Bm (A.36.889)

Collection de 10 Ouvertures
    Arranger unknown
    Harmoniemusik
    EP (Paris, Ebend)

Sacchini, Antonio Maria Gasparo (1730–1786)

Oedipe à Colone (opera, 1786)
    Airs d'Oedipe a Colone
    Arranger unknown
    Six-part *Harmoniemusik*
    EP (Mainz: Schott) [Suite 1, 2] BRD:MZsch

Salieri, Antonio (1750–1825)

  La Fiera di Venezia (opera, 1771)
    La Fiera di Venezia
    Arranger unknown
    Harmoniemusik
    MS A:Ee

  La Dama Pastorella (opera, 1780; later called, *La Cifra*)
    La Cifra
    Arranged by Wendt
    222-02
    MS A:Wn (Sm. 3846)

    La Cifra
    Arranger unknown
    222-02
    MS I:Fc (D.V.501)

    La Ciffra
    Arranger unknown
    Harmoniemusik
    MS A:Ee

    L'Chiffera
    Arranger unknown
    222-02
    MS (Advertized in Traeg's Catalog, Vienna, 1799)

  Der Rauchfangkehrer (opera, 1781)
    Die Rauchfangkehre
    Arranger unknown
    222-02
    MS I:Fc (D.V.483)

    Die Rauchfangkehrer
    Arranger unknown
    222-02
    MS (Advertized in Traeg's Catalog, Vienna, 1799)

  Il ricco d'un giorno (opera, 1784)
    Il ricco d'un giorno
    Arranged by Wendt
    202-02, 2 basset horns
    MS A:Wn (Sm. 3848)

    Il Ricio d'un Giorno
    Arranged by Wendt [Went], 7 movements
    202-02, 2 English horns
    MS CS:K (Nr. 45.K.I.)

La Grotta di Trofonio (opera, 1785)
    La Grotta di Trofonio
    Arranged by Wendt
    222-02
    MS A:Ee

    La Grotta di Trofonio
    Arranger unknown
    2222-02, 2 violas (?), string bass
    MS BRD:Rtt (Salieri 10/V)

    La Grotta di Tronfonio
    Arranged by Wendt [Went], 12 movements
    202-02, 2 English horns
    MS CS:K (Nr. 42b.K.I.)

    Grotta di Triogonio
    Arranger unknown
    222-02
    MS I:Fc (D.V.478)

    La Grotta di Trofonio
    Arranger unknown
    222-02
    MS A:Wn [lost]

    La Grotta di Trofonia
    Arranger unknown
    222-02
    MS (Advertized in Traeg's Catalog, Vienna, 1799)

    La Grotta di Trophonio
    Arranger unknown
    22-02
    MS (Advertized in Traeg's Catalog, Vienna, 1799)

Tarare (opera, 1787; later *Axur re d'Ormus*)
    Axur Re d'Ormus
    Arranged by Wendt
    222-02
    MS CS:Pnm (XLI.B.116)

    Axur Re d'Ormus
    Arranged by Wendt, 17 movements
    202-02, 2 English horns
    MS CS:K (Nr. 43.K.I.); A:Wn (Sm. 3845)

    Ascur, Re di Ormus
    Arranger unknown
    222-02
    MS I:Fc (D.V.484)

Pièces d'Harmonie de l'opera Axur
Arranged by Stumpf
22-02
MS CS:Pnm (XLI.B.138)
EP (Offenbach, André [1796]) BRD:AB

Axur, Re d'Ormus
Arranged by Wendt
Harmoniemusik
MS A:Ee

Suite d'harmonie
Arranged by Mr. Ernest
22-02
EP (Paris, Imbault, Nr. 93) S:Uu (Utl.instr.mus.i.tr.145, 149–151) [missing clarinet 2 and horn 2]

Pièces d'armonie
Arranged by Ernest
22-02
EP (Berlin, Hummel, Nr. 805) DDR:Dl (Mus.3796/F/24a); BRD:TSCH (Gg176)

Axur Re de Ormus
Arranger unknown
.22-02
MS (Advertized in Traeg's Catalog, Vienna, 1799)

Axur Re de Ormus, '8th Collection'
Arranged by Stumpf
22-02
MS (Advertized in Traeg's Catalog, Vienna, 1799)

Axur Re de Ormus
Arranger unknown
222-02
MS (Advertized in Traeg's Catalog, Vienna, 1799)

Il Talismano (opera, 1788)
Il Talismano
Arranged by Wendt [Went], 16 movements
202-02, 2 English horns
MS C:K (Nr. 44.K.I.)

Il Talismanon
Arranger unknown
222-02
MS I:Fc (D.V.484)

Pièces d'Harmonie de Il Talismano
Arranged by Stumpf, 6 movements
22-02
EP (Offenbach, André, Nr. 3115) [Recueil 6] CS:Pnm (XLI.B.133); A:KR, A:Wn; DDR:SWl; CB:Zz; US:Wc; BRD:B (D.MS.197.131.an.3).

Talismann
Arranger unknown
222-02
MS A:Ee

Il Talismando
Arranger unknown
222-02
MS A:Wn [lost]

Talismanno
Arranger unknown
222-02
MS (Advertized in Traeg's Catalog, Vienna, 1799)

Talismann, '6th Collection'
Arranged by Stumpf
22-02
MS (Advertized in Traeg's Catalog, Vienna, 1799)

Palmira, Regina di Persia (opera, 1795)

Palmira
Arranged by Wendt
222-02
MS BRD:DO [may be lost]

Regina di Persia
Arranged by J. Handl, 1 movement
222-02
MS A:Wn (Sm. 0352)

La Palmira
Arranger unknown
222-02
MS I:Fc (D.V.481)

Regina di Persia
Arranged by Wendt? (horn 1 and part of bassoon 1 is in Sedlak's manuscript; the rest apparently by Wendt), 23 movements
222-02
MS A:Wn (Sm. 3847)

Palmira
Arranger unknown
222-02
MS CS:Bm (A.16.668)

Palmira
Arranger unknown
Clarinet and 3 basset horns
MS CS:Pnm

Palmira
Arranger unknown
222-02
MS A:Ee

Falstaff (opera, 1799)
Arranger unknown
222-02
MS I:Fc (D.V.495)

Cesare in Farmacusa (opera, 1800)
Trio and Finale, Cesare in Farmacusa
Arranger unknown
222-02
MS A:Wn (Sm. 3792)

Cesare in Farnuccia
Arranger unknown
222-02
MS I:Fc (D.V.495)

König von England (original unidentified)
Arranger unknown
222-02
MS BRD:DO [may be lost]

Sarsino, ?

Honon (original unidentified)
Duet from Honon
Arranger unknown
22-02
MS CS:KRa (IV.B.127)

Sarti, Giuseppe, 1729-1802

I Contrattempi (opera, 1778)
I Contrettempi
Arranger unknown
222-02
MS I:Fc (D.V.483)

Il Contra Tempo
Arranger unknown (probably Wendt), 29 movements
202-02, 2 English horns
MS CS:K (Nr. 2.K.II.)

I contra Tempi
Arranged by Wendt [Went], 10 movements
202-02, 2 English horns
MS CS:K (Nr. 20.K.I.)

I Contrattempi
Arranger unknown
222-02
MS A:Wn [lost]

Contra Tempi
Arranger unknown
222-02
MS (Advertized in Traeg's Catalog, Vienna, 1799)

Contra Tempi
Arranger unknown
22-02
MS (Advertized in Traeg's Catalog, Vienna, 1799)

Giulio Sabino (opera, 1781)
Guilio Sabino
Arranger unknown, 5 movements
222-22, contrabassoon
MS CS:Bm (A.35.227)

Julio Sabino
Arranged by Wendt [Went], 3 movements
202-02, 2 English horns
MS CS:K (Nr. 18.K.I.)

Giulio Sabino
Arranger unknown
222-02
MS A:Wn [lost]

Fra due Litiganti, il terzo gode (opera, 1782)
Fra due Litiganti
Arranger unknown
222-02
MS I:Fc (D.V.479)

Fra due Litiganti
Arranged by Wendt
222-02
MS A:Wn (Sm. 3849)

Due Littiganti
Arranger unknown
21-02
MS CS:Pnm (XLII.D.89)

Fra e Due littiganti
Arranged by Wendt, 8 movements
202-02, 2 English horns
MS CS:K (Nr. 19.K.I.)

Fai due Litigant
Arranger unknown
22-02
MS (Advertized in Traeg's Catalog, Vienna, 1799)

Fai due Litigant
Arranger unknown
222-02
MS (Advertized in Traeg's Catalog, Vienna, 1799)

Terzetto
Arranged by Wendt?
202-02, 2 English horns
MS A:Wgm (VIII 8579)

Rondo nella Saarti idolo amato
Arranger unknown
222-02
MS PL:LA (2472)

Schaffner, N. A.

Ouverture du Chasse
Arranged by Gambaro
Harmoniemusik
EP (Paris) F:Pn (Vm.27.1620)

Schenk, Johann (1753–1836)

Die Weinlese (opera, 1785)
Arranged by Wendt?, 4 movements
222-02
MS A:Wn (Sm. 3850)

Seyfried, Ignaz Ritter von (1776–1841)

Saul, Konig in Israel (Biblical drama, 1810)
  Saul, Konig in Israel
  Arranger unknown
  222-02
  MS I:Fc (D.V.510)

Saul
Arranger unknown
Six- and nine-part *Harmoniemusik*
EP (Vienna, Haslinger)

Saul König in Israel
Arranged by the composer
222-02
EP (Vienna, Chemischen Druckerey [1810]) A:Wst (M.24772/c)

Saul Konig in Israel
Arranger unknown
EP (Vienna, Steiner, as *Journal Nr. 2*, Nr. 1486 for 222-02, contrabassoon; Nr. 1487 for 22-02)

Richard Löwenherz (original unidentified)
Arranger unknown
222-02
MS I:Fc (D.V.510)

Duet from Mitternacht (opera)
Arranged by Triebensee
222-02
MS A:Wn (Sm. 3739, Jg. I, Oevre 2, Nr. 5)

Duet from Marpissa (opera)
Arranged by Triebensee
222-02
MS A:Wn (Sm. 3739, Jg. I, Oevre 3, Nr. 6)

March aus Alamar der Maure (original unidentified)
Arranged by Triebensee
MS CS:KRa (IV.B.144) [for 21-02]; A:Wn (Sm. 3739, Jg. I, Oevre 1, Nr. 3) [for 222-02]

Solié, Jean Pierre (1755–1812)

Jean et Geneviève (opera, 1792)
   Airs de Jean et Geneviève
   Arranged by Fuchs
   42-02
   EP (Paris, Nadermann, Nr. 172) F:Pn (Vm.27.3937 and Vm.7.6979)

   Airs de Jean et Geneviève
   Arranged by Fuchs
   2022-02
   EP (Paris, Nadermann?) F:Pn (Vm.22.4)

Le jockey (opera, 1796)
> *Ouverture arrangée pour harmonie*
> Arranger unknown
> 2022-02
> EP (Paris, Imbault, Nr. 163) F:Pn (Vm.7.6982 and Vm.27.3935)

> *Suite d'harmonie tirée des airs du Jockey*
> Arranged by Simonet
> 2022-02
> EP (Paris, Imbault, Nr. 222) F:Pn (Vm.27.3911)

Le Chapitre second (opera, 1799)
> *Ouverture arrangee pour harmonie*
> Arranger unknown
> 2022-02
> EP (Paris, Imbault, Nr. O.H.H.171) F:Pn

> *Airs choisis …*
> Arranged by Fuchs
> 2022-02
> EP (Paris, Imbault, Nr. 761) F:Pn (Vm.27.3934)

> *Ouverture de Chapitre*
> Arranger unknown
> Eight-part *Harmoniemusik*
> EP (Paris, Janet et C.)

> *Airs de Chapitre*
> Arranger unknown
> Eight-part *Harmoniemusik*
> EP (Paris, Janet et C.)

Spohr, Louis (1784–1859)

Faust (opera, 1816)
> *Faust Harmonia*
> Arranger unknown, 9 movements
> 222-02, contrabassoon
> MS CS:KRa (IV.B.138)

Jessonda (opera, 1823)
> *Jessanda*
> Arranger unknown, 2 movements
> 222-22, contrabassoon
> MS CS:Bm (A.35.230)

> *Jessonda*
> Arranger unknown
> *Harmoniemusik*
> EP (Leipzig, Peters)

Overture aus Jessonda
Arranger unknown
Harmoniemusik
EP (Leipzig, Peters)

Die Kreuzfahrer (opera, 1845)
8 Pieces de diverses Comedies favorites
Arranged by Schulz [with works by B. Weber]
Six- and seven-part *Harmoniemusik*
EP (Leipzig, Peters)

Spontini, Gasparo (1774–1851)

Milton (opera, 1804)
Airs du Milton
Arranger unknown
Harmoniemusik
EP (Paris, Ebend)

Julie (opera, 1805)
Ouverture de Julie
Arranger unknown
Harmoniemusik
EP (Paris, Erard)

La Vestale (opera, 1807)
La Vestale
Arranger unknown
222-02
MS I:Fc (D.V.511)

Die Vestalin
Arranged by Triebensee
222-02
MS A:Wn (Sm. 3739, Jg. II, Oevre 10 [Act I, 6 movements]; Jg. II, Oevre 11 [Act II, 6 movements]; and Jg. II, Oevre 12 [Act III, 9 movements])

Di Vestalin
Arranger unknown, 7 movements
222-02
MS CS:KRa (IV.B.139)

Vestalin
Arranger unknown, 2 movements
222-22, contrabassoon
MS CS:Bm (A.40.162)

La Vestale
Arranger unknown
222-02, contrabassoon
EP (Vienna, Steiner)

Ouverture du Vestale
Arranged by Etienne Gebauer
2222-121, serpent
EP (Paris) F:Pu (Vm.27.3973)

Vestalinn Nr. III
Arranger unknown
22-02
EP (Vienna, Chem. Druckerey, as *Journal für Sechstimmige Harmonie*) CS:KRa (IV.B.188)

die Vestalin
Arranger unknown
Nine-part *Harmoniemusik*
EP (Vienna, Haslinger)

Airs de la Vestalin
Arranger unknown
Six-part *Harmoniemusik*
EP (Paris, Ebend)

Ouverture de la Vestale
Arranger unknown
Harmoniemusik
EP (Paris, Ebend)

Airs de la Vestale
Arranger unknown
Harmoniemusik
EP (Paris, Erard) [Liv. 1, 2]

Fernand Cortez (opera, 1809)
   Ferdinard Cortez
   Arranger unknown, 12 movements
   222-02, contrabassoon
   MS CS:KRa (IV.B.140)

   Ferdinand Cortez
   Arranger unknown
   222-02, contrabassoon
   EP (Vienna, Steiner)

   Ferdinand Cortez
   Arranger unknown
   Nine-part *Harmoniemusik*
   EP (Vienna, Haslinger)

Ferdinand Cortez
Arranger unknown
Six-part *Harmoniemusik*
EP (Paris, Ebend)

Airs des Dieux Rivaux
Arranger unknown
Harmoniemusik
EP (Paris, Erard)

Starzer, Josef (1726–1787)

Adelheid von Ponthieu (ballet, 1775)
  Adele de Ponthieu
  Arranger unknown
  1202-02
  MS CS:Pnm (XLII.A.226)

  Adelheit v. Ponthieu
  Arranger unknown
  201-02
  MS CS:Pnm (XLII.B.253)

Steibelt, Daniel (1765–1823)

La Journée d'Ulm (original unidentified)
  Arranger unknown
  Six- or ten-part *Harmoniemusik*
  EP (Paris, Janet et C.)

Combat naval (original for piano)
  Combat naval
  Arranged by Göpfert
  222-02, serpent
  EP (Bonn, Simrock; Paris, Simrock, Nr. 346) A:Wmi; CH:N; BRD:AB [missing oboe 1], BRD:HR; DDR:Bds, DDR:Dl; F:Pn (K.1852); H:KE; S:J; US :DW (155)

[Sterbelt] *March and trio* (original unidentified)
  Arranged by Triebensee
  222-02
  MS A:Wn (Sm. 3739, Jg. I, Oevre 9, Nr. 17)

Cinquième pot-pourry
  Arranged by Fuchs
  42-02
  EP (Paris, Nadermann, Nr. 200) F:Pn (Vm.7.6969 and Vm.27.3982) [two copies]

Bataille d'Austerlitz
  Arranged by Fuchs
  Harmoniemusik
  EP (Paris) F:Pn (Vm.27.1593)

Storace, Stephen (1763–1796)

Gli Sposi malcontenti (opera, 1785)
    Sposi Malcontenti
    Arranged by Wendt [Went], 10 movements
    202-02, 2 English horns
    MS CS:K (Nr. 4.K.I.)

    Sposi Malcontenti
    Arranger unknown
    222-02
    MS I:Fc (D.V.488)

    Gli Sposi mal Conlenti
    Arranger unknown
    222-02
    MS (Advertized in Traeg's Catalog, Vienna, 1799)

Cora (opera?)
    Arranger unknown (probably Wendt), 19 movements
    202-02, 2 English horns
    MS CS:K (Nr. 5.K.I.)

Der Ersterwichtig Liebhaber (opera?)
    Arranger unknown (probably Wendt), 6 movements
    202-02, 2 English horns
    MS CS:K (Nr. 6.K.I.)

Strauss, ?

Krapfenwaldelwalzer
    Arranger unknown
    Six- and nine-part *Harmoniemusik*
    EP (Vienna, Haslinger)

Süssmayr, Franz Xaver (1766–1803)

Der Spiegel von Arkadien (opera, 1794)
    Der Spiegel von Arkadien
    Arranged by Triebensee and Wendt? (It appears to me that oboe 1, and Bassoon 1, 2 are in Triebensee's hand for 10 movements, and everything else is perhaps in Wendt's hand)
    19 movements
    222-02
    MS A:Wn (Sm. 3854)

    Spiegel von Arkadien
    Arranger unknown
    222-02
    MS I:Fc (D.V.481)

Spiegel von Arcadien
Arranger unknown
Harmoniemusik
MS BRD:DO [may be lost]

Die neuen Arkadien
Arranged by Schmitt
2222-02, serpent
MS BRD:AB (S.46)

Spiegel von Arkadien
Arranger unknown
222-02
MS (Advertized in Traeg's Catalog, Vienna, 1799)

Spiegel von Arkadien
Arranger unknown
22-02
MS (Advertized in Traeg's Catalog, Vienna, 1799)

Soliman der Zweite (opera, 1799)
    Solymander
    Arranged by Triebensee, 9 movements
    222-02
    MS A:Wn (Sm. 3739, Jg. I, Oevre 10, Nr. 1-9)

Der Retter in Gefahr (cantata, 1796)
    Arranged by Sedlak?
    222-02
    MS A:Wn (Sm. 3853)

Taglioni, Marie (1814–1884, a famous Swedish ballerina, it is not known that she composed)

Pas de Deux from *Divertissiment* (ballet)
    Arranged by Triebensee
    222-02
    MS A:Wn (Sm. 3739, Jg. I, Oevre 3, Nr. 10)

'Pas de Deus' (source unidentified)
    Arranged by Triebensee
    222-02
    MS A:Wn (Sm. 3739, Jg. I, Oevre 10, Nr . 10)

Tarchi, Angelo (1760–1814)

Bachus et Ariani (opera?)
    Arranged by Ruzni, 5 movements
    222-02, contrabassoon
    MS CS:Bm (A.36.877)

1r Suite d'operas comique
    Arranged by Fuchs
    Harmoniemusik
    EP (Paris) F:Pn (Vm.27.1603)

Titl, Anton (1809–1882)

Der Zauberschleier (original unidentified)
    Arranged by Wajacek
    1111-221, contrabassoon
    MS CS:Bm (A.20.929)

Umlauff, Ignaz (1746–1796)

Die schöne Schusterin (opera, 1779):
    Arranger unknown
    -02, 3 basset horns
    MS (Advertized in Traeg's Catalog, Vienna, 1799)

Umlauff, Michael (1781–1842)

Paul et Rosette (ballet, 1806)
    Arranged by Sedlak
    222-02
    MS A:Wn (Sm. 3870)

Aeneas in Carthago (ballet, ca. 1805)
    Arranged by Wendt?, 2 movements
    222-02
    MS A:Wn (Sm. 3869)

Don Ouixotte (original unidentified)
    Arranged by Triebensee, 2 movements
    222-02
    MS A:Wn (Sm. 3791, Nr. 9-10)

Das eigensinnige Landmädchen (ballet, 1810)
    Das eigensinnige Landmädchen
    Arranged by Triebensee
    222-02
    MS A:Wn (Sm. Jg. II, Oevre 7 [12 movements]; Jg. II, Oevre 8 [7 movements]; and Sm. 3795 [13 movements]

    Das Eigensinige Landmädchen
    Arranger unknown, 10 movements
    Harmoniemusik
    MS CS:KRa (IV.B.147)

Vesque von Püttlingen, Johann (1803–1883)

Johanna d'Arc (opera)
    Arranged by J. Hoven [pseudonym of the composer], 12 movements
    222-22, contrabassoon
    MS CS:Bm (A.35.166)

Vogel, Johann Christoph (1756–1788)

Déophon (opera, 1789)
    Demophon
    Arranged by Fuchs
    42-12, serpent; or 22-02
    EP (Paris, Sieber, Nr. 1093) F:Pn

    Démophon
    Arranger unknown
    222-12, serpent; or 22-02
    EP (Leipzig, Kühnel, Nr. 408) BRD:AB
    EP (Leipzig, reprinted by Peters, Nr. 408) BRD:NEhz

    Démophon
    Arranger unknown
    222-02
    EP (Vienna, Hoffmeister [1805])

    Ouverture de Démophon
    Arranger unknown
    22-02
    EP (Paris, Janet et C.)

    Overture aus Démophon
    Arranged by Triebensee
    222-02
    MS A:Wn (Sm. 3739, Jg. I, Oevre 12, Nr. 1)

Vogler, Georg Joseph (1749–1814)

Castore e Polluce (opera, 1787)
    Arranged by Triebensee, Three Acts
    Harmoniemusik
    EP (Vienna, Triebensee)
    Advertized in the AMZ, January, 1804, together with an original 'parthie.'

Wagner, Jakob Karl (1772–1822)

'*Liebe und Freundschaft*'
    Arranged by Sartorius
    Harmoniemusik
    MS BRD:DS [lost in WWII, according to Grove XX, 149]

Weber, Bernhard Anselm (1766–1821)

Die Jungfrau v. Orleans
   Die Jungfrau v. Orleans
   Arranger unknown
   21-02, string bass
   MS BRD:AB (S.52)

   Monolog aus Die Jungfrau
   Arranged by Triebensee
   222-02
   MS A:Wn (Sm. 3739, Jg. I, Oevre 12, Nr. 9)

   Airs de Jungfrau von Orleans
   Arranged by Schulz [together with arias by Spohr and B. Weber]
   Six- or seven-part *Harmoniemusik*
   EP (Leipzig, Peters)

Johanna
   Arranged by Schmitt?, 3 movements
   21-02
   MS BRD:AB (K.8a)

Weber, Carl Maria von (1786–1826)

Preciosa (opera, 1821)
   Overture aus Preciosa
   Arranger unknown
   Nine-part *Harmoniemusik*
   EP (Vienna, Lithographisches Institut)

   Ouverture de Preciosa
   Arranger unknown
   Harmoniemusik
   EP (Paris, Ebend)

Der Freischütz (opera, 1821)
   Freischütz
   Arranged by Flachs
   2222-02
   MS BRD:MÜu (W-Eb-35)

   Der Freischütz
   Arranger unknown
   222-02
   MS A:Wn [lost]

Freyschütz
Arranged by Sedlak, Part I, 12 movements; Part II, 9 movements
222-22, contrabassoon
MS CS:Bm (A.35.242 and A.35.243)

5 Stücke aus dem Freischütz
Arranged by Küffner
1011-02, basset horn
EP (Mainz, Schott) BRD:MZsch

Airs de l'Op. der Freischütz
Arranged by Küffner
Harmoniemusik
EP (Paris, Richault) [Liv. 1–3]

der Freischütz
Arranged by Flachs
2221-02
EP (Leipzig, Hofmeister)

Mélange ou Choix de Morceaux de l'Opéra: der Freischütz
Arranger unknown
1222-02
EP (Paris, Ebend)

Mélange ou Choix de Morceaux de l'Opéra: der Freischütz
Arranger unknown
22-02
EP (Paris, Ebend)

Der Freischütz
Arranger unknown
Seven-part *Harmoniemusik*
EP (London, Boosey)

Der Freischütz
Arranged by Brod
1221-02
EP (Paris, Petit)

Der Freischütz
Arranger unknown
22-02
EP (Paris, Petit)

Euryanthe (opera, 1823)
Euryanthe
Arranger unknown
222-22, contrabassoon
MS NL:M

Euryanthe
Arranger unknown
Nine-part *Harmoniemusik*
EP (Vienna, Steiner; reprinted in Paris, Richault)

Euryanthe
Arranger unknown
1022-02
EP (Mainz, Schott) BRD:MZsch

Oberon (opera, 1826)
    Oberon
    Arranged by Weller
    Ten- or twelve-part *Harmoniemusik*
    EP (Berlin, Schlesinger; reprinted in Paris, Ebend) [Liv.1,2]

    Ouverture d'Oberon
    Arranged by Weller
    Ten- or twelve-part Harmoniemusik
    EP (Paris, Ebend)

Jubel Overture, Cantata for the 50th royal jubilee of King Frederick Augustus I of Saxony
    Arranged by Rummel
    Nine-part *Harmoniemusik*
    EP (Mainz, Schott) BRD:MZsch

'*Lutzows wilde Jagd, und Schwerdtlied*'
    Arranged by Neithardt
    -134, 2 Kenthörner
    EP (Berlin, Schlesinger)

Lorzing
    Arranged by Rugni, 2 movements
    1022-1, basso
    MS CS:Bm (A.20.291)

[Unidentified opera movements]
    Arranger unknown
    222-22, contrabassoon
    MS CS:Bm (A.35.244)

Weigl, Joseph (1766–1846)

Das Petermännchen (opera, 1784)
    Arranger unknown
    222-02
    MS I:Fc (D.V.487)

Il pazzo per forza (opera, 1788)
    Il Pazo per Forza
    Arranged by Wendt [Went], 15 movements
    202-02, 2 English horns
    MS CS:K (Nr. 48.K.I.)

    Pazza par forza
    Arranger unknown
    22-02
    MS (Advertized in Traeg's Catalog, Vienna, 1799)

    Pazzo per forza
    Arranger unknown
    222-02
    MS (Advertized in Traeg's Catalog, Vienna, 1799)

Giulietta e Pierotto (opera, 1794)
    Arranged by Wendt [Went], 12 movements
    202-02, 2 English horns
    MS CS:K (Nr. 46.K.I.)

La Principessa d'Amalfi (opera, 1794)
    Le Principessa d'Amalfi
    Arranged by Wendt
    222-02
    MS A:Wn (Sm. 3855)

    Principessa d'Amalfi
    Arranger unknown
    222-02
    MS I:Fc (D.V.504)

    La Principessa da Malvi
    Arranged by Wendt [Went], 12 movements
    202-02, 2 English horns
    MS CS:K (Nr. 49.K.I.)

    Principessa d'Amalfi
    Arranger unknown
    Harmoniemusik
    MS A:Ee

I solitari (opera, 1797)
    Arranged by Wendt?, 2 movements
    222-02
    MS A:Wn (Sm. 3856)

L'Amor marinaro (opera, 1797)
> *Amor L'Marinaro*
> Arranger unknown
> 222-02
> MS I:Fc (D.V.485)
>
> *L'Amor marinaro*
> Arranger unknown
> 222-02
> MS CS:Pnm (XLII.B.54)
>
> *L'Amor marinaro*
> Arranger unknown
> 22-02
> MS CS:Pnm (XLI.B.126)
>
> *Gli amori marinari*
> Arranged by Stumpf, 6 movements
> 22-02
> EP, (Offenbach, André) [as Recueil 19–20, of 20 recueils] A:KR, A:Wn; DDR:SWl; CH:Zz; US:Wc, US:WS

Vesta's Feuer (opera, 1803)
> *Vesta*
> Arranger unknown
> 222-02
> MS I:Fc (D.V.503)

Die Uniform (opera, 1805)
> *L'Uniforme*
> Arranger unknown
> 222-02
> MS I:Fc (D.V.497)

Kaiser Hadrian (opera, 1807)
> *Kaiser Hadrian*
> Arranger unknown, 5 movements
> 222-22, contrabassoon
> MS CS:Bm (A.35.245)
>
> *Kaiser Adrian*
> Arranger unknown
> 222-02
> MS I:Fc (D.V.504)
>
> *Kaiser Hadrian*
> Arranger unknown, 10 movements
> 222-12
> MS CS:KRa (IV.B.161)

Marsch aus Kayser Hadrian
Arranged by Triebensee
222-02
MS A:Wn (Sm. 3739, Nr. 7); CS:KRa (IV.B.144)

Marsch aus Kaiser Hadrian
Arranger unknown
222-02, contrabassoon
EP (Vienna, Steiner)

Marsch aus Kaiser Hadrian
Arranger unknown
Nine-part *Harmoniemusik*
EP (Vienna, Haslinger)

Adrian von Ostade (opera, 1807)
Arranger unknown
222-02
MS I:Fc (D.V.510)

Das Waisenhus (opera, 1808)
Das Waisenhaus
Arranger unknown
222-02
MS I:Fc (D.V.491)

das Waisenhaus
Arranger unknown, 5 movements
222-02
MS CS:KRa (IV.B.164)

Marsch aus das Waisenhaus
Arranger unknown
222-02, contrabassoon
EP (Vienna, Steiner, Nr. 1114)

Marsch aus das Waisenhause
Arranger unknown
Nine-part *Harmoniemusik*
EP (Vienna, Haslinger)

Die Schweizerfamilie (opera, 1809)
Die Schweizer Familie
Arranger unknown, 5 movements
222-02, contrabassoon
MS CS:Bm (A.35.247)

Die Schwerzerfamilie
Arranged by Triebensee
222-02
MS A:Wn (Sm. 3739, Jg. II, Oevre 1 [Act I, 10 movementsl; Jg. II, Oevre 2 [Act II, 10 movements]

Schweizer Familie
Arranger unknown
22-02
EP (Vienna, K.K. priv. Chem. Druckerie) CS:Pnm (XLI.B.165)

Schweizer Familie
Arranger unknown, 4 movements
22-02
MS CS:Pnm (XLII.F.36)

Schweizerfamilie
Arranger unknown, 13 movements
222-02, contrabassoon
EP (Vienna, Chemishe Druckerey) CS:Bm (A.20.232)

Die Schweitzer Familie
Arranger unknown, 13 movements
22-02
MS CS:KRa (IV.B.168)

Die Schweizerfamilie
Arranged by Ahl, 14 movements
Harmoniemusik
EP (Offenbach, André) [Recueils Nr. 3, 4] A:KR, A:Wn; DDR:SWl; CR:Zz; US:Wc, US:WS [Recueil Nr. 4 only]

Die Schweizer Familie
Arranger unknown
222-02, contrabassoon
EP (Vienna, Steiner, Nr. 1449) [as 'Journal Nr. 1']

Die Schweizer Familie
Arranger unknown
22-02
EP (Vienna, Steiner, Nr. 1448)

die Schweizerfamilie
Arranger unknown
Nine-part *Harmoniemusik*
EP (Paris, Ebend)

die Schweizerfamilie
Arranger unknown
Six-part *Harmoniemusik*
EP (Paris, Ebend)

Pièces d'Harmonie de l'Op. die Schweizerfamilie
Arranged by Barth
1022-02
EP (Leipzig, Hofmeister)

Nachtigall und Rabe (opera, 1818)
Arranged by Starke, 7 movements
222-22, contrabassoon
MS CS:Bm (A.35.246) [incomplete]

Das Sinnbild des menschlichen Lebens (ballet, 1794)
  Das Sinbild
  Arranged by Wendt [Went], 16 movements
  202-02, 2 English horns
  MS CS:K (Nr.177.K.II.), CS:KRa (IV.B.167)

  Das Sinnbild
  Arranger unknown
  22-02
  MS (Advertized in Traeg's Catalog, Vienna, 1799)

  Das Sinnbild
  Arranger unknown
  222-02
  MS (Advertized in Traeg's Catalog, Vienna, 1799)

  Sinnbild des Menschlichen Lebens
  Arranger unknown
  222-02
  MS A:Ee

Die Reue des Pygmalion (ballet, 1794)
  die Reue de Pigmalion
  Arranger unknown
  222-02, contrabassoon
  MS (Advertized in Traeg's Catalog, Vienna, 1799)

  Die Reue des Pygmalion
  Arranged by Wendt
  222-02
  MS A:Wn (Sm. 3872), A:Wgm (VIII 39999)

  Die Reue des Pigmalion
  Arranged by Wendt [Went], 12 movements
  202-02, 2 English horns
  MS CS:K (Nr.47.K.I)

  Die Reue des Pigmalion
  Arranger unknown
  Harmoniemusik
  MS A:Ee

Arrangements for Harmoniemusik 139

Reue des Pigmaleon
Arranger unknown
Harmoniemusik
MS BRD:DO [may be lost]

Die Reue des pymallon
Arranger unknown
22-02
MS (Advertized in Traeg's Catalog, Vienna, 1799)

Richard Löwenherz (ballet, 1795)

Richard Löwenherz
Arranger unknown
222-02
MS BRD:DO [may be lost]

Richard Löwenherz
Arranged by Wendt [Went], 15 movements
202-02, 2 English horns
MS CS:K (Nr.176.K.II)

Richart Löwenherz
Arranger unknown
22-02
MS CS:Pnm (XLI.B.127)

Richard Löwenherz
Arranger unknown
22-02
MS (Advertized in Traeg's Catalog, Vienna, 1799)

Marcia aus Richard Löwenherz
Arranger unknown
22-02
MS (Advertized in Traeg's Catalog, Vienna, 1799)

Richard Löwenherz
Arranger unknown
222-02
MS (Advertized in Traeg's Catalog, Vienna, 1799)

Marcia aus Richard Löwenherz
Arranger unknown
222-02
MS (Advertized in Traeg's Catalog, Vienna, 1799)

Richart Löwenherz
Arranged by Stückel
22-02
MS PL:LA (2315)

Stücke aus Richard Löwenherz und Insel Christina
Arranged by Buchal
21-02
MS PL:LA (2287)

Richard Löwenherz
Arranger unknown
222-02
MS A:Ee

Riccardo
Arranger unknown
Harmoniemusik
EP (Vienna, Hoftheater)
Advertized in the *Wiener Zeitung*, 1796.

Der Raub der Helena (ballet, 1795)
   Raub der Hellena
   Arranger unknown (probably Wendt), 10 movements
   202-02, 2 English horns
   MS CS:K (Nr.178.K.II.)

   Raub der Helene
   Arranger unknown
   222-02
   MS A:Ee

   Raub der Helena
   Arranger unknown
   222-02
   MS BRD:DO [may be lost]

   der Raub helenens
   Arranger unknown
   222-02
   MS (Advertized in Traeg's Catalog, Vienna, 1799)

   Hellena
   Arranger unknown
   Harmoniemusik
   EP (Vienna, Hoftheater)
   Advertized in the *Wiener Zeitung*, 1796

Die Verbrennung und Zestorung der Stadt Troja (ballet, 1796)
   Trojas Brand
   Arranger unknown, 10 movements
   222-02
   MS CS:KRa (IV.B.162)

Incando di Troja
Arranger unknown
222-02
MS BRD:DO [may be lost]

Alonzo e Cora (ballet, 1796)
    Alonzo et Cora
    Arranger unknown
    Harmoniemusik
    MS A:Ee

    Ballo aus Allonso & Cora
    Arranger unknown
    222-02
    MS (Advertized in Traeg's Catalog, Vienna, 1799)

Alcina (ballet, 1798)
    Alcine
    Arranged by Wendt?, 17 movements
    222-02
    MS A:Wn (Sm. 3874)

    Alcine
    Arranger unknown
    Harmoniemusik
    MS A:Ee

    Allcina
    Arranger unknown
    22-02
    MS PL:LA (2314)

    Stücke aus Allcina
    Arranged by Buchal
    22-02
    MS PL:LA (2286)

Clothilde, Prinzessin von Salerno (ballet, 1799)
    Chlotilde
    Arranger unknown
    Harmoniemusik
    MS A:Ee

    Clothilde Prinsesin v. Salerno
    Arranged by Havel
    201-02
    MS CS:KRa (IV.B.165)

Alceste (ballet, 1800)
    Alceste
    Arranged by Wendt?
    222-02
    MS A:Wn (Sm. 3873)

    Alceste
    Arranger unknown, 7 movements
    222-02
    MS BRD:Rtt (Weigl.4)

    Alceste
    Arranger unknown, 15 movements
    22-02
    MS CS:KRa (IV.B.160)

Die Spanier auf der Insel Christina (ballet, 1802)
    I spagnoli nell'isola Cristina
    Arranger unknown
    Harmoniemusik
    MS BRD:DS [cited in Grove XX, 298]

    Die Spanier auf der Insel Christina
    Arranger unknown
    222-02
    MS PL:LA (2316)

    Stücke aus Richard Lovenherz und Insel Christina
    Arranged by Buchal
    21-02
    MS PL:LA (2287)

Die Atheniensische Tänzerin (ballet, 1802)
    Tänzerinn
    Arranger unknown
    22-02
    MS CS:Pnm (XLI.B.285)

    Die Tänzerin
    Arranged by Paul Maschek, 10 movements
    222-02
    MS CS:KRa (IV.B.163)

    Die Tänzerin aus Athen
    Arranged by Sedlak
    222-02
    MS PL:LA (2317)

Piolla (ballet) [and three unidentified operas]
   Arranger unknown
   222-02
   MS A:Wn [lost]

Tiroler Jahrmarkt (ballet)
   Arranger unknown, 2 movements
   22-02
   MS CS:KRa (IV.B.166)

Palmira (original unidentified)
   Arranger unknown
   Harmoniemusik
   EP (Vienna, Hoftheater)
   Advertized in the *Wiener Zeitung*, 1796.

Weigl, Thadeus (fl. 1797–1804, Vienna, brother to Josef Weigl)

Bachus et Ariadne (ballet)
   Bachus et Ariadne
   Arranger unknown
   Harmoniemusik
   MS A:Ee

   Bachus und Ariadne
   Arranged by Triebensee?, 13 movements
   222-02, contrabassoon
   MS CS:K (Nr.179.K.II.) [as *Erster Jahrgang Zweÿte Lieferung*]

   Ariadne e Bacchus
   Arranged by Wendt?, 13 movements
   222-02
   MS A:Wn (Sm. 3875)

Die Huldigung (ballet)
   Arranged by Wendt
   222-02
   MS A:Wn (Sm. 3876)

Die Vermählung im Keller (ballet)
   Vermählung im Keller
   Arranger unknown, 12 movements
   222-02
   MS CS:Bm (A.21.000) [incomplete]

   Die Vermählung im Keller
   Arranger unknown, 11 movements
   Harmoniemusik
   MS CS:Bm (A.35.259) [incomplete]

die Vermählung in Keller
Arranger unknown
222-02
MS (Advertized in Traeg's Catalog, Vienna, 1799)

Die Vermählung im Keller
Arranger unknown
22-02
MS (Advertized in Traeg's Catalog, Vienna, 1799)

Weigl, ?

Ginevra di Scozia (original unidentified; there was a ballet by this name by the choreographer, Ronzi, in Milano in 1800. The music may have been by Joseph Weigl)
Arranger unknown
222-02
MS I:Fc (D.V.494)

10 Arien (original unidentified)
Arranger unknown
201-02
MS CS:KRa (IV.B.169)

Weiss, ?

Amphion (ballet)
Arranged by Triebensee, 1 movement
222-02
MS A:Wn (Sm. 3739, Jg. I, Oevre 2, Nr. 3)

Winter, Peter von (1754–1825)

Henry IV (ballet, 1781)
Arranged by Rosiniack
Harmoniemusik
MS BRD:DO [may be lost]

Helena und Paris (opera, 1782)
Arranged by Sartorius
22-02, contrabassoon
MS BRD:DS (Mus.1025)

Das unterbrochene Opferfest (opera, 1796)
das unterbrochene Opferfest
Arranged by Stumpf
22-02
MS (Advertized in Traeg's Catalog, Vienna, 1799)

Das unterbrochene Opferfest
Arranged by Sartorius
22-02, contrabassoon
MS BRD:DS (Mus.1024)

Unterbrochene Opferfest
Arranger unknown
222-02
MS I:Fc (D.V.493)

Das unterbrochene Opferfest
Arranged by Triebensee?
222-02
MS A:Wn (Sm. 3859) [11 movements], A:Wn (Sm. 3794) [5 movements]

Das Unterbrochene Offerfest
Arranger unknown, 11 movements
22-02
MS CS:KRa (IV.B.177/178)

Das Unterbrochene Opferfest
Arranger unknown
22-02
MS CS:Pnm (XLI.B.128 and SLI.B.131) [two copies]

Das unterbrochene Opferfest
Arranger unknown
Harmoniemusik
MS A:Ee

Das unterbrochene Opferfest
Arranger unknown
22-02
MS PL:LA (2319)

Pièces d'harmonie de l'Opera unterbrochene Opferfest
Arranged by Stumpf
22-02
EP (Offenbach, André, [neuvième recueil, Nr. 1139; reprinted as Nr. 3153; dixieme recueil, Nr. 1140; reprinted as Nr. 3110; onzième recueil, Nr. 1204; reprinted as Nr. 3154; and douzième recueil, Nr. 1205; reprinted as Nr. 3113]) A:KR, A:Wn, A:L [Recueil 10]; BRD:WER1 [Recueil 9 and 10], BRD:OF [Recueil 10 and 12, incomplete], BRD:B [Recueil 11 and 12]; DDR:SWl; CH:Zz, CS:Pnm [Recueil 10, 11, 12]; H:KE [Recueil 10, 11, 12], H:Bn [Recueil 12]; US;Wc, US:WS [Recueil 9, 11, and 12 only]
MS CS:Pnm (XLI.B.142 [Part 1]; XLI.B.141 [Part II]; XLI.B.140 [Part III]; and XLI.B.139 [Part IV])

Babylons pyramiden (opera, 1797)
    Arranger unknown
    222-02
    MS A:Wn [lost]

Das Labirint (opera, 1798)
    Das Labirint
    Arranged by Wendt?, 13 movements
    222-02
    MS A:Wn (Sm. 3858)

    Labirinth
    Arranged by Triebensee, 8 movements
    222-22, contrabassoon
    MS CS:Bm (A.36.880)

    Der Labyrint
    Arranger unknown
    222-02
    MS I:Fc (D.V.497)

    Das Labyrinth
    Arranged by Triebensee [Trübensee], Part I, 14 movements
    222-02, contrabassoon
    MS CS:K (Nr. 50.K.I.)
    Triebensee advertized his arrangement of this work, in two acts, in the AMZ, in January, 1804.

    Das Labirinth
    Arranger unknown, 14 movements
    22-02
    MS CS:KRa (IV.B.176)

    Das Labirinth
    Arranged by Sedlak
    22-02
    MS CS:Pnm (XLI.B.132)

    Das Labyrinthe
    Arranger unknown
    Harmoniemusik
    MS A:Ee

Marie von Montalban (opera, 1800)
    Marie von Montalban
    Arranger unknown
    222-02
    MS I:Fc (D.V.493)

Maria von Matalban
Arranged by Sedlak
22-02
MS CS:Pnm (XLI.B.130)

Marie von Montalban
Arranger unknown
22-02
MS PL:LA (2318)

Stücke aus Montalban und Opferfest
Arranged by Buchnal
22-02
MS PL:LA (2288)

Suitte d'harmonie (Overture only)
Arranger unknown
Harmoniemusik
EP (Paris, Nadermann; reprinted in Genève, Marcillac, Nr. 1233)

Ouverture de Marie de Montalban
Arranger unknown
Harmoniemusik
EP (Paris, Ebend)

Tamerlan (opera, 1802)
   Tamerlan
   Arranged by Triebensee
   222-02
   MS A:Wn (Sm.3739, Jg. III, Oevre 7 [10 movements]; Jg. III, Oevre 8 [10 movements]

   Deuxième suite d'harmonie (12 Arias)
   Arranger unknown
   Harmoniemusik
   EP (Paris, Nadermann; reprinted in Genf, Marcillac) CH:Gpu

Elise Graefin von Kilburg (original unidentified)
   Elise Graefin von Kilburg
   Arranged by Sartorius
   22-02, contrabassoon
   MS BRD:DS (Mus. 1026)

   Elisa (original unidentified)
   Arranger unknown
   222-02
   MS I:Fc (D.V.498)

Brüder von Stauffenberg (original unidentified)
   Arranged by Triebensee, 6 movements
   222-22, contrabassoon
   MS CS:Bm (A.35.249)

Harmonie tirée des ses Opera
   Arranger unknown
   Harmoniemusik
   EP (Paris, Nadermann) [Liv. 1, 2]

Oboe Quartet
   Arranged by Triebensee, 1 movement
   222-02
   MS A:Wn (Sm. 3739, Jg. I, Oevre 12, Nr. 10)

Wranitzky, Paul (1756–1808)

Oberon, König der Elfen (opera, 1789)
   Oberon
   Arranged by Rosiniack
   222-02
   MS BRD:DO [may be lost]

   Pièces d'harmonie
   Arranged by Stumpf, 6 movements
   22-02
   EP (Offenbach, André, recueil 4, Nr. 772; reprinted as Nr. 3108] A:KR, A:Wn; BRD:AB, BRD:B, BRD:OF; DDR:HER, DDR:SWl; CH:Zz; US:Wc

   Pièces d'harmonie
   Arranged by Stumpf, 6 movements
   22-02
   EP (Offenbach, André, recueil 5, Nr. 774; reprinted as Nr. 3109] A:KR, A:Wn; BD:AB, BRD:OF; DDR:SWl; CH:Zz; US:Wc
   These two collections were also advertized in manuscript form in Traeg's Catalog, Vienna, 1799.

Das Waldmädchen (ballet, 1796)
   Waldmädchen
   Arranged by Sedlak?, 13 movements
   222-02
   MS A:Wn (Sm. 3871)

   Das Waldmädchen
   Arranger unknown
   Harmoniemusik
   MS BRD:DO [may be lost]

   Das Waldmädchen
   Arranger unknown, 12 movements
   222-02
   MS (modern score) CS:Pnm (XXVIII.A.277)

Das Waldmädchen
Arranger unknown
22-02
MS CS:Pnm (XLI.A.90)

Das Waldmädchen
Arranger unknown, 12 movements
22-02
MS CS:Pnm (XLI.D.322)

Das Waldmädchen
Arranged by Ignaz Beecke, 13 movements
222-02
MS BRD:HR (III.4.1/2.20.350)

ballo aus das Waldmädchen
Arranger unknown
22-02
MS (Advertized in Traeg's Catalog, Vienna, 1799)

Zingarelli, Nicola Antonio (1752–1837)

Pirro, re d'Epiro (opera, 1791)
   Pirro
   Arranger unknown
   Harmoniemusik
   MS A:Ee

   Pirro
   Arranger unknown, 5 movements
   222-02
   MS CS:KRa (IV.B.180)

   Pirro
   Arranger unknown
   222-02
   MS I:Fc (D.V.494)

   Pirro
   Arranger unknown
   222-02
   EP (Vienna, Pietro Mechetti [ca. 1816]) CS:KRa (IV.B.180)

Giulietta e Romeo (opera, 1796)
   Giuletta e Romeo
   Arranger unknown
   222-02
   MS I:Fc (D.V.485)

Giuletta e Romeo
Arranger unknown, 8 movements
222-02, contrabassoon
MS CS:Bm (A.20.942)

Giulretta e Romeo
Arranged by Ravel
22-02
MS CS:KRa (IV.B.181)

Giulietta e Romeo
Arranger unknown
Harmoniemusik
MS BRD:DO [may be lost]

Giulietta e Romeo
Arranged by Sedlak
22-02
MS PL:LA (2320)

Collections

Deux grandes Pièces, op. 52
Arranged by Rummel
222-02, contrabassoon
EP (Mainz, Schott) BRD:MZsch; CS:KRa (IV.B.126); A:Wgm (VIII 5146)
Contains works by Weber, Dussec and Kalkbrenner.

VIII Stücke aus opern und Ballets
Arranged by Wenusch, 8 movements
Six- or seven-part *Harmoniemusik*
MS A:Wn (Sm. 21790)
Contains works by Wranitzky, Kreutzer, etc.

Aus den besten Opern und Ballett
Arranged by Triebensee, 37 movements
222-02
MS A:Wn (Sm. 3792)
Contains arias by Mayr (6), Zingarelli (3), Mozart (3), Salieri, Paer (9), Weigl (10), and Wranitzky (4).

Die Fee und der Ritter (ballet)
Arranged by Sedlak (his '56th and 57th' work), 12 movements
222-02
MS A:Wn (Sm. 3881); CS:Bm (A.36.872)
Apparently a ballet taken from the works of Rossini, Aiblinger, Mercadante, Pacini, Payer, Pensel, and Romani.

(76) *Stücke fur Harmoniemusik*
Arranged by Widder
1022-02 [Nr. 1–56]; and 1122-02 [Nr. 57–76]
MS BRD:Mbs (Mus.Ms.2603)
Contains works by Rossini, Meyerbeer, Weber, Auber, Mozart, and Johann Strauss.

88 *Stücke* (opera arrangements)
Arranger unknown
22-24, 2 violas (1), string bass
MS BRD:Rtt (Inc. IVa/21/II)

Harmonie für die königliche Tafelmusik
Arranged by Poissl
Harmoniemusik
MS BRD:Mbs [cited in Grove XV, 24]
Contains works by Donizetti, Auber, and Lachner.

89 *Stücke* (opera arrangements)
Arranger unknown
22-02
MS BRD:BAR
Contains works by Rossini, Rosetti, Wanhall, and Gossec.

Miscellanées de la Musique
Arranged by Ruzni, 5 movements
222-12, contrabassoon
MS CS:Bm (A.36.878)
Contains works by Della Maria, Bruni, Weigl, and Winter.

Miscellanées de la Musique
Arranged by Ruzni, 6 movements
222-02
MS CS;Bm (A.35.254)
Contains works by Dramar, Weigl, and Winter.

Miscellanées de la Musique
Arranged by Ruzni, 4 movements
222-02
MS CS:Bm (A.35.255)
Dated December 20, 1817, contains works by Winter, Kauer, and Triebensee.

(Collection)
Arranger unknown
222-22
MS CS:Bm (A.36.892)
Contains works by J. Wilhelm, Schwarz, and Covalovsky.

(Collection)
Arranged by Starke
222-22, contrabassoon
MS CS:Bm (A.35.251)
Contains works by Boieldieu, Starke, Rossini, and Guiliani.

(Collection)
Arranged by Sedlak
222-22, contrabassoon
MS CS:Bm (A.35.209)
Contains works by Rossini, Rode, and Hummel.

(Collection)
Arranged by Starke, 4 movements
1031-221
MS CS:Bm (A.36.660)
Contains works by Adam and Donizetti.

(Collection)
Arranger unknown
222-02, contrabassoon
MS CS:Bm (A.36.877)
Contains works by Weiss and Tarchi.

Harmonie
Arranger unknown, 8 movements
22-02
MS CS:Bm (A.20.038)
Dedicated to 'Prince Waldek,' contains several works by Haydn.

(Collection)
Arranger unknown
222-221, contrabassoon
MS CS:Bm (A.37.337)
Contains works by Lanner and Strauss.

Zwey Rondeaux Concertants
Arranged by Starke
222-22, contrabassoon
MS CS:Bm (A.36.667)
Contains works by Kalkbrenner and Mayseder.

Miscellanées
Arranged by Triebensee, 10 movements
22-12
MS CS:KRa (IV.B.144)
Contains works by Mozart, Pleyel, Seyfried, Diabelli, Paer, Maurer, Weigel, Gretry, Tipsly, and Cherubini.

Suitte d'airs
Arranged by Beinet
Four-part Harmoniemusik
EP (Paris, Imbault [ca. 1795]) S:Uu [missing clarinet 2 and horn 2)
Contains works by Champein, Dalayrac, Framery, Giarnovick, Grétry, Haydn, Monsigny, Salieri, and Vogel.

Amusemens militaire
Arranged by Beinet
222-02
EP (Paris, Bouin, Castagnery & Blaisot [ca. 1788]) S:Uu [missing clarinet 2, horn 2, and both oboes]
Contains works by Gretry, Paisiello, and Salieri.

Première Suite d'airs d'opera comiques
Arranged by Fuchs
2022-02
EP (Paris, Imbault [ca. 1799]); BRD:AB [incomplete]; F:Pn (Vm.7.6965, Vm.27.1603, and Vm.27.1591); US:Cn
Contains works by Bruni, Dalayrac, and Tarchi.

2e Suite d'Airs
Arranged by Fuchs
2022-02
EP (Paris) F:Pn (Vm.27.1584)

Nouvelle suite de pièces d'harmonie
Arranged by Ozi
22-02
EP (Paris, Boyer [ca. 1786–1791]) [as, Nrs. 17–32] F:Pn [Nr. 19, 20 only] and F:Pn (D.16233) [Nr. 6]; BRD:DS; S:Uu [missing 19, 23, 25, and 31]
Contained works by Chapelle, Chardiny, Dalayrac, Deshayes, Gardel, Giroult, Grétry, Haydn, Kreutzer, Martini, Ozi, Paisiello, Philidor, Piccini, Pleyel, Rouget de Lisle, Salieri, Trietto, and Viotti.

Pièces d'harmonie
Arranged by Vanderhagen
22-02
EP (Paris, Le Duc F:Pn [Nr. 15–18, 21]; S:Uu [Nr. 8 missing clarinet 2, horn 2, and bassoon 2; Nr. 24 missing clarinet 2, bassoon 2, and both horns]; YU:Zha
Contains works by Dalayrac, Dezède, Grétry, Monsigny, Paisiello, Sacchini, and Anonymous.

Suitte d'harmonie
Arranged by Vanderhagen
22-02
EP (Paris, Sieber [ca. 1790]) S:Uu [missing clarinet 2 and horn 2]
Contains works by Beffroy de Regny, Dalayrac, Gretry, Mehul, Pleyel, and Anonymous.

Suitte d'airs d'harmonie
Arranged by Vanderhagen
22-02
EP (Paris, Le Roy [ca. 1785]) S:Uu [missing clarinet 2 and horn 2]
Contains works by Grétry, Martini, Piccini, and Sacchini.

(Collection)
Arranged by Courtin
Eight-part *Harmoniemusik*
EP (Paris, Dufant et Dubois)
Contains works by Andreozzi, Martini, Mozart, Sarti, and Zingarelli.

(Collection)
Arranger unknown, 12 movements
1120-02
MS NL:Ura/mZ (M.A.Zcm.2)
Contains works by Grétry, Monsigny, Piccini, Dalayrac, and Dittersdorf.

Works by Unidentified Composers

Dalayrac, Nicolas or Paisiello, Giovanni?

Nina (opera)
Arranged by Wendt [Went], 7 movements
202-02, 2 English horns
MS CS:K (Nr.25.K.I)

Gyrowetz, Adalbert or Persuis, Louis?

Der Zauberschlaf (ballet)
   Der Zauberschlaf
   Arranged by Starke
   222-22, contrabassoon
   MS CS:Bm (A.35.205 [Part I, 5 movements] and A.35.204 [Part II, 8 movements]

   Zauberschlaf
   Arranged by Sedlak, 14 movements
   222-02
   MS A:Wn (Sm. 3867)

Anonymous

Alexandre et Campase de Larisse (ballet)
Arranger unknown
201-02
MS CS:Pnm (XLII.B.139)

Le Baal Angloise (ballet)
Arranger unknown
201-02
MS CS:Pnm (XLII.B.161)

La Bianca e la Rolsa (ballet)
Arranger unknown (probably Wendt), 11 movements
202-02, 2 English horns
MS CS:K (Nr.7.K.II.)

Valses, 'Le bon gout'
Arranger unknown
222-22, contrabassoon, serpent
MS CS:Bm (A.35.232) [incomplete]

Die Eingebildeden Philosophen (opera)
Arranger unknown (probably Wendt), 10 movements
202-02, 2 English horns
MS CS:K (Nr.13b.K.I)

Airs d'opera buffa Fucheria e puntiglio
Arranged by Fuchs
2022-02
EP (Paris, Imbault, Nr. 535) [together with arias by Cimarosa, Bianchi, Palma, and anonymous]

(6) *Menuetti* and (12) *Deutsche aus dem bummen Gartner*
Arranger unknown
201-02
MS (Advertized in Traeg's Catalog, Vienna, 1799)

Le Festin de Piere (ballet)
Arranger unknown
201-02
MS CS:Pnm (XLII.B.291)

Le fête flamende (ballet)
Arranger unknown
201-02
MS CS:Pnm (XLII.B.162)

Rundtanz aus Figaro (ballet)
Arranger unknown
222-02, contrabassoon
EP (Vienna, Steiner, Nr. 960)

Les Horaces (ballet)
Arranger unknown
201-01
MS CS:Pnm (XLII.B.195)

Grosser Marsch aus König Lear
Arranged by J. von Blumenthal
222-02, contrabassoon
EP (Vienna, Steiner, Nr. 1474) E:Mbmc (K.846) [here for 222-12]

Le Lavandaje di Cittera (ballet)
    Le Lavandaje di Cittera
    Arranger unknown
    201-02, 2 English horns
    MS CS:Pnm (XLII.C.256)

    Le Lavandajie de Cittera
    Arranger unknown (probably Wendt), 7 movements
    202-02, 2 English horns
    MS CS:K (Nr.175.K.II)

Das beliebte Lied, 'Mensch, Mensch, Mensch'
Arranger unknown
222-22, contrabassoon
MS CS:Bm (A.36.853)

Messellan
Arranger unknown
222-12
MS CS:BA (193/78-632)

Messano
    Messano
    Arranged by J. Wratni
    202-12
    MS BRD:DS (Mus.Ms.1223/15)

    March v. Messano
    Arranged by J. Wratni
    21-12
    MS BRD:DS (Mus.Ms.1223/15)

La morte di Virginia
Arranger unknown, 6 movements
222-22, contrabassoon
MS CS:Bm (A.35.259)

Die Psyche (ballet)
Arranged by Ruzni, Part II, 12 movements
222-22, contrabassoon
MS CS:Bm (A.36.665)

Der Quacksalber und die Zwerge (ballet)
Arranged by Triebensee
222-02
MS A:Wn (Sm. 3739, Jg. II, Oevre 3 [10 movements]; Jg. II, Oevre 4 [6 movements]

Overture aus Rochus Pumpernickel
Arranger unknown
Ten-part *Harmoniemusik*
EP (Vienna, Haslinger; reprinted by Steiner, Nr. 1211)

La Sposa Persiana (ballet)
Arranger unknown (probably Wendt), 20 movements
202-02, 2 English horns
MS CS:K (Nr. 1.K.II.)

Die Tage der Gefahr (opera)
Arranged by Triebensee, 2 movements
222-02
MS A:Wn (Sm. 3794, Nr. 2–3)

Der Triumph des Vitelius Maximus (ballet), likely by Agostino Belloli
Arranged by Triebensee, 3 movements
222-02
MS A:Wn (Sm. 3739, Jg. I, Oevre 8, Nr. 2–4); BRD:Mbs (Mus.Ms. 2584)

L'uomo negro
Arranged by Osswald
222-22, contrabassoon
MS CS:Bm (A.35.199 [Part I, 10 movements]; A.18.380 [Part II, 6 movements]; A.35.200 [Part III, 5 movements])

Airs du Ballet de Vénus et Adonis
Arranged by Vanderhagen
22-02
EP (Paris, Imbault, Nr. 909) CH:N; F:Pn (Vm.27.4173)

Die Zween Anton (opera)
   Die Zween Anton
   Arranger unknown
   222-02
   MS I:Fc (D.V.488)

   Die Zweÿ Anton oder der Dame Gärtner
   Arranger unknown (probably Wendt), 16 movements
   202-02, 2 English horns
   MS CS:K (Nr.15.K.I.)

[Madame D.]
Airs composés pour le clavecin (original unidentified)
Arranger unknown
22-02
MS F:Pn

Ballo (Original unidentified)
Arranger unknown
201-02
MS CS:Pnm (XLII.C.327)

Beliebter Marsch (original unidentified)
Arranger unknown
222-02
EP (Vienna, Steiner, Nr. 1231)

Condrillon Romance (original unidentified)
Arranger unknown
222-02, contrabassoon
MS CS:Bm (A.36.851)

Sposalizio Allegro (original unidentified)
Arranger unknown
222-02
MS I:Fc (D.V.496)

(Unidentified opera)
Arranger unknown
222-02
MS CS:Bm (A.36.848)

(Unidentified opera)
Arranger unknown
222-22, contrabassoon
MS CS:Bm (A.35.266) [incomplete]

Pièces d'Harmonie
Arranged by F. Baer
22-02)
EP (Offenbach, André) [as '18.recueil'] BRD:Bhm (6936)

(Unidentified opera)
Arranged by Josepf Heinrich
Harmoniemusik
Advertized in AMZ, 1832 (according to MGG).

Airs d'Opéra buffa
Arranged by Fuchs
Eight-part *Harmoniemusik*
EP (Paris, Janet et C.) [Liv. 1, 2]

Airs d'Opéra comique
Arranged by Fuchs
Eight-part *Harmoniemusik*
EP (Paris, Ebend)

2me Suite d'Airs
Arranged by Fuchs
2022-02
EP (Paris, Imbault, Nr. 794) F:Pn (Vm.7.6966); BRD:AM

Pot-pourri
Arranged by Fuchs
42-02
EP (Paris, Nadermann, Nr . 202) F:Pn

Douze ariettes
Arranged by Hoffmeister
21-02
EP (Berlin, Hummel; reprinted in Amsterdam; *au grand magazin de musique*, Nr. 826) CS:Pnm

L'opéra comique
Arranged by Jörg
22-02
EP (Mainz, Schott) BRD:MZsch

12 Piecen
Arranged by Jörg
Harmoniemusik
EP (Mainz, Schott) BRD:MZsch

Ouvertures et Airs
Arranged by Ozi
Harmoniemusik
EP (Paris, Nadermann) [Liv. 1–32]

Misscelans für 1816
Arranged by Starke, 13 movements
222-02
MS CS:KRa (IV.B.141)

Overture
Arranged by Stumpf
22-02
MS DDR:HER (Mus.N.1=11), [missing clarinet 2 and bassoon 1]

Pièces d'harmonie
Arranged by Vanderhagen
22-02
EP (Paris, Le Duc) F:Pn [Nr. 15–18, 21]; S:Uu [Nr. 8, missing clarinet 2, horn 2 and bassoon 2; Nr. 14, and Nr. 24, missing clarinet 2, horn 1 and 2, bassoon 2]; YU:Zha

1ère [-12ème] Suitte des amusements militaires
Arranged by Vanderhagen
22-02
EP (Paris, Le Duc) S:Uu (Suites 1, 2, 4, 9, 12 [missing clarinet 2 and horn 2])

[Ière-4e] Suitte des amusements militaires
Arranged by Vanderhagen
22-02
EP (Paris, La Chevardière; reprinted in Lyon, Castaud) F:BO [Suite 1], F:Pn [Suite 4]

Pot-pourri
Arranged by Vanderhagen
Eight-part *Harmoniemusik*
EP (Paris, Imbault, Nr. 685) F:Pn [two copies, here for 1022-02]

Airs de l'Opéra buffa
Arranged by Vanderhagen
Six-part *Harmoniemusik*
EP (Paris, Janet et C.)

Franzosische Stücke aus Opern
Arranger unknown (probably Wendt), 21 movements
202-02, 2 English horns
MS CS:K (Nr.8.K.I)

(Pieces from various ballets)
Arranged by Wendt
222-02
MS A:Wgm (VIII 41158)

Diverisi Opern Arien
Arranged by Wendt [Went]
22-02
MS CS:Pnm (XLI.B.115)

Vari Pezzi degli Balli
Arranged by Wendt [Went]
22-02
MS CS:Pnm (XLII.E.319)

PART 2

WIND BAND AND WIND ENSEMBLE LITERATURE OF THE CLASSICAL PERIOD

Austria–Bohemia

(Collections)

(30) *Partitas*
21-02
MS BRD:DO (Mus.Ms.1551)
Contains works by Wenzel Piehl (Nr. 1–51), Francesco Alessio
  (Nr. 52–93), and Franz Aspelmayer (Nr. 95–131).

(10) *Parthien*
1-02, 2 English horns
MS CS:KRa (IV.B.199)
Contains 6 multiple movement works by Neuman and 4 multiple
  movement works by 'Handke, Mauritius.'

Anonymous

Adagio
2002-02
MS CS:Pnm (XL.F.364)

Alle Mande in C
21-02
MS CS:K (Nr.239.K.II.) [missing horn 2 and clarinet 1]

Animas Fidelium
SATB, 2201-22
MS CS:Pnm (XLVI.F.44)

Aria funebris
SATB, 21-02
MS CS:Pnm (IX.C.64)

Arioso e Menuetto
22-01
MS (Advertized in Traeg's Catalog, Vienna, 1799)

Auszüge
3022-42, timpani
MS CS:Pnm (XL.F.308)

Auszüge
3042-22, timpani
MS CS:Pnm (XL.F.238)

Auszüge
1021-32, timpani
MS CS:Pnm (XL.E.352)

Begräbnisgesang
SATB, 22-02
MS A:Wn (Sm. 9118)

Cassation
Solo flute, with 202-02, 2 taliae
MS CS:Pnm (XLII.B.188)

Concerto for Bb Clarinet
222-02
MS A:Wgm (VIII 2506); US:DW (4)
Voxman identified this work with Beer.

Deutsche Messe, 9 movements
SA, 2020-02, organ
MS CS:KRa (VI.A.17)

Hier liegt var dei

Divertimento
201-02
MS CS:Pnm (XLII.B.146)

Divertimento Militaire ('de Differends Auteurs')
222-02
MS CS:Pnm (XLII.B.46)

Divertimento in D
222-22, timpani, cinelli
MS CS:Pnm (XLII.A.332)

Divertimento
22-22
MS CS:Pnm (XL.E.340)

(2) *Divertimento a Trée*
1-02
MS CS:Pnm (XXII.E.61/17 & 61/18)

Divertimento, 2 movements
1022-12
MS CS:KRa (IV.B.194)

Divertimento in G
201-02
MS CS:Pnm (XXII.E.61/44)

Divertimento in D
202-02
MS CS:Pnm (XXII.E.61/46)

AUSTRIA-BOHEMIA 165

Divertimento in C
201-02
MS CS:Pnm (XXII.E.61/49)

Divertimento, 3 movements
21-, basset horn
MS CS:KRa (IV.B.195)

Eccosse
222-02
MS CS:Pnm (XLII.C.401)

'Gott auf dein Wort erscheinen'
SATB, -022, organ, string bass
MS CS:Ksm (C.644)

Hymne auf die Harmonie
Harmoniemusik
EP (score, city unknown) A:Wn (M.S.36780)

Hymnus pro Solemni
SATB, 222-22
MS CS:KRa (no shelf-mark)

Iste confessor

Sammlung aller Märsche und Kriegslieder des Österr. Aufgebotes
222-02
EP (Vienna, Sauer)
Advertized in the *Wiener Zeitung*, August 23, 1797.

(6) *Märsche von Verschiedenen Meistern*
222-02
MS CS:Pnm (XLII.B.320)

Marsche
2222-
MS A:Wgm (VIII 38672)

Marsch des Iöbl: zweyten Bürger Regiments in Wien
EP (Vienna, Kunst- und Industrie-Compotior, Nr. 517) A:Wn
This work was also advertized in Traeg's Catalog, Vienna, 1799,
for 222-02.

*Den Manen des gefallenen Volkes von Unterwalden nid dem Walde, am
9ten Herbstmonat 1798*
2022-02 (muted horns)
EP (city unknown, 1799) CH:EN

(24) *Märsche*
222-02
MS (Advertized in Traeg's Catalog, Vienna, 1799)

March
222-02
MS (Advertized in Traeg's Catalog, Vienna , 1799)

(24) *Marcie Turchesi*
222-22, Tamb. grande
MS (Advertized in Traeg's Catalog, Vienna, 1799)

Marcia
22-02
MS (Advertized in Traeg's Catalog, Vienna, 1799)

Trauer Marsch
22-02
MS A:Wn (Sm. 346, ch. XIX. 5 fol)

Marcia Funebre
222-02
MS A:Wn (Sm. 652)

(2) *Märsche*
222-02
MS A:Wn (Sm. 3787)

Märsche (1767)
202-02, 2 violas (?)
MS A:GÖ (MS.2970)

Marsch de l'Artillerie Tambourette
201-02
MS CS:Pnm (XXII.E.61/25)

Menuetto
201-02
MS CS:K (Nr.237.K.II.) [missing oboe 2, both horns]

Minuetto
201-02
MS CS:K (Nr.259.K.II.)

Pange lingua
SSATBB, 21-02
MS A:Wn (Sm. 657)

(10) *Partitas*
202-02, 2 talie [Nr. 1]; 2-02, 2 talie [Nr. 2–10]
MS A:Wgm (VIII 8541)

Parthia
22-02
MS A:Wn (Sm. 0353, ch. XIX, 11 fol)

AUSTRIA-BOHEMIA 167

Parthia in A
202-02
MS (Advertized in Traeg's Catalog, Vienna, 1799)

(6) *Partitta*
201-02
MS (Advertized in Traeg's Catalog, Vienna, 1799)

Parthia in D
201-03
MS (Advertized in Traeg's Catalog, Vienna, 1799

Parthia
2021-02
MS (Advertized in Traeg's Catalog, Vienna, 1799)

Parthia
2 oboes or 2 clarinets, with 2-12
MS (Advertized in Traeg's Catalog, Vienna, 1799)

(2) *Partitte Turchesi*
222-22, 2 piccolos, Tamb. piccolo, Trianglo, Tamb. grande, Cinelli
MS (Advertized in Traeg's Catalog, Vienna, 1799)

Parthia in G
202-02
MS CS:Pnm (XXII.E.61/43)
This and the following works were originally part of a large collection of wind music from the Jana Pachty estate, in addition there are a number of partitas for 21-, under (XXII.E.61/19, 20, 21, 22, 23, 24).

Parthia in E♭
202-02
MS CS:Pnm (XXII.E.61/54)

Parthia in E♭
1-02, 2 English horns
MS CS:Pnm (XXII.E.61/26)

Partita in F
1-02, 2 English horns [elsewhere listed as 2 talie]
MS CS:Pnm (XXII.E.61/27)

Parthia in F
21-02
MS CS:Pnm (XXII.E.61/28)

Parthia in C
22-02
MS CS:Pnm (XXII.E.61/29)

Parthia in C
202-02
MS CS:Pnm (XXII.E.61/30)

Parthia in F
21-02
MS CS:Pnm (XXII.E.61/31)

Paradi Parthia in D
201-02
MS CS:Pnm (XXII.E.61/32)

Parthia in D
201-02
MS CS:Pnm (XXII.E.61/33)

Partitta
201-02
MS CS:Pnm (XXII.E.61/34)

Partitta
201-02
MS CS:Pnm (XXII.E.61/35)

(2) *Partitte*
201-02
MS CS:Pnm (XXII.E.61/36)

Parthia
201-02
MS CS:Pnm (XXII.E.61/37)

Parthia in D
201-02
MS CS:Pnm (XXII.E.61/38)

Parthia in C
201-02
MS CS:Pnm (XXII.E.61/39)

Parthia in C
201-02
MS CS:Pnm (XXII.E.61/40)

Parthia in C
201-02
MS CS:Pnm (XXII.E.61/41)

AUSTRIA-BOHEMIA 169

Partia in G
202-02
MS CS:Pnm (XXII.E.61/42)

Parta in D
202-02
MS CS:Pnm (XXII.E.61/45)

Parthia in G
202-02
MS CS:Pnm (XXII.E.61/47)

Parthia in D
202-02
MS CS:Pnm (XXII.E.61/48)

Parthia in D
201-02
MS CS:Pnm (XXII.E.61/50)

Partia in G
202-02
MS CS:Pnm (XXII.E.61/51)

Parthia in A
202-02
MS CS:Pnm (XXII.E.61/52)

Parthia in E♭
202-02
MS CS:Pnm (XXII.E.61/53)

Partia
201-02
MS CS:Pnm (XLII.A.349)

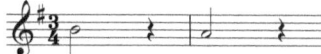

Parthia Pastoralis
201-02
MS CS:Pnm (XLII.C.219)

Parthia in C
201-02
MS CS:Pnm (XLII.A.74)

Parthia ala Camera
1-02, 2 English horns
MS CS:Pnm (XLII.E.339)

Partia
21-02
MS CS:Pnm (XIII.A.214)

Parthia ala Camera in E♭
1-02, 2 English horns
MS CS :Pnm (XLII.B.307)

(4) *Parti*
1-02, 2 talie ['Due Tally, Due Cornny et Fagatto'l
MS CS:Pnm (XLII.B.251)

Parthia in D
201-02
MS CS:Pnm (XLII.B.110)

(20) *Partie*
21-02
MS CS:KRa (IV.B.197)

[C. M.] *Parthia* (1776), 4 movements
22-02
MS CS:KRa (IV.B.201)

[C. M.] *Parthia* (1776), 4 movements
22-02
MS CS:KRa (IV.B.202)

Parthia in G, 4 movements
202-02
MS CS:KRa (IV.B.203)

Parthia in F, 4 movements
202-02
MS CS:KRa (IV.B.204)

Parthia in C, 4 movements
202-02
MS CS:KRa (IV.B.206)

Parthia in B♭
202-02, 2 English horns
MS CS:K (Nr.228.K.II.)

Parthia in E♭
1-02, 2 English horns
MS CS:K (Nr.231.K.II.)

Parthia in E♭
2-02, 2 English horns
MS CS:K (Nr.233.K.II.)

(6) *Poloneso e* (2) *Masur* [Mazurka]
222-02, contrabassoon
MS CS:Pnm (XX.F.107)

Polonoise
21-02
MS (Advertized in Traeg's Catalog, Vienna, 1799)

[Adolph I.K.H.P.] *Quadrille* in E♭
221-02
MS CS:Pnm (XLII.E.299)

Sextetto (1800)
22-02
MS A:Sca (Hs.421)

Sonatini
202-02
MS CS:Pnm (XXII.E.61/43)

(6) *Variatione* ('Nr. 3')
Solo clarinet, with 212-02
MS A:Wgm (VIII 2531); US:DW (35)

Alessio, Francesco

Parthia in B♭
21-02
MS BRD:DO (Mus.Ms.1551, Nr. 52–56)

Parthia in B♭
21-02
MS BRD:DO (Mus.Ms.1551, Nr. 57–61)

Parthia in B♭
21-02
MS BRD:DO (Mus.Ms.1551, Nr. 62–66)

Parthia in E♭
21-02
MS BRD:DO (Mus.Ms.1551, Nr. 67–70)

Parthia in E♭
21-02
MS BRD:DO (Mus.Ms.1551, Nr. 71–75)

Parthia in F
21-02
MS BRD:DO (Mus.Ms.1551, Nr. 76–79)

Parthia in E♭
21-02
MS BRD:DO (Mus.Ms.1551, Nr. 80–83)

Parthia in E♭
21-02
MS BRD:DO (Mus.Ms.1551, Nr. 84–88)

Parthia in E♭
21-02
MS BRD:DO (Mus.Ms.1551, Nr. 89–93)

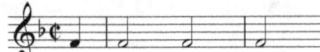

Parthia in F
202-02
MS CS:Pnm (XXXII.A.99)

Most of these works by Alessio in CS:Pnm have additional clarinet parts, in a somewhat later hand, intended as replacements for the 'talie' parts. The library also contains numerous works for 21- by Alessio.

Parthia in C
222-02
MS CS:Pnm (XXII.A.35)

Cassatio in E♭
2-02, 2 talie
MS CS:Pnm (XXII.A.64)

(4) *Parthia* in E♭
2-02, 2 talie
MS CS:Pnm (XXII.A.59, 61, 62, and 63)

Parthia in G
2-02, 2 talie
MS CS:Pnm (XXII.A.60)

(3) *Parthia* in B♭
202-02
MS CS:Pnm (XXII.A.65, 66, and 76)

Parthia in C
202-02
MS CS:Pnm (XXII.A.67)

(3) *Parthia* in D
202-02
MS CS:Pnm (XXII.A.69, 70, and 71 [the latter is missing both oboe parts])

Parthia in D
202-02
MS CS:Pnm (XXII.A.68)

(2) *Parthia* in F
202-02
MS CS:Pnm (XXII.A.72 [missing oboe 2], and 73)

(2) *Parthia* in G
202-02
MS CS:Pnm (XXII.A.74 and 75)

(8) *Parthia* in B♭
22-02
MS CS:Pnm (XXII.A.44, 45, 46, 50, 52, 54, 55, and 57)

(6) *Parthia* in E♭
22-02
MS CS:Pnm (XXII.A.47, 48, 49, 51, 53, and 56)

(4) *Parthia* in C
202-02; with 22-02 given as an option
MS CS:Pnm (XXII.A.33, 34, 39, and 58)

(7) *Parthia* in F
202-02; with 22-02 given as an option
MS CS:Pnm (XXII.A.36, 37, 38, 40, 41, 42, and 43)

Cassatio
202-02, 2 violas (?)
MS CS:Pnm (XXII.A.77)

Amantino, ?

Divertimento in B♭
201-02
MS CS:Pnm (XXII.A.98) [missing oboe 2]

Divertimento in C
201-02
MS CS:Pnm (XXII.A.94)

Divertimento in E♭
201-02
MS CS:Pnm (XXII.A.95)

Divertimento in G
201-02
MS CS:Pnm (XXII.A.96)

Divertimento in F
201-02; with 21-02 given as an option
MS CS:Pnm (XXII.A.91)

Divertimento
201-02; with 21-02 given as an option
MS CS:Pnm (XXII.A.93)

(5) *Divertimento*
201-02
MS CS:Pnm (XXII.A.92, 99 [missing the bassoon], 100, 101, and 102)

Divertimento in A
201-02
MS CS:Pnm (XXII.A.97)

Ascherl, ?

Marsch
1021-12, drum
MS CS:Pnm (XLII.F.193)

Aspelmayer, Franz (1728–1786)

Partitta di Campagnia in F
202-02
MS CS:Pnm (XLII.A.216); BRD:DO (Mus.Ms.1551, Nr. 99–102) [for 201-02]

Partitta di Campagnia in D
221-02
MS CS:Pnm (XXII.A.216)

Partitta di Campagnia in D
202-02
MS CS:Pnm (XXII.A.235)

Partitta di Campagnia in A
202-02
MS CS:Pnm (XXII.A.226)

Partitta di Campagnia in G
202-02
MS CS:Pnm (XXII.A.225)

(6) *Partitta di Campagnia* in F
202-02
MS CS:Pnm (XXII.A.194, 196, 197, 201, 203, and 213)

(5) *Partitta di Campagnia* in F
201-02
MS CS:Pnm (XXII.A.195, 204, 214, 240, and 249)

Partitta di Campagnia in B♭
201-02
MS CS:Pnm (XXII.A.217)

Partitta di Campagnia in C
201-02
MS CS:Pnm (XXII.A.242)

(3) *Partitta* in D
202-02
MS CS:Pnm (XXII.A.230, 233, and 238)

Partitta a 2 chori in D
402-04
MS CS:Pnm (XXII.A.251)

Partitta da Camera in F
21-02
MS CS:Pnm (XXII.A.215)

(2) *Partitta* in F
201-02
MS CS:Pnm (XXII.A.211 and 237)

(3) *Parthia*
Harmoniemusik
MS A:Ee

Partitta in G
201-02
MS CS:Pnm (XLII.C.64); BRD:DO (Mus.Ms.1551, Nr. 103–107)

Partitta in G
201-02
MS CS:Pnm (XLII.A.227)

Partitta in D
201-02
MS CS:Pnm (XLII.A.203)

Partitta in D
201-02
MS CS:Pnm (XLII.B.191)

(8) *Partitta di Campagna* in C
201-02
MS CS:Pnm (XXII.A.199, 200, 202, 205, 206, 208, 209, and 210)

(4) *Partitta di Campagna* in G
201-02
MS CS:Pnm (XXII.A.241, 245, 246, and 248)

(5) *Partitta* in C
201-02
MS CS:Pnm (XXII.A.198, 207, 212, 218, and 219)

(3) *Partitta* in G
2o1-02
MS CS:Pnm (XXII.A.227, 229, and 232)

Partitta di Campagnia in B♭
1-02, 2 English horns
MS CS:Pnm (XXII.A.222)

(2) *Partitta di Campagnia* in E♭
1-02, 2 English horns
MS CS:Pnm (XXII.A.220 and 221)

Partitta
2001-02
MS CS:Pnm (XLII.B.140)

Partitta in G
2001-02
MS CS:Pnm (XLII.C.175)

Partitta in A
2001-02
MS CS:Pnm (XLII.C.102); BRD:DO (Mus.Ms.1551, Nr. 124–127)

Partitta in C
2001-02
MS CS:Pnm (XLII.C.105)

Partitta in C
2001-02
MS CS:Pnm (XLII.A.328)

Partitta in C
2001-02
MS CS:Pnm (XLII.C.173)

Partitta in G
2001-02
MS CS:Pnm (XLII.A.82)

Partitta in G
2001-02
MS CS:Pnm (XLII.D.92)

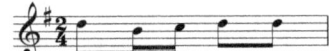

Partitta in G
2001-02
MS CS:Pnm (XLII.C.293); BRD:DO (Mus.Ms.1551, Nr. 128–131) [here in E♭]

Concertino (1786)
202-02, 2 talii
MS A:Wgm (VIII 8544)

(2) *Partitas* (in F and D)
201-02
MP (Leuckart)

Partita in F
21-02
MS BRD:DO (Mus.Ms.1551, Nr. 95–98)

Partita in F
21-02
MS BRD:DO (Mus.Ms.1551, Nr. 99–102); CS:Pnm (XLII.A.216)

Partita in F
21-02
MS BRD:DO (Mus.Ms.1551, Nr. 103–107); CS:Pnm (XLII.C.64)

Partita in F
21-02
MS BRD:DO (Mus.Ms.1551, Nr. 108–111)

Partita in A
21-02
MS BRD:DO (Mus.Ms.1551, Nr. 112–115)

Partita in A
21-02
MS BRD:DO (Mus.Ms.1551, Nr. 116–119)

Partita in A
21-02
MS BRD:DO (Mus.Ms.1551, Nr. 120–123)

Partita in A
21-02
MS BRD:DO (Mus.Ms.1551, Nr. 124–127); CS:Pnm (XLII.C.102)

Partita in E♭
21-02
MS BRD:DO (Mus.Ms.1551, Nr. 128–131); CS:Pnm (XLII.C.293)

Avertal, ?

(3) *Partitta*
2021-22, Tamborino, Tamb. Turc., Piati
MS (Advertized in Traeg's Catalog, Vienna, 1799)

Parthia
2022-, and 2 'Cor. Trombe'
MS (Advertized in Traeg's Catalog, Vienna, 1799)

Parthia
21-12; and 2 'Pfiffari'
MS (Advertized in Traeg's Catalog, Vienna, 1799)

Turcia
2022-2
MS (Advertized in Traeg's Catalog, Vienna, 1799)

Bärr, ? (Beer), Joseph (1744–1811)

Variatione
22-02
MS CS:KRa (IV.B.2)

Bayer, ?

Landler
222-02
MS CS:Pnm (XX.F.23)

Bém, Vaclav

Parthia
202-02 .
MS CS:Pnm (XXII.B.15)

Bitsch, ?

Pièces d'Harmonie
22-02
MS (Advertized in Traeg's Catalog, Vienna, 1799)

Bono, Giuseppe (1710–1788)

Partitta ala Camare
1-02, 2 English horns
MS CS:K (Nr. 243.K.II.)

Parthia in E♭
1-02, 2 English horns
MS CS:K (Nr. 244.K.II.)

Parthia in E♭
1-02, 2 English horns
MS CS:Pnm (XLII.C.50)

Parthia in E♭
1-02, 2 English horns, 2 violas (?)
MS CS:Pnm (XLII.C.274)

Parthia in F
201-02
MS CS:Pnm (XLII.C.26)

Parthia in F
1-02, 2 English horns
MS CS:Pnm (XLII.C.191)

Parthia in C
1-02, 2 English horns
MS CS:Pnm (XLII.C.25)

Parthia in C
201-02
MS CS:Pnm (XLII.C.317)

Parthia, 'Nr. 1' in C
1-02, 2 English horns
MS CS:Pnm (XLII.A.300)

Parthia in C
201-02
MS CS:Pnm (XLII.C.176)

Parthia in C
201-02
MS CS:Pnm (XLII.B.164)

Brixi, Frantisek (1732–1771)

Intermezzo
2-02, 2 talie
MS CS:Pnm (XXII.B.80)

Parthia in E♭
1-02, 2 talie
MS CS:Pnm (XXII.B.79)

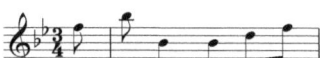

Parthia in E♭
1-02, 2 talie
MS CS:Pnm (XXII.B.81)

Parthia in D
202-02
MS CS:Pnm (XXII.B.82)

'Chamber works for winds'
202-02 and 222-02
MS CS:Pk [cited by MH; this library was closed during my residence in Prague, thus I cannot confirm this information.]

Brusek, Joseph

Parthia
22-02
MS CS:Pnm (XXIX.D.207)

[Bruscheck] *Parthia*
222-02
MS A:Wn (Sm. 562)

[Brussechek] *Variatzione*
22-02
MS CS:KRa (IV.B.5)
Contains 7 variations and a coda.

[Bruzzek] *Salve Regina*
SAB, 222-02
MS I:MOe (Mus.D.38)

[Bruczeck) *Salve Regina*
Eight voices and winds
MS I:Fc (A.1033)

Buchna, ?

Todten-Marsch
22-02
MS CS:KRa (III.B.233)

Cartellieri, Antonio (1772–1807)

Divertimento, Nr. 1
222-02, contrabassoon
MS A:Wn (Sm. 3615); US:DW (340)
A:Wgm (VIII 8868); US:DW (345)

Divertimento, Nr. 2
222-02, contrabassoon
MS A:Wn (Sm. 3615); US:DW (341)

Divertimento, Nr. 3
222-02, contrabassoon
MS A:Wn (Sm. 3615); US:DW (342)
A:Wgm (VIII 8867); US:DW (343)

Cejka, Valentin

Divertimento
201-02
MS CS:Pnm (XXII.B.184)

Divertimento
202-02
MS CS:Pnm (XXII.B.185)

Divertimento
202-02
MS CS:Pnm (XXII.B.186)

Cigler, ?

Parthia in F
2 0 1 - 0 2
MS CS: Pnm (XXXII.A.101)

Cisler, ?

Parttia
2 2 - 0 2
MS A:Wn (Sm. 3096)

Cremitasch, ?

Parthia
2 2 - 0 2
MS A:Wn (Sm. 571, ch. XIX, fol. 6)

Czeyka, Valentin (b. 1769)

Walzer & (3) *Ländler*
Harmoniemusik
MS I:Mc [cited in Eitner]

Dittrichstein, Graf Moritz (1775–1864)

Minuetto
2001-, 2 basset horns, 2 English horns
MS A:Wgm (VIII 8548)

Discher, J

Quintetto, 4 movements
2 2 - 0 2
MS CS:KRa (IV.B.16)

Partie alla Camera, 5 movements
2 2 - 0 2
MS CS:KRa (IV.B.15)

Partia alla Camera, 4 movements
2 2 - 0 2
MS CS:KRa (IV.B.14)

Partie ala Camera, 'Nr. 9,' 4 movements
2 2 - 0 2
MS CS:KRa (IV.B.13)

Partie ala Camera, 'Nr. 4,' 4 movements
2 2 - 0 2
MS CS:KRa (IV.B.12)

Dousa, Karl

Missa in honoren St. Venceslai
SATB, -202
MS CS:Pnm (VIII.E.40)

Drechsler, Josef (1782–1852)

Marcia Mor. di Nelson
222-02
MS (hand of Druschetzky)
H:Bn (Ms.Mus.1529); US:DW (331)

Drosler, ?

(12) *Ländler*
22-02
MS CS:KRa (IV.B.19)

Druschetzky, Georg (1745–1819)

Adagio & Allegro
222-02
MS H:Bn (Ms.Mus.1529); US:DW (331)

(2) *Concerti*
Solo clarinet, with 22-02
MS H:Bn [cited in MGG, which also mentions 32 movements for 3 basset horns]

Der Frühling, Nr. 1
SATB, 222-02
MS H:Bn (Ms.Mus.1538); US:DW (328)

Der Frühling, Nr. 2
SATB, 222-02
MS H:Bn (Ms.Mus.1539); US :DW (329)

Des Herrn Zmeskals Tact Messer Wiener Zoll
222-02
MS H:Bn (Ms.Mus. 1519); US:DW (115)
An educational work demonstrating one of the pre-metronome devices for establishing relative time.

(2) *Marches* (French *Zapfenstreich* and March for the French Division of General Gudon)
222-02
MS H:Bn (Ms.Mus.1527); US:DW (82)

Marche du Couronnement de L'Empereur Napoleon à Paris
222-02, contrabassoon
MS H:Bn (Ms.Mus. 1528); US:DW (45)

Marsch
222-02
MS H:Bn (Ms.Mus.1530)

Regimentsoboisten Marsch
202-02; or 22-02
MS BRD:Mbs (Mus.Ms.3672)

Mass
222-221, contra [missing vocal parts?]
MS H:Bn (Ms.Mus.1536); US:DW (327)

Miserere
2-02, with 2 clarinets alternating on basset horns
MS H:Bn (Ms.Mus.1598); US:DW (335)

Motetto
222-02, voices and strings ad lb.
MS H:Bn (Ms.Mus.1600); US:DW (48, 319, 319a)

Offertorium de St. Stephan
('Adagio con un Imitazione')
222-22, organ (voices missing?)
MS H:Bn (Ms.Mus.1582); US:DW (354)

Partita ('echo')
222-02
MS A:Wgm (VIII 38670); US:DW (111)

(17) *Partiten*
201-, English horn, basset horn
MS A:Wgm (VIII 8536)

(24) *Partiten*
202-02
MS A:Wgm (VIII 8537)

Partita in C
202-02
MS A:Wn (Sm. 2919); BRD:Rtt (Sammelband 8, Nr. 9–12) [for
    21-02, in A]

Parthia
22-02
MS A:Wn (Sm. 567)

Partitta Berdlersgarn
222-02, 'violino pigoia und tamborino'
MS A:Wn (Sm. 11377)

Partita in A
21-02
MS BRD:Rtt (Sammelband 8, Nr. 58–61)
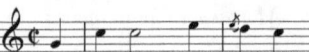

Partita in A
21-02
MS BRD:Rtt (Sammelband 8, Nr. 66–69)
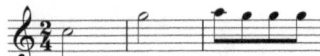

Partita in E♭
21-0'2
MS BRD:Rtt (Sammelband 8, Nr. 78–81)

Partita in E♭
21-02
MS BRD:Rtt (Sammelband 8, Nr. 87–90)

Partita in E♭
21-02
MS BRD:Rtt (Sammelband 8, Nr. 91–94)

Partita in A
21-02
MS BRD:Rtt (Sammelband 8, Nr. 9-12); A:Wn (Sm. 2912) [in C]

Partita in F
22-02
MS CH : GLiceo

Parthia in E♭ (ca. 1780)
22-02
MS CH:Zz (AMG XII.103, A–E)

Parthia in Eb ('Concertand')
22-02
MS CH:Zz (AMG XII.700, A–E)

Parthia: Concertand
22-02
MS CS:Zz (AMG XII.701, A–E)

Parthia
222-02
MS CS:Pnm (XXII.C.42)
According to MGG, there are 100 partitas by Druschetzky in
    CS:Pnm; I could find only the works listed below)
EP (Vienna, Torricella)
Advertized in the *Wiener Zeitung*, 1784.
MP (Vienna, Doblinger, DM 269)

Parthia
222-02
MS CS:Pnm (XXII.C.40)
EP (Vienna, Torricella)
MP (Vienna, Doblinger, DM 268)

Parthia
222-02
MS CS:Pnm (XXII.C.39)
EP (Vienna, Torricella)
MP (Vienna, Doblinger, DM 267)

Parthia
222-02
MS CS:Pnm (XXII.C.41)
EP (Vienna, Torricella)
MP (Vienna, Doblinger, DM 266)

Parthia
222-02
MS CS:Pnm (XXII.C.38)
EP (Vienna, Torricella)
MP (Vienna, Doblinger, DM 265)

Parthia
222-02
MS CS:Pnm (XXII.C.43)
EP (Vienna, Torricella)
MP (Vienna, Doblinger, DM 264)

Parthia in B♭
22-02
MS CS:Pnm (XLI.B.112)

Partitta in G
102-02, 3 basset horns
MS CS:Pnm (XLII.E.41)

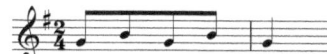

Partitta a la Camera in G
101-02, 3 basset horns
MS CS:Pnm (XLII.E.35)

Partitta in G
2-02, 3 basset horns
MS CS:Pnm (XLII.E.223)

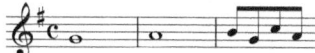

Partitta a La Camera in G
2-02, 3 basset horns
MS CS:Pnm (XLII.E.222)

Partitta in G
102-02, 3 basset horns
MS CS:Pnm (XLII.E.221)

Partitta in G
102-02, 3 basset horns
MS CS:Pnm (XLII.E.227)

Parthia in F
1201-02
MS CS:Pnm (XLII.E.226)

Parthia in A minore
1201-02
MS CS:Pnm (XLII.E.230)

Partitta in C
1201-02 .
MS CS:Pnm (XLII.E.288)

Partitta in G
1201-02
MS CS:Pnm (XLII.E.237)

Parthia in C
'Concertino a Flauto,' 201-02
MS CS:Pnm (XLII.E.284)

Parthia in C
1201-02
MS CS:Pnm (XLII.E.285)

Partitta in C
201-02
MS CS:Pnm (XLII.E.286)

Partitta in G
1201-02
MS CS:Pnm (XLII.E.287)

Partitta
222-02
MS CS:Pnm (XX.F.106)

Partia in C
222-02
MS CS:Pnm (XXVII.B.84)

[*Partita*] in B♭
222-02
MS CS:Pnm (XII.E.343)

Parthia in F
22-02
MS CS:KRa (IV.B.20)

Partia in F
Harmoniemusik
MS CS:K [cited in MGG; I could not find this work there]

Parthia in E♭
222-02
MS DDR:WRgs (Noten-sgl. Goethe Nr. 518)

Parthia in E♭
22-02
MS PL:LA (2291)

Partita in F
201-02
MS CS:BMahr [cited in MGG]

Partita in F
202-02
MS CS:Bm
MP (Prague, MAB, Nr. 35)

Partitta
Solo timpani, 222-02
MS H:Bn (Ms.Mus.1516)
According to MGG, there are some 70 partien in this library; I am familiar only with the following [in 1983, in 2012 there are many more].

Parthia
222-02 (players alternate on 'Klachter, Bruma marina, Layer, Span. Fidl, Tudlsak, citer, and Tiroli')
MS H:Bn (Ms.Mus.1569)

Partita
222-02
MS I:GI (SS.A.2.12)

Parthia
201-02
MS (Advertized in Traeg's Catalog, Vienna, 1799)

Parthia
222-02
MS (Advertized in Traeg's Catalog, Vienna, 1799)

Punschlied
SATB, 222-02
MS H:Bn (Ms.Mus.1541; US:DW (112)

Sensucht
SATB, 222-02
MS H:Bn (Ms.Mus.1537); US:DW (330)

(6) *Themes*, each with 6 Variations
22-02
MS CS:KRa (IV.B.21)

Variations on a March Theme by Count Louis de Szechny
222-02
MS H:Bn (Ms.Mus.1530); US:DW (84)

Variationen
222-02
EP (Vienna, Torricella)
Advertized in the *Wiener Zeitung*, 1784)

Theme and Variation
Harmoniemusik
MS CS:K [cited in MGG; I did not find this work]

Variazioni in B♭
222-02
EP (city unknown, perhaps published by Torricella) H:Bn; A:M

Zrini Ungaria
222-02
MS H:Bn (Ms.Mus.1534)

Dusek, Frantisek (1731–1799)

Marsch in D
21-32, timpani
MS CS:Pnm (VIII.F.40)

Parthia (1762)
202-02
MS CS:Pnm (XXII.C.119)

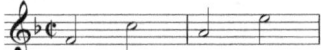

Partitta
202-02
MS CS:Pnm (XXII.C.120)
Under XXVI.C.2 one will find a modern MS score, which I believe is made from these parts.

Partitta
202-02
MS CS:Pnm (XXII.C.120b)

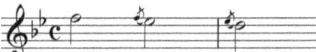

Partitta
202-02
MS CS:Pnm (XXII.C.121)

AUSTRIA-BOHEMIA 189

Partitta
202-02
MS CS:Pnm (XXII.C.122)

Partitta
202-02
MS CS:Pnm (XXII.C.123)

Partitta
202-02
MS CS:Pnm (XXII.C.124)

Partitta
202-02
MS CS:Pnm (XXII.C.125)

Partitta
202-02
MS CS:Pnm (XXII.C.126)

Partitta
202-02
MS CS:Pnm (XXII.C.127)

Partitta
202-02
MS CS:Pnm (XXII.C.128)

Partitta
202-02
MS CS:Pnm (XXII.C.129)

Partitta
202-02
MS CS:Pnm (XXII.C.130)

Parthia
202-02
MS CS:Pnm (XXII.C.131)

Parthia
202-02
MS CS:Pnm (XXII.C.132)

Parthia
202-02
MS CS:Pnm (XXII . C.133)

Partitta
202-02
MS CS:Pnm (XXII.C.134)

Parthia
201-02
MS CS:Pnm (XXII.C.135)

Parthia
202-02
MS CS:Pnm (XXII.C.136)

Parthia
202-02
MS CS:Pnm (XXII.C.137)

Parthia
202-02
MS CS:Pnm (XXII.C.138)

Parthia
202-02
MS CS:Pnm (XXII.C.139)

Parthia
202-02
MS CS:Pnm (XXII.C.140)

Parthia
202-02
MS CS:Pnm (XXII.C.141)

Parthia
202-02
MS CS:Pnm (XXII.C.142)

Parthia
201-02
MS CS:Pnm (XXII.C.143)

Parthia
201-02
MS CS:Pnm (XXII.C.144)

Parthia
202-02
MS CS:Pnm (XXII.C.145)

Parthia
202-02
MS CS:Pnm (XXII.C.146)

Parthia
202-02
MS CS:Pnm (XXII.C.147)

Parthia
202-02
MS CS:Pnm (XXII.C.148)

Parthia
202-02
MS CS:Pnm (XXII.C.149)
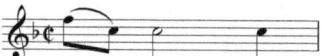

Parthia
202-02
MS CS:Pnm (XXII.C.150)

Parthia
202-02
MS CS:Pnm (XXII.C.151)

Parthia
202-02
MS CS:Pnm (XXII.C.152)

Partia
202-02
MS CS:Pnm (XXII.C.153)

Partia
202-02
MS CS:Pnm (XXII.C.154)

Partia
202-02
MS CS:Pnm (XXII.C.155)
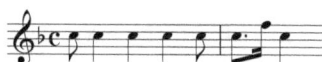

Partia
202-02
MS CS:Pnm (XXII.C.156)

Parthia in A
202-02
MS CS:Pnm (XL.D.436)

Parthia in B♭
202-02
MS CS:Pnm (XL.D.437)

Parthia in F
202-02
MS CS:Pnm (XL.D.438)
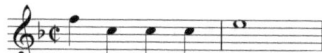

Parthia in C
202-02
MS CS:Pnm (XLII.E.149)

Partia in D
202-02
MS CS:Pnm (XXXII.A.104)

Parthia in A
202-02
MS CS:Pnm (XLII.E.143)

Parthia in F
202-02
MS CS:Pnm (XLII.E.135)

Parthia in F
202-02
MS CS:Pnm (XLII.E.151)

Parthia
202-02
MS CS:Pnm (XXXII.B.8)

Parthia in B♭
202-02
MS CS:Pnm (XLII.E.134)

In CS:Pnm there are also a number of compositions for 201- by this composer.

[Duscheck] *Parthia* in B♭
22-02
MS BRD:F (Mus.Ms.1558)

Parthia
201-02
MS CS:Bm
MP (MAB, 1958)

[Tuschek] (4) *Parthien*
Harmoniemusik
MS BRD:DO [may be lost]

Ermitasch, ?

Parthia
22-02
MS A:Wn (Sm. 571)

Esmeister, ?

Partitta in C
202-02, timpani
MS CS:Pnm (XLII.C.202)

Partitta in C
201-02, timpani
MS CS:Pnm (XLII.A.214)

Partitta in F
202-02
MS CS:Pnm (XLII.A.215)

Fischer, ?

Todten Marsch in E minor
22-02
MS CS:Pnm (II.F.125)

Fischer, Thomas

Il Couraggio
Solo oboe, solo English horn, 202-02
MS A:Wgm (VIII 2283); US:DW (46)

Freundthalier, ?

Divertimento
21-02
MS (Advertized in Traeg's Catalog, Vienna 1799)

Harmoniestücke
2 basset horns and 2 bassoons
MS (Advertized in Traeg's Catalog, Vienna 1799)

Harmoniestücke
21-, basset horn
MS (Advertized in Traeg's Catalog, Vienna 1799)

Divertimento
21-02, basset horn
MS (Advertized in Traeg's Catalog, Vienna 1799)

Gassmann, Florian (1729–1774)

Partita in E♭
21-02
MS BRD:Rtt (Sammelband 8, Nr. 113–117)

Partita in E♭
21-02
MS BRD:Rtt (Sammelband 9, Nr. 104–107)

[*Parthia*]
201-02
MS CS:Pnm (XXXII.C.246)

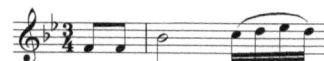

Parthia in C
202-02
MS CS:Pnm (XLII.E.200)

Partita in E♭
21-02
MS BRD:Rtt (Sammelband 8, Nr. 100–103); BRD:Rtt (Inc. IVa/31/I, Nr. 4)

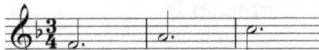

Partita in E♭
21-02
MS BRD:Rtt (Sammelband 8, Nr. 108–112)

Partita in E♭
21-02
MS BRD:Rtt (Sammelband 8, Nr. 30–34); BRD:Rtt (Inc. IVa/31/I, Nr. 5)

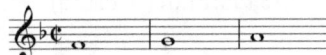

Partita in E♭
21-02
MS BRD:Rtt (Sammelband 8, Nr. 38–42); BRD:Rtt (Inc. IVa/31/I, Nr. 1)

Partita in E♭
21-02
MS BRD:Rtt (Sammelband 8, Nr. 21–24); BRD:Rtt (Inc. IVa/31/I, Nr. 2)

The second movement of this second copy bears the note, 'Madame la Comtesse de Wallerstein.'

Partita in E♭, 5 movements
21-02
MS BRD:Rtt (Sammelband 8, Nr. 1–4); BRD:Rtt (Inc.IVa/31/I, Nr. 6), BRD:Rtt (Gassmann 8) [here, 13 movements for 22-02, 2 violas (?)]

Gebel, ?

(2) *Harmonie*, op. 11
22-02
EP (Vienna, Steiner)

Golabek, ?

Partita
21-02 [cited in Hellyer]

Griessbacher, Reimund (Director of the *Harmoniemusik* for Prince Grassalkowitz in Vienna in 1796)

Allegro und Romance
22-02
MS DDR:SWl (MS.2212)

Grot, ?

Parthia
22-02
MS A:Wn (Sm. 347, ch.XIX, 12 fol.)

Gyrowetz, Adalbert (1763–1850)

Aria Russe
22-02
MS CS:KRa (IV.B.27)

Divertimento in D
Harmoniemusik
MS A:M

'Lasst Fenisens Lob'
Voice, 1022-1, guitar, 2 timpani
MS DDR:Ds
This work was performed under Carl Maria von Weber's name during Act III, Scene 3, of *Gastons Randgesang* and is incorrectly known as his work.

Nocturno in Dis
22-02
MS CS:KRa (IV.B.30)

Parthia in B♭
222-02, contrabassoon
MS CS:Pnm (XX.F.12)

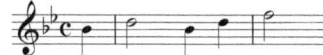

Parthia in E♭
222-02, contrabassoon
MS CS:Pnm (XX.F.11)

Parthia, 5 movements
22-02
MS CS:KRa (IV.B.28)

(7) *Partien*
Harmoniemusik
MS BRD:DO [may be lost]

(4) *Parth.*
21-02
MS (Advertized in Traeg's Catalog, Vienna, 1799)

(12) *Kleine Partien*
Brass instruments [cited in MGG]

Quintetto
-02, 3 basset horns
MS (Advertized in Traeg's Catalog, Vienna, 1799)

Serenade, op. 3, nr. 1
21-02
MS CS:Pnm (V.B.179) NL:Ura/mZ (M.A.Zcm.20); [missing clarinet 2] CH:Zz (AMG XIII.7090. A-D)
EP (Offenbach, André, Nr. 315, Nr. 1) BRD:Bu; DDR:Dlb; USSR:Lsc; DK:A
EP (Paris, Imbault [1796])
EP (Paris, Janet et C.)

Serenade, op. 3, nr. 2
21-02
MS NL:Ura/mZ (M.A.Zcm.20) [missing clarinet 2]; CH:Zz (AMG XIII.7090, A-D)
EP (Paris, Offenbach, André, Nr. 315) BRD:Bu; DDR:Dlb; USSR:Lsc; DK:A
EP (Paris, Imbault [1796])
EP (Paris, Janet et C.)

Deux sérénates, op. 5
21-02
EP (Berlin, Hummel, Nr. 819) BRD:Mmb

Serenade, op. 7
Nine-part *Harmoniemusik*
EP (Offenbach, André)

Serenade, op. 32
21-02
EP (Offenbach, André)

Walses
Eight-part *Harmoniemusik*
EP (Paris, Sieber)

Hanschke

Partia in E♭
22-02
MS CS:Pnm [cited by SJK]

AUSTRIA-BOHEMIA 197

Harke, Friedrich

(6) *Märschen*
222-12, contrabassoon
MS PL:LA (2606)

Hattasch [Hataš], Dismas [Jan] (1724–1777)

Parthia Pastoritia in C
202-02
MS CS:Pnm (XLII.E.261)

Parthia Pastoritia in D
201-02
MS CS:Pnm (XLII.E.262)

Parthia in D
2021-02
MS CS:Pnm (XLII.E.292)

Parthia Pastoritia
201-02
MS CS:Pnm (XLII.E.296)

Parthia
201-02
MS CS:Pnm (XLII.E.291)

Parthia
2020-02
MS CS:Pnm (XLII.E.294)

Parthia
201-02
MS CS:Pnm (XLII.E.295)

Parthia Pastoritia in F
201-02
MS CS:Pnm (XLII.E.263)

Parthia in F
201-02
MS CS:Pnm (XLII.E.293)

Haydn, Franz Josef (1732–1809)

Adagio in E♭ (not in Hoboken)
1122-02
MS I:Fc [cited in HA]

Andante (not in Hoboken)
21-02
MS (Advertized in Traeg's Catalog, Vienna, 1799)

Divertimento in G (Lukavec), 5 movements
(Hoboken II, 3)
202-02
MS CS:Pnm (XLII.D.35), CS:KRa (IV.B.198) [dated 1766],
    CS:KRa (IV.B.38)
MP (Vienna, Doblinger DM 84)

Divertimento in F (Hoboken II, 4)
21-02 .
MS [apparently lost]

Divertimento in F (Hoboken II, 5)
21-02
MS [lost in this form, but survives as a *Quintetto* for baryton]

Divertimento in C, (Lukavec) in 5 movements
(Hoboken II, 7)
202-02
MS BRD:Rtt (J. Haydn 90); CS:KRa (IV.B.36), CS:KRa
    (IV.B.198) [dated '1766']; US:DW (377)
MP (Vienna, Doblinger DM 31); (London, Musica Rara)

Divertimento ['Nr. 8'] (Hoboken II, 12)
Probably 2-02, 2 English horns
MS [apparently lost]

Divertimento ['Nr. 11'] (Hoboken II, 13)
'a Sei'
MS [apparently lost]

Divertimento (Lukavec) ['Nr. 9'] (Hoboken II, 14)
22-02
MS (autograph) USSR:Lk ['Divertimento, Giuseppe Haydn
    761']; A:Wgm (VIII 23669)
MP (Vienna, Doblinger DM 32)

Divertimento (Lukavec) ['Nr. 14'] (Hoboken II, 15)
202-02
MS (autograph) A:Harrach Archives [incomplete after eighteenth bar, fifth movement]; CS:KRa (IV.B.198) [dated '1766'], CS:Pnm (XLII.D.33); A:Wgm, A:M [arranged for string quartet]
MP (Vienna, Doblinger DM 29)

Feld Parthie ex A (Hoboken II, 20 bis)
Instrumentation unknown
MS [lost, known only through an entry in Haydn's catalog, given
    without incipit]

AUSTRIA-BOHEMIA 199

Divertimento (Lukavec) 5 movements (Hoboken II, 23)
MS (autograph) BRD:B (Ms.auto. Haydn 8) [only fourth
    and fifth movements are autograph] A:Wn, A:Wgm, A:M
    [arranged for string quartet]; CS:K (Piaristische Slg.),
    CS:KRa (IV.B.39), CS:KRa (IV.B.198) [dated '1766,'
    as *Parthia*]
MP (Vienna, Doblinger DM 30)

Divertimento, 4 movements (Hoboken II, 41)
222-02
MS DDR:Dlb (Mus. 3356-P-522), DDR:ZI (Sigl. Exner)
EP (Breitkopf & Härtel, c. 1782, as Nr. 3 in (6) *Divertimenti*)
MS (score) A:Wgm [copy by Pohl of this print]
MP (Vienna, Universal Edition, 1931)
This and the following five works are generally taken as spurious.

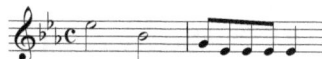

Divertimento, 5 movements (Hoboken II, 42)
222-02
MS DDR:Dlb (Mus.3356-P-521), DDR:ZI (Sigl. Exner)
EP (Breitkopf & Härtel, ca. 1782, as Nr. 2 in (6) *Divertimenti*)
MS (score) A:Wgm [copy by Pohl of this print]

Divertimento, 4 movements (Hoboken II, 43)
222-02
MS DDR:Dlb (Mus.3356-P-525), DDR:ZI (Sigl. Exner)
EP (Breitkopf & Härtel, ca. 1782, as Nr . 5 in (6) *Divertimenti*)
MS (score) A:Wgm [copy by Pohl]
MP (Mainz, Schott, ed. May)

Divertimento, 4 movements (Hoboken II, 44)
203-02, serpent
MS DDR:Dlb (Mus.3356-P-525) [for 202-02], DDR:ZI (Sigl.
    Exner) [for 202-02]
EP (Breitkopf & Härtel, ca. 1782, as Nr. 6 in (6) *Divertimenti*)
MS (score) A:Wgm [copy by Pohl of this print]

Divertimento, 4 movements (Hoboken II, 45)
203-02, serpent
MS DDR:Dlb (Mus.3356-P-523) [for 202-02], DDR:ZI (Sigl.
    Exner) [for 202-02]
EP (Breitkopf & Härtel, ca. 1782, as Nr. 4 in (6) *Divertimenti*)
MS (score) A:Wgm [copy by Pohl of this print]

Divertimento, 4 movements (Hoboken II, 46)
203-02
MS A:Wgm (VIII 39900) ['mit St. Anthony']; DDR:Dlb
    (Mus.3356-P-520) [for 202-02], DDR:ZI (Sigl. Exner)
    [for 202-02]

EP (Breitkopf & Härtel, ca. 1782, as Nr. 1 in (6) *Divertimenti*)
MS (score) A:Wgm [copy by Pohl of this print]
MP (Leipzig, Schuberth, 1932); (Leipzig, Peters, ed. Boudreau)

Partie (missing in Hoboken)
202-02
MS CS:KRa (IV.B.198) [dated '1766']

Partie (Lukavec, Hoboken II.D.18)
202-02
MS CS:KRa (IV.B.198) [dated '1766']
MP (Vienna, Doblinger DM 33)

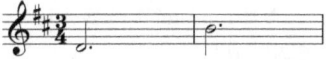

Divertimento ['Feldparthie Nr. 8'] (missing in Hoboken)
202-02
MS CS:Pmn
MP (Vienna, Doblinger DM 66)

Divertimento in D (probably Lukavec, Hoboken II.D.23)
202-02
MS CS:Pmn (XLII.D.32, 'Clam-Gallias')
MP (Vienna, Doblinger DM 86)

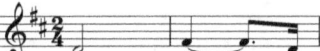

Parthia ['del Sigre Hayd'] (Hoboken II.Eb.12)
222-02
MS A:Wgm

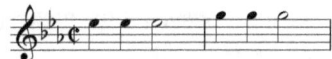

[*Parthia*] (Hoboken II.Eb.13)
222-02
MS (Pohls Nacblass) A:Wgm; US:DW (400)

Parthia ['del Sigre Hayd'] (Hoboken II.Eb.14)
222-02
MS A:Wgm

(2) *Parthien* (Hoboken II.Eb.16)
222-02
MS BRD:B [only one Partita survives]

Suite (Hoboken II.Eb.17)
22-02
MS BRD:B (Mus.Ms.10000)

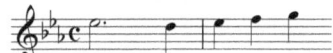

Parthia ['Sigre Hayd'] (Hoboken II.F.7)
222-02
MS A:Wgm; CS:K; US:DW (245); DDR:HER (Mus.C.16=7) [for 222-02], DDR:HER (Mus.N.1=3) [for 222-02]; CS:Pu (59-R-16) [for 22-02]
EP (Simrock, Nr. 262, as *Harmonie*) A:Wgm; S:J; B:Bc; CS:Pnm
MP (Leipzig, Kahnt, 1902)

Grove, VIII, 378, suggests the composer may be Wranitzky.

Divertimento (Hoboken II.F.12)
202-02
MS CS:K (Nr. 240.K.II) ['Del Sig. Hayden']
MP (London, Musica Rara, ed. Janetzky)
Grove, VIII, 378, calls this spurious.

Deux Parthies (missing in Hoboken)
22-02
MS [cited in J]

Divertimento (Hoboken II.G.3)
202-02
MP (Vienna, Doblinger DM 84)

Partita, 6 movements (Hoboken II.G.8)
201-02
MS CS:KRa (IV.B.37) [dated '1766']

Divertimento in G (Lukavec, missing in Hoboken)
202-02
MS CS:KRa (IV.B.198)
MP (Vienna, Doblinger DM 85)

Divertimento in D (Lukavec, missing in Hoboken)
202-02
MP (Vienna, Doblinger DM 66)

Parthia in G, 4 movements (missing in Hoboken)
201-02
MS CS:Bm (A.19.005)

Parthie ['del Sig Hayden'] (Hoboken II.Bb.7)
22-02
MS CS:Bm (A.19.095); US:Mor
Hellyer and Landon find this work elsewhere under 'Mozart' and 'Joseph Morris.'

Divertimento [1760] (Concordance unknown)
202-02
MS A:Wgm (VIII 40898)

Divertimento in E♭ (Concordance unknown)
222-02
MS A:Wgm (VIII 40899)

Parthia in E♭ (Concordance unknown)
222-02
MS A:Wgm (VIII 39998)

Parthia in E♭ (Concordance unknown)
222-02
MS A:Wgm (VIII 41159)

Parthia in F (Concordance unknown)
222-02
MS A:Wgm (VIII 40752)

(2) *Partie* (Concordance unknown)
Harmoniemusik
MS CS:KRa (R.I.27) [under 'XII Parthien']

Echo
2000-
MS DK:Kk (Giedde Coll. Mu. 6207.3179 [II, 11])

Introduzione
1222-022, contrabassoon
MP (*Haydn Gesamtausgabe*)
This is an independent overture to the second part of the *Seven Last Words*.

March in C
1222-12, serpent, Tamburo
MS (autograph) Stockholm: Private library of R. Nydahl
This is an arrangement by Haydn, taken from the second movement of Symphony 100, (cited in Grove, VIII, 374).

March ['Derbyshire Nr. 1'] (Hoboken VIII, 1)
22-12, serpent [percussion, but with staves not filled in]
MS (autograph) H:Bn (eig.Ms.Nr. 136; Inv. F. Nr. 240)
EP (London, Simpkins, 1794) GB:Lbm; US:R
EP (Kühnel, Nr. 489 [1806]) H:KE, H:Bn; DDR:ZI
EP (Vienna, Eder, Nr. 268) H:Bn [for 22-102]
MP (Vienna, Doblinger DM 34/5)

March ('Derbyshire Nr. 2') (Hoboken VIII 2)
MS (autograph) A:Eh (Slg. Sandor Wolf)
EP (London, Simpkins, 1794) GB:Lbm; US:R
EP (Kühnel, Nr. 489 [1806]) H:KE, H:Bn; DDR:ZI
EP (Vienna, Eder, Nr. 268) H:Bn [for 22-102]
MP (Vienna, Doblinger DM 34/6)

March für den Prinzen von Wales (Hoboken VIII, 3)
22-12, serpent
MS (autograph) GB:Lrs
MP (Vienna, Doblinger DM 34/4)

Ungarischer National-Marsch (Hoboken VIII, 4)Incipit
222-12
MS (autograph) H:Bn (eig.MS.Nr.39) [may now be Mus. Ms.I.43a]
MP (Vienna, Doblinger DM 34/7)

March (Hoboken VIII, 6)
22-02
MS (autograph) CS:Pn
MP (Vienna, Doblinger DM 34/3)

Marche Regimento de Marshall (missing in Hoboken)
202-02
MS (autograph) F:Pn; CS:Pnm [dated 1771]
MP (Vienna, Doblinger DM 34/1 and 34/2)

March in E♭ (Hoboken VIII, 7)
22-12, serpent
MS (autograph) GB:Lbm [incomplete, 8 bars only]; A:Eh

Marsch in G (missing in Hoboken)
202-02
MP (London, Musica Rara, ed. Janetzky)

March ['de me, giuseppe Haydn 1795']
MS (autograph) H:Bn (Ms.Mus.I.43b)

Haydn, Johann Michael (1737–1806)

Divertimento in D, 5 movements dated Salzburg, March 9, 1786
202-02
MS H:Bn [previously A:Ee]
MP (Vienna, Doblinger, DM 312)

Divertimento in C
1-02, 2 basset horns
MS [lost, according to Grove]

Divertimento in D, 6 movements (ca. 1787)
1101-01
MS A:Wgm
MP (Leipzig, 1960, under *Hofmeister Studienwerk*)

Harmonie, Nr. 1
222-02
EP (Kühnel)
Advertized in AMZ, in 1803.

Libera
STB, 22-02
MS CS:Pnm (X.A.69)

March Collection
22-02
Advertized in AMZ, in 1803.

Türkischer Marsch, dated Salzburg, August 6, 1795
2222-22, Piatelli, Tamburo
MP (DTO, XXIX)

Marcia a piu stromenti, dated April 22, 1803
Instrumentation unknown
MS (autograph score) BRD:Mbs (Mus.Ms.447)

Deutsche Messe
SATB, 2222-22, timpani, organ
MS A:Wn (Sm. 22260); I:MOe (Mus.D.169) [may be a different work]

Deutsche
SATB, 2200-02, organ
MS CH:E (Th.123, 31)

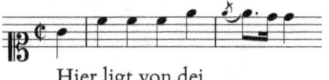
Hier ligt von dei

Heiligen Messe
SATB, 22-02, organ
MS [incomplete] A:Wn (Sm. 20001 and 20002)
Carries the note, 'Gesange bey dem Heiligen Mess Opfer in der KK Landesfürstt: Hadtpfarrkirche.'

Missa St. Hieronymus
Vocies with 202-003
MS BRD:Mbs (Mus.Ms.1289) [some wind parts missing]

Partita in F, dated Pressburg, December 22, 1762
21-02
MS [lost, according to Grove]

Terzetto, 'Yluc piae mentes'
STB, 22-02
MS CS:Pnm (X.A.50)

Hoschna, Jacob Phil.

Parthia in F
201-02
MS CS:Pu (59-R-165)

Huber, Jakub

Missa choralis in G
SATB, 200-02, organ
MS CS:Pnm (XXXVII.D.22)

Missa choralis in C
SATB, 201-02, organ
MS CS:Pnm (XXXVII.D.23)

Kammel, ?

Serenata
101-02
MS CS:Bm [cited by Hellyer]

Serenata in G
202-02
MP (MAB, Nr. 35)

Kauer, Ferdinand (1751–1831)

Nelsons grosse Seeschlacht
Harmoniemusik
EP (Vienna, ca. 1798) [cited in Grove, IX, 830]

Partita
202-02
MS A:Wn (Sm. 2943)

Partita
202-02
MS A:Wn (Sm. 2944)

Kirsten, ?

Partita
2001-02, 2 taille
MS CS:Pnm (XLII.C.204)

Partita
2001-02, 2 taille
MS CS:Pnm (XLII.C.201)

Knezek, Vaclav (1745–1806)

Partita in B♭
22-02, 2 violas (?), string bass
MS BRD:Rtt (Knezek, 14)

Partita in B♭
22-02, 2 violas (?), string bass
MS BRD:Rtt (Knezek 13)

Knorr, Bernhard, Freiherr von (Vienna, eighteenth century)

Quintet
1001-02, English horn
MS A:Wgm [cited by Eitner]

Koschevitz, Josef

(6) *Hongroises*
2221-02
MS [cited by MGG]

(6) Hongroises
Arranged by Druschetzky
222-02, contrabassoon
MS [cited by MGG]

Kotterz, ?

Parthia
202-02
MS CS:Pnm (XXXII.A.103)

Kozeluch, Jan Antonin (1738–1814)

Cassation
21-02
MS CS:Pnm (XXX.B.14)

Kozeluch, Leopold (1752–1818)

Divertimento in D ('Nr. 1')
22-02
MS CS:Pnm (XXXII.A.87) [missing clarinet 2]

Divertimento in D ('Nr. 2')
22-02
MS CS:Pnm (XXXII.A.88)

Divertimento in E♭ ('Nr. 3')
22-02
MS CS:Pnm (XXXII.A.89)

Divertimento in E♭
22-02, piano
MS A:Wn (Sm. 11390)

Divertimento in E♭
22-02, piano
MS A:Wn (Sm. 11391)

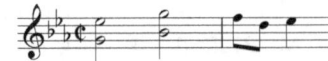

Divertimento in E♭
22-02, piano
MS BRD:W (Vogel, 141)

Harmonie, Nr. 2
222-02, contrabassoon
EP (Bonn, Simrock, Nr. 270; reprinted in Leipzig, Breitkopf & Härtel) BRD:Bds; US:Wc

AUSTRIA-BOHEMIA 207

Musica Militaire
Instrumentation unknown
MS I:Fc (D.6.53)

Marsch für das Corps des Handelstandes von Wien
Harmoniemusik
EP (Augsburg, Gombert) CS:Pnm (XLI.D.279)
Also advertized in Traeg's Catalog, Vienna, 1799, in manuscript under 'der Freywilligen des handelsstand in Wien,' for nine-part *Harmoniemusik*.

Prag
MS (autograph piano score)
A:Wn (Sm. 2091)
A collection of pieces for military band, including marches and a theme and variations.

Parthia in B♭
222-02
MS DDR:HER (Mus.C.19=1)

Parthia in F
2022-02
MS BRD:W (Ms. Vogel 141) BRD:HR (III.4.1/2.fol. 356); USSR:Lk (Jus.209e) [as 'Nr. 23. Parthia']
The manuscript reads, 'Cassazion ... angeschafft für die braunschweigische Musikgesellschaft 1796 durch aldefeld,' for 1022-02, 2 violas(?).

Parthia in C minor, 4 movements
221-02
MS CS:KRa (IV.B.60) [as Pardia ala Camera, by 'J: Goschelock']

Parthia in D minor, 4 movements
221-02
MS CS :KRa (IV. B.61, 'Nr. 2')

Parthia in D minor, 4 movements
221-02
MS CS:KRa (IV.B.63) 'Nr. 4')

Parthia in F
22-02
MS CS:Bm (A.31.764)

Parthia in B♭, 4 movements
222-02
MS CS:KRa (IV.B.65, as 'Nr. 6: Partie ala Camera ... Goscheluch')

Parthia in B♭, 4 movements
Solo oboe, with 222-02
MS CS:KRa (IV.B.64, as 'Nr. 6: Partie ala Camera
    ... Goscheluck')

Parthia in B♭, 3 movements
222-02
MS CS:KRa (IV.B.62)

Parthia in F
2022-02
MS USSR:Lk (Jus.209b, as 'Nr. 22') BRD:Mbs (Mus.Ms. 6854)
    [here for 222-02, contrabassoon]; US:DW (225)

Quintet in E♭
21-02
MS CS:Pk (1.c.4769)
Jerkowitz lists this work under *Parthia* in E♭ for 22-02.

Krasa, ?

Parthia in E♭
22-02
MS CS:Pnm (XLI.B.160)

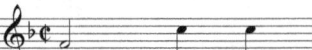

Parthia in B♭
22~02
MS CS:Pnm (XLI.B.159)

Kreith, Karl (d. 1809)

Partita in B♭, op. 57
22-02
EP (Vienna, Eder, Nr. 199)
H:KE (663/VIII)

Partita in E♭, op. 63
21-02
EP (Vienna, Eder, Nr. 201) H:KE (664/VIII), H:Bn (Z.43657)
Jerkowitz gives this works as 22-02.

Partita in B♭, op. 58
22-02
EP (Vienna, Eder, Nr. 202) H:Bn (Z.43656)

Partita in D, op. 59
21-02
EP (Vienna, Eder, Nr. 203) H:KE (665/VIII)
Jerkowitz gives this works as 22-02.

Partita in E♭, op. 60
21-02
EP (Vienna, Eder) [Advertized in the *Wiener Zeitung*, March 17, 1802]
Jerkowitz gives this work as 22-02.

Partitta in B♭
222-02
EP (Vienna, Eder) [Advertized in AMZ in 1807]

Armonia
Harmoniemusik
EP (Vienna, T. Mollo [Artaria], Nr. 130 [1801]; reprinted in Vienna by Torricella]

Marcia per i morti, op. 52
222-02, contrabassoon [Basso]
EP (Vienna, Eder)
Advertized in the *Wiener Zeitung*, October 17, 1801.

Andantino, 'Der Trompetenstoss,' op. 51
222-12
EP (Vienna, Eder)
Advertized in the *Wiener Zeitung*, October, 17, 1801.

VI *Märsche*
21-02, timpani
EP (Vienna, Eder, Nr. 126) H:Bn

Marsch ('Für das neu errichtete Wiener Scharfschützen Korps')
1222-32, Grosse Trommel, Teller sammt Czinellen, Kleine Trommel
EP (Vienna, Eder, Nr. 122 A:Wn

Deux marches in B♭, op. 95
222-02
EP (Vienna, Eder, Nr. 452) H:KE [missing both bassoon parts]

Regimentsmarsch
Harmoniemusik
EP (Vienna, Eder)
Advertized in the *Wiener Zeitung*, September 1, 1802.

(12) *Original aufzüge für die K.K. Regimenter zu Pferd*
-5
EP (Vienna, Eder)
Advertized in the Wiener Zeitung, September 1, 1802.

Musique harmonique
222-02
MS DDR:Bds [Hausbibl., 432]

Partita in E♭
222-02
MS BRD:DO (Mus.Ms.1109)
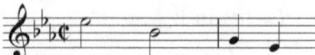

Partita in E♭
222-02
MS BRD:DO (Mus.Ms.1110)
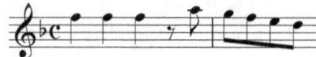

Partita in B♭
222-02
MS BRD:DO (Mus.Ms.1108)

The 1804 catalog of this library lists two more partitas, now lost.

Partitta in C
22-02
MS [cited by Jerkowitz]

Partita
222-02
MS I:Gi[1] (SS.B.1.10) US:DW (77)

(3) *Parth.*
21-02
MS (Advertized in Traeg's Catalog, Vienna, 1799)

(12) *Parthien*
222-02
MS (Advertized in Traeg's Catalog, Vienna, 1799)

Partita in E♭
21-02
MS CS:Pnm (XXII.D.183)

Partita in E♭
21-02
MS CS:Pnm (XXII.D.184)

Partita in D minor
222-02
MS CS:Pnm (XXII.D.185)

Partita
21-02
MS CS:Pnm (XI.E.158)

Kucharž, Johann Baptist (1751–1829)

(Various) *Partitas*
Harmoniemusik
MS [cited in MGG]

Laube, Antonin (1718–1784)

Te Deum
SATB, -23, timpani, organ
MS [cited in MGG]

Parthia in D
202-02
MS CS:Pnm (XLII.E.58)

Parthia in C
202-02
MS CS:Pnm (XLII.E.59)

Parthia in C
202-02
MS CS:Pnm (XXII.D.198)

Parthia in D
202-02
MS CS:Pnm (XXII.D.197)

Parthia in G
202-02
MS CS:Pnm (XXII.D.196)

Parthia in F
202-02
MS CS:Pnm (XXII.D.194)

Parthia in E♭
202-02
MS CS:Pnm (XXII.D.190)

Parthia in D
202-02
MS CS:Pnm (XXII.D.191)

Parthia in D
202-02
MS CS:Pnm (XXII.D.192)

Parthia in A
202-02
MS CS:Pnm (XXII.D.193)

Parthia in F
202-02
MS CS:Pnm (XXII.D.195)

Parthia in D
202-02
MS CS:Pnm (XLII.E.89)

Linek, Jiri

Fanfare (1785)
-4, timpani
MS CS:MH (Hu.1)

Lorentz, ?

(3) *Parthia* in C
202-02
MS CS:Pnm (XXII.D.215, 220, 225)

(3) *Parthia* in F
202-02
MS CS:Pnm (XXII.D.216, 221, 226)

(2) *Parthia* in B♭
202-02
MS CS:Pnm (XXII.D.217, 222)

(2) *Parthia* in G
202-02
MS CS:Pnm (XXII.D.218, 223)

(2) *Parthia* in D
202-02
MS CS:Pnm (XXII.D.219, 224)

Parthia in F
202-02
MS CS:Pnm (XXXII.B.149)

Lutter, ?

Parthia
22-02
MS A:Wn (Sm. 600)

Malzat, Ignaz (1757–1804)

Parthia (1799)
1021-12
MS (autograph score) A:Sca (Hs.242); US:DW (401; 7)

Parthia
21-02
MS A:KR [cited by Hellyer]

(3) *Parth.*
21-02
MS (Advertized in Traeg's Catalog, Vienna, 1799)

Divertimento per L'armonia
222-02, English horn
MS (Advertized in Traeg's Catalog, Vienna, 1799)

Matiegka, W.

(6) *Aufzüge*
-421, timpani
MS CS:Ksm

(6) *Aufzüge* ('Regenschoir in Wien')
Solo clarino with -222, timpani
MS CS:Ksm (C.306)

Maÿer, Franz

Parthia, 7 movements
202-02
MS CS:KRa (IV.B.88)

Parthia in Hoch C, 7 movements
202-02
MS CS:KRa (IV.B.89)

Parthia, 3 movements
202-02
MS CS:KRa (IV.B.87)

Parthia, 3 movements
Solo oboe, with 202-02
MS CS:KRa (IV.B.90)

Parthia, 5 movements
202-02
MS CS:KRa (IV.B.91)

Mederitsch, Johann (1752–1835)

Chor der Tempelherrn
SATB, 2021-002, organ
MS [cited in S]

Mering, ?

Parthia in C
1-2, 2 English horns
MS CS:Pnm (XLII.B.55)

Michl, Joseph (1745–ca. 1815)

Laudate Pveri (ca.1770)
SATB, 200-22, timpani, organ
MS BRD:Mbs (Mus.Ms.2357)

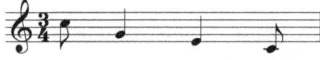

Polonaise concertante
1022-02
MS B:Lc (261-2.L-VI)

Milling, ?

Partie (1776)
202-02
MS CS:KRa (IV.B.198)

Parthia
201-02
MS CS:KRa (IV.B.205)

Misik, Frantisek

Parthia
202-02
MS CS:Pnm (XXII.D.278)

Partitta
201-02, 2 talia
MS CS:Pnm (XVII.B.300)

Partitta
202-02, 2 tallie
MS CS:Pnm (XXVII.E.53)

Partitta in B♭
1-02, 2 talie
MS CS:Pnm (XXII.D.262)

Partitta in B♭
1-02, 2 talie
MS CS:Pnm (XXII.D.263)

Partitta in B♭
1-02, 2 tallie
MS CS:Pnm (XXII.D.264)

Partitta in F
201-02, 2 talie
MS CS:Pnm (XXII.D.265)

Partitta
201-02, 2 tallie
MS CS:Pnm (XXII.D.266)

Partitta in C
201-02, 2 tallie
MS CS:Pnm (XXII.D.267)

Partitta
201-02, 2 tallie
MS CS:Pnm (XXII.D.268)

Partitta in F
201-02, 2 English horns
MS CS:Pnm (XXII.D.269)

Partia
201-12, 2 talie
MS CS:Pnm (XXII.D.273)
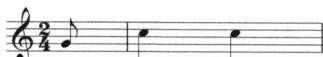

Partitta
202-02, 2 tallie
MS CS:Pnm (XXII.D.270)

Partia in F
201-02, 2 talie
MS CS:Pnm (XXII.D.271)

Partia in C
201-02, 2 talie
MS CS:Pnm (XXII.D.272)

Partitta in F
201-02, 2 talie
MS CS:Pnm (XXII.D.274)

Partitta
202-02
MS CS:Pnm (XXII.D.275)
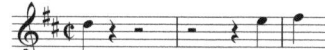

Parthia
201-02
MS CS:Pnm (XXII.D.276)

Partitta in D
202-02
MS CS:Pnm (XXII.D.277)

Monn, Giovanni

Musica Turchese
201-22, timpani, Tamburo grand, Piatti
MS (Advertized in Traeg's Catalog, Vienna, 1799)

Moravetz, ?

Parthia
222-02
MS (Advertized in Traeg's Catalog, Vienna, 1799)

Mozart, Wolfgang Amadeus (1756–1791)

Divertimento in B♭, K.159b (formerly K.186)
222-02, 2 English horns
MS (autograph, composed in March, 1773) BRD:B [perhaps lost], BRD:B (Mus.Ms.15313)
MP (Dover, in score)

Divertimento in E♭, K.159d (formerly K.166)
222-02, 2 English horns
MS (autograph, composed March 24, 1773) BRD:B [perhaps lost], BRD:B (Mus.Ms.15312) [perhaps lost]
MP (Dover, in score)

Divertimento in F, K.213, composed July, 1775
202-02
MS BRD:Mbs (Mus.Ms.1704), BRD:B (autograph) [perhaps lost], BRD:B (Mus.Ms.15317), BRD:B (Mus.Ms.15310, Nr. 1) [MS by Fuchs]; CS:Pu (M.1/28 Slg. A. Fuchs)
EP (Offenbach, André, Nr. 1504, as Nr. 1 under *Cinq divertissemens*) A:Wgm, A:Sm, A:Wn-h, A:Wst; BRD:MGmi, BRD:OF; (Reprinted in Paris, Mme Duhan, Nr. 1504), F:Pn
MP (Dover, in score)
MP (Breitkopf & Härtel, as *Divertimento Nr. 8*)

Divertimento in B♭, K.240, composed July, 1776
202-02
MS BRD:B (autograph) [perhaps lost], BRD:B (Mus.Ms.15318), BRD:B (Mus.Ms.15310, Nr. 2) [MS by Fuchs], BRD:Mbs (Mus.Ms.1705); CS:Pu (M.1 28/2, Slg. A. Fuchs)
EP (Offenbach, André, Nr. 1504, as Nr. 2 under *Cinq divertissemens*) A:Wgm, A:Sm, A:Wn-h, A:Wst; BRD:MGmi, BRD:OF; (Reprinted in Paris, Mme Duhan, Nr. 1504), F:Pn
MP (Dover, in score)
MP (Breitkopf & Härtel, as *Divertimento Nr. 9*)

Divertimento in E♭, K.240a (formerly K.252), composed January, 1776
202-02
MS (autograph) BRD:B [perhaps lost], BRD:B (Mus.Ms.15310, Nr. 3) [MS by Fuchs], BRD:Mbs (Mus.Ms.1706); CS:Pu (M.1 28/4, Slg. A. Fuchs)

EP (Offenbach, André, Nr. 1504, as Nr. 2 under *Cinq divertissemens*) A:Wgm, A:Sm, A:Wn-h, A:Wst; BRD:MGmi, BRD:OF; (Reprinted in Paris, Mme Duhan, Nr. 1504), F:Pn
MP (Dover, in score)
MP (Breitkopf & Härtel, as *Divertimento Nr. 12*)

Divertimento, K.240b
2000-5, timpani
MS (autograph) F:Bibl.de l'Institute de France; BRD:B (Mus. Ms.15315)
MP (Dover, in score)

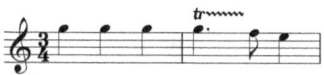

Divertimento in F, K.253, composed August, 1776
202-02
MS (autograph) BRD:B [perhaps lost], BRD:B (Mus.Ms.15321), BRD:B (Mus.Ms.15310, Nr. 4) [MS by Fuchs], BRD:Mbs (Mus.Ms.1707); CS:Pu (M.1 28/6, Slg. A. Fuchs)
EP (Offenbach, André, Nr. 1504, as Nr. 2 under *Cinq divertissemens*) A:Wgm, A:Sm, A:Wn-h, A:Wst; BRD:MGmi, BRD:OF; (Reprinted in Paris, Mme Duhan, Nr. 1504), F:Pn
MP (Dover, in score)
MP (Breitkopf & Härtel, as *Divertimento Nr. 13*)

Divertimento in B♭, K.270, composed January 1777
202-02
MS (autograph) BRD:B [perhaps lost], BRD:B (Mus.Ms.15310, Nr. 5) [MS by Fuchs], BRD:B (Mus.Ms.15322) [for 22-02], BRD:Mbs (Mus.Ms.1708); CS:Pu (M.1/28/5, Sgl. A.Fuchs)
EP (Offenbach, André, Nr. 1504, as Nr. 2 under *Cinq divertissemens*) A:Wgm, A:Sm, A:Wn-h, A:Wst; BRD:MGmi, BRD:OF; (Reprinted in Paris, Mme Duhan, Nr. 1504), F:Pn
MP (Dover, in score)
MP (Breitkopf & Härtel, as *Divertimento Nr. 14*)

Divertimento in E♭, K.271g (formerly K.289), composed in 1777
202-02
MS (autograph) GB [in private hands] BRD:B (Mus .Ms. 15325), BRD:B (Mus.Ms. 15310, Nr. 1) [MS by Fuchs], BRD:Mbs (Mus.Ms.1709); CS:Pu (M.1/28/1, Slg. A. Fuchs)
MP (Dover, in score)
MP (Breitkopf & Härtel, as *Divertimento Nr. 16*)

Gran Partita K.370a (formerly K.361), composed in February, 1784
222-04, 2 basset horns, string bass
MS (autograph) US:Wc; BRD:B (Mus.Ms. 15338, 15351/1 [two copies], 15424, and 15424/1, BRD:Rtt; A:Wgm (VIII 17361) [Köchel Nachlass MS score], US:DW (302); CS:Pu (M.I.29), US:DW (309); CS:Pnm (XX.F.55) [missing oboe 2]

EP (Vienna, Bureau d'Arts et d'Industrie, Nr. 62, as *Grande serenade*) A:Wgm (VIII 17361), US:DW (304); A:Wn-h; CS:Zz; CS:Bm (A.19.495, CS:K; BRD:Mbs; I:Fc, I:Mc; S:Skma

[*Gran Partita* for eight winds, K.Anh.182]
MS BRD:B (Mus.Ms.15351, Nr. 1) [MS by Jahn], BRD:B (Mus. Ms.15338) [Movements 5, 4, and 6], BRD:DO (Mus.Ms.1359) [Movements 1, 2, 3, and 7], BRD:Rtt (W.A.Mozart, 19) [for 222-02, string bass, with an additional trio for the second minuet], BRD:F (Mus.Hs.221) [Movements 1, 2, 3, and 7], BRD:F (Mus.Hs.222) '[Movements 5, 4, and 6]; CS:Pu (M.1/31) [*Parthia II*, MS by Traeg, ca. 1792, movements 5, 4, and 6], US:DW (42); CS:Pu (M.1/31) [*Parthia IV*, MS by Traeg, ca. 1792, movements 1, 2, 3, and 7], US:DW (44); CS:Pnm (XX.F.S5) [for 222-02, contrabassoon]; A:Ee [arranged by Heidenrieich]

EP (Leipzig, Breitkopf & Härtel, Nr. 61 [1801], as numbers 1 and 3 of *Trois Pièces d'harmonie* [Nr. 2 is K.C.17.01) A:Sm, A:Wgm [two copies], A:Wn-h; CS:Bm (A.19.490); DDR:Dmb, DDR:ZI [missing horns and bassoons]; I:Fc; US:DW (418)

EP (Bonn, Simrock, Nr. 994) [for 222-02, contrabassoon] A:Wn-h; B:Bc, BRD:HR; S:Skma

MP (Peters, ed., Einstein)

Gran Partita for six winds
MS CH:E (Th.91, 18/1, 3) [for 202-02]

Gran Partita for String Quintet
MS A:Wgm (IX 14156) [for string quintet] US:DW (306)
EP (*Gesamtausgabe*, as K.46)
EP (Peters, Nr. 3704 and 3705, as *Deux quintuors de violon, arrangés pour Ie piano à quatre mains,* arranged by R. Enke) A:Wgm, US:DW (307)

Gran Partita for Chorus
EP (Vienna, Artaria, Nr. 784, as 'Chor' [*Quis te comprehendat*], for SATB, solo violin, two violins, viola, 2 horns, organ, contrabass) A:GÖ, A:Ssp, A:Wgm, A:Wn; CH:Zz; CS:Bm, CS:Pk; F:Po; H:SFc; S:Skma, YU:Lu

Gran Partita for Piano-forte
EP (Vienna, Traeg, Nr. 44, as *Différentes petites pièces pour le fortepiano*) A:Wn, A:Wst

Gran Partita as Symphonie Concertante
EP (Offenbach, André, Nr. 1506, as *Sinfonie concertante* for 2 violins, flute, 2 oboes, 2 clarinets, 2 bassoons, 2 horns, alto and basse, arranged by F. Gleissner) A:Wn; BRD:BFb, BRD:Mbs, BRD:OF, BRD:Tes; DDR:ZI; GB:Lcm; H:P

Gran Partita as Quintet
EP (Hamburg, Böhme, as *Grand quintetto* for piano, oboe, violin, viola, violoncelle, arranged by C. F. G. Schwencke) B:Bc; CH:E; BRD:Bhm [incomplete]; US:DW (308)

Partita in E♭, K.375, composed in 1781
222-02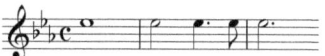
MS BRD:B (autograph), BRD:B (Mus.Ms.15310, Nr. 7), US:DW (301); BRD:KNmh (Formerly Catalog Nr. 184) [autograph for fragment of first movement, present location unknown]; CS:KRa (R.1.27/1), CS:Pnm (Slg.Kacina), CS:Pu (59-R-9)
EP (Offenbach, André, Nr. 1 [1792], reprinted ca. 1810 as Nr. 2882) A:Wgm, A:Wn-h, A:Wst; BRD:KNh, BRD:NEhz, BRD:OF; S:Skma; US:Wc

Partita, K.375, for six winds
22-02
MS BRD:B (autograph), US:DW (301); BRD:B (Mus.Ms.15310, Nr. 7) [MS by Fuchs] ; I:Gi(l) (C.2.3.7.Sc.35); CS:Pnm (XLI.B.155); PL:LA (2295)
EP (Offenbach, André, Nr. 530, as 'Sérénade, Oeuvre 27me') A:M; F:Pc; GB:Lbm; CH:E (Th. 86, 14) [MS copy]; DDR:LEm (Becker 111.12.12) [MS copy]
EP (Leipzig, Breitkopf & Härtel, Nr. 202, as 'Pièce d'harmonie') A:Sm, A:Wgm, A:Wn; CS:Bm; BRD:LÜh, BRD:Mbs; DDR:ZI; GB:Lbm

Partita, K.375 as String Quintet
EP (Vienna, Artaria, Nr. 821, as 'Grand Quintetto, Nr. 7,' for five strings)
A:Wst; CS:K; BRD:Mbs, BRD:HL (second edition); DDR:LEm, DDR:MEIr; DK:Kmk; GB:Lbm (second edition); H:Bn; US:BE, US:Wc
EP (reprinted by T. Mollo, in Vienna, Nr. 821) CS:Bu
EP (reprinted by T. Mollo, in Vienna, Nr. 1244) A:Wgm, A:Wn, A:Wst; CS:BRnm

Partita, K.375 as String Quintet
EP (Amsterdam, Steup, Nr. 22, as *Quintuor* for five strings) A:Wgm; BRD:Bhm, BRD:MZsch; NL:At, NL:DHgm

Partita K.375 as String Quintet
EP (Paris, Sieber, Nr. 82, as 'Quintetto concertant' for five strings)
CH:Gc
EP (Paris, Sieber, Nr. 82, reprinted as Nr. 1 of *Deux quintettis*) BRD:Mbs; F:Pn

Partita K.375 as a Piano Trio
EP (Mainz, Zulehner, Nr. 1, as 'Trio, op. 77,' for piano, violon and cello)
A:Wgm [piano only]; B:Br [piano only]; BRD:LB, BRD:Mbs; GB:Lbm

Partita, K.384a (formerly K.388), composed in 1784
222-02
MS BRD:B (autograph), US:DW (303); BRD:B (Mus.Ms.15339) [MS by Fuchs for 202-02, 2 English horns], BRD:F (Mus. Hs. 220); A:Wgm (VIII 8570b) [for 202-02, 2 English horns]; CS:Pu (M./1/302) [score], CS:Pu (59-R-10), CS:Bm (A.16.818)
EP (Leipzig, Kühnel, Nr. 900, as *Ottetto*) A:Wn-h; BRD:HR, BRD:HEhz; DDR:Dmb, DDR:RUI; S:Skma
EP (Offenbach, André, Nr. 2883, as *Sérénade*) A:Wgm, A:Wst; BRD:AB, BRD:F, BRD:OF; CS:Pnm (XL.B.124); US:Wc
EP (Offenbach, André, Nr. 2883, reprinted as *Zwei Serenaden*) A:Wgm, A:Wn-h

Partita, K.384a/388 for string Quintet
EP (Berlin, Hummel; reprinted in Amsterdam, *au grand magaziu de musique et aux adresses ordiuaires*, Nr. 818, as 'Grand quintetto' for five strings) NL:DHgm

[Fragment of an Andante], K.384B
222-02
MS (autograph) A:Wgm

[Fragment of a March], K.384b
222-02
MS (autograph) CH: Private collection of Dr. Georg Walter, Zurich

[Fragment of an Allegro], K.384c
222-02
MS A:Sm (Nr. 54) DDR:Bds (Mus.Ms.15589)

'Adagio,' K.484a (formerly 411)
20-, 3 basset horns
MS (autograph) BRD:B [may be lost]
EP (Offenbach, André) CS:Pnm (V.B.103)

[Fragment of an Allegro assai], K.484b, formerly K.Anh.95
20-, 3 basset horns
MS (autograph) A:Sm (Nr.53)

[Fragment of an Adagio], K.484c, formerly K.Anh.93
10- 3 basset horns
MS (autograph) A:Sm (Nr. 52)

[Fragment of an Allegro], K.484e
Six parts, one marked 'basset horn'
MS [lost]

Divertimento, K.C.17.01 (formerly K.Anh.226)
222-02

MS BRD:B (Mus.Ms.15351, Nr. 2) [MS Jahn], BRD:B (Mus. Ms.15351, Nr. 1) [MS Fuchs, for 242-02]; CS:Bm (A.12.793) [for 22-02], CS:KRa (R.1.27/III); I:Fc (Hr. 477.B.II) [for six winds]; A:KR (H.38.46) [under 'Puscbmann, Giu.'] CH:E (Th. 91, 18/Nr. 2) [for 22-02]

EP (Leipzig, Breitkopf & Härtel, Nr. 61 [1801]) A:Sm, A:Wgm, A:Wn-h; CS:Bm; DDR:Dmb, DDR:ZI [clarinets only]; I:Fc; US:DW (418)

MP (London, Musica Rara; Peters)

Divertimento, K.C.17.02 (formerly K.Anh.227)
222-02

MS BRD:B (Mus.Ms.15351, Nr. 4) [MS Jahn], BRD:B (Mus. Ms.15310, Nr. 6) [MS Fuchs, for 22-021; CH:E (Th. 91, 18/ Nr. 4) [for 22-02]; F:Pn (Vma.ms.262) [for 22-02]

EP (Leipzig, Breitkopf & Härtel, Nr. 65 [1801]) A:Wm, A:Wn-h; CS:Bm; DDR:Dmb; H:KE

MP (Peters; Schott)

Divertimento, K.C.17.03 (formerly K.Anh.228)
222-02

MS BRD:B (Mus.Ms.15351, Nr. 5) [MS Jahn], US:DW (38); BRD:DO (Mus. 1592) [under 'Pleyel', BRD:Bbm (11521 [score] and 11248 [parts]); CH:E (Th. 91, 18/Nr. 5) [for 22-02]

EP (Leipzig, Breitkopf & Härtel, Nr. 65 [1801])

Divertimento, K.C.17.04 (formerly K.Anh.224)
222-02

MS BRD:B (Mus.Ms.15310/1, Nr. 3) [MS Fuchs]; CS:Pu (*Parthia III* by Traeg, ca. 1792), US:DW (43)

Partita, K.C.17.05 (formerly K.Anh.225)
222-02

MS BRD:B (Mus.Ms.15310/1, Nr. 2) [MS Fuchs], BRD:Bbm (11620 and 11260) [two copies]; CS:Pu (MS by Traeg, ca. 1792), US:DW (41)

Variationen, K.C.17.06
22-02

MS CS:KRa (R.21.g)

'Adagio-Allegro,' K.C.17.07
222-02
MS CS:Pu (M.1/31) [Traeg copy, ca. 1792], US:DW (110); CS:Pnm [cited by Hellyer]

Parthia in F, K.C.17.08
22-02
MS CS:Bm (A.16.817)

Sextet, K.C.17.09
22-02
MS CS:Bm (A.14.282), CS:Pu [under 'Haydn,' *Ordo militaris Crucigerorum cum rebea stella in pedepontis Pragensia*]; US:WS [under 'Haydn'], US:BETm [under 'Jos. Morris']

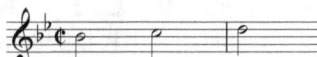

Parthia, K.C.17.10
22-02
MS A:Wn (Mus.Ns.622) [not here, according to Hellyer]; BRD:DO (Mus.1597, 1571, and 1574) [under 'Pleyel']; GB:Ob [under 'Haydn,' in Brooks *36 Select Pieces*], GB:Lbm (RM21.d.2)[under 'Pleyel']

(6) *Variations* in F
22-02, contrabassoon
MS CS:Pnm (XL11.F.770)

(5) *Parthia*
222-02
MS (Advertized in Traeg's Catalog, Vienna, 1799)

(32) 'Movements attributed to Mozart'
2202-02
MS BRD:HR (III.4.1/2.40.499)

AUSTRIA-BOHEMIA 223

Partita, 8 movements
222-02
MS CS:Bm (A.19.489)

(2) *Parthien* (unidentified)
Harmoniemusik
MS A:Ee

Pièces d'Harmonie (original is K.497)
222-02
MS (Lobkovic Archiv X.g.f.70); US:DW (414)

Alma dei, K.277
Arranged by Ferdinand Schubert
Voices with 1201-22, timpani
MS KNmh (formerly Catalog Nr. 307, current location unknown)

Pièce d'Harmonie, K.386c (formerly K. 407, original for horn and four strings)
22-02
EP (Breitkopf & Härtel [first *Gesamtausgabe*, 1805] A:Wgm, A:Wn; CH:Zz; CS:Bm; BRD:Mmb

Müller, Wenzel (1767–1835)

(Works for Harmoniemusik)
MS A:Gk [uncataloged]

Mülling, ?

Parthia in B♭
201-02
MS CS:Pnm (XXII.E.l)

Myslivecek, Josef (1737–1781)

Partita in E♭
222-02
MS BRD:DO (Mus.Ms.1597, Nr. 5); CH:OLu (II.322459)
MP (MAB, Vol. 55, Nr. 2)

Partita in E♭
222-02
MS BRD:DO (Mus.Ms.1597, Nr. 6); CH:OLu (II.322459)
MP (MAB, Vol. 55, Nr. 1)

Partita in B♭
222-02
MS BRD:DO (Mus.Ms.1597, Nr. 7); CH:OLu (II.322459)
MP (MAB, Vol. 55, Nr. 3)

Neubauer, Franz Christoph (ca. 1760–1795)

Partita in G
222-02
MS BRD:DO (Mus.Ms.1423)

Partita in B♭
222-02
MS BRD:DO (Mus.Ms.1424) [missing clarinet 2]

Partita in E♭
222-02
MS BRD:DO (Mus.Ms.1425)

Partita in B♭
222-02
MS BRD:DO (Mus.Ms.1426)

Partita in E♭
222-02
MS BRD:DO (Mus.Ms.1427)
The catalog of this library lists another Partita, now lost.

Parthia, Nr. 2
222-02
MS DDR:RUl (RH.Nr.14)

Parthia, Nr. 3
1122-02, Quart-bassoon
MS DDR:RUl (RH.Nr.13)

Harmonia, Nr. 1 ('Parthia 4 und 5'), 10 movements
222-02
MS DDR:RUl (RH.Nr.15)

Parthia, Nr. 5
1222-02, contrabassoon
MS DDR:RUl (RH.Nr.16)

Partita in F
222-02
MS BRD:Rtt (Neubauer 6)

Parthia
2042-02, contrabasse
MS NL:Ura/mZ (M.A.Zcm 4, Nr. 4)

Partita in G
222-02
MS I:Gi(1) (SS.G.1.14.[H.8]); US:DW (80)

(5) *Parthien*
21-02
MS A:KR [cited by Hellyer]

(6) *Parthien*
1122-02, string bass
MS BRD:DS [lost in WWII]

Neuhauser, ?

Marcia Turcica
1222-22, timpani
MS (Advertized in Traeg's Catalog, Vienna, 1799)

Neumann, Anton (1740–1776)

Partita
1-02, 2 English horns
MS CS: Bm, Pum, or KRa [cited by Grove, XIII, 125]

(6) *Partitas*
MS CS:KRa (IV.B.199) [cited by Schnall]

Nudera, Vojtech

Parthia in B♭
21-02
MS CS:Pum (X.C.91)

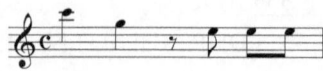

Ordonez, Carlo (1734–1786)

Octet
202-02, 2 English horns
MS CS:K [cited in Grove, XIII, 703; MGG lists CS:KRa]
The *Wiener Diarium*, 1779, mentions a performance of a Serenade, *Das Denkkmal des Friedens*, for two wind orchestras with a total of 31 players during a fireworks display in the Prater.

Partitta Turc
201-22, timpani, Tambour, Piatti
MS (Advertized in Traeg's Catalog, Vienna, 1799)

Panizza, Giovanni

Sextet
1021-02
EP (Vienna, Artaria) A:Wgm (VIII 5193)

Piccinni, Nicola (1728–1800)

Raffael Marcia, des löblich StändischenFrenkorps
222-02
MS (Advertized in Traeg's Catalog, Vienna, 1799)

Pichl, Wenzel (1741–1805)

Harmonie
21-02
MS DDR:SWl (Pichl, W.5)

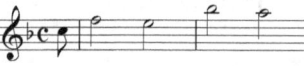

Parthia
221-02
MS DDR:SWl (Pichl, W.4)

Parthie
2 Chalemaux, Taille, Fagotto
MS A:GÖ (MS.2873)

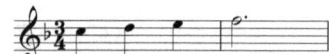

(6) Parties
21-02
MS DDR:HER (Mus.C.23=3)

AUSTRIA-BOHEMIA 227

(12) *Partitas*
21-02
MS BRD:DO (Mus.Ms.1551, Nr. 1-51)

Partitta in D
201-02
MS CS:Pnm (XII.E.59)

Partitta d'stromenti a fiato in D
201-02
MS CS:Pnm (XII.E.58)

Partitta in A
201-02
MS CS:Pnm (XII.E.57)

Jagd. Partitta in C
202-02
MS CS:Pnm (XII.E.56)

Partitta in F
202-02
MS CS:Pnm (XII.E.55)

Partitta in C
202-02
MS CS:Pnm (XII.E.54)

Partitta in F
22-02
MS CS:Pnm (XII.E.53)

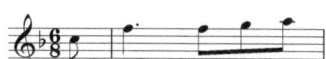

Partitta in F
201-02
MS CS:Pnm (XII.E.52)

Partitta in F
201-02
MS CS:Pnm (XII.E.51)

Partitta in F
22-02
MS CS:Pnm (XII.E.50)

Partitta in F
22-02
MS CS:Pnm (XII .E.49)

Pastorelle
22-02
MS CS:Pnm (XII.E.48)

Partitta in F
201-02
MS CS:Pnm (XII.E.47)

Partitta in C
201-02
MS CS:Pnm (XII.E.46)

Parthia in B♭
21-02
MS CS:Pnm (XXXIV.A.82)

Parthia in D
202-02
MS CS:Pnm (XLII.E.272)

Divertimento in B♭
22-02
MS CS:Pnm (XXXII.A.302)

Pleyel, Ignaz (1757–1831)

Parthia in E♭
222-02, contrabassoon
MS CS:Pnm (XX.F.57)

Parthia in E♭
22-02
MS CS:Pnm (XX.F.56)

Parthia, 4 movements
22-02
MS CS:KRa (IV.B.114)

Parthia, Nr. VI, 3 movements
22-02
MS CS:KRa (IV.B.113)

Partita, 5 movements
1222-02, contrabassoon
MS CS:Bm (A.35.206)

Partita in B♭
222-02
MS BRD:DO (Mus.Ms.1570)

Partita in E♭
222-02
MS BRD:DO (Mus.Ms.1571), BRD:DO (Mus.Ms.1597)

Partita in B♭
222-02
MS BRD:DO (Mus.Ms.1572)

Partita in B♭
222-02
MS BRD:DO (Mus.Ms.1573)

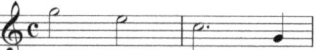

Partita in F
222-02
MS BRD:DO (Mus.Ms.1574)

Partita in E♭
222-02
MS BRD:DO (Mus.Ms.1575)

(6) *Pieces d'Harmonie*
222-02
MS BRD:DO (Mus.Ms.1592)

Partita in E♭
222-02, contrabassoon
MS BRD:HR (III.4.1/2.20.361) US:DW (430)

Serenade in F
2222-221, serpent, percussion
MS BRD:Rtt (Sammelband 14, Nr. 56–59)

Rondo
111-12, serpent
MS BRD: SW1 (MS. 4280/8)

Parthia in E♭
22-02
MS PL:LA (2296)

Sextet
111-02, piano
MS A:Wgm [cited by Eitner]

Sextet
Wind Instruments
MS BRD:Bds (Mus.Ms.Auto.J.Pleyel 2)

Serenade in F
2 oboes or flutes, 22-02, contrebasse ad lib
EP (Bonn, Simrock, Nr. 980) [Liv. 1] BRD:Bds

Serenade in F
2 oboes or flutes, 22-02, contrebasse ad ll.b
EP (Bonn, Simrock, Nr. 981) [Liv. 2] BRD:HR; I:Fc

Trois harmonies
22-02
EP (Vienna, Chemische Druckerei, Nr. 1557) [Nr. 1] A:Z

Trois harmonies
22-02
EP (Vienna, Chemische Druckerei, Nr. 1558) [Nr. 2] A:Z;
   CH:E; BRD:WERl

Trois harmonies
22-02
EP (Vienna, Chemische Druckerei , Nr. 1559) [Nr. 3] A:Z;
   CH:E, CS:Pum (XLI.B.113) [The first of these works also
   appears in MS under XLII.F.36, Nr. 15]; BRD:WERl

Hymn to Liberty
Solo voice, 22-02
EP (Paris, under *Hymnes de la Revolution Française*) F:Pn (H2.15,
   Nr. 9)

Pièces d'harmonie. tirés des oeuvres de Mr Pleyel
Arranged by Mr. Bisch
22-02
EP (Offenbach, André, Nr. 470) DDR:HER [clarinet 1 only];
   S:Skma [clarinet 1 only]

Suite de morceaux, tirés des oeuvres de Mr. J. Pleyel
Arranged by Mr. Bisch
EP (Paris, Imbault, Nr. 262) S:Uu [missing clarinet 2 and horn 2]

Posselt, Franz

Partitta
101-02, viola (?)
MS CS:Pnm (XLII.E.298)

Prachensky, Joaues (Jeau, Jounis)

Parthia Turika
222-02
MS A:Wgm (VIII 38671)

Parthia Turcika (1798)
3222-22, timpani
MS A:Wgm (VIII 39979) US:DW (344)

Parthia Turika (1800)
222-02, 2 piccolo, pagel, Zinellen
MS A:Wgm (VIII 39978)

Parthia Turika (1801)
222-02, 2 piccolo, pagel, Zinellen
MS A:Wgm (VIII 39985)

Puschman, Joseph

Partitta, 4 movements
Solo flute, 22-02
MS CS:KRa (IV.B.115)

Partitta, 4 movements
22-02
MS CS:KRa (IV.B.117)

Partitta, 5 movements
21-02
MS CS:Bm (A.19.697)

Partitta, 4 movements
22-02
MS CS:KRa (IV.B.116)

(3) Partien
22-02
MS (Advertized in Traeg's Catalog, Vienna, 1799)

Relluzi, ?

Parthia, 4 movements
201-02
MS CS:KRa (IV.B.118)

Righini, Vincenzo (1756–1812)

Armonia (1797)
222-02, string bass
MS BRD:B (RKZ-B-15); US:DW (429) [parts]
An extraordinarily long and difficult work!

Partita in E♭, 5 movements
222-02
MS BRD:Rtt (Righini 12)

Serenata en harmonie
22-02
EP (Augsburg, Gombert) A:Wgm (VIII 5200); BRD:B

(2) *Serenati*
22-02
MS (Advertized in Traeg's Catalog, Vienna, 1799)

Serenade in E♭
222-02
MS A:Wgm (VIII 39990) BRD:Rtt; US:WS

Sonata
22-:02
MS A:Wgm (VIII 21579)

Rindl, Hermann

Prüfungslied (July 23, 1799)
SATB, 2022-2, timpani
MS CS:Pnm (XLVI.F.107)

Prüfungslied (July 21, 1800)
SATB, 2222-2, timpani
MS CS:Pnm (XLVI.F.106)

Roller, ?

(6) *Partie* (1766)
202-02
MS CS:KRa (IV.B.198)

Partitta, Nr. 7, 3 movements
22-22
MS CS:KRa (IV.B.119)

Partitta, Nr. 3, 3 movements
22-22
MS CS:KRa: (IV.B.120)

Parthia, 3 movements
22-02
MS CS:KRa (IV.B.120)

Partia Campania, 4 movements
22-02
MS CS:KRa (IV.B.121)

Partia a 10 Voce, Nr. 6, 4 movements
222-02, 2 violas (?)
MS CS:KRa (IV.B.122)

Parthia, Nr. 4, 3 movements
22-22
MS CS:KRa (IV.B.123)

Parthia, 3 movements
22-22
MS CS:KRa (IV.B.124)

Röser, Johann Georg (1740–1797)

Tantum ergo
SATB, 222-02, organ
MS B:Bn (Mus.Ms.1187)

(Works for Harmoniemusik)
MS [cited in MGG]

Salieri, Antonio (1750–1825)

Armonia della Notte
222-02
MS A:Wn (Sm. 3756); US:DW (6)

Cassazione in C
202-02, 2 English horns
MS A:Wgm (VIII 8542)

Quintet
201-02
MS (autograph) F:Pn [cited by Hellyer]

Quintet, 4 movements
201-02
MS (autograph) CS:Pnm (W8, 97)
Carries the note, 'composto per il Senatore di Roma il Principe
    D. Abondro Rezzonico as Sig. Luigi Fuchs.'

Quintet
201-02
MS (autograph) A:Wn (Sm.3758)
Carries a note, 'Picciola Seranata d'Ant. Salieri Milano 1778.

(11) *Marches*
Nr. 1: 222-12, contrabassoon
Nr. 2: -2, 3 timpani
Nr. 3: -8, 4 timpani
Nr. 9: -2 [a fanfare]
MS A:Wn (Sm. 4472)

Marsch
222-22
MS (autograph) A:Wn (Sm.4471); US:DW (332)

Parade Marsch
222-22, singer
MS (autograph) A:Wn (Sm. 4471); US:DW (332)

(4) *Serenades*
Nrs. 1-3: 2202-02 (Andante Maestoso, Minuetto allegro; Larghetto, Allegro assai; Minuetto non troppo Allegro, Allegro assai)
Nr. 4: 222-02 (Cantabile ma non troppo Adagio, Andantino Spiritoso)
MS (autograph) A:Wn (Sm. 3759); US:DW (24-27)

Serenade in C, 2 movements
2202-02, string bass
MS BRD:Rtt (Salieri 1/I)

Serenade in F, 2 movements
2202-02, string bass
MS BRD:Rtt (Salieri 1/II)

Schmidbauer, ?

Partitta, 4 movements
201-02
MS CS:Bm (A.20.096)

Partitta, 4 movements
201-02
MS CS:Bm (A.20.097)

Schöringer, Carl

Parthia
201-02
MS CS:Bm (A.20.893)

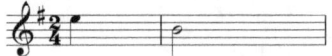

Schuester, ?

(4) *Partie* (1766)
202-02
MS CS:KRa (IV.B.198)

Parthia, 4 movements
202-02
MS CS:KRa (IV.B.133)

Parthia, 6 movements
201-02
MS CS:KRa (IV.B.130)

Parthia, 5 movements
201-02
MS CS:KRa (IV.B.129)

AUSTRIA-BOHEMIA 235

Parthia, 4 movements
201-02
MS CS:KRa (IV.B.131)

Parthia, 4 movements
201-02
MS CS:KRa (IV.B.132)

Schwarz, ?

(11) *Märsche für die ganze Türkische Musick oder neun-stimmige Harmonie*
1242-421, post-horn, contrabassoon, grand tambour, petit tambour
EP (Vienna, Chemische Druckerei, Hr. 2254) BRD:Mmb

Simon, ?

Partita
2001-02, 2 taille
MS CS:Pnm (XLII.D.103)

Partita
2001-02, 2 taille
MS CS:Pnm (XLII.D.102)

Partita
2001-02, 2 taille
MS CS:Pnm (XLII.D.100)

Partita
2001-02, 2 taille
MS CS:Pnm (XLII.C.228)

Spergen, ?

Parthia in C
202-02
MS (Advertized in Traeg's Catalog, Vienna, 1799)

Stadler, Anton (1753–1812)

(Partitas for six winds)
ME [lost, mentioned in the 1785 records of the 'Crowned Hope' Masonic Lodge in Vienna]

Stadler, Josef de Wolfersgrun

(12) *Tadeschi pour Musique d'Harmonie*
22-02
MS A:Wn (Sm. 11169)

Stadler, Maximilian (1748–1833)

Hoch du mein Vaterland
Four-part chorus and Harmoniemusik
MS A:Wgm [cited by Eitner]

Starzer, Josef (ca. 1726–1787)

Musica di Camera
30-32, timpani
MS A:GO (MS.2901)
Composed for the 'Regina di Moscovia.'

Musica da Camera (5 pieces)
2000-5, timpani
MS DDR:Bds [lost]

Les 3 Sultanes
201-02
MS CS:Pnm (XLII.C.179)

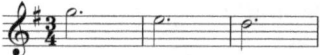

Le Matin et Soir
222-02
MS A:Wgm (VIII 39992); US:DW (67); CS:K (Nr.258.KII.) [for 202-02, 2 English horns]

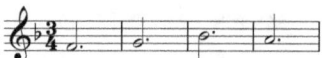

Concerto
21-02
MS
Performed in a 1780 concert of the Wiener Tonkünstler Societät, according to Hellyer.

Steffani, ?

(6) *Parthien*, op. 1
21-02
EP (Hummel) [cited by Hellyer]
MS BRD:B [cited by SJK]

Stepán, Josef (1726–1797)

Harmonie in E♭
21-02
MS DDR:SWl [cited by Eitner, MGG and Grove]

Harmonie in D
222-02
MS DDR:SWl [cited by Eitner, MGG and Grove]

Serenata
Harmoniemusik
MS CS:Pnm [cited by Grove, XVIII, 120; I could not find this work there]

(6) *Partitas*
222-02
EP (Breitkopf & Härtel Catalog of 1785–1787)

Strouhal, Padre Bernard

Parthia in C
201-02 [parts marked 'a.2.']
MS CS:Pnm (XXXII.B.19)

Parthia in A
201-02 [parts marked 'a.2.']
MS CS:Pnm (XXXII.B.26)

Parthia in A
201-02 [parts marked 'a.2.']
MS CS:Pnm (XXXII.B.25)

Parthia in B♭
201-02 [parts marked 'a.2.']
MS CS:Pnm (XXXII.B.20)

Parthia in B♭, 'La Quaglia'
202-02 [parts marked 'a.2.']
MS CS:Pnm (XXXII.B.21)

Parthia in B♭, 'La Parussola'
202-02 [parts marked 'a.2.']
Ms CS:Pnm (XXXII.B.22)

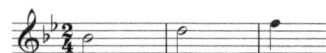

Parthia in B♭
201-02 [parts marked 'a.2.']
Ms CS:Pnm (XXXII.B.23)

Parthia in B♭
201-02 [oboes and bassoon marked 'a.2.']
MS CS:Pnm (XXXII.B.24)

Parthia in C
201-02 oboes and bassoon marked 'a.2.']
Ms CS:Pnm (XXXII.B.16)

Parthia in D
201-02 [oboes and bassoon marked 'a.2.']
MS CS:Pnm (XXXII.B.14)

Parthia in D
201-02 [parts marked 'a.2.']
Ms CS:Pnm (XXXII.B.15)

Parthia in F, 'La Zampagna'
202-02 [parts marked 'a.2.']
MS CS:Pnm (XXXII.B.11)

Parthia in F
201-02 [parts marked 'a.2.']
MS CS:Pnm (XXXII.B.12)

Parthia in G
201-02 [parts marked 'a.2.']
MS CS:Pnm (XXXII.B.9)

Parthia in G, 'Il Cuco'
'Flauto il cuco,' 202-02
MS CS:Pnm (XXXII.B.10)

Parthia in F
201-02
MS CS:Pnm (XXXII.B.13)

Parthia in C, 'Il Echo con Adieu'
202-02 [parts marked 'a.2.']
MS CS:Pnm (XXXII.B.17)

Parthia in C, 'Le Galline Cioche'
202-02 [parts marked 'a.2.']
MS CS:Pnm (XXXII.B.18)

Süssmayer, Franz (1766–1803)

March in C
222-12
MS (autograph); US:DW; GB:Lbm (Add.32181)

Marsch für Militarmusik
MS DDR:Bds [cited by Eitner]

Marcia, der Studenten in Wien
222-02
MS (Advertized in Traeg's Catalog, Vienna, 1799)

Thern, Carl

Wachtparade
222-02
MS A:Wgm (VIII 40640)

Umlauf, Ignaz (1746–1796)

'Musik von Bergleuten,' independent work within the opera,
   Die Bergknappen
202-02
MP (DTO, XVIII)

Vanerovsky, ?

Litaniae
SATB, 21-22, timpani
MS CS:Pnm (XVIII.A.107)

Parthie
22-02
MS CS:Pnm (XLII.F.36, Nr. 4)

Parthie
22-02
MS CS:Pnm (XLII.F.36, Nr. 6)

Requiem
SATB, 22-02
MS CS:Pnm (XVIII.A.162)

Vanhal, Johann Baptist (1739–1813)

Breves et faciles Hymn
SATB, 21-02
MS A:Wn (Sm. 2799)

Divertimento in C
201-02
MS CS:Pnm (XLII.E.246)

Divertimento in C
201-02
MS CS:Pnm (XLII.E.247)

Divertimento in C
201-02
MS CS:Pnm (XLII.E.248)

(4) *Marches*
22-02
MS BRD:F (Mus.Hs.1170)

March
22-02
MS BRD:F (Mus.Hs.1172)

Partita in E♭
21-02
MS BRD:Rtt (Sammelband 8, Nr. 35–37)

Parthie
22-02
MS CS:Pnm (XLII.F.36, Nr. 5)

Parthia in E♭
201-02
MS CS:Pnm (XLII.E.325) [according to SJK, there are two works under this number]

(6) *Quintets*
201-02
EP (Breitkopf & Härtel, Catalog of 1771, supplement 6)

Serenade
1202-02 [bassoon 1 and horn 2 are marked 'a.2.']
MS CS:Pnm (XXXII.A.390)

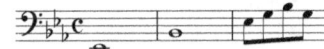

Vogel, Pater Cajetan (1750–1794)

Parthien für Blaser [cited in MGG and Grove, XX, 55]

Démophon Overture
42-02
MS F:Pn (Musique d'harmonie, paquet 30a [Pierre])
EP (Sieber, arranged by Fuchs) [for 42-12, serpent]; F:Pn (Musique d'harmonie, paquet 11 [Pierre])

Wallner, Vinzenz (1769–1799)

Raccolta di IV notturni, un canone con variazioni, una Marcia, un adagio per armonia solo (1796)
Chorus, 1-22
MS A:Wgm [according to MGG]

Weigart, Francesco

Partitta, 5 movements
201-02
MS CS:KRa (IV.B.156)

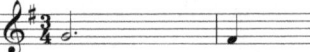

Partitta, 5 movements
201-02
MS CS:KRa (IV.B.157)

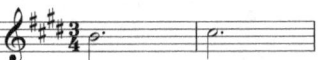

Partitta, 5 movements
201-02
MS CS:KRa (IV.B.158)

Partitta, 5 movements
201-02
MS CS:KRa (IV.B.152)

Partitta, 5 movements
201-02
MS CS:KRa (IV.B.159)

Partitta, 5 movements
201-02
MS CS:KRa (IV.B.153)

Partitta, 5 movements
201-02
MS CS:KRa (IV.B.155)

Partitta, 5 movements
201-02
MS CS:KRa (IV.B.154)

Weigl, Joseph (1740–1820)

Marsch
222-02
MS BRD:HR [according to SJK]

Parthie
Harmoniemusik
MS A:Ee

Partia in B♭
222-02
MS BRD:Bds (Mus.Ms.22940)

Wendt (Went, Vent), Johann (1745–ca. 1809)

Parthia in F
202-02, 2 English horns
MS CS:K (Nr.229.K.II.)

Parthia in C
202-02, 2 English horns
MS CS:K (Nr.230.K.II.)

Parthia in E♭
1-02, 2 English horns
MS CS:K (Nr.232.K.II.), CS:Pnm (XLII.E.317) [as *Parthia a la Cammara*, Nr. 1]

Parthia in E♭
1-02, 2 English horns
MS CS:K (Nr.234.K.II.), CS:Pnm (XLII.E.316)

Parthia ala Camera
1-02, 2 English horns
MS CS:K (Nr.235.K.II)

Parthia in E♭
1-02, 2 English horns
MS CS:K (Nr.236.K.II)

Parthia in F
202-02, 2 English horns
MS CS:K (Nr.241.K.II)

Parthia in B♭
202-02, 2 English horns
MS CS:K (Nr.242.K.II)

Parthia in C
202-02, 2 English horns
MS CS:K (Nr.245.K.II)

Parthia in B♭
202-02, 2 English horns
MS CS:K (Nr.246.K.II)

Parthia in F
202-02, 2 English horns
MS CS:K (Nr.247.K.II)

Parthia in F
202-02, 2 English horns
MS CS:K (Nr.248.K.II)

Parthia in C
202-02, 2 English horns
MS CS:K (Nr.249.K.II)

(18) *Pièces*
202-02, 2 English horns
MS CS:K (Nr.250.K.II)

Parthia in F
202-02, 2 English horns
MS CS:K (Nr.251.K.II)

Parthia in F
202-02, 2 English horns
MS CS:K (Nr.252.K.II)

Parthia in F
202-02, 2 English horns
MS CS:K (Nr.253.K.II)

AUSTRIA-BOHEMIA 243

Parthia in G
202-02, 2 English horns
MS CS:K (Nr.254.K.II)

(17) *Pièces*
202-02, 2 English horns
MS CS:K (Nr.255.K.II)

(12) *Pièces*
202-02, 2 English horns
MS CS:K (Nr.256.K.II)

Parthia in E♭
201-02
MS CS:Pnm (XLII.E.33)

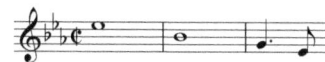

Parthia alla Camera
201-02
MS CS:Pnm (XLII.E.103)

Parthia in D
201-02
MS CS:Pnm (XLII.E.315)

Parthia in E♭
1-02, 2 English horns
MS CS:Pnm (XLII.E.31S)

Oktet
222-02
MS CS:Bm (A.35.133)

(6) *Parthien*
Harmoniemusik
MS A:Ee [cied by HI]

Parthia in E♭
222-02
MS A:Wgm (VIII 39988); US:DW (34)

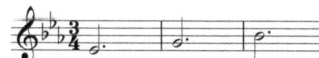

(3) *Parthia* in F; (3) *Parthia* in C; *Parthia* in E♭; (2) *Parthia* in B♭; and (2) *Parthia* in C minor
202-02, 2 English horns
MS A:Wgm (VIII 8539)

Parthia in E♭
222-02
MS DDR:Bds (Mus.Ms.23010/15)

Parthia in E♭
222-02
MS DDR:RUl (RH.W55)

Pièces en harmonie
42-0
EP (Paris, Nadermann, Nr. 133); F:Pn [two copies]

Pièces en harmonie
42-02
EP (Paris, Nadermann, Nr. 134); BRD:Tu; F:Pn

Pièces alla Camera
201-02; alternate version given as 1-02, 2 basset horns
MS (Advertized in Traeg's Catalog, Vienna, 1799)

(6) *Parth.*
22-02
MS (Advertized in Traeg's Catalog, Vienna, 1799)

(2) *Partitte*
222-02
MS (Advertized in Traeg's Catalog, Vienna, 1799)

Willy, Jean

Barthia Pastorelle, 3 movements
202-02
MS CS:KRa (IV.B.173a)

Barthia, 3 movements
202-02
MS CS:KRa (IV.B.173b)

Parthia a la Parade (1766), 4 movements
202-02
MS CS:KRa (IV.B.174)

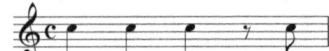

Barthia, 3 movements
202-02
MS CS:KRa (IV.B.172)

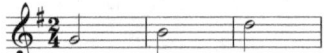

Barthia, 3 movements
202-02
MS CS:KRa (IV.B.171)

Divertimento, 3 movements
2-02 [the parts, however, are for viola, bassoon, and 2 horns]
MS CS:KRa (IV.B.175)

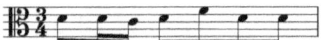

Barthia, 3 movements
202-02
MS CS:KRa (IV.B.170)

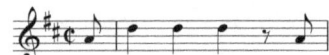

Winter, Peter von (1754–1825)

Partita in E♭
222-02
MS BRD:DO (Mus.Ms.1597, Nr. 2)

Parthia in E♭
22-02
MS CS:Pnm (XLI.B.129)

Parthia-Harmonie, Nr. 1
222-02, contrabasson
MS DDR:LEm (Becker III.11.67)

Parthia-Harmonie, Nr. 4
22-02
MS DDR:LEm (1 an Becker III.11.67)

Parthia in Dis
22-02
MS PL:LA (2298)

Partita
222-02
EP (Vienna, Bureau d'Arts et d'Industrie, Nr. 442; perhaps reprinted by Breitkopf & Härtel in Leipzig, as it was so advertised in AMZ in January, 1805). A:Wgm (VIII 5221), US:DW (49); CS:Bm (A.20 .257), CS:Pk; BRD:HEms; DDR:Bds, DDR:RUl; H:KE

Nun danket alle Gott
SATB, 2101-02
MS BRD:Mbs (Mus.Ms.2668)

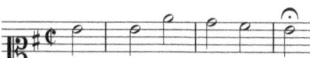

O könnt ich dich
SATB, 2022-02
MS BRD:Mbs (Mus.Ms.2667)

Veni Sancte Spiritus
SATB, 2202-02
MS BRD:Mbs (Mus.Ms.2663)

Wranitzky, Anton (1761–1820)

(4) *Jagdmärsche*
22-02
MS CS:Pnm (X.h.b.6)
MP (Bratislava, Supraphon)

(2) *Jagermärsche*, 'in the French Style'
222-12, contrabassoon
MS CS:Pnm (X.h.b.7)
MP (Bratislava, Supraphon)

(6) *Märsche*
222-12, contrabassoon
MS CS:Pnm (X.h.b.8)
MP (Bratislava, Supraphon)

Wranitzky, Paul (1756–1808)

Divertimento, 'La Chasse'
2222-02, timpani, grand tambour
EP (Offenbach, André, Nr. 2425) A:Wgm; DDR:Bds [cited by Eitner]

Parthia in F
222-02
MS BRD:DO (Ms.Mus.2062)

Zapf, Johann Hepomuk

Parthia in B♭
222-02
MS A:Wgm (VIII 8914)

Ziha, ?

Partitta in F
201-02
MS CS:Pnm (XLII.E.189)

Partitta in D
201-02
MS CS:Pnm (XLII.E.188)

Partitta in D
201-02
MS CS:Pnm (XLII.E.187)

Partitta in C
201-02
MS CS:Pnm (XLII.E.186)

Partitta in C
201-02
MS CS:Pnm (XLII.E.185) [cited by SJK]

Zimmermann, Anton (1741–1781)

Parthia
22-02
MS A:Wgm (VIII 8571)

Parthia
Seven winds
MS A:Wgm [cited by Grove XX, 687; and Eitner]

Parthia in C
21-002
MS CS:Bm [cited by Grove XX, 687]

Parthia in C
21-02
MS CS:Bm [cited by Grove XX, 687]

Parthia in E♭
1-02, 2 English horns
MS CS:Bm [cited by Grove XX, 687]

Parthia in G
201-02
MS CS:Bm [cited by Grove XX, 687]

Zoëdler, ?

Parthia in F
1-02, 2 English horns
MS CS:Pnm (XLII.C.156)

Belgium

Anonymous

Marche des Patriotes de Mons (1790)
Marche des Volontaires de Bruxelles (1790)
Marche des Patriotes de Louvain (1790)
Marche des Patriotes de Gand (1790)
EP (Brussels, in Edmond Vander Straeten, *La Musique aux Pays-Bas*, V, 65ff.) [in piano score]

Gehot, Joseph

(24) *Military Pieces*
21-02
EP (London, Napier) [Vol. 3] DDR:SWl (Mss. 2011) [missing clarinets]

Denmark

Croebelis, Domingo

Quartet, 3 movements
4000-
MS DK:Kk (Mu.7302.2240)

Schall, Claus

Carasel Musique (1791)
Nr. 1. *Harmonie*, for 222-02
Nr. 2. for -3, timpani
Nr. 3. for 2022-22, 2 piccolos, percussion
MS DK:Sa (R.237)
Carries the following note: 'Das Carasel ist so eingerichtet, wie es im Jahre 1791 zu Copenhagen im Koenigl.Reithause ist gehaltet worden. Die Musique zur Schild und Tanz-tour ist componiret vom Hem Schall, Concert-Meister bey der koenigl. daenischen Capelle. Die musique zu den Maerschen, Ring- und Kopftour ist gesetzt vom Hr. Skalk, Hoboisten bey der koenigl. daenischen Lieb-Garde zu Fus.'

England

Anonymous

(2) *Divertimenti*
202-02, 2 basset horns; some with flutes substituting for oboes, some with additional serpent.
MS GB:Lbm (R.M.21.d.2)

(19) *Pieces*
202-02, 2 basset horns; some with flutes substituting for oboes, some with additional serpent.
MS GB:Lbm (R.M.21.d.3)

(65) *Pieces*
202-02, 2 basset horns; some with flutes substituting for oboes, some with additional serpent.
MS GB:Lbm (R.M.c.32-40)

(24) *Military Pieces*
Oboes or clarinets, 2-02
EP (London, Longman & Broderip) DDR:SWl (C.h.20)

XXIV Favourite Marches
Unknown
EP (London, ca. 1770–1771) GB:Lbm (b.78.b)

A Second Collection of (24) Favourite Marches
For his Majesty's Foot & Horse Guards
220-02, bass [has thorough-bass figures]
EP (London, C. & S. Thompson, 1775) GB:Lbm (A.226); US:DW (743)

(8) *Military Concertos*
2222-02
EP (London, R. Bremner) DDR:SWl (C.h.37)

(4) *Concerti Militari*
201-22
EP (Breitkopf & Härtel, Catalog of 1771, Supplement 6)

(13) *Military Concertos*
121-02
EP (London, Bremner) GB:Lbm; US:DW (417)
EP (Reprinted, Breitkopf & Härtel, Catalog of 1775, Supplement 10)
DDR:DWl (344)

ENGLAND 251

A New Set of Military Pieces for a Full Band ('Composed in India ...
   His Majesties 33rd Regt.')
2041-12, Serbando [serpent]
EP (London, T. Key) DDR:SWl (C.h.30)

(6) Marches
1032-121, serpent, cymbal
EP (London, Wm. Napier) GB:Lbm, US:DW (750)

[R.I.] Marches
Band
EP (London, Bremner, ca. 1770) GB:Lbm (B.79/1)

The Arch Duke Charles of Austria March
Band
EP (London, Longman & Broderip, ca. 1797) GB:Lbm (G.133/72)

The Slow and Quick March of the Mid-Lothian Artillery
21-02
EP (city and publisher unknown) GB:En (Glen 347-37/1),
   US:DW (775)

Abingdon, 4th Earl of (1740–1799)

A Selection of Twelve Psalms and Hymns (inspired by the Revelation
   of St. John)
Chorus, with 222-02, timpani
EP (London) [cited by Grove]

Abington, William

Royal East India Slow March (1777)
Dedicated to Colonel Ingles, of same
22-12, serpent
EP (London, Culliford, Rolfe & Barrow) GB:Lbm (h.3213.k.[1]),
   US:DW (720)

Royal East India Quick March
22-12, serpent
EP (London, Culliford,Rolfe & Barrow)
MS GB:Lbm (g.133.[1]), US:DW (721)

Arundall, Robert (Gallway, Lord Viscount)

Two favorite minuets
21-02
EP (London, Smart)
MS GB:Lbm (b.55.b.[2])

Ashley, Josiah

Royal Dorsetshire March, 1797
2021-22
EP (London, Bland & Weller)
MS GB:Lbm (g.133.[2])
'Repeatedly Performed before their Majesties at Weymough and Composed expressly for that occasion.'

Attwood, Thomas (b. 1765)

The Third Regiment of Royal East India Vol. (Slow and fast marches)
Band
EP (London?)
MS GB:Lbm (g.443.3.[1])

Piece
31-02
MS GB:Lbm [cited in Grove]

Divertimento (in collaboration with Pleyel and Storace)
202-02, 2 basset horns, serpent
MS GB:Lbm [cited in Grove]

(2) *Royal Exchange Marches*
2022-12, serpent
EP (London, J. Dale)
MS GB:Lbm (g.133.[3]), US:DW (735)
'Dedicated to Lt. Col. Birch and the rest of the Officers of the Royal Exchange or 1st Regiment of Loyal London Volunteers.'

Baillie, R. Miss, of Mellerstone

A Favorite March (ca. 1795)
21-12
EP (Edinburgh, Stewart) GB:En (Glen 347-19), GB:Gu; US:NYp, US:DW (772)
'For the Edinburgh Volunteers, Performed at the Review of the Corps on Saturday, Nov. 22, 1794,'

Barthelémon, François-Hippolyte (1741–1808)

The Prince of Wirtemberg's March
Band
EP (London, Longman & Broderip)
MS GB:Lbm (g.133.[5]), GB:Ob

ENGLAND 253

Beckford, Mons. de

Marche
221-02
MS (score) GB:Cfm (32.F.25)

Beckford, William (1759–1844, a student of Mozart)

March
222-02
MS GB:Cfm (Mus.Ms.154)

Blackwell, J. G.

A grand divertimento; Military March
'Haub., 2 clarinets, 2 flutes, etc.'
MS GB:Lbm [cited by Eitner]

Bridgeman, Charles (organist at Hertford)

(8) *Marches for the Hertfordshire Vol.*
22-12, 2 fifes
EP (London, Broderip & Wilkinson)
MS GB:Lbm(g.137.[28])
'Dedicated to Marquiss of Salisbury.'

Brooks, James

(36) *Select pieces for a Military Band* (ca. 1797)
EP (London, Culliford GB:Lbm [cited by Eitner],
   GB:Ob (Mus.61.d.2[6])

Busby, Thomas (1755–1838)

The Field of Honor March (1798)
EP (London, Hookhan & Carpenter, as
British Military Journal Nr. 1 GB:Lbm (under, 'Ten Original
   Marches for the British Military Journal,' P.P.4050.ga),
   US:DW (727)

The Triumph March (1799)
2021-22, serpent
EP (London) GB:Lbm US:DW (729)

British Valour March (1798)
2022-22, serpent
EP (London, Hookham & Carpenter, as *British Military Journal
   Nr. 2*) GB:Lbm; US:DW (728)

Cantelo, ? (a collector)

(24) *American country dances as danced by the British during their winter quarters at Philadelphia, New York, & Charles Town ... with six minuetts*
Piano [with wind instrument incipits]
EP (London, Longman & Broderip GB:Lbm (b.53.[2]); US:DW (176)

Chapman, Richard

The Overture & favorite airs from the popular entertainments of the Bastile, and Naval Review, as performed at the Royal Circus
Instrumentation unknown
EP (London) GB:Lbm (H.129.[11]), GB:Ob, GB:Lge; US:NYp

Coleman, John

Twelve slow and twelve quick marches as now in use in the Garrison of Gibraltar
2022-12, 2 'pifes'
EP (London, Broderip, ca. 1796) GB:Lbm (G.376.[14]); ERIE:Dn [harpsichord only]

Dibdin, Charles

(2) *Marches*
22-22, bassi
MS (autograph) GB:Lbm (Add.30950); US:DW (768)

March in C
22-022
MS (autograph) GB:Lbm (Add.30952)

March in B♭
21-022
MS (autograph) GB:Lbm (Add.30953)

(8) *British War Songs*
One voice with military band [cited in Grove, V, 427]

Dixon, William (b. ca. 1760)

Four services in score ('with accomp. for flutes & oboes, and a bassoon or cello, designed for the use of country choirs')
EP (London, composer) GB:Lbm (G.502.[1]), GB:Cu

Eastland, Edwin

(12) *Marches*
Two flutes or clarinets, with 201-
EP (London, Longman & Broderip) GB:Lbm (b.60.[2]), GB:Ob

Ebdon, Thomas (1738–1811)

Favourite March (ca. 1795)
Unknown
EP (London?) GB:Lbm (g.133.[14])

Eley, C. F.

Coldstream Regt. Favorite Troop (1784)
22-12; optional version for 2000-, guitar
EP (London, Longman & Broderip) GB:Lbm (g.133.[15]);
  US:DW (702)

Favorite Short Troop
21-12
EP (London) GB:Lbm (h.726.3.[6])
'Performed by the Duke of York's new Band ... Coldstream
  Regiment of Guards.'

Hercules & Omphale March (1794)
222-12, serpent [ad lib.]
EP (London, G. Smart) GB:Lbm (g.133.[19]); US:DW (704)
'As performed in the Pantomime by Eley, Late Master of
  the Band'

March in Cymon, a short Troop (1785)
22-12, optional version for 2000-
EP (London, Longman & Broderip) GB:Lbm (g.133.[16]);
  US:DW (703)

(12) *Select Military Pieces*
22-12
EP (London, composer) GB:Lbm (b.80); US:DW (45)
Dedicated to the Duke of York; as performed by Coldstream
  Regiment of Guards.'

A Second Set of (8) Military Pieces
22-12, 2 oboes alternating with 'flute Terzio'
EP (London, Longman & Broderip) GB:Lbm; US:DW (746)

A Third Set of (8) Military Pieces
222-12
EP (London, Longman & Broderip) GB:Lbm; US:DW (747)

Essex, Timothy

Royal Westminster Volunteers March
1022-12, serpent, timpani
EP (London, Longman & Broderip) GB:Lbm (g.133.[21]),
  GB:Ob; US:DW (724)
'Dedicated to Col. Robertson and the rest of the officers and the
  Brother Soldiers of the Corps, as performed by the Duke of
  York's Band.'

Hampstead Loyal Assoc. March (1797)
1022-12, sepent, timpani
EP (London, Longman & Broderip) GB:Lbm (g.133.[20]),
  GB:Ob; US:DW (722), Bp
'Dedicated to the Captain Commandant and the rest of the officers and Gentlemen of the Corps, as performed by the Duke
  of York's Band.'

Angus Fencibles March & Quick Step
Band'
EP (London, composer, ca. 1795) GB:Lbm (g.133.[22])

Grand March (composed for 'Sir John De la Pole')
Original unknown
EP (London, Longman & Broderip) GB:Lbm (g.133.[24]) [piano
  only], US:DW (763)

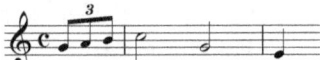

Fergus, John

Grand March (1794)
22-02
EP (Edinburgh, composer) GB:En (Glen 347-33), GB:Lbm
  (H.1568.b/4); US:DW (770)
'Dedicated to the Royal Glasgow Volunteers.'

Flack, Casper

(36) *Military Divertimenti* (1793)
21-02
EP (London, composer) GB:Ckc; DDR:Bds (Hausbibl., Nr. 395)
  [now lost]

Godfrey, W.

The Thrush (ca. 1785)
Solo piccolo, with 22-02, serpent
EP (London, H. Robinson GB:Lbm (h.111.[12]); US:DW (707)

Gov, Nathaniel (1763–1831)

Ramsay Maule of Panmure's (March)
21-12
EP (Edinburgh, Stewart) GB:En (Glen 347-28); US:DW (771)

Griesbach, Charles ('of their Majesties Band of Musicians')

(12) *Military Divertimentos*
42-12, serpent
EP (London, Smart) GB:Lbm (h.129.[3]); US:DW (748)
'For a full band, which occasionally may be performed by a small band of 22-02. Composed for the use of their majesties Band and dedicated to the Prince of Wales.'

(12) *Mil. Divertimentos, a third set*
EP (London, Broderip) [cited by Hellyer]

Hargrave, Henry

Five concertos
Bassoon and strings; optional version for bassoon ensemble
EP (London, composer) GB:Lbm (h.210.j.[1])

Hartmann, ?

A Set of Military Pieces
Band?
EP (London, Smart) [cited by Hellyer]

Herschel, Friedrich Wilhelm (1738–1822, the famous astronomer/oboist)

Deus concertos militaires in E♭
202-22 [cited by F]

Andantino
202-02, 2 basset horns
MS GB:Lbm [cited by Grove, VIII, 522, where it is suggested this may be an anonymous arrangement]

Hewitt, James (1770–1827, in the United States after 1792)

(4) *Ouick Marches*
22-12
EP (London, Preston) GB:Lbm (g.157.[29]), GB:Ob; US:DW (732)
'Composed for and dedicated to William Phillips Inge, Esq., Captain Commandant of the Litchfield Loyal Assoc.'

Hill, Frederic (organist at Loughborough)

Leicester Quick-Step (ca. 1780)
21-02, with a Trio for 2 fifes and drums
EP (London, composer) GB:Lbm (g.133.[26]); US:DW (725)
'Dedicated to Col … and the Yeomanry, Cavalry and Infantry of the County of Leicester.'

Three Military Pieces for full Band (dedicated to 'the honourable Mrs. Mynell') [cited in S]

Hill, John (1724–1797)

Hill's Church music … interspersed with proper symphonies
EP (London, Bland) [Vol. I, II] GB:Lbm (H.3117), GB:Lcm

Hindmarsch, J. (d. 1796)

Earl of Uxbridge March (1795)
2020-12, basso
EP (London, Longman & Broderip) GB:Lbm (g.133.[26★]); US:DW (712)
'As performed by the Staffordshire Band and dedicated to the Earl of Uxbridge.'

Hoberecht, J. L.

A Grand Military Piece (ca. 1799)
42-02, serpent
EP (London, Goulding, Phipps & D'Almainc) GB:Lbm (h.3213.k.[7]); US:DW (759)
A concert work.

Holden, Smollet

A Collection of Quick & Slow Marches …
Instrumentation unknown
EP (Dublin, Cooke) ERIE:Dn

Hummel, Karl

Marsch
'Mil-Musik'
EP (London, ca. 1770) GB:Lbm [cited by Eitner]

Kauntze, George

The Downfall of Paris Quick Step
2020-, piano
EP (London, composer, ca. 1800) GB:Lbm (H.1994.e./2)

King, Matthew Peter (1733–1823)

The Mary-Le-Bone March (1794)
EP (London, Booth) GB:Lbm (g.133.[32]); US:DW (710)

The Siege of Valenciennes (ca. 1794)
22-12
EP (London, Longman & Broderip) GB:Lbm (g.133.[31]);
  US:DW (711)
'Dedicated to the Duke of York.'

The British March (1798)
1222-12, 2 fifes, serpent, timpani, long drum, side drum
EP (London, Longman & Broderip) GB:Lbm (g.133.[33]);
  US:DW (726)

The Princess of Wales Minuett
Instrumentation unknown
EP (London, Longman & Broderip) [cited in MGG]

Kollmann, August Friedrich (ca. 1756–1829)

A New March
Instrumentation unknown
EP (London, Dale) GB:Lbm (g.133.[34]); US:DW (763)
  [piano version]

Legier, John Bernard

(13) *Sets of Military Pieces* [cited in S]

Longman & Broderip (Publishers)

The Clarinet instructor ... To which is added ... a guintetto for horns. clarinets and a bassoon.
EP (London, Longman & Broderip) GB:Lbm (b.161.i.);
  US:Wc, US:BE

Mackintosh, Robert (1745–1807)

Edinburgh Vol. March (ca. 1794)
21-12
EP (Edinburgh, composer) GB:En (Glen 347-12); US:DW (777)
'Dedicated to Sir James Stirling, Bart., Loard Provost & Lord
  Lieutenant of Edinburgh.'

Mahon, John (1749–1834)

Slow and Quick Marches ('for the Oxford Association Military
  Band') [ca. 1797, cited in Grove, XI, 533]

McLean, J. M. (of the 29th Regiment)

(2) *The Bagshot March(s)* (1795)
22-12, 2 fifes
EP (London, Longman & Broderip) GB:Lbm (g.133.[40], for a 'Quick' march) and (H.1568.b.[10] for the 'Slow' march); US:DW (713)
Dedicated to the Earl of Harrington.

Brighton Camp March
221-12, serpent
EP (London, Longman & Broderip) GB:Lbm (g.133.[42]); US:DW (714)
Dedicated to the Prince of Wales

Brighton Camp Quick March (1795)
21-12, serpent
EP (London, Longman & Broderip) GB:Lbm (g.133.[43]); US:DW (715)
Dedicated to the Prince of Wales

Miller, M.

(12) *Military Marches*
22-22, serpent
EP (London, Longman & Broderip) GB:Lbm (b.81); US:DW (744)
Composed for and dedicated to the Royal Family

Monckton, Robert (1726–1782)

Lady Galway's Minuet
Miss Buckley Mathew's Minuet
21-02
EP (London, Smart) GB:Lbm [cited by SJK]

Oliver, J .A.

Quarante divertissements militaires (for the '2. Schottischen Inf. Regiment')
22-02
EP (London, ca. 1792) [cited in F]

Oswald, James (1711–1768)

The Hessian & Prussian Night Pieces & Marches (ca. 1762)
[cited in MGG]

(55) *Marches for the Militia* (ca. 1765)
GB:Lbm (g.79.b.[5])

Percival, John ('Master of the Band')

Bristol Volunteer Troop (1799)
21-12, serpent
EP (London, Broderip & Wilkinson) GB:Lbm (g.133.[47]);
US:DW (730)

Powell, Thomas (b. 1776)

Grand March and Rondo ('as performed by the military band at
Vauxhall Gardens') [cited in S]

Raimondi, Ignazio (1737–1813, in London after 1790)

Six grand marches
Military band
EP (London, composer) GB:Cu, GB:Gu, GB:Lbm, GB:Ob;
US:NYp, US:R

Six grand Marches
Military band
EP (London, Monzani) GB:Lbm

Rathgen, A.

(7) *Sonate*, op. 1
21-02
EP (Breitkopf & Härtel Catalog of 1775, Supplement 10)

(6) *Military Divertimentos*
21-02
EP (Botz, ca. 1780) GB:Ckc

Rawlings, J. A.

A Grand Military March (ca. 1780)
222-12, timpani
EP (London, composer) GB:Lbm (g.133.[48]); US:DW (701)
'As performed by the royal Highness Regiment.'

Reid, John, General (1721–1807)

(12) *Marches*
21-02
EP (London, Preston, 1778) GB:Lbm (b.79.1.)

A Second Set of Six Solos
Oboe or flute, with 21-02
EP (London, Bremner, 1778) [cited by MGG]

Reinagle, Joseph (1762–1825)

(2) *Oxford University Volunteers Marchs* (1776)
21-02, with alternate version for 2000-
EP (London, Goulding) GB:Lbm (g.272.u.[20]); US:DW (706)
'Dedicated to the Colonel, officers and other Gentlemen of the
   Oxford University Volunteers.'

Rockeman & Alters

Six Sonatas ('as performed in the Militia')
21-02
EP (London, Thompson, 1773) GB:Lbm (b.206), GB:Ckc

Rogers, ?

(24) *Divertissements*
21-02
EP (Böhme; reprinted Pleyel) [cited by Hellyer]

Rose, J. H.

The 1st battn Breadalbane fencibles new march
22-12
EP (Edinburgh, Johnson) GB:DU

Tay side fencibles slow and quick March
21-12
EP (Edinburgh, composer) GB:DU, GB:Gu, GB:Lbm (g.133.
   [50]) [for piano], GB:Ob

Russell, W.

Guildford Volunteers March
Band
EP (London, Longman & Broderip, ca. 1795) GB:Lbm (g.133.[51])

Salner, G. P.

St. Helena Slow March
2042-12, piccolo, timpani, tamborine, side drum, serpent
EP (London, Riley) GB:Lbm; US:DW (733)
'Dedicated to Capt. Den. Taaffe, Island St. Helena.'

Schetky, Johann Georg (1740–1820)

(12) *Slow Airs* and (12) *Reels and Strathspeys*
2021-12
EP (London, ca. 1800) GB:En

(Collection of) *Marches, Quicksteps, Slow and Lively Scotch Airs*
Piccolo, 2 fifes, and 2 bugles
EP (Edinburgh, ca. 1806 GB:En [cited in Grove, XVI, 637]

Schroeder, H. B.

Earl of Radnor Slow March
22-12, serpent, timpani
EP (London, Longman & Broderip) GB:Lbm (g.133.[56]),
   US:DW (716); GB:Gu, GB:Ob

Earl of Radnor Quick March
Military band
EP (London, Longman & Broderip, GB:Lbm (g.133.[54])

Duke of York Quick March (1795)
22-12, serpent, timpani
EP (London, Longman & Broderip) GB:Lbm (g.133.[55]),
   US:DW (718); GB:Ob

West London Slow March (1795)
22-12, serpent, timpani
EP (London, Culliford, Rolfe & Barrow) GB:Lbm (g.133.[53]),
   US:DW (719)
'Dedicated to the Colonel and officers of the West London Militia.'

West London Quick March (1796)
22-12
EP (London, Culliford, Rolfe & Barrow) GB:Lbm (g.133.[58])

Berkshire Militia Troop March (1795)
22-12
EP (London, Longman & Broderip) GB:Lbm (g.133.[56]),
   US:DW (717); GB:Ob

A favorite Quick March
Military band
EP (city unknown, probably London) GB:Lbm [cited in RISM, perhaps the same as g.133.[55]

Skillern (Publisher)

Compleat instructions for the fife … with a collection of the most celebrated marches, airs, &c. perform'd in the Guards and other regiments
EP (London, T. Skillern) US:Wc [contains works by Wiedeman and anonymous]

Smart, Timothy

(24) *Select military pieces*
22-02
EP (London, Fentum) DDR:SWl (Mss. 5872/4) [here clarinet 2 and horn 2 only]

Spencer, Capt. John

Oxfordshire Militia Troop (1793)
2032-12, serpent
EP (London, Smart) GB:Lbm (h.1568.b.[21]), US:DW (709)

Stevens, Richard John Samuel (1757–1837)

(2) *Marches*
Military band
MS GB:Cfm [cited in MGG]

Storace, Stephen (1763–1796)

'Hope a distant Joy disclosing,' from the opera, *La Cameriera Astuta* (Act I, finale)
SSTB 2222-02 US:DW (159)

Tebay, J.

The Bath volunteer's March (ca. 1785)
22-02
EP (London, T. & W. M. Cahusac) GB:Lbm (h.1568.b.[22]), US:DW (105)

Thompson (Publisher)

The Compleat tutor for the fife ... with a collection of celebrated marchs and airs
EP (London, Thompson, ca. 1770) GB:En, GB:Gm [incomplete]
Contains works by Randel, Wiedeman, and Anonymous.

Troop, A.

(3) *Scotch Quick-Steps des Regiments, 'Duke of Albany Highlanders'*
Military band
MS DDR:Bds (Hausbibl., Nr. 385)

Webb, William (Isle of Wight)

The Loyal Isle of Wight Volunteers Slow March
42-12
EP (London, Preston) GB:En (Glen 347-16), US:DW (773)
'Dedicated to Capt. Joseph Fitzpatrick.'

ENGLAND 265

Weideman, Charles Frederich (d. 1782)

Old Buffs March (ca. 1760)
201-02
EP (London) GB:Lbm (H.1601.a.[112])

Weigh, Jolin

(2) *Marches*
22-02
EP (Newcastle, composer) GB:Lbm

Wesley, Samuel

March in D (1777)
202-02, serpent
MS (autograph) GB:Lbm (Add.35007, ff.237r–238r)

Wivill, Zarubbabel

Berkshire Militia March (1793)
2222-02
EP (London, Longman & Broderip) GB:Lbm (g.133.[64]),
    US:DW (708); GB:Gu, GB:Ob; US:Wc
'Composed at the desire of the Earl of Radnor.'

Worgan, James (the younger)

Essex March (1799)
1222-22, timpani
EP (London, Longman & Broderip) GB:Lbm (g.133.[67]),
    US:DW (731); GB:Ob

Hark! the loud drum ('A song for the new militia. To a march for
    trumpets, drums, hautboys and bassoons')
EP (London, Johnson) GB:Lbm

French March
Military band
EP (London, Longman & Broderip, ca. 1800) GB:Lbm (G.139/54)

Wright, Thomas (1763–1829)

Newcastle Slow & Quick Marches
21-02
EP (city unknown) GB:En (Glen 347-37/2), US:DW (774)

West York March
Military band
EP (London, Goulding GB:Lbm (H.1568.b.[24])

East York Militia March
Military band
EP (London, Goulding) GB:Lbm (H.1568.b.[23])

(2) *Marches for the Volunteer Corps of Newcastle upon Tyne*
21-02
EP (London, Goulding, ca. 1795) GB:En (Glen E.L.86.1-22)

ADDENDUM:

Anonymous (Mozart)

The Duke of York's New March
222-02
EP (London, Preston) GB:En (Glen 347-15); US:DW (776)
'As performed by his Royal Highness Band.'

Freeman, Thomas Augustine

The Earl of Carlisle's March
22-02
EP (London, Longman & Broderip) GB:Lbm (g.271.t.[11])

France

Anonymous

Les aires ordinaires de la musique que l'on joue dans la messe des Corsses (1772)
22-02, tambour
MS BRD:DS (Mus.1186 [score] and Mus.1187 [parts]); US:DW (198)
Contains nine titles, such as *Les Marches de la galenterre*.

Journal de Musique Militaire
2020-2, fifres, tambours
EP (Strassbourg, Reinh.) DDR:SWl [cited in Eitner]

6eme Marche (celle des Mousquetaires)
22-02
EP (Paris, Castagnery) DDR:SWl

1re (-5me. 7me. 8me) Marche
21-02
DDR:SWl [Nr. 1 is missing clarinet 1 and bassoon; Nr. 3 is missing clarinet 1; Nr. 4 is missing horn 2]

(8) Marche celle des Gardes françoises
21-02
EP (Paris, Castagnery) DDR:SWl (C.h.31)

(2) Marche religieuse
42-02
MS F:Pn (Musique d'harmonie, paquet 30a)

Marche
1232-121, serpent, cymbales, grosse caisse, timpani
MS F:Pn (Musique d'harmonie, paquet 50)

Marche
1232-121, serpent, cymbales, grosse caisse, timpani
MS F:Pn (Musique d'harmonie, paquet 50)

Marche
1232-121, serpent, cymbales, grosse caisse, timpani
MS F:Pn (Musique d'harmonie, paquet 50)

Marche
1232-, serpent, cymbals, grosse caisse, timpani
MS F:Pn (Musique d'harmonie, paquet 50)

d' Adrien l'Aîné

Hymne à la Victoire, sur l'évacuation du territoire
Bass, chorus, with 2222-221, 2 piccolos, serpent, timpani, 'tambour turc,' and string bass

Baronville, ?

Nouvelles batteries de l'ordonnance des dragons de France
Military band
EP (Paris?, Mme Berault) F:Pa

La nouvelle ordonnance des dragons
Military band
EP (Paris, Bayard, 1756) F:Pa

Baudron, Antoine (1743–1834)

Cinquieme Suite du Concert Militaire
22-02 or 202-02
EP (composer, 1769) [cited in MGG]

Bédard, Jean-Baptiste (1765–ca. 1815)

Potpourri Connus
22-02
EP (Paris, Decombe) US:Wc

Beinet, ?

Suites. Airs und Pot-pourri
Pot Pourris [Liv. 1, 2]
Suites [Liv. 1, 2, 3, 4]
22-02
EP (Parjs' Imbault, ca. 1796) [cited in G2]

Berton, Henri Montan (1767–1844)

Marche militaire
2022-12, serpent
EP (Paris, Magasin de musique, Issue 12, Nr. 3) F:Pn (H2.12.3), US:DW (638)

Hymne pour la fete de l'Agriculture
Solo voice, chorus, 1022-223, serpent, timpani, triangle, and 'tambour turc.'
EP (Paris, *Hymnes de la Revolution Francaise*) F:Pn (H2.35, Nr. 11 and D.16082); US:DW (549)

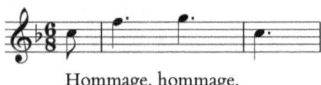

Hommage, hommage,

FRANCE 269

Bisch, ?

Recueil de marches et pas redoublés
22-02, piccolo, serpent, bass drum, Cimbales
MS DDR:Bds (Hausbibl., Nr. 399)

Blasius, Matthiew Frédéric (1758–1829)

Suite d'Harmonie, 7 movements
22-02
EP (Paris, Imbault) F:Pn (Vm.7.6962, Vm.7.10530,
    and Vm.7.10532)

Ouverture
2222-223, serpent
EP (Paris, Magasin de musique, Issue 8, Nr. 1) F:Pn (H2.8,1 and
    H2.125,a-n); US:DW (620)

(4 Volumes) *Harmonie Militair*
EP (Paris, Gaveaux) F:Pn (Vm.27.214/1-4)

Harmonie
Six-part *Harmoniemusik*
EP (Paris, Pleyel) [cited in MGG]

Journal d'Harmonie
EP (Paris, Leduc) [Vol. 10, cited in MGG]

Messe in A
Tenor, Baritone, and Bass soli, with *Harmoniemusik*
MS I:Mc

Bordoux, Jean Ernest

Nouveau Marche
222-12
MS DDR:Bds (Mus.Ms.2237)

Brunett, Gaéton (?Gaetano Brunetti, ca. 1740–1809)

Deux livres d'harmonies pour les danses de chevaux des fetes publiques
EP (Paris?) [cited in F]

Cambini, Giovanni (1746–1825)

Marche Militaire
MS (score) BRD:DS [cited by Eitner]

Le pas de charge républicain
SSATB, 21-22, serpent, tambour
EP (Paris, Boyer) F:Pn (Vm.7.7081 and Vm.7.16761)

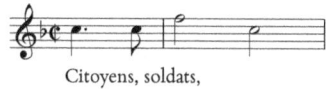

Citoyens, soldats,

Hymn to the Supreme Being
Solo voice, 21-021 or 201-021
EP (Paris, Boyer) F:Pn (Vm.7.7064)

Ordre éternal,

Hymn to the Supreme Being
Solo voice, 222-021, serpent, organ
EP (Paris, Imbault) F:Pn (Vm.7.7056)

Ame de L'univers;

Hymn to Victory
Solo voice, 21-022 or 201-022
EP (Paris, Boyer) F:Pn (Vm.7.7065)

Peuple triomphateur

Hymn to Victory
Solo voice, 2 oboes or clarinets, bassoons, trombones, serpentoni
EP (Paris, Imbault) F:Pn (Vm.7.7061)

O! de la liberté

Ode on the Two Young Heros, Barra and Viala
Solo voice, 21-022, basse
EP (Paris, Imbault) F:Pn (Vm.7.7063)

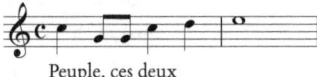
Peuple, ces deux

Hymn to Virtue
Solo voice, 222-022, organ
EP (Paris, Imbault) F:Pn (Vm.7.7057)

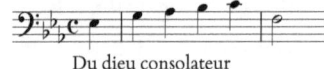
Du dieu consolateur

Hymn to Liberty
Solo voice, 222-022, serpents, organ
EP (Paris, Imbault) F:Pn (Vm.7.7058)

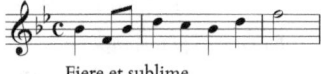
Fiere et sublime

Hymn to Equality
Solo voice, 221-022, serpents, organ
EP (Paris, Imbault) F:Pn (Vm.7.7059)

Don précieux

Les rois, les grands, les prêtres
Solo voice, 22-02, serpents, basse
EP (Paris, Imbault, 1793) F:Pn (Vm.7.7062 and Vm.7.16755)

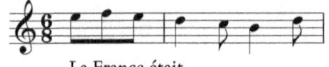
La France était

Ode on the Victories
Solo voice, 22-022, serpentoni, basso
EP (Paris, Imbault) F:Pn (Vm.7.7060)

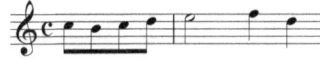
L'airain belliqueux

Catel, Charles Simon (1773–1830)

Ouverture
2022-221, serpent, timpani
EP (Paris, Magasin de musique, Issue 1, Nr. 1); F:Pn (Vm.7.7019); US:DW (616)
MP (Mercury Music, as *Overture in C*)

FRANCE 271

Ouverture
2022-223, 2 piccolos, serpent, timpani
EP (Paris, Magasin de musique, Issue 10, Nr. 1); F:Pn (B2.10,1); US:DW (621)
MP (Mercury Music, as *Overture in F*)

Symphonie
22-223, 2 piccolos, serpent, timpani, bass drum
EP (Paris, Magasin de musique, Issue 14); F:Pn (H2.127 a-q and H2.127 aa-pp)

Symphonie militaire
22-121, 2 piccolos, serpent, cymbals, bass drum
EP (Paris, Magasin de musique, Issue 5, Nr. 1); F:Pn (H2.5,1 and Vm.7.7043); US:DW (614)
MS F:Pn (H2.128 a-l)
MP (Atlantic Music Supply)

Marche militaire
22-22, 2 piccolos, serpent, cymbals, bass drum
MS F:Pn (Cons.743)
EP (Paris, Magasin de musique, Issue 1, Nr. 3;); F:Pn (H2.1,3); US:DW (625b)

Pas de manoeuvre
22-12, 2 piccolos, serpent
EP (Paris, Magasin de musique, Issue 1, Hr. 4); F:Pn (Vm.7.7022 and H2.1,4); US:DW (639)

Marche militaire
22-12, 2 piccolos, serpent
EP (Paris, Magasin de musique, Issue 3, Nr. 3); F:Pn (vm.7.7033 and H2.3,3); US:DW (628)

Marche militaire
22-12, 2 piccolos, serpent
EP (Paris, Magasin de Musique, Issue 4, Nr. 4); F:Pn (H2.4,4 and Vm.7.7040); US:DW (629)

Marche militaire
22-12, 2 piccolos, serpent
EP (Paris, Magasin de Musique, Issue 5, Nr. 3); F:Pn (H2.5,3 and Vm.7.7045); US:DW (630)

Marche militaire
22-12, 2 piccolos, serpent
EP (Paris, Magasin de Musique, Issue 8, Nr. 3); F:Pn (H2.8,3); US:DW (631)

Ode patriotique
Three-part male chorus, 2022-223, tuba curva, serpent, timpani
MS F:Pn (Musique nationale, paquet 46) [missing trombone 3]

La Seine qui vit

Ode sur le vaisseau, 'le Vengeur'
Bass voice, 22-02
EP (Paris, Collection Époques); F:Pn (H2.15, Nr. 26)

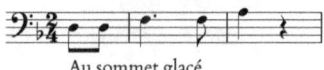
Au sommet glacé

Hymne à l'Être supreme
Solo voice, 22-02
EP (Paris, Collection Epoques); F:Pn (H2.15, Nr. 23)

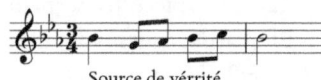
Source de vérrité

Hymne à la victoire, sur la bataille de Fleurus
Solo voice, 2022-221, serpent
EP (Paris, Magasin de Musique, Issue 5, Nr. 5) F:Pn (H2.5,5, Vm.7.7047, and Vm.16773)
EP (Paris, Collection Epoques) [for solo voice, 22-02]; F:Pn (H2.15, Nr. 27)

C'est en vain

The Battle of Fleurus
Three-part male chorus, 22-223, 2 piccolos, serpent, timpani
EP (Paris, Magasin de Musique, Issue 7, Nr. 2 and Issue 8, Nr. 2); F:Pn (H2.7,2 and H2.8,2); US:DW (558)

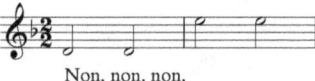
Non, non, non,

Hymn to Liberty
Solo voice, 22-02
EP (Paris, Collection Epoques); F:Pn (H2.15, Nr. 7)

De chêne et de

Ode on the Situation of the Republic during the 'tyrannie d'cemvirale'
Solo voice, 22-02
EP (Paris, Collection; Époques) F:Pn (H2.15, Nr. 29)

O vaisseau de l'Etat

Hymn for August 10
Four-part chorus, 22-223, 2 piccolos , serpent, tuba curva, buccin, timpani, bass drum, tambour turc, cymbals
EP (Paris, Magasin de Musique, Issue 16); F:Pn (H2.35, Nr. 9), US:DW (510)
EP (Paris, Collection Epoques) [for chorus, 22-02]; F:Pn (H2.15, Nr. 9)

Jeunes guerriers,

Hymn for the Republican banquet, for the Festival of Victory
Solo voice, four-part chorus, 2 flutes or 2 oboes, with 22-223, serpent, timpani
MS F:Pn (Musique National H2.95 a-g)
EP (Paris, Collection Époques) [for Solo voice, 22-02]; F:Pn (H2.15, Nr. 36)

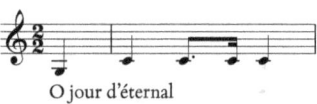
O jour d'éternal

Hymn to the Sovereignty of the People
Solo voice, 22-02
EP (Paris, Collection Époques); F:Pn (H2.15, Livre second, Nr. 3)

Salut époque

FRANCE 273

Cherubini, Luigi (1760–1842)

Hymn to the Pantheon
Three-part male chorus, 22-223, 2 piccolos, serpent, timpani, gong, bass drum
EP (Paris, Magasin de Musique, Issue 12, Nr. 2); F:Pn (H2.12,2); US:DW (578)

Restes sacrés

Hymn to Fraternity
Four-part chorus, 22-24, 2 piccolos, serpent, bass drum, cymbals, tambour turc
MS (score) DDR:Bds (Bottée de Toulmon, Nr. 116/2)
EP (Collection Époques) [for solo voice, 22-02]; F:Pn (H2.15, Nr. 31)

Nous avons chanté

Hymn for August 10
Four-part chorus, 22-223, 2 piccolos, serpent, buccin, tuba curva, cymbals, bass drum
MS (autograph) F:Pn (Cons.10948)
MS (score) DDR:Bds (Bottée de Toulmon, Nr. 116/3)
MS (parts) F:Pn (Musique nationale, paquet 16 and H2.31)
EP (Paris, Collection Époques) [for solo voice, 22-02]; F:Pn (H2.15, Nr. 15)

S'il en est qui

Hymn to Victory
Solo voice, 22-223, 2 piccolos, tuba curva, serpent, bass drum, timpani ,
MS (score by Pierre) F:Pn (Vm.7.7945)
MS (parts) F:Pn (H2.99 a-v)
EP (Paris, Leduc) [choral parts only]; F:Pn (V.7.m.a.2545)

Fille terrible

Funeral Hymn on the Death of General Hoche
Four solo voices, three-part male chorus, 2022-223, 2 piccolos, serpent, timpani
MS (score) DDR:Bds (Bottée de Toulmon, Nr. 116/5)
MS (parts) F:Pn (H2.34)
EP (Paris, Collection Époques) [for solo voice, 22-02]; F:Pn (H2.15, Nr. 38)

Du haut de la voûte

Le Salpêtre républicain
Solo voice, 22-02
EP (Paris, Collection Époques); F:Pn (H2.15, Nr. 21)
MS (score) DDR:Bds (Bottée de Toulmon, Nr. 116/7)

Descendons dan nos

Ode sur le 18 fructidor
Three-part male chorus, 22-223, 2 piccolos, serpent, timpani, string bass
MS (autograph) F:Pn (Cons.10948)

O jour d'éternelle

MS (score) DDR:Bds (Bottée de Toulmon, Nr. 116/6)
MS (parts) F:Pn (Musique Nationale, paquet 18 and B2.32)
EP (Paris, Collection Époques) [for solo voice, 22-02]; F:Pn (H2.15, Nr. 37)

Hymne pour la fête de la Jeunesse, 10 germinal
Voice, 22-02
EP (Paris, Collection Époques); F:Pn (H2.15, Livre second, Nr. 4)
MS (score) DDR:Bds (Bottée de Toulmon, Nr. 116/8)

De l'hiver

Fête de la Reconnaissance, 10 prairial
Voice, 22-02
EP (Paris, Collection Époques); F:Pn (H2.15, Livre second, Nr. 6)
MS (score) DDR:Bds (Bottée de Toulmon, Nr. 116/9)

Paré de verdure

Della Maria, Pierre-Antoine (1769–1800)

Pièces d'harmonie
22-02
EP (Mainz, Schott, Nr. 231) BRD:MZsch

Deshayes, Prosper (d. 1815)

Premiere suite d'harmonie
22-02
EP (Paris, Imprimerie du Conc.); F:Pn; CS:Pnm

Devienne, François (1759–1803)

Ouverture
222-221, 2 piccolos, serpent, timpani
EP (Paris, Magasin de Musique, Issue 7, Nr. 1); F:Pn (H2.7, 1); US:DW (619); DDR:WRtl

Hymn to the Eternal
Voice, 22-02
EP (Paris, Collection Époques); F:Pn (H2.15, Nr. 25)

Il flétrissait

Le Chant du retour
Voice, 22-02, 2 piccolos, timpani
MS [lost, mentioned in a communication by Legrand, historian to the Army of the Rhein, dated May 31, 1797]

La paix couronne

Duernoy, Frédéric (1765–1838)

Pas de manoeuvre
22-12, 2 piccolos, serpent
EP (Paris, Magasin de Musique, Issue 4, Nr. 5); F:Pn (H2.4,5 and Vm.7.7041); US:DW (642)

Eler, André-Frédéric (1764–1821)

Ouverture
222-223, 2 piccolos, serpent, timpani
EP (Paris, Magasin de Musique, Issue 16); F:Pn (H2.44, Hr. 7; H2.130A, a-w; H2.130B, a-q); US:DW (624)

Ode on the Situation of the Republic in May, 1799
Voice, 22-02
EP (Paris, Collection Époques); F:Pn (H2.15, Nr. 41)

Quel est ce vaisseau

(6) *Walses*, (1) *Anglaise*
22-02 [cited by Grove, VI, 112]

(3) *Quatuors*, op. 11
1011-01 [cited by Grove, VI, 112]

Esch, Louis von

Airs Champêtres, op. 4
111-02, string bass
MS F:Pn [cited by Eitner]

Feray, Abbé (fl. ca. 1792)

Strophes on the Anniversary of the Just Punishment of the Last King of France
Chorus, 222-02
MS [lost]

Flaska, Joseph (1706–1772)

Musique d'harmonie and some *Marches*
EP (Böhme) [cited by F]

Foignet, Charles Gabriel (1750–1823)

Messe en symphonie
Chorus and Military orchestra [cited by MGG]

Friedem, ?

(2) *Sextets*, op. 1
22-02
EP (Paris, Lemoine) [cited by Hellyer]

Fuchs, Georg-Friedrich (1752–1821)

Airs Patriotiques, 1798
2022-12, percussion
MS [lost, cited in Grove]

Le carillon national, Ah: Ca ira, dictum populaire
22-02
EP (Paris, Sieber) BRD:AB

Divertissement
Six-part *Harmoniemusik*
EP (Paris, Gaveaux) [Liv. 1]

(6) *Fanfares*
-421, timpani
EP (Paris, Hentz; reprinted by Jouve); F:Pn (Vm.27.1585 and Vm.27.1595)

1ère Harmonie (without further subtitle)
42-12, serpent, percussion [according to Grove]
EP (Paris, Nadermann)

2ème Harmonie ('le Siège de Lille')
42-12, cymbals, bass drum
EP (Paris, Nadermann; reprinted by Ebend)

Harmonie Nr. 2
42-02
EP (Paris, Cousineau); CS:Pnm (XLII.A.212)

3ème Harmonie ('le Siège de Thionville')
42-12, serpent, percussion [according to Grove]
EP (Paris, Nadermann; reprinted by Ebend)

4ème Harmonie ('1'Entrée des Français à Mayence')
42-12, serpent, percussion [according to Grove]
EP (Paris, Ebend)

5ème Harmonie ('la Bataille de Gemmapes et la prise de la ville de Mons')
42-12, bass drum
EP (Paris, Nadermann; reprinted by Ebend); BRD:Tu [for 42-12, contrabassoon]

(Harmonie) *Ouverture du Camp de Grand-Pré*
Instrumentation uncertain
EP (Paris, Nadermann); F:Pn (Vm.7.6977 and Vm.27.1876)

(Harmonie) *Airs du Camp de Grand-Pré*
42-02
EP (Paris, Nadermann); F:Pn (Vm.7.6978 and Vm.27.1875)

(Harmonie) *La Bataille de Marenzo*
1022-121, serpent, percussion
EP (Paris, composer); F:Pn (Vm.27.1594)
This consists of one long, programmatic movement dedicated 'a Bonaparte.'

Harmonie, op. 50
Instrumentation unknown
EP (Paris, Janet et C.; reprinted by Decombe)

Harmonie
Twelve-part Harmoniemusik
EP (Paris, Leduc)

Marche en pas redoublé de la landwehr de la ville de Vienne
Harmoniemusik
EP (Paris, Janet et C.); F:Pn (Vm.27.1587)

Marche de la Garde nationale de la Vienne
Harmoniemusik
EP (Paris, Ebend); F:Pn (Vm.27.1586)

Marches et Pas redoubles de la Garde imperiale d'Autriche
Harmoniemusik
EP (Paris, Pleyel)

Marches et Pas redoubles
Six-part *Harmoniemusik*
EP (Paris, Sieber); BRD:AB

(6) *Marches et* (6) *Pas redoubles*
Harmoniemusik
EP (Paris, Hentz) [Liv. 1, 2]

Marches et Pas redoubles
Harmoniemusik
EP (Paris, Nadermann) [1ère Suite]

Marches et Pas redoubles dedides au Regiment du Roi
Harmoniemusik
EP (Paris, Ebend) [Liv. 1, 2]

(3) *Marches et* (3) *Pas redoubles*
Harmoniemusik
EP (Paris, Frere)

(3) *Marches royales, Vive Henry IV, Charmante Gabrielle, Ou peuton etre mieux, et God save the King*
Harmoniemusik
EP (Paris, Hentz)

104me Suite militaire ('marche pas redoublée et fanfares à plusieurs inst. à vent')
EP (Paris, Sieber, Nr. 1497); BRD:AB

(12) *Nocturnes*
1-02
EP (Paris, Lemoine); F:Pn (Vm.17.340)

Parthie
Harmoniemusik
MS A:Ee

Pas redoublé
Musique militaire
EP (Paris, Carli)

(4) *Pas redoublé*, (4) *Contredanses et* (4) *Walses*
Harmoniemusik
EP (Paris, Ebend) [Liv. 1–4]

Potpourri, 6 movements (based on works of Blasius)
42-02
EP (Paris, Nadermann); F:Pn (Vm.7.6967)

Potpourri, 1 movement (based on 'Richard')
42-02
EP (Paris, Nadermann); F:Pn (Vm.18.151)

Potpourri, 1 movement (based on *Nina* by 'Paësielle')
42-02
EP (Paris, Nadermann); F:Pn (Vm.7.6968)

(3) *Quartets*
11-02
EP (Paris, Nadermann & Boyer); F:Pn (Cons.A.34.04)
The Conservatoire library also has (3) *Trios-concertants*
   for clarinets
EP (Paris, Sieber père), under Vm.17.342.

Walses
Eight-part Harmoniemusik
EP (Paris, Sieber)

(12) *Walses 'à grande Harmonie'*
EP (Paris, Ebend)

Walses fav. de la Reine de Prusse
Harmoniemusik
EP (Paris, Ebend)

Gambaro, V.

Ouverture
1022-121, serpent, timpani, string bass
EP (Paris, Gambaro); F:Pn (Vm.27.1621 and Vm.27.1625)

(4) *Suites*
1030-121, serpent, percussion
EP (Paris, Gambaro); F:Pn (Vm.27.1623/1-4)

Gébauer, François René (1773–1844)

(6) *Suites* (each called *Harmonie*)
Eight-part *Harmoniemusik*
EP (Paris, Leduc)

(6) *Marches*
EP (Paris); F:Pn (Vm.27.1740)

(3) *Marches* ('pour l'entrée Louis XVIII')
EP (Paris); F:Pn (Vm.27.174l)

March (Collection)
EP (Paris)
F:Pn (Vm.27.1742) [MGG cites 35 marches by Gebauer, without the source; perhaps this collection contains most of them]

Marches a l'usages des Musique Militaires
22-02
EP (Paris); BRD:DS [cited by Eitner]

Pas de manoeuvre
22-12, serpent, 2 piccolos
EP (Paris, Magasin de musique, Issue 5, Nr. 4); F:Pn (H2.5, 4 and Vm.7.7046); US:DW (643)

Pas de manoeuvre
22-12, serpent, 2 piccolos
EP (Paris, Magasin de musique, Issue 8, Nr. 4); F:Pn (H2.8, 4); US:DW (644)

(3) *Quintets*
1111-01
MS F:Pn (L.2554)

(3) *Quartets*
1101-, English horn
MS F:Pn (L.2552)

(3) *Quartets*
1011-01
EP (Paris, Pleyel); CS:Pom (XLI.C.145)

Gébauer, Michel-Joseph, père

(12) *Marches nouvelles exécutées à l'occasion des grandes parades*
Instrumentation unknown
EP (Vienna, Weigl, Nr. 1100); A:Wgm

(5) *Marches de la Garde Imp. françoise*
Instrumentation unknown
MS DDR:Bds (Mus.Ms.7205)

Marche militaire
22-12, 2 piccolos, serpent
EP (Paris, Magasin de musique, Issue 9, Nr. 3); F:Pn (H2.9,3); US:DW (637)

Pas de manoeuvre
22-12, 2 piccolos, serpent
EP (Paris, Magasin de musique, Issue 9, Nr. 4); F:Pn (H2.9,4); US:DW (645)
According to MGG, Gebauer composed more than 200 marches.

1re Suite de douze fanfares ou Marches
-4, timpani
EP (Paris, Lemoine); F:Pn (Vm.7.7098)

Gossec, François Joseph (1734–1829)

Andante Larghetto in C minor
22-02
MS (autograph) F:Pn (MS.1436/1), US:DW (269)
A note in Gossec's hand reads, 'This piece may take the place of the andante in a symphony in case another one is needed; it will go very well before the allegro of the symphony in the other [now lost] book.'

Concertanta
1111-01
MS B:Bc [cited in Grove, VII, 562–563]

Symphony, 3 movements
22-02
MS (autograph) F:Pn (MS.1436/2); US:DW (267)

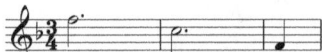

La Bataille (Largo: l'appel des trouppes; Marche fierement et marque; Allegro molto; la mellee ou attaque; Gaümont: la victoire)
22-02
MS (autograph) F:Pn (MS.1491 a-f); US:DW (266)
A note on the manuscript reads, 'composée pour Mour le Prince de Condé a Chantilli et executée chaque jour par les musicians pendant son souper devant Mgr le Duc d'Orleans et le Roi Louis XV pendant leur dejour a le chateau.'

La grande chasse de Chantilli
22-02
MS (autograph) F:Pn (MS.1436)
MS (parts) F:Pn (MS.1490 a-f); US:DW (268)

Chasse d'Hÿlas et Silvie faite par Gossec a Chentilli
(incidental music for a staged dramatic production, produced at Chantilly, November 7, 1768)
22-02
MS (autograph) F:Pn (MS.1436); US:DW (170)
MP (Heugel, 1970) F:Pn (H.32060)

Symphonie militaire
222-22, 2 piccolos, serpent, timpani, bass drum
EP (Paris, Magasin de musique, Issue 2, Nr. 1); F:Pn (H2.2,1 and Vm.7.7025); US:DW (611); DDR:WRtl
MP (Mercury Music; and William Schaefer, University of Southern California)

Symphonie in C
222-023, tuba curva, serpent, buccin, 2 piccolos, timpani
MS F:Pn (H2.154)
MP (Mercury Music)

Concertante
Solo 2221-02, accompanied by 1-203, timpani
MS F:Pn (Musique d'harmonie, paquet 13) [incomplete]

Marche lugubre
22-223, 2 piccolos, serpent, tam-tam, bass drum, caisse roulante voilée
MS F:Pn (Bibl.Cons.Partitions [Pierre]; Musique d'harmonie, paquet 37 [tam-tam only])
EP (Paris, Magasin de musique, Issue 12); F:Pn (H2.12,1; and H2.143 a-q)
MP (Columbo, as 'Number 4' in *Gossec Suite*)

Marche religieuse
2022 12, serpent
EP (Paris, Magasin de musique, Issue 6, Nr. 3); F:Pn (H2.6,3 and Vm.7.7050); US:DW (626)

Marche funèbre
22-223, 2 piccolos, serpent, tuba curva, tam-tam, 'drum or timpani'
MS F:Pn (H2.14)

Marche victorieuse
22-12, 2 piccolos, serpent
EP (Paris, Magasin de musique, Issue 6, Nr. 4); F:Pn (H2.6,4 and Vm.7.7051); US:DW (632)

Marche
22-12, 2 piccolos, serpent
EP (Paris, Magasin de musique, Issue 10, Nr. 3); F:Pn (H2.10,3); US:DW (634)

Marche
22-12, 2 piccolos, serpent
EP (Paris, Magasin de musique, Issue 11, Nr. 3); F:Pn (H2.11,3), US:DW (635)

Te Deum
Three-part chorus, 222-223, 2 piccolos, 2 'alto,' serpent, bass drum, 'tonnerre,' cymbal, snare drum
MS (autograph) F:Pn (MS.1.430); US:DW (318)

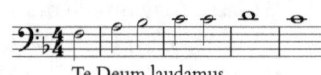
Te Deum laudamus

Domine Salvum
Three-part chorus, 222-223, 2 piccolos, 2 'alto,' serpent, bass drum, 'tonnerre,' cymbal, snare drum
MS (autograph) F:Pn (MS.1.430) [appendix]

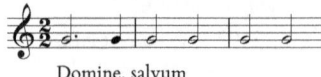
Domine, salvum

Hymn for July 14
Three-part chorus, 2022-223, serpent
EP (Paris, Magasin de musique, Issue 17); F:Pn (H2.35, Nr. 17); US:DW (502)

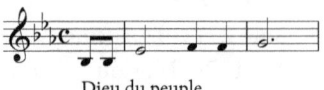
Dieu du peuple

Hymne sur la translation du corps de Voltaire au Pantheon
Solo voice, 22-02
F:Pn (H2.52)

Ce ne sont plus

Patriotic Chorus
Three-part chorus, 222-223, serpent, 'petites et grandes trompes antiques,' timpani
MS (autograph) F:Pn (Cons.10947); US:DW (573)
A note in Gossec's hand reads, 'in the absence of clarinets, the violins may transpose.'

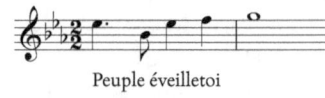
Peuple éveilletoi

Choeur à la liberte
Four-part chorus, 1022-043, piccolo, serpent, timpani
MS F:Pn (H2.103 a-r and H2.68)

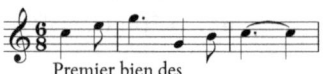
Premier bien des

National Round
Four-part chorus, 1022-043, piccolo, serpent, timpani
MS F:Pn (H2.103 a-r)
EP (Paris, Collection Époques) [for solo voice, 22-02]; F:Pn (H2.125, Nr. 8)

L'innocence est

Funeral Hymn
MS [lost, mentioned in contemporary newspapers]

Patriotic Chorus
Three-part chorus, 222-223, 2 piccolos, serpent, buccin, tuba curva, bass drum, cymbals
MS (autogrph) F:Pn (Cons.10947)
EP (Paris, Magasin de musique, Issue 2, Nr. 2) [omitting trombones 1, 2, buccin, tuba curva]; F:Pn (H2.2,2 and Vm.7.7026); US:DW (576)

Salut et respect

Hymn to Liberty
Four-part chorus, 22-223, 2 piccolos, serpent, timpani
EP (Paris, Magasin de musique, Issue 15) F:Pn (H2.35, Nr. 8); US:DW (503)

Vive à jamais

Hymn to Liberty
Four-part chorus, 22-103, piccolo, serpent
MS F:Po (Nr. 350)
EP (Paris, Magasin de musique, Issue 5, Nr. 2) [with additional horns, large or small flutes given as optional, and missing trombones 1, 2]; F:Pn (H2.5, 2; H2.101 a-n; and Vm.7.7044); US:DW (506)

Touchant réveil

Hymn to Nature
Chorus, 22-203, piccolo, serpent, timpani
MS F:Po (Nr. 350)
EP (Paris, Magasin de musique, Issue 10, Nr. 2); F:Pn (H2.10, 2 and H2.35, Nr. 5); US:DW (507)

Divinité tutélaire

[?] for chorus, 22-223, 2 piccolos, serpent, timpani
MS F:Po [lost]

Hymn to the Statue of liberty
Three-part chorus, 2-22, piccolo
MS F:Pn (Musique d'harmonie, paquet 2bis); US:DW (508)

Quel peuple immense

Auguste et consolante

Air des Marseillais
Three-part chorus, 22-22, 2 piccolos, serpent, timpani
MS F:Po (Nr.350); F:Pn (H2.49, 4; H2.151,8a8b; and H2.55)

Siècles fameux

Hymn to the Supreme Being
Four-part chorus, 2222-223, 2 piccolos, buccin, tuba curva, serpent, bass drum, cymbals, tambour turc
MS (autograph) F:Pn (Cons.10946) [Movements 1, 5 only]; US:DW (536)

Source de véreté

Hymn to the Supreme Being
Four-part chorus, 2222-223, 2 piccolos, buccin, tuba curva, serpent, bass drum, cymbals, tambour turc
MS F:Pn (Cons.10946)
EP (Paris, Magasin de musique, Issue 4, Nr. 2) [missing buccin and tuba curva]; F:Pn (H2.4,2 and Vm.7.7039)

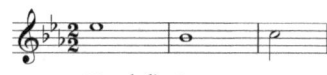
Père de l'univers

Hymn to the Supreme Being
Solo and chorus, with 2222-223, 2 piccolos, serpent
EP (Paris, Magasin de musique, Issue 4, Nr. 3) F:Pn (H2.4,3 and Vm.7.7038); US:DW (537
EP (Paris, Collection Époques) [for solo voice, 22-02]; F:Pn (H2.15, Nr. 22)

Père de l'univers

Hymn to Jean-Jacques Rousseau
Solo voice, 22-02
EP (Paris, Collection Époques) F:Pn (H2.15, Nr. 32)

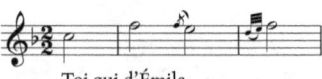
Toi qui d'Émile

Chant funèbre sur la mort de Ferraud
Solo, chorus, 2222-243, serpent
MS F:Pn (H2.100 a-p)

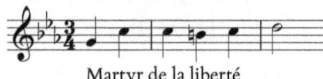
Martyr de la liberté

Hymn to Humanity
Chorus, 2022-223, serpent, string bass
MS F:Pn (Musique nationale, paquet 26)

O mère des vertus

Aux mânes de la Gironde
Soli, chorus, 2232-243, 2 piccolos, serpent, timpani, string bass
MS (autograph) F:Pn (Cons.10947)
MS (parts) F:Pn (Musique nationale, paquet 24)

Par mi ces funèbres

Hymn to Victory
Chorus, 222-223, 2 piccolos, buccin, tuba curva, serpent, timpani
MS (autograph) F:Pn (Cons.10947)
MS (parts) F:Pn (Musique nationale, paquet 44)

La peuple dans la

Hymn for the Celebration of Victory
Solo, chorus, 2222-223, tuba curva, serpent, timpani
MS (autograph) F:Pn (Cons.10947)
MS (parts) F:Pn (Musique nationale, paquet 25)

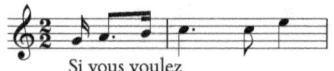
Si vous voulez

Honauer, Leonz (fl. in Paris ca. 1760–1778)

Suite de Pièces in B♭
22-02, piano
MS DDR:SWl (Honauer, L.1)

Suite de Pièces in E♭
22-02, piano
MS DDR:SWl (Honauer, L.2)

Suite de Pièces
22-02, clavecin
EP (Paris, ca. 1770) DDR:Bds [cited by Eitner]

Horix, ?

Marche des Français sur les bords de la Grande-Bretagne
2122-223, percussion
MS [lost, known only from a memorandum dated March 28, 1798, signed by Cherubini and Méhul]

Jadin, Hyacinthe (1769–1800)

Ouverture
22-12, 2 piccolos, serpent
EP (Paris, Magasin de musique, Issue 13); F:Pn (H2.47); US:DW (623)
MS F:Pn (H2.132 a-m)
MP (Columbo)

Hymn for January 21
Solo voice, 22-02
EP (Paris, Collection Époques) F:Pn (H2.15, Nr. 20)

Les flammes de l'Etna

Hymn to Agriculture
Solo, chorus, 222-223, piccolo, serpent
MS (score) F:Pn (Cons.10949)
MS (parts) F:Pn (H2.20)

Assez longtemps

Jadin, Louis Emmanuel (1768–1853)

(3) *Sextuors concertans*
22-02
EP (Paris, Dufant & Dubois, Nr. 546); A:Wgm

(3) *Quintetti concertans*
Oboe or clarinet, with 1001-01, piano
EP (Paris, Janet & C., Nr. 1209, 1210); A:Wgm

Harmonie
22-02
EP (Paris, Leduc)

Harmonie par Musique Militaire
EP (Paris, Leduc) [Journal Liv. 2 and 6]

Symphonie
22-221, 2 piccolos, serpent
MS F:Pn (H2.133A a-l and H2.133B a-l)
EP (Paris, Magasin de musique, Issue 4, Nr. 1-); F:Pn (H2.4,1 and Vm.7.7037); US:DW (613)
EP (Paris, Ebend)
MP (Shawnee; Friedrich Hoffmeister-Verlag)

Ouverture
2222-221, 2 piccolos, serpent, timpani
EP (Paris, Magasin de musique, Issue 6, Nr. 1) F:Pn (H2.6, 1 and Vm.7.7048); US:DW (618)
EP (Paris, Schlesinger)

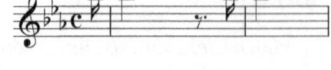

Marche
22-12, 2 piccolos, serpent
EP (Paris, Magasin de musique, Issue 7, Nr. 3); F:Pn (H2.7,3); US:DW (636)

Pas de manoeuvre
22-12, 2 piccolos, serpent
EP (Paris, Magasin de musique, Issue 7, Nr. 4); F:Pn (H2.7,4); US:DW (646)

Hymn of the Freed Slaves
Voice, 22-
EP (Paris, Magasin de musique, Issue 3, Nr. 6); F:Pn (H2.3,6 and Vm.7.7036); US:DW (652)

Au jour plus pur

Hymn to J.-J. Rousseau
Chorus, 2022-22, serpent
MS F:Pn (H2.18 and H2.108 a-m)

Enfin sur les bords

Kreutzer, Rodolphe (1766–1831)

Ouverture, Journée de Marathon
22-121, 2 piccolos, serpent, timpani
EP (Paris, Magasin de musique, Issue 9, Nr. 1); F:Pn (H2.9,1); US:DW (656)

Lamberti, Louis (b. 1769)

Pièces en harmonie
EP [lost, cited by F]

Langlé, Honoré François (1741–1807)

(6) *Sinfonie*, op. 1
22-02
EP (Paris, 1776-1782) [cited in *MGG* and Grove, X, 452]

Hymn to the Eternal
Solo voice, 22-02
EP (Paris, Collection Époques); F:Pn (H2.15, Nr.24)

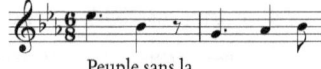
Peuple sans la

Lefèvre, Jean Xavier (1763–1829)

Ouverture
122-02, piccolo, serpent, tuba curva, buccin, string bass
MS F:Pn (Musique d'harmonie, paquet 22)

(6) Marches and (6) *Pas redoublés*
2022-12, serpent, cymbals, bass drum
EP (Paris, Imbault) F:Pn (Vm.7.7100)

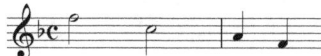

Marche militaire
22-121, 2 piccolos, serpent, timpani
EP (Paris, Magasin de musique, Issue 2, Nr. 3); F:Pn (H2.2,3 and Vm.7.7027); US:DW (627)

Pas de manoeuvre
22-121, 2 piccolos, serpent
MS (score) F:Pn (Cons.10947)
EP (Paris, Magasin de musique, Issue 2, Nr. 4) F:Pn (H2.2,4 and Vm.7.7028); US:DW (640)

Hymn
2222-223, serpent, timpani
MS [lost, cited in a document of 1795]

Hymn to Agriculture
Solo, chorus, 2022-223, serpent
MS (score) F:Pn (Cons.10949)
MS (score and parts) F:Pn (Musique nationale, paquet 30)

Mère commune

Lesueur, Jean François (1760–1837)

Hymn of the Triumphs of the French Republic
222-02, bass drum, cymbal
MS F:Pn (Cons.Mus.pour inst. à vent, paquet 39)
This seems to be an instrumental version of the following work which I could not actually find in the library.

Hymn of the Triumphs of the French Republic
Chorus, 2222-223, serpent, timpani
EP (Paris, Magasin de musique, Issue 9, Nr. 2); F:Pn (H2.9,2); US:DW (559)

Quand des montagnes

Patriotic Scene
Male chorus, 2224-243, 2 piccolos, serpent, tuba curva, string bass timpani
MS F:Pn (Musique nationale, paquet 34) [missing some choral parts and all band parts except the first clarinet]

C'est peu d'avoir

Chant du IX thermidor (July 27)
Solo voice, 22-02
EP (Paris, Collection Époques) F:Pn (H2.15, Nr. 30)

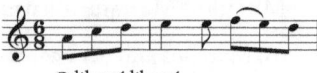
Levons nous, un

Hymn for the Inauguration of a Temple of Liberty
Voice, 22-02
EP (Paris, Collection Époques) F:Pn (H2.15, Nr. 17)

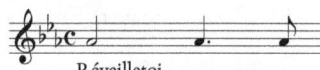
O liberté liberté

Chant dithyrambique
Solo voice, 22-02
EP (Paris, Collection Époques) F:Pn (H2.15, Nr. 39)

Réveilletoi

Hymn for the Festival of Agriculture
Solo voice, 22-02
EP (Paris, Collection Époques) F:Pn (H2.15, Livre second, Nr. 7)

Allons ami de labour

Hymn for Old Age
Voice, 22-02
MS (autograph?) F:Pn (MS.4713)
EP (Paris, Collection Époques) F:Pn (H2.15, Livre second, Nr. 10)

Ce jour est le jour

Lorenziti, Bernardo (fl. in Paris, late eighteenth century)

Canon ou divertissement
22-
EP (Paris, David); H:KE; S:Skma

Martini, Johann [known as Martini el Tedesco] (1741–1816)

Hymn to the Republic
Chorus, 2222-221, 2 piccolos, serpent, bass drum, cymbals, string bass
EP (Paris, Magasin de musique, Issue 22); F:Pn (Cons., Musique nationale, paquet 35)
EP (Paris, Collection Époques) [for solo voice, 22-02]; F:Pn (H2.15, Livre second, Nr. 1)

Que nos voix

Triumphal Hymn for the Festival of September 22
Chorus, 1222-021, piccolo, serpent, bass drum, cymbals, string bass
MS F:Pn (Cons., Musique nationale, paquet 43)

Chantons!

Méhul, Étienne (1763–1817)

Ouverture
22-221, 2 piccolos, serpent, timpani
MS F:Pn (D.7.855); US:DW (368)
MS (parts) F:Pn (H2.135 a-q)

EP (Paris, Magasin de musique, Issue 3, Nr. 1) F:Pn (H2.3,1 and Vm.7.7031); US:DW (617)

MP (Southern Music Corp.)

Le Chant du départ
Solo, Chorus, 22-2, serpent, timpani
EP (Paris, Magasin de musique, Issue 6 Nr. 2) F:Pn (H2.6,2 and Vm.7.7049); US:DW(597)
EP (Paris, Collection Époques) [for solo voice, 22-02] F:Pn (H2.15, Nr. 16)

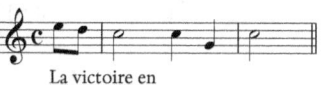
La victoire en

Le Chant des victories
Chorus, 222-223, serpent, buccin, cymbals, bass drum, string bass
EP (Paris, Collection Époques) [for Solo voice, 22-02]; F:Pn (H2.15, Nr. 28)

Fuyant ses villes

Funeral Hymn for Feraud
Voice, 22-223, 2 piccolos, serpent
MS F:Pn (Cons., Musique nationale, paquet 38 and Fol.y.688)
EP (Paris, Collection 'Epoques) [for solo voice, 22-02] F:Pn (H2.15, Nr. 33)

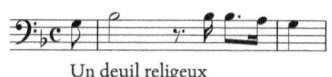
Un deuil religeux

Hymne du IX thermidor (July 27)
Voice, 22-02
EP (Paris, Collection Époques) F:Pn (H2.15, Livre second, Nr. 8)

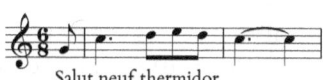
Salut neuf thermidor

Hymn of the Twenty-Two
Solo, chorus, 22-223, 2 piccolos, buccin, serpent, string bass, timpani, bass drum, cymbals
MS F:Pn (Cons., Musique nationale, paquet 37)
EP (Paris, Collection Époques) [for solo voice, 22-02] F:Pn (H2.15, Nr. 35)

Républicains dont

Le chant du retour
Voice, 22-02
EP (Paris, Collection Époques) F:Pn (H2.15, Nr. 40)

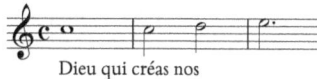
Contemplez nos

Hymn for the Festival of Marriage
Voice, 22-02
EP (Paris, Collection Époques) F:Pn (H2.15, Livre second, Nr. 5)

Dieu qui créas nos

Millingre, ?

Suite pour 1a Harmonie, op. 1
Nine-part *Harmoniemusik*
EP (Paris, 1794) [cited in S]

Minoja, Ambrogio (b. 1752)

March and Funeral symphony (composed in honor of General Hoche [for which he] obtained from General Buonaparte the prize of a gold medal.) [cited in S]

Mitscha, Francois Adam (1746–1811)

Pièces d'harmonie
222-02
EP [cited in F]

Ozi, Etienne (1754–1813)

(32) *Nouvelles suites de pièces d'harmonie*
22-02
EP (Paris, 1783-1791) [cited in Grove, XIV, 40]

Marches et Pas redoublés
EP (Paris, Nadermann) [Cah.33]

Pas de manoeuvre
22-12, 2 piccolos, serpent
EP (Paris, Magasin de musique, Issue 3, Nr. 4) F:Pn (H2.3,4 and Vm.7.7034); US:DW (641)

Pas de manoeuvre
22-12, 2 piccolos, serpent
EP (Paris, Magasin de musique, Issue 12, Nr. 4) F:Pn (H2.12,4); US:DW (648)

Hymne à l'hymen pour la célébration des marriages
Two voices, 22-02
EP (Paris, Collection Époques) F:Pn (H2.15, Livre second, Nr. 11)

Dieu d'hymen reçois

Pujolas, ?

Nouvelles marches militaires à plusieurs instruments [Nr. 1]
242-22, serpent, caisse, cimballes
EP (Paris, Sieber) F:Pn
EP (reprinted: Paris, Imbault) DDR:HER

Nouvelles marches militaires à plusieurs instruments [Nr.2]
2042-12, serpent, timpani
EP (Paris, Sieber) F:Pn
EP (reprinted: Paris, Imbault) DDR:HER; F:Pn

Nouvelles marches militaires à plusieurs instruments [Nr.3)
222-12, 2 fifres, timpani, caisse

EP (Paris, publisher undetermined) F:Pn

Nouvelles marches militaires à plusieurs instruments [Nr. 4]
42-14, serpent, 2 fifres, caisse, cimballes, serpent
EP (Paris, Imbault) F:Pn

Nouvelles marches militaires à plusieurs instruments [Nr. 5]
42-14, 2 fifres, sepent, caisse, cimballes
EP (Paris, Imbault) F:Pn

Nouvelles marches militaries à plusieurs instruments [Nr. 6]
42-14, 2 fifres, serpent, caisse, cimballes
EP (Paris, Imbault) F:Pn

Nouvelles marches militaires à plusieurs instruments [Nr. 7]
42-12, 2 fifres
EP (Paris, Imbau1t) F:Pn

Nouvelles marches militaires à plusieurs instruments [Nr. 8]
22-12, 2 fifres, serpent, caisse, cimballes
EP (Paris, Imbault) F:Pn

Riegel, Henri Joseph (1741–1799)

Parthia
201-02
MS CS:Pnm (XLII.B.215)

Rigel, père

Hymn to Liberty
Chorus, 22-22, piccolo, serpent, timpani, string bass
MS F:Pn (Cons.10949 and Musique nationale, paquet 39)

Toi dont le bras

Röser, Valentin (1735–1782)

Andante Grazioso
2002-02, 2 basset horns
MS GB:Lbm [cited by SJK]

*Essai d'instruction à l' usage de ceux qui composent p. la Clarinette et le
    Cor avec des remarques sur l'harmonie et des exemples a 2 clarin. 2
    Cors et 2 Bassons*
MS F:TO
EP (Paris, Le Menu); B:Br

Suite de Pièces d'harmonie
22-02

EP (Paris, Sieber, 1782) BRD:DS [cited by Eitner]; DDR:Dlb
[cited by Eitner as '12 Pieces']

Suite d'Harmonie des Opera
22-02
EP (Paris, Sieber) F:Pn (Vmg.14853)

(56 Sets) *Divertissements militaires*
22-02
EP (Paris, Sieber, 1771-1782) BRD:DS [Sets 39, 42, 50, 55, 56,
lost in WWII]; DDR:SWl [one example]

Ire Suite des Ariettes
22-02
EP (Paris, Bérault, 1771)

Suite des Airs
22-02
EP (Paris, Bérault, 1772)

XVI *Marches et Airs*
22-02
EP (Berlin, Hummel)

Rouget de Lisle, Claude-Joseph (1760–1836)

Marche des Marseillois, arranged by Gossec
2022-022, timpani
EP (Paris, Imbault) F:Pn

Où courent ces

Roland à Roncevaux
Chorus (?), 21-22, serpent
MS F:Pn (Cons., Musique nationale, paquet 30b and 40)
EP (Paris, Collection Époques) [for solo voice, 22-02] F:Pn
(H2.15, Nr. 11)

Rousseau, Jean Jacques (1712–1778)

Collection (4 *Airs* for 2 clarinets; *Air for le fifre avec les
tambours; Air pour la musique* [221-01])
MS CH:Genf, Société J.J.Rousseau (MS.R.15)

Deuxieme Air pour la Musique
222-02
MS F:Pn; US:DW (437)

Air for 2 clarinets, 'composés pour le marquis de Belfroy'
MS F:Pn (Rés.Vm.7.667, Nr. 3493)

Sòlere, Etienne (1753–1817)

Ouverture
22-12, 2 piccolos, serpent
EP (Paris, Magasin de musique, Issue 11, Nr. 1) F:Pn (H2.11,1);
  US:DW (622)

Solié, Jean Pierre (1755–1812)

Pas de manoeuvre
22-12, 2 piccolos, serpent
EP (Paris, Magasin de musique, Issue 10, Nr. 4) F:Pn (H2.10,4);
  US:DW (647)

Widerkehr, J. C. (1759–1823)

(10?) *Simphonie concertantes*
1112-01, cello
EP (Paris, Imbault) F:Pn [cited by Eitner]

Germany

Anonymous

(4) *Aufzüge* (ca. 1780)
Two four-part brass choirs, timpani
MS BRD:WEY (675)

Aufzüge (ca. 1800)
Nine-part brass
MS BRD:WEY (676)

Aufzüge (ca. 1780)
Ten-part brass
MS BRD:WEY (677)

Aufzüge (ca. 1780)
Eight-part brass
MS BRD:WEY (678) [missing Choir II, clarino 1]

Allegretto con Variazioni
2021-02
MS DDR:Dlb (2/P/2) [cited by SJK]

Allemande
122-12
MS DDR:SWl (592)

Andante
1222-02, serpent
MS DDR:Z (XLIX, 156)

Andante maestoso
2222-02, serpent
MS DDR:SWl (568/2) [cited by SJK]

(6) *Angloises*
22-12
MS DDR:SWl (561)

Allegretto
2222-02, serpent
MS DDR:SWl (568/3) [cited by SJK]

Cantate, 'Auf den Abzug des Herrn'
SSAATB, 2021-021
MS DDR:AG (63)

Cantata, 'Singet dem Herrn ein neues Lied'
SATB, 2101-11, clav., organ, timpani
MS DDR:GOL (Nr. 26)

Choral, 'O komm zu uns verheissner Geist' (1797)
S, 222-22, timpani, organ
MS DDR:SWl (A.f.4)

Concerto
1-02, 2 oboe d'amore
MS BRD:BÜu (Rheda MS.876)

(13) *Military Concerti*
221-02
EP (Breitkopf & Härtel, 1775 Catalog)

(4) *Military Concerti*
201-22
EP (Breitkopf & Härtel, 1771 Catalog)

[L. v. L] *Divertimento*, 15 movements
2001-02
MS BRD:DO (Mus.Ms.353/1) [missing both flutes]

(3) *Divertimenti* in E♭
22-02
MS BRD:F (Mus.Hs.1560, 1561, and 1562)

Harmonie, 2 movements (ca. 1790)
202-1
MS BRD:DS (Mus.Ms.1223/9)

Journal de Musique militaire
22-02
EP (Storck); DDR:SWl (MS.3014)

(5) *Märsche* (one marked, *Saxon Grenediergarde*)
222-02
MS BRD:Mbs (Mus.Ms.3668)

(250) *Marches*
Four to six winds
MS BRD:DS (Mus.Ms.1224)

(200 *Märches*) *Die Königlich Preusische Ordonance* (ca. 1776–1771)
MS BRD:DS (Mus.Ms.1222 and 1225) [two copies, many are incomplete in only two parts]

Parade Marsch (1788, '*Elector Sächischen Reg.*')
MS (autograph) CS:Pnm (XXII.F.374)

(6) *Marcia*
201-12
MS DDR:SWl (C.h.15)

(6) *Märsche*
202-12
MS DDR:SWl (C.h.1) [missing bassoon 1]

(5) *Märsche ('von Leib-Regiment')*
220-02
MS DDR:SWl (C.h.6)

Mariata bella Truppa Municipals
2001-221
MS (score) DDR:SWl (MS.575c)

(4) *Märsche*
201-12
MS DDR:SWl (MS.575b)

(3) *Märsche, Allegro, Ecoss, Walzer*
-4, timpani
MS DDR:SWl (MS.575d)

(8) *Märsche für Türkische Musick*
2022-221, percussion
EP (Offenbach, André) [Vol. 2]; CS:KRa (IV.B.192)

Marsch
201-12
MS DDR:SWl (C.h.17)

(24) *Märsche*
Instrumentation uncertain
MS DDR:SWl (548/6) [here only oboe 2, bassoon 2, and horn 2]

(4) *Vergatterungen* and (1) *Zapfenstreich*
2020-, 2 pfeiffe, small drum
MS DDR:SWl (C.h.28) [some parts missing]

Marsch ('Du Roy de Prusse')
201-1
MS DDR:SWl (C.h.29)

Zapfenstreich
3023-441, percussion
MS DDR:SWl (C.h.50)

Friedensmarsch
1222-22, percussion
MS DDR:SWl (C.h.59)

(Collection)
1. *Marsch* for 2222-12
2. *Andante* for 2222-12, percussion
3. *Allegretto* for *Blasinstrumete*
4. *Quadrille* for *Blasinstrumente*
MS DDR:SWl (C.h.26)

Marcia con Minuetto
22-03
MS DDR:SWl (572)

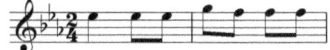

(3) *Märche*
1022-121, contrabassoon
MS BRD:F (Mus.Hs.1173)

Märche Collection
22-02
MS BRD:F (Mus.Hs.1171)

Marsch
222-22
MS BRD:DS (Mus.Ms.1223/11) [missing bassoon 2]

Marsch
201-2
MS BRD:DS (Mus.Ms.1223/30)

(2) *Märsche*
MS BRD:DS (Mus.Ms.1223/13)
Carries the note, 'Alte Dessauer und des Fürst Moritzinsen Reg. Diese Märche erhielt Ich von dem Hautobisten ersteren Regiments, modo Thadden.'

(2) *Märsche*
222-22
MS BRD:DS (Mus.Ms.1223/20)
('Gen. Konig' and 'Gen. Bornstadt,' ca. 1790–1800)

Märsche (for 'Exelenz: Moellendorff')
Nr. 1 for 21-12
Nr. 2 for 221-12
MS BRD:DS (Mus.Ms.1223/22)

Marsch Julius Caesar ('pour tout la Musique turque Du Regiment d'alsase,' ca. 1790)
2021-22, serpent
MS BRD:DS (Mus.Ms.1223/6)

Märsche
202-2
MS BRD:DS (Mus.Ms.1223/18)

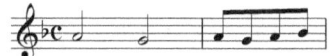

Marsch ('f.KK Inft. Reg.v.Ligne')
2022, bass
MS BRD:DS (Mus.Ms.1223/5)

Marc Graz (ca. 1780)
20-22, bass
MS BRD:DS (Mus.Ms.1223/3-4)

Marche ('von der Armee des Bouonaparte')
22-12
MS BRD:DS (Mus.Ms.1223/16)

(2) *Marches* ('für Princess Amalia v. Prussia and Prince Christian v. Hessen')
41-22
MS BRD:DS (Mus.Ms.1223/21)

March (ca. 1770)
202-1
MS BRD:DS (Mus.Ms.1223/18)

(2) *Märsche* ('Wilhelmus v. Nassau' and 'al is ons Prinsje nog 200 Kley')
222-22
MS BRD:DS (Mus.Ms.1223/8a, b)

Marsch (ca. 1800)
3041-22
MS BRD:DS (Mus.Ms.1223/25)

Marche ('du quinzieme Reg. d'Angletterre') (ca. 1790)
2 clarinets or oboes, 2 horns or trumpets, and bassoon
MS BRD:DS (Mus.Ms.1223/26)

Marche (ca. 1790)
22-12
MS BRD:DS (Mus.Ms.1223/28)

Marche a. 9 Parth:
222-12
MS BRD:DS (Mus.Ms.1223/29)

Marche ('Regiment Sr. Exctenz v. Moellendorf')
221-12
MS BRD:DS (Mus.Ms.1223/22)

Menuett
202-12
MS DDR:SWl (C.h.53)

Menuet & Gavotte
202-12
MS DDR:SWl (552) [cited by SJK]

GERMANY 299

Partita in C
222-02, contrabassoon
MS BRD:DO (Mus.Ms.1531)

Parthia
2021-02
MS DDR:HER (Mus.B.10=17)

Parthia
22-02
MS DDR:HER (Mus.B.10=18)

(6) *Partiten*
MS DDR:HER (Mus.N1=19) [incomplete, only 1-02 is present]

Partia, 3 movements
22-12
MS DDR:SWl (C.h.10)

Parthie in D
201-12
MS DDR:SWl (557)

(2) *Partittas* ('Nr. III, V')
211-02
MS BRD:KA [cited by SJK]

Parthia in C
21-12
MS DDR:Dlb (1/F/32) [cited by SJK]

Partita in E♭
21-02
MS BRD:TSCH (Gg 99)

Partita in E♭
21-02
MS BRD:TSCH (Gg 99)

Parthia
1022-02
MS BRD:F (Mus.Hs.1564)

Parthia ('Transporta del Henrico Ehrenfried')
222-02
MS BRD:F (Mus.Hs.1556)

Partita (1773)
21-02
MS BRD:Rtt (Inc.IVa/31/I, Nr. 3)

Partita (1773)
21-02
MS BRD:Rtt (Inc.IVa/31/I, Nr. 9)

Partita (1773)
21-02
MS BRD:Rtt (Inc.IVa/31/I, Nr. 10)

Partita (1773)
21-02
MS BRD:Rtt (Inc.IVa/31/I, Nr. 11)

Partita (1773)
21-02
MS BRD:Rtt (Inc.IVa/31/I, Nr. 12)

Partita (1773)
21-02
MS BRD:Rtt (Inc.IVa/31/I, Nr. 13)

Partita (1773)
21-02
MS BRD:Rtt (Inc.IVa/31/I, Nr. 14)

Partita (1773)
21-02
MS BRD:Rtt (Inc.IVa/31/I, Nr. 17)

Partita in E♭ (ca. 1790), 11 movements
22-24, 2 violas (?), string bass
MS BRD:Rtt (Inc.IVa/16/I)

Partita in E♭ (ca. 1790), 14 movements
('favorite von Rudolf und Wack')
22-02, 2 violas (?), string bass
MS BRD:Rtt (In c.IVa/8) [missing bassoon 1]

Romanze (ca. 1780)
12-02
MS BRD:Rtt (Inc.IVa/24)

Rondo
200-02
MS DDR:SWl (C.h.41a)

Serenade, 7 movements
2220-2
MS BRD:Mbs (Mus.Ms.7612) [apparently missing parts]

(20) *Stücke*
200-12, basso
MS BRD:DS (Mus.Ms.1188)

Variations (on 'O du Ueber Augustin')
2022-02
MS DDR:SWl (613)

Walzer
122-1
MS DDR:SWl (600/1)

Anonymous Compiler

Divertissiment
22-02
MS DDR:SWl (C.h.40)
Contains a *Presto* ('Mons. Roeser'), a *Siciliano* ('Mons. Rathgen')
and a *Polonaise* ('Mons. Martini')

Altenburg, Johann Ernst (b. 1734)

*Versuch einer Anleitung zur heroisch-musikalischen Trompeter-
und Pauker-Kunst*
EP (Halle, Hendel, 1795); A:Wgm; B:Br; DDR:Dlb, Bds, LEm;
BRD:Hs; GB:Lbm (c.251)
Contains a *Concerto* -7, timpani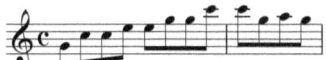
MP (Brass Press, 1974); US:DW (433)

Amalie, Prinzessin v. Preussen (1723–1787, sister to Frederick the Great)

March ('Pour le Rég. der Gen. F. de Millendorf')
201-3
MS DDR:Bds (Mus.Ms.Amalie, 1)

(3) *Märsche*
1. 'Pour de Régiment du Comte Lottum, March 29, 1767'
2. 'Pour de Rég. d. Gen. Bülow, August 14, 1767'
3. 'Pour de Rég. d. Gen. Saldern, May 16, 1769'
201-01
MS DDR:Bds (Mus.Ms.Amalie, 2)

Apell, Johann (1754–1832)

(12) *Notturni*
Blasinstrumente
MS [cited in F]

Bach, Johann Christian (1735–1782)

(6) *Divertissements*
21-02
EP (Paris) [cited in G2]

(3) *Marsch*
1. 'du Regiment Ie Prince'
2. 'du Regiment Ie Braun'
3. 'du Regiment Ie Wurmb'
221-02, cembalo
MS DDR:SWl (Bach, J.C.13)
MP (Hamburg, Hans Sikorski, 1956)

Due Marce ('di Cavallelria e d'Infanteria Ie Prince Wallis de la Gran Bretagna d'un Regimento di Dragoni')
222-02
MS DDR:Bds (Mus.Ms.381)

(2) *Marches* (from *Scipione*)
Military band
EP (London, Dale, 1785)

(2) *Märsche* in E♭ (for the Bataillon Garde-Regiment, Hanover)
222-02
MS DDR:Bds (Hausbibl.386)

(6) *Symphonies*
22-02
MS US:PHf; GB:Lbbc
EP (London, Longman and Broderip, ca. 1780); GB:Lbm
   (R.M.16.b.17.[2] and R.M.17.b.1.[15]) [two copies]
MP (Leipzig, Friedrich Hofmeister, 1957); GB:Lbm (h.423.e.[6])

(4) *Symphonies*
22-02
EP (Cooke, ca. 1779?); ERIE:Da
MP (London, Boosey & Hawkes, 1957, as 'Four Quintets');
   GB:Lbm (b.211)

Bach, Johann Christoph Friedrich (1732–1795)

Septett (ca. 1780)
122-02
MS BRD:Buc [cited by MGG]
MP (Breitkopf & Härtel)

Bach, Karl Philipp Emanuel (1714–1788)

(2) *Märsche*
202-02
MS B:Bc (Wotquenne 187)
MP (Parrhysius, 1952)

(2) *Marche*
201-02
MS B:Bc (Wotquenne 6370)

March, 'Für die Arche'
-3, timpani
MS B:Bc (W.12,465)

(6) *kleine Stücke oder Märsche* (Wotquenne 185)
222-02
MS US:PHf; US:DW (378)

(6) *kleine Stücke oder Märsche*
222-02
MS B:Bc (Wotquenne 6369)

(2) *kleine Stücke*
22-02
MS B:Bc (Wotquenne 186)

(6) *kleine Sonaten*
2022-02
MS B:Bc (Wotquenne 184); A:Wn (Sm.5525)
MP (London, Musica Rara); GB:Lbm (c.140.ww.[1]);
    US:DW (381)

(6) *Piccolo Sonate*
2021-02
MS B:Bc (Wotquenne 6367)

Bachmann, Anton (1716–1800)

Allegro and Andante
222-1
MS DDR:Bds (Hausbibl., Nr. 333)

Marsch
22-1
MS DDR:Bds (Hausbibl., Nr. 82)

Marsch
222-1
MS DDR:Bds (Hausbibl., Nr. 83)

Marsch
222-02
MS DDR:Bds (Hausbibl, Nr. 84)

Marsch
122-1
MS DDR:Bds (Hausbibl., Nr. 85)

Marsch
22-1
MS DDR:Bds (Hausbibl., Nr. 86)

Janitschareumarsch and a *March* with text
MS DDR:Bds (Hausbibl., Nr. 95) [lost]

Marsch
Harmoniemusik
MS DDR:MERZ (49.F/10)

Marsch
-3
MS DDR:Bds (Hausbibl., Nr. 231)

Backofen, Johann Georg (1768–1830)

'Works for Harmoniemusik'
EP (Breitkopf & Härtel, 1796) [cited in MGG]

Barth, Christian (1735–1809)

Grand Sinfonie pour instruments à vent, op. 10, in 3 movements
2222-241, serpent, timpani
EP (Offenbach, André)
BRD:DS [lost in WWII]

Baumgarten, C. Gotthilf von (1741–1813)

(30) *Aufzüge fur eine Principal Trompete, erste und Zweyte Ripientrompete und Pauken, zum Gebrauch für Cavalleréregimenter*
EP (Berlin and Amsterdam, Hummel, Nr. 1037) S:L

Beecke, Ignaz von (1733–1803)

Partita in E♭, 5 movements
1121-02
MS BRD:BR (111.4.1/2.40.98)

Parthia
2222-02, string bass
MS BRD:Rtt [cited by Hellyer]

Benda, ?

Dragoner-Marsch
202-1, timpani
MS (score) DDR:Bds (Hausbibl., Nr. 232)

Bender, H.

(6) *Piècen fur Kavalleriemusik*
MS DDR:Bds (Hausbibl., Nr. 233)

Bordorf, Jean Erneste

Nouveau Marsch (ca. 1800)
222-12
MS BRD:B (Mus.Ms.2337)
Carries the note, 'Marchand de Musique a Lewin.'

Boser, ?

Partia in C, Nr. 1 (1768)
2001-02, 2 talia
MS DDR:Z (Mus.VI, 1)

Partia in G, Nr. 2 (1768)
2001-02, 2 talia
MS DDR:Z (Mus.VI, 2)

Partia in C, Nr. 3 (1768)
2001-02, 2 talia
MS DDR:Z (Mus.VI, 1/3)

Partia in F, Nr. 5 (1768)
2001-02, 2 talia
MS DDR:Z (Mus.VI, 1/4)

Partia in G, Nr. 6 (1768)
2001-02, 2 talia
MS DDR:Z (Mus.VI, 1/5)

Partia in C, Nr. 7 (1768)
2001-02, 2 talia
MS DDR:Z (Mus.VI, 1/6)

Partia in F, Nr. 8 (1768)
2001-02, 2 talia
MS DDR:Z (Mus.VI, 1/7)
Eitner reported finding two more works in this collection which are apparently now lost.

Braun, Johann (1753–1795)

Harmoniestücke
EP (Berlin, Hummel, 1792) [cited in G2]

Brösel, ?

Parade a 5 (ca. 1780)
202-1
MS BRD:DS (Mus.Ms.1223/1)

Parade a 7 (ca. 1780)
203-1
MS BRD:DS (Mus.Ms.1223/2)

Parade a 5
202-1
MS BRD:DS (Mus.Ms.1223/24)

Bucholtz, Johann Gottfried (d. 1800?)

(3) *Partie* (1766)
202-02
MS CS:KRa (IV.B.198)

Bühler, Franz (1760–1824)

Veni creator spiritus
Four voices, 1021-02
MS (autograph) BRD:Mbs (Mus.Ms.3205)

Buschmann, ?

Parthia in E♭
22-02
MS BRD:Rtt (Buschmann 1)

Partita in E♭ (ca. 1760)
22-02
MS BRD:Rtt (Buschmann 2)

Buttstett, Franz (1735–1814)

Quintet (1793)
22-01, viola (?)

(12) 'Pieces for Wind Instruments'
(12) *Choral variations*
1010-001, cornett, organ
MS [lost, these works are cited in Grove, III, 524]

Cannabich, Johann Christian (1731–1798)

The Installation Slow March (for the 3rd Regiment of Guards)
EP (London?); GB:Lcm, GB:Lcs

Celestino, Eligio (1739–1812)

[title unknown]
201-12
MS DDR:SWl (Celestino.4)

Cramer, Wilhelm (1746–1799)

Rondo (ca. 1790)
222-02
MS BRD:Rtt (Cramer 1)

Croes, Henri-Joseph (1758–1842)

Andantino
1222-02, 2 viola (?), string bass
MS BRD:Rtt (Sammelband 32, Nr. 2)

Andantino and Allegro
1242-121, serpent, 2 viola (?),
MS BRD:Rtt (Sammelband 18, Nr. 39)

Divertimento in B♭
202-22, basse
MS BRD:Rtt (H.de.Croes 11)

Divertimento, 20 movements
20-22
MS BRD:Rtt (Inc.IVa.26/II)

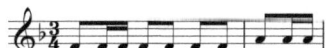

Divertimento, 12 movements
20-22
MS BRD:Rtt (Inc.IVa/26/I)

Divertimento
22-24, 2 viola (?), string bass
MS BRD:Rtt (H.de.Croes 18)

Douze moreceaux
22-02, 2 viola (?), string bass
MS BRD:Rtt (H.de.Croes 9)

Douze Marceaux ('comp. a Tischingen, 1788')
20-22
MS BRD:Rtt (H.de.Croes 7)

Partita in E♭, 12 movements
20-22
MS BRD:Rtt (H.de.Croes 1)

Partita in E♭, 12 movements
20-22
MS BRD:Rtt (H.de.Croes 2)

Partita in E♭, 12 movements
20-22
MS BRD:Rtt (H.de.Croes 3)

Partita in E♭, 12 movements
20-22
MS BRD:Rtt (H.de.Croes 4)

Partita in E♭, 12 movements
20-22
MS BRD:Rtt (H.de.Croes 5)

Partita in E♭, 14 movements
20-22
MS BRD:Rtt (H.de.Croes 6)

Partita in B♭, 12 movements
22-02, 2 viola (?), string bass
MS BRD:Rtt (H.de.Croes 10)

Partita in E♭, 12 movements
22-24, 2 viola (?), string bass
MS BRD:Rtt (H.de.Croes 12)

Partita in E♭, 10 movements
22-24, 2 viola (?), string bass
MS BRD:Rtt (H.de.Croes 13)

Partita in E♭, 9 movements
22-02, 2 viola (?), string bass
MS BRD:Rtt (H.de.Croes 15)

Partita in E♭
22-02, 2 viola (?), string bass
MS BRD:Rtt (H.de.Croes 17)

Partita in E♭
22-22, timpani
MS BRD:Rtt (H.de.Croes 23)

Partita in B♭, 12 movements
22-02, 2 viola (?), string bass
MS BRD:Rtt (H.de.Croes 33)

Partita in B♭, 12 movements
22-02, 2 viola (?), string bass
MS BRD:Rtt (H.de.Croes 34)

Partita in B♭, 11 movements
22-02, 2 viola (?), string bass
MS BRD:Rtt (H.de.Croes 35)

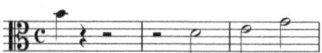

Partita in B♭
22-02, 2 viola (?), string bass
MS BRD:Rtt (H.de.Croes 36)

Partita in E♭, 10 movements
222-04, 2 viola (?), string bass
MS BRD:Rtt (H.de.Croes 37)

Partita in E♭, 6 movements
1242-121, serpent, 2 viola (?)
MS BRD:Rtt (Sammelband 18, Nr. 19ff)

Partita in F
1242-121, serpent, 2 viola (?)
MS BRD:Rtt (Sammelband 18, Nr. 37ff)

Romance
1242-121, serpent, 2 viola (?),
MS BRD:Rtt (Sammelband 18, Nr. 38)

Danzi, Franz (1763–1826)

Pot-pourri, op. 45
1202-02
EP (?); BRD:HEms

Sestetto
22-02
MS BRD:Rtt (Danzi 6)
MP (Sikorski, 1965)

Deiselbach, ?

Parthia in B♭
222-02
MS BRD:F (Mus.Hs.1656)

Diez, Johann (1711–1793)

Lauda Sion
SATB, -4, timpani, organ
MS BRD:WS (MS.171) [version for SATB, -601, flügelhorn, bombard, timpani, organ]

Dittersdorf, Karl ditters von (1739–1799)

(2) *Partitta* in D
202-02
MS CS:Pnm (XXII.B.250, 254)

(2) *Partitta* in C
202-02
MS CS:Pnm (XXII.B.251, 252)

Partitta in G
202-02
MS CS:Pnm (XXII.B.249)

Partitta in E♭
202-02
MS CS:Pnm (XXII.B.253)

(2) *Partia* in A
202-02
MS CS:Pnm (XXII.B.258, 259)

Partia in G
202-02
MS CS:Pnm (XXII.B.260)

Partitta in F
202-02
MS CS:Pnm (XXII.B.264) [incomplete]

Partia in E♭
201-02
MS CS:Pnm (XXII.B.261)

(2) *Parthia* in D
201-02
MS CS:Pnm (XXII.B.187, 262)

Parthia in G
201-02
MS CS:Pnm (XXII.B.263)

(4) *Partitta* in D
201-02
MS CS:Pnm (XXII.B.243, 245, 247, 257)

GERMANY 311

(2) *Partitta* in B♭
201-02
MS CS:Pnm (XXII.B.244, 248)

(2) *Partitta* in F
201-02
MS CS:Pnm (XXII.B.246, 241)

Partitta in E♭
201-02
MS CS:Pnm (XXII.B.255)

Partitta in C
201-02
MS CS:Pnm (XXII.B.240)

Partitta in B♭ ('Nr. 3')
1-02, 2 English horns
MS CS:Pnm (XXII.B.242)

Partitta in C
1201-02
MS CS:Pnm (XXII.B.256)

Partita in B♭
201-02
MS CS:Pnm (XXXII.C.103)

Partitta in B♭
201-02
MS CS:Pnm (XXXII.B.145)

Partita in F
201-02
MS CS:Pnm (XXXII.B.139)

Parthia in D
201-02
MS CS:Pnm (XLII.B.187)

Partitta in G
202-02
MS CS:Pnm (XXXII.B.141)

Partitta in G
202-02
MS CS:Pnm (XXXII.B.142)

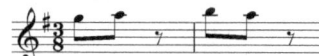

Partita in G
202-02
MS CS:Pnm (XXXII.B.140)

Partitta in C
202-02
MS CS:Pnm (XXXII.B.147)

Partitta in E♭
201-02
MS CS:Pnm (XXXII.B.146)

Cassatio
4000-
MS CS:Pnm (XLII.D.8)

(2) *Partitas*
202-02
MS A:K

Divertimento
222-
MS A:Wgm (VIII 8871)
MP (Sikorski, 1954) [for 221-]

(12) *Parth.*
22-02
MS (Advertized in Traeg's Catalog, Vienna, 1799)

(7) *Partite*
202-02
MS DDR:Bds (Hausbibl., Nr. 335)

(3) *Partite*
Nr. 1:1201-02
Nr. 2:402-22
Nr. 3:2202-22, timpani
MS DDR:Bds (Hausbibl., Nr. 336)

(2) *Parthien*
2221-02
MS DDR:Bds [cited by M]

Partia in C
201-02
MS DDR:HER (Mus.C.13=1)
Carries a note suggesting flute as an option for oboe 1 and violin as an option for oboe 2!

Parthia in B♭
201-02
MS DDR:Dlb [cited by SJK]

Parthia in B♭
201-02
MS DDR:LEm (Mus.3411.P.5)

Partita in E♭, 5 movements (ca. 1770)
202-02
MS BRD:Rtt (Sammelband 8, 53-57), [for 21-02] BRD:Rtt (Dittersdorf 39) [for 22-02, 2 violas (?), in 12 movements], BRD:DO (Mus.Ms.332) [as 'Parthie']

Parthia
222-02
MS BRD:Mbs (Mus.Ms.1723); US:DW (255)

Partita in D
202-02
MS GB:Lbm (R.M.21.a.13.[2])
MP (Musica Rara, 1958)

(12) *kleine Stücke*
22-02
MS BRD:Rtt [cited by SJK]

Notturno
4000-
MS DK:Kk (Giedde Coll., Mus.6503.1860 [IV, 3])
MP (Schott, 1969)

Donninger, Ferdinand (1716–1781)

Partita in B♭, 10 movements
22-02, 2 violas (?)
MS BRD:Rtt (Donninger 18)

Döring, Johann Friedrich (1766–1840)

Des Jahres erster Morgen Lied zum Neujahrstag
SATB, -204, timpani, organ
MS BRD:BNu (MS.98)

Drobisch, ?

(6) *Angloises neuves*
22-22, clavicembalo
MS DDR:SWl (MS.1704)

Droste-Hülshoff de Vischering, Max von

(16) *Dances* (menuets, allemandes, country dances, cottillion)
2020-12, timpani [some dances the flutes double on clarinet, oboe, and piccolo]
MS BRD:Rheda (MS.178)

Das Hallelujah von Pfeffel
Four soloists, chorus, 22-021
EP (Berlin, Logier); BRD:Mbs; NL:At

Druot, ?

Partita in B♭
22-02, 2 violas (?), string bass
MS BRD:Rtt (Druot 1)

Eberwein, Christian (1750–1810)

Musique d'harmonie
(4) *Partien*
2112-02
MS BRD:DS [cited in MGG and Hellyer]

Ebell, H.

Partita
222-02
MS PL:Wbu (Ka. 4, 5, 6)

Ehmann, ?

Marsch
42-12, 2 piccolos, serpent
MS DDR:Bds (Hausbibl., Nr. 98a)

Eichner, Ernest (1740–1777)

Divertissement
222-02
MS GB:Lbm (R.M.21.d.4.Nr. 10); US:DW (333)

Divertissement
222-02
EP (Paris, Mme Bérault); BRD:MÜu

(2) *Divertissement*
22-02 [cited in MGG]

Divertimento Militiare
21-02 _
EP (Advertized in Goetz's Catalog, Mannheim and Frankenthal)
  [cited in Grove, VI, 81]

Divertimento
222-02
MS BRD:BÜu (E-Ich-70)

(Divertimento) 'Delia'
222-02
EP (Dublin, Rhames) [cited in MGG]

Parthia
222-02
EP (Advertized in Cramer's *Magazin der Musik* of 1783)

Eisner, Carl

Sextett, Nr. 2
1111-02, basset horn
MS (autograph) DDR:Dlb [cited in SJK]

Ernst, François (fl. 1786)

Harmoniemusik [cited in G2]

Eschstruth, Hans von (1756–1792)

(12) *Marches*, op. 4
212-02, bass continuo
EP (Advertized in Cramer's *Magazin der Musik* of 1783)

Feldmayr, Georg (1757–1818)

Partita in F (ca. 1790)
201-02, viola (?)
MS BRD:DO (Mus.Ms.419)

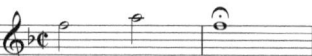

Partita in G (ca. 1785)
2212-02, string bass
MS BRD:HR (III.4.1/2.40.472)

Partita in F (1786)
2122-03, string bass
MS BRD:HR (III.4.1/2.40.473)

Partita in F, 10 movements
201-02, viola (?)
MS (autograph) BRD:HR (III.4.1/2.40.475)
MS (autograph, fifth movemnt); BRD:HR (III.4.1/2.40.478)
MS BRD:DO (Mus.Ms.420)

Parthia Concerto
201-02, viola (?)
MS BRD:BR (III.4.1/2.40.476)
MS BRD:DO (Mus.Ms.421) [as 'parthia concertante']

Partita in D ('nel mese d'April, 1790')
2222-03, string bass
MS (autograph) BRD:BR (III.4.1/2.40.479)
MS BRD:BR (III.4.1/2.40.589)

Partita in E♭ (ca. 1795), 18 movements
22-02
MS (autograph) BRD:BR (III.4.1/2.40.480)

Partita in F
2122-03, string bass
MS (autograph) BRD:HR (III.4.1/2.40.481)

Partita in F
2222-03, viola (?)
MS (autograph) BRD:BR (III.4.1/2.40.502)
MS BRD:HR (III.4.1/2.40.595)

Partita in F (1798), 8 movements
202-02, 2 violas (?), string bass
MS BRD:BR (III.4.1/2.20.584)

Partita in F (ca. 1778)
2222-03, string bass
MS (autograph) BRD:BR (III.4.1/2.20.585)

Partita in F (ca. 1785)
201-02, viola (?)
MS BRD:BR (III.4.1/2.20.586)

Partita in F (ca. 1788)
2222-03, string bass
MS (autograph) BRD:BR (III.4.1/2.20.587)

Partita in D (1797)
1212-13, string bass
MS (autograph) BRD:BR (III.4.1/2.20.588)

Parthia in G
2202-03, string bass
MS BRD:BR (III.4.1/2.20.590) [cited in SJK]

Partita in D (1790)
2222-02
MS BRD:BR (III.4.1/2.20.591)

Partita in G (ca. 1786)
2202-03, string bass
MS (autograph) BRD:BR (III.4.1/2.20.592)

Partita in F
2122-03, string bass
MS (autograph) BRD:BR (III.4.1/2.20.593)

Partita in D (1794)
2222-12, string bass, timpani
MS BRD:BR (III.4.1/2.20.594)

Partita in D (1795)
1212-13, cello
MS (autograph) BRD:BR (III.4.1/2.20.596)

(4) *Partien*
201-02, viola (?)
MS BRD:DO [may be lost]

Fiala, Josef (ca. 1754–1816)

Partia
Four winds
MS A:Wgm [cited by SJK]

Parthia in E♭
1-02, 2 talie
MS CS:Pnm (XLII.E.48)

Partthia in E♭
1-02, 2 talie
MS CS:Pnm (XLII.E.52)

Parthia in G
202-02
MS CS:Pnm (XXXII.A.100)

Divertimento in F
202-02
MS CS:Pnm (XLII.E.249)

Partita
201-02
MS CS:Pnm [copy in BRD:DO (Mus.445), according to SJK]

Divertimento in E♭ ('Nr. 1,' ca. 1780)
22-03, 2 English horns
MS BRD:DO (Mus.Ms.427)

Divertimento in E♭ ('Nr .1 ,' ca. 1780)
21-03, 2 English horns
MS BRD:DO (Mus.Ms.428)

Divertimento in E♭ ('Nr.3,' ca. 1780)
2-03, 2 English horns
MS BRD:DO (Mus.Ms.429)

Divertimento in B♭ ('Nr.2')
21-02, 2 English horns
MS BRD:DO (Mus.Ms.430)

Divertimento in E♭ ('Nr. 3')
21-02, 2 English horns
MS BRD:DO (Mus.Ms.431)

Divertimento in E♭ ('Nr. 11,' 1780)
2-03, 2 English horns
MS BRD:DO (Mus.Ms.432)

Divertimento in F
202-02
MS BRD:DO (Mus.Ms.433)

Divertimento in D ('Nr.4')
221-02
MS BRD:DO (Mus.Ms.434)

Divertimento in B♭ ('Nr. 6')
21-02, 2 English horns
MS BRD:DO (Mus.Ms.435)

Divertimento in G
202-02
MS BRD:DO (Mus.Ms.436)

Divertimento ('Nr .6')
221-02
MS BRD:DO (Mus.Ms.437)

Divertimento ('Nr .6')
202-02
MS BRD:DO (Mus.Ms.438)

Divertimento in B♭ ('Nr. 6')
21-02, 2 English horns
MS BRD:DO (Mus.Ms.439)

Partita in E♭
222-03
MS BRD:DO (Mus.Ms.440)

Partita in E♭
21-03, 2 talie
MS BRD:DO (Mus.Ms.441)

Partita in E♭
21-02, 2 English horns
MS BRD:DO (Mus.Ms.442)

Partita in F
2202-02
MS BRD:DO (Mus.Ms.443)
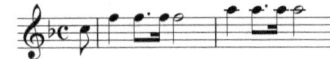

GERMANY 319

Partita in G
2202-02
MS BRD:DO (Mus.Ms.444)

(3) *Partitas*
1-02, 2 English horns
MS BRD:DO (Mus.Ms.447, 448, 449) [cited by Hellyer]

Divertimento in A
222-02
MS BRD:DO (Mus.Ms.451) [missing oboe 1 and bassoon 2]

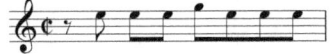

Divertimento
1-02, English horn
MS (Advertized in Traeg's Catalog, Vienna, 1799)

Fischer, Heinrich Wilh.

Trauer Marsch
Harmoniemusik
MS DDR:SWl (MS.1870)

Fischer, Johann Christian (1733–1800)

Triumphmarsche
222-02, Trommel, Triangel, Becken
MS DDR:Bds (Hausbibl., Nr. 99)

Fischer, J.

Partita in E♭ (ca. 1780), 13 movements
22-02, 2 violas (?), string bass
MS BRD:Rtt (Fischer 9)
MS BRD:Rtt (Sammelband 8, 43–47) [dated 1770, in 5 movements, for 21-02]

Partita in E♭
21-02
MS BRD:Rtt (Sammelband 8, 70–77)

Partita in E♭
21-02
MS BRD:Rtt (Sammelband 8, 13–16)

[Tischer]

Partita in E♭
21-02
MS BRD:Rtt (Sammelband 8, 95–99)

[Ficher]

Partita in E♭
21-02
MS BRD:Rtt (Sammelband 8, 82–86)

Forstmeyer, Ehrenfried Andreas (1730–1787)

(2) *Partitas*
21-02
MS BRD:DO (Mus.Ms.472)

(2) *Parthien*
21-02
MS BRD:DO (Mus.Ms.473,474) [cited by Hellyer]

Fränzl, Ignaz (1736–1811)

Partia
222-02
MS BRD:DS [cited by SJK]

Frederick II (1712–1786, 'the Great')

Hohenfriedberger Marsch
Mollwitzer Marsch
Military band [cited by V]

Fricke, Elias Christian, Editor

Neue Sammlung Englischer Tänze
2200-22, timpani
EP (Lübeck, Iversen, 1776); GB:Lbm; DDR:SWl

Frontzel, ?

Parthia
222-02
EP (Advertized in Cramer's *Magazin der Musik*, 1783)

Gleissner, Franz (1759–1818)

Journal de Musique militaire
Eight-part *Harmoniemusik*
EP (Munich, Götz); BRD:MÜu

Missa
Voices and winds
MS BRD:DO [may be lost]

(6) *Pièces d'harmonie*
1021-02
EP (Offenbach, André, Nr. 3890); BRD:OF

Gloger, ?

Anweisung für Tamboure und Pfiefer ('nach Noten zu erlernen')
MS DDR:Bds (Hausbibl., Nr. 251)

Göller, ?

Partita in E♭, 12 movements
MS BRD:DO (Mus.Ms.542) [the BRD:DO catalog of 1804 lists two such works]

Göttling, ?

(6) *Harmoniestücke*
122-02
MS BRD:Bds [cited by Hellyer]

Graaf, C. E.

Die Schlacht bei Austerlitz
Turkische Musik
MS DDR:Bds (Hausbibl., Nr. 312)

Gräfe, Johann Friedrich (1711–1787)

Marsch
Winds [cited in Grove, VII, 613]

Grenser, Johann Friedrich (1758–1794)

Partita, Nr. 1
21-02
MS (score) DK:Kk (Mu.7410.0831)

Partita, Nr. 2da
21-02
MS (score) DK:Kk (Mu.7410.0832)

Partita, Nr. 3tia
21-02
MS (score) DK:Kk (Mu.7410.0833)

Partita, Nr. 4ta
21-02
MS (score) DK:Kk (Mu.7410.0834)

Partita, Nr. 5
21-02
MS (score) DK:Kk (Mu.7410.0835)

Partita, Nr. 6
21-02
MS (score) DK:Kk (Mu.7410.0836)
Another copy, in score, of these six works made by F.
   Keyper ('Contra Bassista Amico suo') can be found in
   DK:Kk (Mu.6506.1833).

Parthia (ca. 1800)
Eight-part *Harmoniemusik*
MS DDR:Z (Mus.Ms.500) [only 12-02 is extant]

Gretsch, Johann Konrad (1710–177)

Partita in E♭
21-02
MS BRD:Rtt (Inc.IVa/31/I, Nr. 7, [29–35])

Partita in E♭
21-02
MS BRD:Rtt (Inc.IVa/31/I, Nr. 15, [83–89])

Gross, ?

Echo, 5 movements (ca. 1770)
202-1, with echo oboe
MS BRD:DS (Mus.Ms. 1223/23)

Gruner, Nathanel Gottfried (1732–1792)

Herr, wie du willst
Chorus, 22-02
MS [cited by MGG]

Günther, Carl Friedrich

Sammlung von Kriegs-Märschen der Churfürstlich Sachsischen Armee
Piano score
EP (Leipzig); A:Wn; DDR:Hau

(20) *Märsche der Königlich Preussischen Armee*
Piano score
EP (Leipzig); A:Wgm; GB:Lbm

(12) *Märsche*
Ten-part military band
MS DDR:Bds (Hausbibl., Nr. 460)

GERMANY 323

Hammer, Carl Anton

Partita in E♭ (ca. 1800)
121-02
MS BRD:ZL
The second movement carries a note, 'da Haydn.'

Harbordt, Gottfried (1768–1837)

Trauer Marsch
21-02, 2 timpani 'con sordini'
MS BRD:DS (Mus.518)

Hasse, ?, perhaps Johann Adolph (1699–1783)

Prussian Army March Nr. 68
Military band
MS DDR:Bds (Hausbibl., Nr. 11) [lost]

Geschwindmärsche ('Volhynischen Leib-Garde-Regiments')
Military band
MS (score) DDR:Bds (Hausbibl., Nr. 452)

Hauff, Wilhelm Gottlieb

(6) *Sextuers* (ca. 1776–1777)
22-02
MS BRD:F (Mus.Hs.1567)

Häusler, Ernst (1761–1837)

National Marche e Aria Francois Saira
2222-22, piccolo, percussion
MS BRD:HR (III.4.1/2.20.360)

(2) *Kirchencantaten*
One for *Harmoniemusik*; one for orchestra
MS (score) BRD:As [cited by Eitner]

(6) *Notturni*
2-02
EP (Leipzig, Breitkopf & Härtel); DDR:SWl (MS.2524)

Der Tag beginnt
Four singers, wind instruments
MS [cited by MGG]

Fantasie
Singer, piano, 20-02
MS [cited by MGG]

Kirchen-Musik (1799)
SATB, 101-02, cello
MS (autograph) BRD:Mbs

Hennig, ?

(3) *Märsche für Gardehautboisten* ('89th Regiment')
Military band
MS DDR:SWl (MS.2674)

Hertel, Johann Wilhelm (1727–1789)

(6) *Märsche*
Wind instruments
MS (score) DDR:SWl [cited by Grove, VIII, 524 and Eitner]

Herzogin von Braunschweig (Philippine Charlotte, sister to Frederick the Great)

Regiments-Marsch
222-1
MS DDR:Bds (Hausbibl., Nr. 43)

Marsch (1751)
202-1
MS DDR:Bds (Hausbibl., Nr. 39)

Hiller, Johann Adam (1728–1804)

Herr Gott dich loben mir
SATB, trumpets, trombones, timpani
EP (Leipzig, Muller, 1790); DDR:LEm

Himmel, Friedrich Heinrich (1765–1814)

Marches, op. 34
22-2, 2 'sept-flutes,' serpent, tambour
EP (Leipzig, Kühnel); A:Wgm

Marsch vom 2. Bataillon Garde
221-1
MS DDR:Bds (Hausbibl., Nr. 56) [lost]

Terzetto
SST, wind instruments, harmonika
EP (Leipzig, Kühnel)

Trauer-Cantate (for the funeral of Friedrich Wilhelm II)
'Quartetto,' for SSTB, 22-2, 3 timpani
'Chorale,' for 2202-224, timpani
EP (Dresden) US:DW (175)

Hummel, Johann Barnard

(2) Militarmärsche
222-22
MS DDR:Bds (Hausbibl., Nr. 108)

Hoffmeister, Franz Anton (1754–1812)

Parthia
222-02
MS A:Wgm (VIII 39983)

Parthia ('Nr. VI')
222-02
MS A:Wgm (VIII 39982)

Variations
22-02
MS A:Wgm
EP (Leipzig, Hoffmeister, Nr. 151); A:Wgm (VIII 9268)

Parthia
222-02
MS (Advertized in Traeg's Catalog, Vienna, 1799)

Divertimento
222-02
MS (Advertized in Traeg's Catalog, Vienna, 1799)

(2) Echo Parthia
22-02
MS (Advertized in Traeg's Catalog, Vienna, 1799)

(3) Parthia
11-01, with 'echo' ensemble of 11-01
MS CS:Pnm [cited by SJK]

Parthia
22-02
MS CS:Pnm (XLII.F.36, Nr. 12)

Parthia, Nr. 1
22-02
MS CS:Pnm (XLI.B.119)

Parthia, Nr. 2
22-02
MS CS:Pnm (XLI.B.118)

Parthia, Nr. 3
22-02
MS CS:Pnm (XLI.B.117)

Parthia, Nr. 1, 3 movements
222-02
MS CS:KRa (IV.B.45)

Parthia, Nr. 2, 4 movements
222-02
MS CS:KRa (IV.B.46)

Parthia, Nr. 3, 3 movements
222-02
MS CS:KRa (IV.B.44)

Parthia in Dis, Nr. V, 3 movements
22-02
MS CS:KRa (IV.B.42); US:DW (370)

Pardia alla Camera, Nr. 8, 3 movements
222-02
MS CS:KRa (IV.B.48)

Pardia, Nr. 13, 4 movements
222-02
MS CS:KRa (IV.B.49)

Pardia alla Camera, Nr. 14, 4 movements
222-02
MS CS:KRa (IV.B.47)

Parthia in Dis, 4 movements
22-02
MS CS:KRa (IV.B.53)

Parthia in Dis, 4 movements
22-02
MS CS:KRa (IV.B.52)

Parthia in Dis, 3 movements
22-02
MS CS:KRa (IV.B.51)

Parthia in Dis, 3 movements
22-02
MS CS:KRa (IV.B.43)

Parthia in D minor, 4 movements
202-02
MS CS:KRa (IV.B.54)

Parthia in E♭ Concertans, 3 movements
22-02
MS CS:KRa (IV.B.50)

GERMANY 327

Harmonie
222-02
EP (Paris); BRD:DS [cited by Eitner]

Partita in B♭
222-02
MS BRD:DO (Mus.Ms.1679, as 'Nr. 7' under '6 Partitas by Rosetti')

Partita
22-02
MS BRD:DO (Mus.Ms.767, Nr. 1)

Partita
22-02
MS BRD: (Mus .Ms. 767, Nr. 2)

Partita
22-02
MS BRD:DO (Mus.Ms.767, Nr. 3)

Partita
22-02
MS BRD:DO (Mus.Ms.767, Nr. 4)

Partita
222-02
MS DDR:Bds [cited by Eitner]

Parthia, Nr. 15
222-02
MS DDR:RUl (RH-H.143)

[title unknown]
2022-02
MS DDR:RER (Mus.N.1–15) [here only clarinet 1, flute 2, and horn 1]

Parthie
222-02
MS NL:Ura/mZ (M.A.Zcm 26, Nr. 1)

Parthie
222-02
MS NL:Ura/mZ (M.A.Zcn 26, Nr. 2)

Parthie
222-02
MS NL:Ura/mZ (M.A.Zcn 26, Nr. 3)

Parthie
222-02
MS NL:Ura/mZ (M.A.Zcn 26, Nr. 4)

Parthie
222-02
MS NL:Ura/mZ (M.A.Zcn 26, Nr. 5)

Parthie
222-02
MS NL:Ura/mZ (M.A.Zcn 26, Nr. 6)

Parthia in E♭
222-02
MS PL:WRH [cited in SJK]

Parthia, Nr. 4, in F
-02, 3 basset horns
MS PL:LA (2270)

Parthia, Nr. 5, in F
-02, 3 basset horns
MS PL:LA (2271)

Parthia in E♭
22-02
MS PL:LA (2292)

Parthia in F, Nr. 6
1-02, 3 basset horns
MS PL:LA (2293)

Parthia in E♭
22-02
MS US:WS [cited by SJK]

Harmonie
222-02
EP (London, Broderip & Wilkinson, ca. 1800);
    GB:Lbm (H.114/8)

Parthia
Harmoniemusik
MS A:Ee

Holler, Augustin (1745–1814)

Divertimento
21-22, 2 piccolos, timpani

MS BRD:Mbs (Mus.Ms.73S6)

Parthia in F
2020-02, viola (?), string bass
MS BRD:Mbs (Mus.Ms.7437)

(12) *Avertissementes* (Allemandes)
2021-02, percussion
MS BRD:Mbs (Mus.Ms.7356)

Holzbauer, Ignaz (1711–1783)

Divertimento pro cassatione, 6 movements
2-02
MS CS:KRa (IV.B.55)

Holzinger, ?

Missa
Voices and winds
MS BRD:DO [may be lost]

Jahn, August Wilhelm Friedrich

Reveille, Vergatterung, Zapfenstreich
2 pfieffen and 2 clar(ini)
MS (score) DDR:SWl (MS. 2950)

Jetschmann, ?

Parade- und Geschw.-Marsch
222-12
MS DDR:Bds (Hausbibl., Nr. 53)

Kaffka, Wilhelm (1751–1806)

Divertimento in E♭
22-02, 2 violas (?), string bass
MS BRD:Rtt (W. Kaffka 1)

Keil, Johann (?)

Parthia, Nr. 12
222-02, Quart-bassoon
MS DDR:RUl (RH-K.37)

Kirchner, Johann Heinrich (1765–1831)

(4) *Cantatas* ('zu den Rudolstädter Sittenfesten der Jahre 1795-1800')
Chorus and winds [cited in MGG]

Kolb, Stefan (b. 1743)

Divertimento in E♭
22-24, 2 violas (?), string bass
MS BRD:Rtt (Klob 14)

Contradantz (ca. 1780)
22-02, 2 violas (?)
MS BRD:Rtt (Klob 17)

Partita in E♭ (ca. 1770), 4 movements
21-02
MS BRD:Rtt (Sammelband 8, 17–20)
BRD:Rtt (Klob 16) [for 22-02, 2 violas (?), in 12 movements]

Partita in E♭, 13 movements
22-02, 2 violas (?), string bass
MS BRD:Rtt (Klob 19)
A note indicates these movements were taken from
 Haydn symphonies.

Partita in E♭
21-02
MS BRD:Rtt (Sammelband 8, 62–65)

Partita in E♭ (ca. 1790), 12 movements
22-02, 2 violas (?), string bass
MS BRD:Rtt (Klob 4)

Partita in B♭
22-02, 2 violas (?), string bass
MS BRD:Rtt (Klob 3)

Partita in B♭, 10 movements
22-02, 2 violas (?), string bass
MS BRD:Rtt (Kolb 5)

Vaudeville (ca. 1790)
22-24, 2 violas (1), string bass
MS BRD:Rtt (Klob 18)

Koch, Heinrich Christoph (1749–1816)

Choralbuch für die Hofkirche
Harmoniemusik [mentioned in AMZ, 1816, cited in MGG]
(3) *Pas redoubles par Musique militaire*, op. 48
EP (Mainz, Schott); BRD:MZsch

Köhler, Gottlieb Heinrich (1765–1833)

(3) *Parthien*
22-02
EP (Leipzig, Becker, 1798); DDR:Dlb [cited by SJK]

König, M.

Marsch
222-1
MS DDR:Bds (Hausbibl., Nr. 109)

(6) *Halberstädtische Märsche*
122-1
MS DDR:Bds (Hausbibl., Nr. 110)

Kopprasch, Wilhelm (1750–1832)

Serenata in C, Nr. 11
222-22, Quart Fagot, timpani
MS DDR:RUl (RH-K72)

(6) *Sonates*
-223
EP (Leipzig, Peters); BRD:DS [lost in WWII]

Kospoth, Otto (1753–1817)

Parthie
Harmoniemusik
MS CS:Pnm (XLII.F.36, Nr. 1)

Serenata, op. 19
Oboe or flute, 2 bassoons, 2 basset horns, piano or harpsichord
EP (Offenbach, André, 1794) [cited in Grove, X, 215]

Kühnau, Johann Christoph (1735–1805)

Te Deum [ca. 1784] (*'Herr Gott! dich loben wir'*)
Trumpets or cornetts, trombones, organ
MS DDR:Bds [cited in MGG]

Kuntzen, Adolph Karl (1720–1781)

(6) *Märsche*
301-2
MS DDR:SWl (MS.3284)

Marsch
201-12
MS DDR:SWl (MS.3283)

Kunzen, Friedrich Ludwig (1761–1817)

Chorale, 'O Jesu Christ, Guds Salvede' (ca. 1790–1800)
Voice, 222-223
MS (autograph) DK:Kk (Mu.6506.1138)

Kunzer, ?

(6) *Deutsche Tanze*
Harmoniemusik
MS BRD:DO [may be lost]

Kurzweil, Franz

Partita, Nr. 1 in E♭
222-02
MS BRD:DO (Mus.Ms.767)

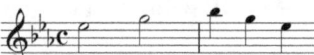

Partita, Nr. 2 in B♭
222-02
MS BRD:DO (Mus.Ms.767)

Partita, Nr. 3 in B♭
222-02
MS BRD:DO (Mus.Ms.767)

Partita, Nr. 4 in E♭
222-02
MS BRD:DO (Mus.Ms.767)

Partita, Nr. 5 in B♭
222-02
MS BRD:DO (Mus.Ms.767)

Partita, Nr. 6 in E♭
222-02
MS BRD:DO (Mus.Ms.767)

Partita, Nr. 7 in B♭
222-02
MS BRD:DO (Mus.Ms.767)

Lehman, Frederick Adolph von

(6) *Marches*, op. 4
'l'instr. a vent' [cited in S]

Liber, Joseph Anton (1732–1809)

Divertimento in E♭
22-24, 2 violas (?), string bass
MS BRD:Rtt (Liber 4)

GERMANY 333

Loewe, Johann Heinrich (b. 1766)

Notturno, op. 5
2001-02, 2 'altos,' basse
EP (Offenbach, André, Nr. 1930); BRD:OF

Loibl, Benedikt Anselm OSB (1766–1822)

Parthia in E♭
22-02
MS BRD:Kbs (Mus.Ms.7511)

Ludwig IX, Landgr. von Ressen-Darmstadt (1719–1790)

(54) *Märsche*
Instrumentation unknown
MS BRD:DS (Ms.Mus.1354 [3 Grenadier-märsche];
    Ms.Mus.1222, Nr. 9–12, 17, 40, 42, 44, 46–52, 58–60, 63, 65,
    70–74; Ms.Mus.1225, Nr. 9–12, 17, 41, 44, 46–52, 58–60, 62,
    63, 67–71, 80; MS.Mus.1223; and Ms.Mus.1224)
According to Eitner, before WWII one could find nearly 90,000
    such marches in BRD:DS.

Martinides, Carlo (1731–1794)

Partita in E♭ (ca. 1770)
21-02
MS BRD:Rtt (Sammelband 8, 25–29)

Maier, L. (fl. 1782)

Parthia in C
222-22, Quart-fagotto, timpani
MS DDR:RUl (RH-M81)

Partia
222-02
MS DDR:Dlb (Mus.3309-P-1)

Main, ?

Sextour, op. 9
22-02
EP (Augsburg, Gombart); DDR:SWl (35058)

Maurer, ?

Variations sur un air Russe
1022-02, string bass
EP (Hofmeister) [cited by Hellyer]

Mauser, ?

(2) Parthia
222-02
MS (Advertized in Cramer's *Magazin der Musik*, 1783)

Meder, Johann Gabriel

(6) Marches
21-02
EP (Berlin, Hummel, Nr. 914, ca. 1795); CS:Pnm

Molke, Graf von

Des Grossen Kurfursten Reitermarsch
Arranged by Lehmann
MS DDR:Bds (Hausbibl., Nr. 18) [lost]

Müller, August Eberhard (1767–1817)

Cantatine zu Familienfesten
Four singers, Chorus, 222-02
EP (Leipzig, Hoffmeister, Nr. 917); A:Wgm; CH:E; BRD:Bhm

Naumann, Johann Gottlieb (1741–1801)

Erster Marsch ('des Regiments von Kalckstein')
22-02
MS DDR:Bds (Hausbibl., Nr. 62)

(2nd) Marsch ('von Kalckstein')
121-02
MS DDR:Bds (Hausbibl., Nr. 63)

(6) Marsche
Wind instruments
MS (autograph) DDR:Bds (Mus.Ms.Auto.J.G.Naumann 13)

Quartetto
SSTT, 2023-02
MS DDR:Bds (Mus.Ms.15956)

Nopitsch, Christoph (1758–1824)

Ariette ('Augsburg, c. 1790')
Seven voices and winds [cited by Grove, XIII, 175]

Pachta, ?

Sinfonia (ca. 1780)
201-02 [cited by Hellyer, quoting Wurzbach's *Biographisches Lexikon*]

Panoitschka, ?

Parthia
22-02
MS BRD:F (Mus.Hs.1559)

Pfeilstücker, Nicolas

(3) *Walzer*
Militarmusik
MS BRD:Mbs [cited by SJK]

Piticchio, ?

Quintet (1779)
201-02
MS DDR:Bds [cited by Hellyer]

Pirch, G. von ('Lieutenant im Regiment, von Graevenitz')

Marsche
222-12
MS BRD:Bds (Hausbibl., Nr. 123)

(6) *Märsche*
222-02
MS BRD:Bds (Hausbibl., Nr. 123a)

Pokorny, F. X. (1729–1794)

Partita in E♭ (ca. 1760)
20-03
MS (autograph) BRD:Rtt (Pokorny 182/7)

Presto Assai in D (ca. 1770)
202-2, timpani
MS (autograph) BRD:Rtt (Pokorny 196)

Reicha, Joseph (1746–1795)

Partita in D (ca. 1784)
2222-02, string bass
MS (autograph) BRD:HR (III.4.1/2.40.496)

Partita in D (ca. 1782)
221-02
MS (autograph) BRD:HR (III.4.1/2.40.495)

Partita in D (ca. 1783)
2222-02
MS (autograph) BRD:HR (III.4.1/2.40.489); US:DW (413)

Partita in D (ca. 1780, 'a fluto solo')
1221-02
MS (autograph) BRD:HR (III.4.1/2.40.492)

Partita in D (ca. 1782)
2222-02, string bass
MS (autograph) BRD:HR (III.4.1/2.40.497), BRD:HR (III.4.1/2.40.477) [under 'Feldmayr']

Partita in D (ca. 1783)
2222-03, string bass
MS (autograph) BRD:HR (III.4.1/2.40.651)

Partita in E♭ (1783)
222-02, string bass
MS (autograph) BRD:HR (III.4.1/2.40.494)

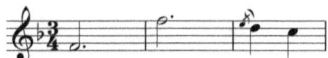

Partita in E♭ (1782)
222-02
MS (autograph) BRD:HR (III.4.1/2.40.491)

Partita in F (ca. 1780)
1221-02
MS (autograph) BRD:HR (III.4.1/2.40.498)

Partita in F
2222-02
MS (autograph) BRD:HR (III.4.1/2.40.570)

Partita in F (1783)
222-03, string bass
MS (autograph) BRD:HR (III.4.1/2.40.490)

Partita in E♭ (1782)
221-02
MS (autograph) BRD:HR (III.4.1/2.40.493)

Reichardt, Johann Friedrich (1752–1814)

Der May: ein Wettgesang (1780)
Two voices, 2203-02 [cited by Grove, XV, 707]

Reichelt, F. G. (d. 1798)

Parthie
22-02 [cited in S]

Rellstab, Johann Carl Friedrich (1759–1813)

(12) *Marsche*
222-1, with -02, timpani ad lib; alternate version for piano
[cited in MGG; lost according to Grove, XV, 732]

Riepel, Josef (1709–1782)

Divertimento in E♭
22-02, 2 violas (?), string bass
MS BRD:Rtt (Riepel 21)

Richter, Anton

Overture
1022-02
MS A:Wgm (VIII 38550)

Sextet
1021-02
MS A:Wgm (VIII 37678)

Serenade
1021-02
MS A:Wgm (VIII 37680)

Ritter, (?Georg, 1748–1808)

(4) *Parthien*
22-02
MS A:Wn (Sm.622)

(12) *Kleine Stücke*
1122-02
MS US:Wc

Roetscher, Sen.

Marsch (with 'Gesang')
4022-22, percussion
MS BRD:Bds (Hausbibl., Nr. 54) [lost]

Marsch
222-02
MS BRD:Bds (Hausbibl., Nr. 126)

Marsch
222-02
MS BRD:Bds (Hausbibl., Nr. 128)

Marsch (1799)
222-1
MS BRD:Bds (Hausbibl., Nr. 129)

Lied am Geburtstage Friedrich Wilhelm III (1806) ['von den Waisen-
   kindern gesungen']
MS BRD:Bds (Hausbibl., Nr. 264) [lost]
The melody is taken from BRD:Bds (Hausbibl., Nr. 54).

Roger, ?

(20) *Divertissements en Harmonie*
21-02
EP (Pleyel); DDR:Dlb [cited by SJK]

Rolle, Christian Carl

Das Herr Gott dich loben wir
-304, timpani, organ
EP (Berlin, Winter, 1765); BRD:Sl; DDR:LEm; F:Pn [organ
   only]; US:Wc

Rong, Wilhelm Ferdinand (fl. ca. 1720)

(6) *Marsche*
2002-02, 2 basset horns
MS BRD:Bds (Hausbibl., Nr. 131)

Marsch (1789)
222-1
MS BRD:Bds (Hausbibl., Nr. 131a)

Rosetti, Franz Anton (1750–1792)

(7) *Partitas* (Kaul II, 2-7, 16)
101-02, 2 English horns
MS A:Wgm (VIII 8538)

Partia in E♭
222-02
MS A:Wgm (VIII 39991); BRD:DO (Mus.Ms.767, Nr. 6,
   under 'Kurzweil')

Partita in E♭
222-02
MS BRD:DO (Mus.Ms.1679, Nr. 1)

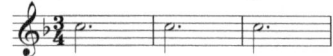

Partita in E♭
222-02
MS BRD:DO (Mus.Ms.1679, Nr. 2)

Partita in E♭
222-02
MS BRD:DO (Mus.Ms.1679, Nr. 3); A:Wgm (VIII 8538, Nr. 6) [for 102-02, 2 English horns]

Partita in E♭
222-02
MS BRD:DO (Mus.Ms.1679, Nr. 4)

Partita in E♭
222-02
MS BRD:DO (Mus.Ms.1679, Nr. 5)

Partita in E♭
222-02
MS BRD:DO (Mus.Ms.1679, Nr. 6)

Partita in E♭ (Kaul I, 35 as 'Sinfonia in E♭')
222-02
MS BRD:DO (Mus.Ms.1597, Nr. 3)
EP (Pleyel and Simrock); BRD:DS, BRD:Brüder-Unität, Herrnhut (Mus.C1:17), BRD:KNh

Septetto [ca. 1780] (Kaul II, 20 Eb), 9 movements
1121-02
MS BRD:DO (Mus.Ms.1664); A:KR (H.38.45) [in 4 movements]
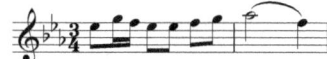

Sextetto [ca. 1780] (Kaul II, 3 Eb)
121-02
MS BRD:DO (Mus.Ms.1676), BRD:DS [lost in WWII], BRD:DO (Mus.Ms.1679, Nr. 6) [for 222-02]; A:Wgm (VIII 8538, Nr. 3) [for 102-02, 2 English horns]

Sextetto [ca. 1780] (Kaul II, 2 Bb)
121-02
MS BRD:DO (Mus.Ms.1657), BRD:DS [lost in WWII]; A:Wgm (VIII 8538, Nr. 5), [for 102-02, 2 English horns]; US:DW (142) [MP]

Sextetto [ca. 1780] (Kaul II, 5 Eb)
121-02
MS BRD:DO (Mus.Ms.1675), BRD:DO (Mus.Ms.1679, Nr. 4) [for 222-02]; A:Wgm (VIII 8538, Nr. 4) [for 102-02, 2 English horns]

Sextetto (Kaul II, 7 Eb)
121-02
MS BRD:DO (Mus.Ms.1669), BRD:Rtt (Schacht 79/1),
 BRD:DO (Mus.Ms.1679, Nr. 5) [for 222-02]; A:Wgm (VIII
 8538, Nr. 4) [for 102-02, 2 English horns]

Partita in F ['1785, mese di Settembre'] (Kaul II, 13 F)
2221-03, string bass
MS (autograph, 'pour la Chasse') BRD:HR (III.4.1/2.40.284),
 BRD:HR (III.4.1/2.40.487), BRD:HR (III.4.1/2.20.597),
 BRD:HR (III.4.1/2.571)

Partita in D [1781] (Kaul II, 8 D)
221-02
MS BRD:HR (III.4.1/2.40.484)

Partita in D (Kaul II, 9 D)
221-02
MS BRD:HR (III.4.1/2.40.485)

Partita in D (Kaul II, 10 D)
221-02
MS BRD:HR (III.4.1/2.40.486)
MP (Kneusslin, 1954) US:DW (141)

Partita in F (Kaul II, 16 F)
301-02, string bass
MS BRD:HR (III.4.1/2.40.488), BRD:DO (Mus.Ms.1679, Nr.
 1) [for 222-02]; A:Wgm (VIII 8538, Nr. 2) [for 102-02, 2
 English horns]; US:DW (140) [MP]

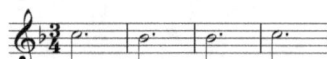

Partita in F (Kaul II, 15 F)
2221-03, string bass
MS BRD:HR (III.4.1/2.20.598)

Partita in F (Kaul II, 12 F)
2222-02
MS BRD:HR (III.4.1/2.20.599)
MP (G. Schirmer, 1964)

Partita in D (Kaul II, 11 D)
2221-02, string bass
MS ('mese di febraro 1784') BRD:HR (III.4.1/2.20.600);
 US:DW (374)

Partita in D (Kaul II, 14 D)
2212-02, string bass
MS BRD:HR (III.4.1/2.20.601)

Parthia (Kaul II, 6 Eb, for '2 oboes concertante,' with 22-02)
222-02
MS (autograph) BRD:Mbs (Mus.Ms.1723); A:Wgm (VIII 8538,
 Nr. 7); BRD:DO (Mus.Ms.1679, Nr. 2)

Divertimento
Nine winds
MS BRD:Mbs [cited in Grove, XVI, 207]

Harmonie
222-02
MS DDR:HER (N.1=8) [here only 21- extant]
EP (Paris, Pleyel, Nr. 102); DDR:HER (Mus.C.1=17)

Parthia in B♭
222-02
MS DDR:RUL (RB.R.93); BRD:DO (Mus.Ms.767, Nr. 7, under 'Hoffmeister')

Parthia (Kaul II, 22 Eb)
21-02
MS CS:Pnm (XIV.E.58); BRD:DO (Mus.Ms.1830, under 'Sperger')

Partita
201-02, 2 basset horns, 2 violas, string bass
MS GB:Lbm (RK 21.d.3, Vol. 2)

Parthia in B♭ (not in Kaul)
21-02
MS GB:Lbbc [cited by SJK]

Parthia, Nr. 12 (not in Kaul)
2-22
MS PL:WRu [cited in SJK]

Partitta (not in Kaul)
21-02
MS US:WS [bassoon only]

Tafel-Musik
Solo oboe, 21-02
MS BRD:Bds (Hatlsbibl., Nr. 338) [lost]

Parthia
Solo oboe or flute, 21-02
MS (Advertized in Traeg's Catalog, Vienna, 1799)

(6) *Sonatas*
2022-02 [cited by V]

Quintetto (Kaul II, 17 Eb)
1111-, taille
MS BRD:HR (III.4.1/2.40.285); BRD:Mbs
EP (Breitkopf & Härtel, Catalog of 1782–1784, Supplement 15)
MP (Kneusslin, 1961; Presser, 1962)
Hellyer calls this the earliest known work for five single winds.

(2) *Partitas* (and some transcribed opera arias for the wedding of Princess Briederike to the Duke of York, in Berlin, September 29, 1791)
222-02 [lost, cited by Hellyer]

Rudolph, Anton (b. 1742)

Partita in F (ca. 1780)
1-02, 2 basset horns, 2 violas (?), string bass
MS BRD:Rtt (Rudolph 1)

Partita in D (1779)
20-22
MS (autograph) BRD:Rtt (Rudolph 2)

Partita in E♭
20-22
MS BRD:Rtt (Rudolph 3) [only 2 clarini parts extant]

Partita in E♭ ('Nr. 8')
21-02
MS BRD:Rtt (Inc.IVa/31/I, Nr. 36–40)

Partita in E♭ ('Nr. 16, in Echo')
21-02
MS BRD:Rtt (Inc.IVa/31/I, Nr. 90–95)

Partita
'Janitscharmusik'
MS DDR:Bds (Hausbibl., Nr. 339)

Sacher, Josef

Feldpartie (ca. 1770)
22-02
MS BRD:F (Mus.Hs. 1566)
MP (Cologne, Hans Gerig)

Schacht, Theodor von (1748–1823)

Allemande & (11) Variations
22-24, 2 violas (?), string bass
MS (autograph) BRD:Rtt (Schacht 86/II); BRD:Rtt (Inc. IVa/21/I) [with additional movements]

(2) *Anglaises Favorites* (1793)
22-24, 2 violas (1), string bass
MS BRD:Rtt (Schacht 87/II)

Harmonie (ca. 1790), 18 movements
121-02
MS (autograph) BRD:Rtt (Schacht 72)

(6) *Notturni*
STTB, 222-02, cembalo
EP (no city or date known); DDR:Bd, DDR:Dlb; H:Bn

Partita in D (1794)
2242-12, Tamburo Turco, Tamburo, Tamburino, triangle, Piatti 'Turchi'
MS BRD:Rtt (Schacht 77)

Partita in C, 12 movements
22-24, 2 violas (?), string bass
MS BRD:Rtt (Schacht 162)

Partita in E♭ (ca. 1790)
121-02
MS (autograph) BRD:Rtt (Schacht 79/I)

Partita in E♭ (ca. 1790), 12 movements
22-24, 2 violas (?), string bass
MS BRD:Rtt (Schacht 163)

Partita in G (1789), 12 movements
22-02, 2 English horns
MS (autograph) BRD:Rtt (Schacht 74)

Partita in B♭, 13 movements
22-02, 2 violas (?), string bass
MS BRD:Rtt (Schacht 161)

Partitta d'Armonica (ca. 1790), 12 movements
222-02
MS (autograph) BRD:Rtt (Schacht 73/II)

Partita in B♭, 12 movements
22-02, 2 violas (?), string bass
MS BRD:Rtt (Schacht 160)

Partita in F, 13 movements
22-24, 2 violas (1), string bass
MS (autograph) BRD:Rtt (Schacht 80/III)

Theme and (48) Variations
22-22, 2 violas (?), string bass
MS BRD:Rtt (Schacht 84) [unfinished]

Theme and (2) Variations
22-02, 2 violas (?), string bass
MS BRD:Rtt (Schacht 79/II)

Turco
1041-12, triangle, tschinelli, tamburo
MS (autograph) BRD:Rtt (Schacht 78)

Scheinpflug, Christian (1722–1770)

(16) *Partiten*
MS DDR:RUl (S.151-166) [cited in MGG, where the instrumentation is given as 'Bläser u. Str.']

Schmidt, ?

Parthia
21-02
MS [cited by Hellyer]

Schmitt, ?

Scherzo
1022-02
EP (Offenbach, André) [cited by Hellyer]

Schneider, ?

(12) *Harmonien*
2022-02
MS DDR:Bds [cited by Hellyer]

(6) *Pièces d'harmonie*
EP (Gombart) [cited by Hellyer]

Schmittbaur, Joseph Aloys (1718–1809)

Divertimento ('per usirsi alla Tavola')
2202-02, 2 piccolos
MS BRD:KA (MS.891)

Divertimento
232-02
MS DDR:SWl [cited by M]

Divertimento in C
222-12
MS DDR:SWl [cited by Eitner]

(3) *Divertimentos militaires*
22-02 and 21-02
MS [cited by Hellyer]

Partita in F (ca. 1770)
21-02
MS BRD:RH (Mus.Ms.701)

Partita
22-02
MS BRD:MÜu [here only clarinet 1, incomplete]

Schoeps,?

Partiten
201-02
MS PL:Wbu (Ka 17)

Schön, ?

Parthia
201-02
MS CR:E [cited by Eitner]

Parthia
201-02
MS DDR:Bds [cited by Hellyer]

Schubert, Joseph (1757–1837)

Partion
Eleven-part *Harmoniemusik*
(many) *Harmonie-Suiten*
Nine-part *Harmoniemusik* [these cited in G2]

Schwegler, Johann David

(4) *Quatuors*
2000-02
EP (Leipzig, Breitkopf & Härtel, Nr. 347) S:Skma

Sigl, Georg

Deutsche Messe in C
Three voices, 201-02, organ
MS BRD:BB (MS.151)

Partita in E♭ (ca. 1780)
22-02
MS (autograph) BRD:Rtt (Sigl 1)

Partita in B♭
22-02
MS BRD:Rtt (Sigl 2)

Partita in B♭
22-02
MS BRD:Rtt (Sigl 3)

Partita in E♭
22-02
MS BRD:Rtt (Sigl 4)

Partita in B♭
22-02
MS BRD:Rtt (Sigl 5)

Partita in E♭ (1770)
21-02
MS BRD:Rtt (Sammelband 8, 48–52); BRD:Rtt (Sigl 6) [for 22-02, 2 violas]

Partita in E♭
21-02
MS BRD:Rttl (Sammelband 8, Nr. 5–8)

Parthia, 5 movements
21-02
MS CS:KRa (IV.B.134)

Parthitta, Nr. 1, 5 movements
21-02
MS CS:KRa (IV.B.135)

Parthitta, Nr. 2, 3 movements
22-02
MS CS:KRa (IV.B.136)

Parthia in E♭
1-02, 2 English horns
MS CS:Pnm (XLII.C.192)

Simonetti, ?

Dresdner Redouten Menuetten e Trios (1767)
2200-02, 2 piccolos, basse
EP (Breitkopf & Härtel, Catalog of 1767)

Sixt, Johann Abraham (1757–1797)

(6) *Allemandes*
222-02
MS BRD:DO (Mus.Ms.1863) [cited in MGG]

Sommer, Johann Mattias

Pieze, 10 movements (ca. 1780)
22-24, 2 violas (?), string bass
MS BRD:Rtt (Sammelband 26)

Sperger, Johann Matthias

(2) *Parthia*
202-02
MS A:KR [cited by Hellyer]

(5) *Parthien*
201-02
MS BRD:DO (Mus.Ms.1826-1830)
Hellyer attributes Mus.Ms.1830 to Rosetti.

Partita in F
222-12
MS BRD:DS (Mus.Ms.1233)

(5) *Parthien*
201-02
MS CS:KRa [cited by SJK]

(5) *Parthia*
201-02
MS B:Bn [cited by SJK]

[title unknown]
Chorus, 1201-02
MS (autograph) DDR:SWl (MS.5327)

Adagio in E♭
222-02
MS DDR:SWl (5189/15)

Cassatio in D
1201-02
MS DDR:SWl (5188/4)

Divertimento in C
222-12, serpent
MS DDR:SWl (5190/22)

Parthia in G
222-02
MS DDR:SWl (5189/1)

Parthia in B♭
211-02
MS DDR:SWl (5189/14)

Parthia in A
202-02
MS DDR:SWl (5189/30)

Parthia in A
202-02
MS DDR:SWl (5189/48)

Parthia in B♭
202-02
MS DDR:SWl (5189/43 and 5189/43a)

Parthia in B♭
202-02
MS DDR:SWl (5189/44)

Parthia in B♭
202-02
MS DDR:SWl (5189/45)

Parthia in C
202-02
MS DDR:SWl (5189/21)

Parthia in C
202-02
MS DDR:SWl (5189/49)

Parthia in C
202-02
MS DDR:SWl (5189/50)

Parthia in D
202-02
MS DDR:SWl (5189/11)

Parthia in D
202-02
MS DDR:SWl (5189/47)

Parthia in D
202-02
MS DDR:SWl (5189/54)

Parthia in F
202-02
MS DDR:SWl (5189/46)

Parthia in F
202-02
MS DDR:SWl (5189/51)

Parthia in G
202-02
MS DDR:SWl (5189/53)

Parthia in G
202-02
MS DDR:SWl (5189/55)

Parthia in E♭
22-02
MS DDR:SWl (5189/2)

Parthia in C
22-02
MS DDR:SWl (5189/4)

Parthia in E♭
22-02
MS DDR:SWl (5189/3)

Parthia in D
201-02
MS DDR:SWl (5189/52)

Parthia in B♭
201-02
MS DDR:SWl (5189/18)

Parthia in B♭
201-02
MS DDR:SWl (5189/23)

Parthia in B♭
201-02
MS DDR:SWl (5189/28)

Parthia in B♭
201-02
MS DDR:SWl (5189/31)

Parthia in C
201-02
MS DDR:SWl (5189/9)

Parthia in C
201-02
MS DDR:SWl (5189/20)

Parthia in C
201-02
MS DDR:SWl (5189/25)

Parthia in C
201-02
MS DDR:SWl (5189/27)

Parthia in C
201-02
MS DDR:SWl (5189/37)

Parthia in C
201-02
MS DDR:SWl (5189/40)

Parthia in D
201-02
MS DDR:SWl (5189/22)

Parthia in D
201-02
MS DDR:SWl (5189/34)

Parthia in D
201-02
MS DDR:SWl (5189/35)

Parthia in D
201-02
MS DDR:SWl (5189/38)

Parthia in D
201-02
MS DDR:SWl (5189/39)

Parthia in E♭
201-02
MS DDR:SWl (5189/26)

Parthia in E♭
201-02
MS DDR:SWl (5189/41)

Parthia in F
201-02
MS DDR:SWl (5189/12)

Parthia in F
201-02
MS DDR:SWl (5189/13)

Parthia in F
201-02
MS DDR:SWl (5189/19)

GERMANY 351

Parthia in F
201-02
MS DDR:SWl (5189/24)

Parthia in F
201-02
MS DDR:SWl (5189/32)

Parthia in F
201-02
MS DDR:SWl (5189/42)

Parthia in G
201-02
MS DDR:SWl (5189/10)

Parthia in G
201-02
MS DDR:SWl (5189/17)

Parthia in G
201-02
MS DDR:SWl (5189/33)

Parthia in A
201-2
MS DDR:SWl (5189/16)

Parthia in B♭
201-2
MS DDR:SWl (5189/36)

Parthia in C
201-2
MS DDR:SWl (5189/29)

Parthia
21-02
MS DDR:SWl (5189/5a)

Parthia in E♭
21-02
MS DDR:SWl (5189/6)

Parthia in E♭
21-02
MS DDR:SWl (5189/7)

Parthia in E♭
21-02
MS DDR:SWl (5189/8)

Parthia in F
21-02
MS DDR:SWl (5189/5)

Spiller, ?

Partia
222-22
MS DDR:Z [cited by Eitner]; DDR:LEt [cited by Hellyer]

Stamitz, Karl (1745–1801)

(7) *Parties*
2222-02
MS DDR:Bds (Hausbibl., 340); DDR:Dlb [cited by Eitner]; GB:Lcm [cited by M]; US:DW (415)

(12) *Sérénades*, op. 28
2001-02
EP (Den Haag, Hummel, 1785); GB:Lbm (G.1065.d.[2])
MP (Sikorski, 1962)

March
202-02, 2 basset horns
MS GB:Lbm [cited by SJK]

Sextet, op. 14
22-02
EP (Paris, Sieber, ca. 1790); GB:Lbm [cited by SJK]

Divertimento a 2 chori
Instrumentation unknown
MS (score) BRD:DS [cited by Eitner]

(4) *Divertissements*
22-02
EP (La Haye et Amsterdam, Hummel); DDR:Bds [cited by Eitner; lost according to Grove, XVIII, 65]

(19) *Stücke fur 10 Blaser* (1795, 'fur den Zaren v. Russland')
MS [lost, cited in MGG and Grove, XVIII, 65]

(16) *Stücke fur Blaser und türk. Musik* (composed in 1801 for the Prince of Wales)
MS [lost, cited in MGG and Grove, XVIII, 65]

(16) *Märsche für 12 Blaser*
MS [lost, cited in MGG and Grove, XVIII, 65]

Steinfeld (Steinfeldt), Albert Jacob

(6) *Quatuors*, op. 20
2 Clarinets, 2 horns or trumpets, timpani
EP (Offenbach, André, Nr. 1575); BRD:Tu [clarinet parts only]

Stengel, F. von

[title unknown]
21-22
MS BRD:DS [cited by SJK; Eitner gives 20-22, basse]

Stranensky, ?

(6) *Parthien* (ca. 1800)
222-02
MS BRD:W
MP (EDM, XIV)
According to G2, Stranensky sent a harmonie work to the Kaiser of Russia in 1800 and received a gift of a golden '*emaillierte Tabatiere.*'

Stumpf, Johann Christian (d. 1801)

(2) *Parthia*
22-02
MS CS:Pnm (XLI.B.134), DDR:SWl (MS .5102) [Nr. 1, under 'Harmonie']
EP (Offenbach, André) [Nr. 1 only]; CS:Pnm (XLI.B.135a)

Tag, Christian Gotthilf (1735–1811)

Cantata, '*Schaffe in mir Gott ein neues Herz*'
SATB, 200-2, organ
MS PL:GDj (Ms.Joh.422)

Cantata, '*Man singet mit Freuden*'
S, 200-2, timpani, organ
MS PL:GDj (Ms.Joh.423)

Choral Vorspiel zu Vom Himmelhoch
122-02, organ
MS DDR:Bds (Mus.Ms.21615)

Gloria
SATB, 'Blasmusik'
MS (score) DDR:Bds (Mus.Ms.21598)

Parthia in C
2223-22, timpani
MS DDR:LEm (Poel.Mus.Ms.326)

Tausch, Franz (1762–1817)

(5) *Märsche und 1 Choral für die russische Garde*
Thirteen vocal and nine wind parts
EP (Paris, Ebend)

(6) *Märsche fur die preussische Garde*
Ten-part military band
EP (Berlin, Schlesinger)

(6) *Quartuors*, op. 5
2-02, 2 basset horns
EP (Orangeburg, Werckmeister); I:Fc (B.3109)

Serenata
22-02
MS DDR:Bds (Hausbibl., Nr. 341)

(13) *Pieces in Quator*, op. 22
21-01
EP (Berlin, Schlesinger)

Toeschi, Carlo Guiseppe (1724–1788, in Germany after 1752)

La Chasse Royale
22-02
MS F:Pa [cited by SJK]

Touchemoulin, Joseph (1727–1801)

Divertimento in E♭
22-24, 2 violas (?), string bass
MS BRD:Rtt (Touchemoulin 13a)

Trost, J. G. M.

Parthia
6-02
MS DDR:Z (Catalog.738)

Ulbrecht, Franz Joseph

(5) *Sätze*
21-22
MS BRD:KA

Ungelenk, ?

(4) *Partitas*
202-02
EP (Breitkopf & Härtel, Catalogs of 1778, Supplement 12, and 1782–1784, Supplement 15)

Vogler, Georg Joseph [Abbé], (1749–1814)

Auf unsern besten König
SATB, 222-02
MS (autograph) BRD:Mbs (Mus.Ms.1710)

Dixit Dominus
SATB, 200-22, timpani
MS (autograph) DDR:Bds (Mus.Ms.Auto.G.F.Vogler 2)

Hessische Vaterunser
SATB, 2222-023, contrabassoon
MS BRD:DS (Mus.Ms.1151 and 1151/a)

Wagner, Carl (1772–1822)

Marsch von den Gens d'Armes (ca. 1790)
-6, timpani
MS BRD:DS (Mus.Ms.1223/10)

Walter, G.

(6) *Airs en Var.conc.*
222-02
EP (Paris, Pleyel, 1797) [cited in G2]

Parthia
22-02
MS BRD:F (Mus.Hs.1555)

Weber, ?

(11) *Partien*
Harmoniemusik
MS BRD:DO [may be lost; listed in the library's 1804 catalog, according to Hellyer]

Weilland, ?

Harmonie
222-02
EP (London, Broderip & Wilkinson); GB:Lbm (h.125/20), GB:Ob

Harmonie
222-02
EP (Paris, Pleyel, 1797); BRD:DS [lost in WWII]

Harmonie
222-02
MS HL:DHgm

Weiss, Wenzel

Marsch und Echo
222-02
MS DDR:Bds (Hausbibl., Nr. 145)

Werttig, Joseph

(6) *Märsche*
222-1
MS DDR:Bds (Hausbibl., Nr. 146)

(24) *Märsche*
222-32, 2 piccolos, 2 fifes, serpent
MS DDR:Bds (Hausbibl., Nr. 147)

(12) *Pièces*
222-1
MS DDR:Bds (Hausbibl., Nr. 342)

Wineberger, Paul (1758–1821)

Partita in C ('Messe di Febrario 1789, P. W. Wallerstein')
2222-12, string bass
MS BRD:HR (III.4.1/2.20.340)

Partita in D (1785)
2222-02, string bass
MS (autograph) BRD:HR (III.4.1/2.40.89)

Partita in D (September, 1785)
2222-03, string bass
MS (autograph) BRD:HR (III.4.1/2.40.95)

Partita in D ('occassione del Giorno/natalizio di … prince Wallerstein, 1788')
2222-03, string bass
MS (autograph) BRD:HR(III.4.1/2.20.342)

Partita in D (1788)
2222-03, string bass
MS (autograph) BRD:HR (III.4.1/2.20.349)

Partita in D (1784)
2221-03, string bass
MS (autograph) BRD:HR (III.4.1/2.40.90)

Partita in E♭
21-02
MS BRD:HR (III.4.1/2.40.93)

Partita in E♭ (1782), 12 movements
21-02
MS (autograph) BRD:HR (III.4.1/2.40.91)

Partita in F (1787)
2212-02, string bass
MS BRD:HR (III.4.1/2.20.336)

Partita in F (1783)
221-03
MS (autograph) BRD:HR (III.4.1/2.20.335)

Partita in F (for a Wallerstein baptismal, 1794)
2222-02, string bass
MS (autograph) BRD:HR (III.4.1/2.20.345)

Partita in F (1786)
2122-03, string bass
MS (autograph) BRD:HR (III.4.1/2.20.337)

Partita in F
2222-02, string bass
MS BRD:HR (III.4.1/2.20.343)

Partita in F
Solo oboe, 2022-04, string bass
MS BRD:HR (III.4.1/2.20.346); DDR:SWl (Wineberger 1)

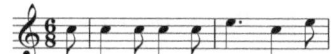

Partita in G
2212-02, string bass
MS BRD:HR (III.4.1/2.20.347)

Partita in G (1788)
2222-04, string bass
MS (autograph) BRD:HR (III.4.1/2.20.338)

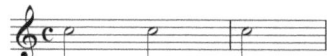

Partita in G
2222-03
MS BRD:HR (III.4.1/2.40.92)

Partita in G
2122-02, string bass
MS BRD:HR (III.4.1/2.20.341)

Partita in G (1786)
2122-04, string bass
MS (autograph) BRD:HR (III.4.1/2.20.348)

Parthia
2222-03, string bass
MS BRD:Mbs (Mus.Ms.6411)

Parthia
2122-04, Violono
MS (score) DDR:SWl (Wineberger 2)

Serenade in D, 10 movements
2222-03
MS BRD:HR (III.4.1/2.20.339) [missing clarinets]

Witt, Friedrich (1770–1836)

Partita in E♭
1122-02, string bass
MS BRD:HR (III.4.1/2.20.602)

Partita in F (March 1, 1790)
2222-02, string bass
MS (autograph) BRD:HR (III.4.1/2.20.604)

Partita in F (February 2, 1791)
2222-02
MS (autograph) BRD:HR (III.4.1/2.20.605)

Partita in E♭ (1790)
1222-02, string bass
MS BRD:HR (III.4.1/2.20.603)

Pièces d'harmonie
32-121, serpent
EP (Mainz,Schott, Catalog of 1878); BRD:MZsch

Wolf, Franz Xaver

(2) *Serenates*
22-02
MS (Advertized in Traeg's Catalog, Vienna, 1799)
EP (Offenbach, André, Nr. 836) BRD:W [missing bassoon 2]

(2) *Quintuors*
22-02
EP (Breslau, Holaufer)

Wölfl, Joseph (1773–1812)

(6) *Sonatas*, op. 3
202-02
MS (autograph) A:Sca

Yost, Michel (1754–1786)

Suito (ca. 1780)
121-02
MS BRD:RH (MS.436)

Zobl, ?

Partita
22-02
MS BRD:F

Zumsteeg, Johann Rudolf (1760–1802)

(5) *Pieces*
Variations
Wind instruments [cited in Grove, XX, 717]

Zwing, M.

(3) *grandes pièces d'harmonie militaires*
32-221, serpent, piccolo, percussion
EP (Worms, Kreitner, Hr. 193); BRD:HR

(6) *Pièces*
1021-02, 'alto'
EP (Mannheim, Heckel)
EP (Worms, Kreitner); BRD:DS [cited by Eitner], BRD:HR 384

The Netherlands

Anonymous Collections

(12) *Compositions*
2232-22, serpent
MS NL:Ura/mZ (M.A.Zcm 1) [missing oboe 2] Contains 9 marches (by Riess, Mankell, Rauscher, etc), and a version of 'God save the King.'

(23) *Sonatas* and (11) [short works]
-004
MS NL:Ura/mZ (M.Aa.Zcm 10)

Mankell, Hermann (fl. late eighteenth century)

Divertissement, 12 movements
22-02
MS NL:Ura/mZ (M.A.Zcm 27)
EP (Hamburg, Günther & Böhme); GB:Ckc

Divertissemento
2022-02, contrebass (in E♭!)
MS NL:Ura/mZ (M.A.Zcm 4, Nr. 1)

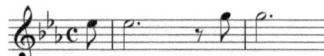

Divertissemento
2022-02, contrebass (in E♭)
MS NL:Ura/mZ (M.A.Zcm 4, Nr. 2)

Divertissemento
2022-02, contrebass (in E♭)
ME NL:Ura/mZ (M.A.Zcm 4, Nr. 3)

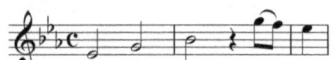

Divertissement, 10 movements
21-02
MS NL:Ura/mZ (M.A.Zcm 28)

(2) *Marches*
2032-12, string bass
MS NL:Ura/mZ (M.A.Zcm 3)

Parthia (1794)
2022-02
MS NL:Ura/mZ (M.A.Zcm 30, Nr. 1)

Parthia (1794)
2022-02
MS NL:Ura/mZ (M.A.Zcm 30, Nr. 2)

Parthia (1794)
2022-02
MS NL:Ura/mZ (M.A.Zcm 30, Nr. 3)

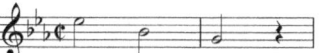

Suite de pièces d'harmonie, 20 movements
2022-02
MS NL:Ura/mZ (M.A.Zcm 29)

(6) *petits pièces trés faciles*
1022-02
EP (Advertized in AMZ, 1799) [cited in G2]

Serenata
22-02
EP (Advertized in AMZ, 1799) [cited in G2]

Rouwyzer, François Léonard (1737–1827)

(Sacred music for voices and winds) [cited in Grove, XVI, 278]

Ruloffs, Bartholomeus (b. 1740)

Musique militaire
201-02
EP (Amsterdam, Hummel); CS:Pnm (XLII.A.210)

Italy

Anonymous

Gloria
TTB, 202-02, Bassi, organ
MS I:Vcr (Busta II.N.25)

(12) *Partiten*
201-02
MS I:Vmc (Busta 1-8-N.1)

Real Ordinanze Italiano
2020-02, drum
MS I:Nc (22.2.20)

Sinfonia
1201-02, Basso
MS I:MOe (Mus.D.642)

Aber, Giovanni (flutist, 1779, La Scala)

(8) *Quintets*
2001-02
MS I:Mc [cited by Eitner]

Alessandri, Felice (1742–1798)

Marsch (1791)
221-1
MS DDR:Bds (Hausbibl., Nr. 78)

Anfossi, Pasquale (1727–1797)

Non temer non son piú Amante
200-02
EP (Venezia, Scataglia, 1773); DDR:SWl; F:Pn

Baldan, Angelo (1747–1804)

(2) *Credos*
TTB, 101-02, organ
MS I:Vcr (Busta III N. 53, 54)

Credo (1789)
TTB, 201-22, organ
MS I:Vmc (N.42)

Bertoni, Ferdinando (1725–1813)

(2) Credos
Three voices, seven winds
MS I:Vsmc

Gloria
Three voices, nine winds
MS I:Vsmc

Pastorale e Gloria
SATB, winds
MS (score) I:Bc

Credo
TTB, 101-02, organ
MS I:Vcr (Busta IV N. 62)

Bertuzzi, A.M.

Credo
Two voices, six winds, organ
MS I:Vsmc

Kyrie
Two voices, six winds, organ
MS I:Vsmc

Besozzi, Carlo (b. 1738)

Partita in F
201-02
MS CS:Pnm (XLII.A.213)

Partita in F
201-02
MS CS:Pnm (XLII.A.208)

(24) Sonaten
202-02
MS A:Wgm (VIII 8535)

Sonata in F
201-02
MS CS:Pnm (XLII.C.174)

Braccini, Luigi

Miserere
Four voices, wind instruments
MS I:Fc (A.29)

Briscoli, Domenico

Symphony, 'The German and French'
2021-12
EP (Dublin, Holden); GB:Lbm (h.1570.e); US:DW (108)

Symphony, 'The Italian'
2021-12
EP (Dublin, Holden); GB:Lbm (h.1570.e); US:DW (107)

Symphony, 'The Conversation of the Five Nations'
2021-12
EP (Dublin, Holden); GB:Lbm (h.1570.e); US :DW (109)

The Battle of Egypt
Military band
EP (Dublin); GB:Lbm (g.138.[9]) [here piano only]

Ciuffolotti, Vincenzo

Motetto (1796)
SATB, wind instruments, basso
MS I:Nc

De Maio, Gian Francesco

Salve
Soprano, wind instruments
MS (score) I:Nc (22.4.1)

Devasini, ?

Sestetto
1121-01 [cited in F]

Furlanetto, Bonaventura (1730–1817)

Alma Redemptoris
Tenor, ten winds, organ
MS I:Vsmc

Beatus Vir
Three voices, seven winds, organ
MS I:Vsmc

Gloria
SSB, 402-22, organ
MS I:Vcr (Busta V N.98)

Kyrie
SSB, 402-22, organ
MS I:Vcr (Busta V N.99)

Tantum ergo
TTB, 201-02, organ
MS I:Vcr (Busta VI N.115)

Credo
SSB, 221-12, organ
MS I:Vcr (Busta V, N.88)

Gallignani, G.

Suonatina
1112-01
MS I:Bc

Gandini, A.

Tantum Ergo
Tenor, wind instruments
MS I:MOe (Mus.D.93)

Gazzaniga, Giuseppe (1743–1818)

Quoniam
Bass, seven winds, organ
MS I:Vsmc

Gherardeschi, Guiseppe (1759–1815)

(3) *Quintetti* (dedicated to 'Cav. Luigi Cellesi')
201-02
MS (autograph) I:PS (B.124.8)

Miserere (1786)
SATB, wind instruments
MS (autograph) I:PS (B.78.2)

Marcia
1-02
MS (autograph) I:PS (B.179.31)

Grazioli, Giovanni Batta (1746–1820)

Credo
Three voices, six winds, organ
MS I:Vsmc

Jommelli, Nicolo (1714–1774)

Le frondi l'erbe
Soprano, chorus, 200-02, continuo
MS GB:Lbm [cited in Grove, IX, 694]

Messa di Requiem solenne
Voices and wind instruments
MS I:Fc (Chiesa di S. Gaetano, E.1019)

Marche de la Garde à pied
201-1
MS DDR:SWl (MS.3009)

March
2021-12, 'tschinken, tymbalo'
MS BRD:HR (III.4.1/2.20.380)

March
201-2
MS BRD:DS (Mus.Ms.1224, S.398, a-l)

Gambaro, ?

Harmonie, op. 5
22-02 [cited by Hellyer]

Lorenzini, Raimondo (1730–1806)

(6) *Nocturns*
21-02, serpent
MS DDR:Bds [cited by SJK]

Mazzorin, ?

Tantum Ergo
Bass solo, TTB chorus, 202-12, organ
MS I:Vcr (Busta X.N.140)

Montferini, ?

(6) *Partien* (1782)
222-02
MS [cited in Gl]

Montorlo, Antonio

Che Fernando
SS, 21-02
MS I:Mc [cited in Eitner]

Paisiello, Giovanni (1740–1816)

March of the First Consul
Instrumentation unknown
EP (Paris, Buffet-Crampon)

(16) *Divertimenti*
2021-02
MS USSR:Mcm [cited in Grove, XIV, 102]

Musica funèbre ('composta all'occasione della morte del genera le Hoche')
MS F:Pn [cited by Eitner]

Marcia Militaire (1798)
2121-002, serpent, percussion
MS (autograph) [present location unknown]

Paluselli, Stefan (1748–1805)

Missa in Dominicam Palmarum
Chorus and five wind instruments [cited in MGG]

Proprien fur den Palmsonntag
Chorus and six wind instruments [cied in MGG]

(4) *Partiten*
[cited in MGG]

Divertimento
Wind instruments [cited in MGG]

Piticchio, Franceso

Quintetto
201-02
MS (autograph) DDR:Bds [cited in Eitner]

Piticchiio, Pietro

(15) *Quintets*
201-02 [cited in F]

(6) *Harmoniepiecen*
402-02 [cited in F]

Rampini, Domenico (d. 1816)

Kyrie
Three-part chorus, 12 winds, organ
MS I:Vsmc [cited in Grove, XV, 578]

Roth, Sinforiano

Marcia della guardia Real Svizera del Re di Napoli (c. 1750)
21-02
MS BRD:Rtt (Roth 1)

Marcia (ca. 1750)
21-02
MS BRD:Rtt (Roth 2)

Storaro, ?

Marcia
Eleven winds with organ

[title unknown]
Seven winds
MS (both, scores) I:Vsmc

Toja, Giovanni

Serenata
1121-02
MP (Ricordi)

Vignali, Gabriele

Piaghe adorate
TTB, wind instruments
MS I:Bl [cited in Eitner]

Canzone, 'al mirarti in mezzo assiso'
TTB, wind instruments
MS I:Bl [cited in Eitner]

Canzone, 'O bella mia speranzi'
Three voices and wind instruments
MS I:Bl [cited in Eitner]

Zoncada, Giovanni

Partita
Solo oboe, 22-02
MS I:Gi(1) (SS.B.1.10.[R.8]); US:DW (47)

Poland

Czeyka, Valentin (b. ca. 1769)

Marches militaires
MS [cited in F]

Flemming, Wilhelm

Partie
21-22
MS PL:WRü [cited by SJK]

Golabek, Jakub (1739–1789)

Partita
21-02
MP (Krakau, Polskie Wydawnictwo Muzyczne, 1962)

Parzízek, Alexis Vincent (b. 1748)

Nocturne (pour des inst. à vent) [cited in F]

Stefani, Jean l'aine (1746–1829, in Poland from 1771)

(6) *Parties,* op. 1
21-02
EP (Berlin, Hummel); DDR:Bds [cited in Eitner]

Spain

Espinosa, Manuel
    (Collection of band music dated 1761)
    MS (score) E:Mn (M.2791)
    Contains approximately 20 works, bound together here, for the
        Spanish cavalry.

Switzerland

Anonymous

(54) *Introduzioni alla Pompa*
-3, timpani
MS CR:E (Th.185, 1)

(3) *Intrade*
-32, timpani, organ
MS CH:E (Th.54, 21)

(36) *Quintets* (1797)
21-02
MS CH:E (Th.86, 4)

(8) *Kleine Stücke*
21-02
MS CH:E (Th.62, 6)

(34) *Allemands*
21-02
MS CH:E (Th.62, 9)

(43) *Kleine Stücke*
1012-02
MS CH:E (Th.51, 40)

(12) *Marsche*
12-02
MS CH:E (Th.5l, 40)

(21) *Intrade*
-22, timpani, organ
MS CH:E (Th.51, 42)

Marche Del Dauphine, Nr. 3, in C minor, 'con Adagio di Schwartz,' Nr. 4
21-12, Bass Drum
MS CH:E (Th.59, 11)

(12) *Aufzüge*
-3, timpani
MS CH:E (Th.60, 5)

Marche religioso, Nr. 6
1020-222, timpani
MS CH:E (Th.60, 21)

Intrada, Nr. 1 (1787, 'per la Festa di Pasqua')
Oboe or clarinet, -42, timpani, 2 organs
MS CH:E (Th.60, 23)

Intrada, Nr. 2 (1796, 'per la Festa di Pentecote')
20-32, timpani, 2 organs
MS CH:E (Th.60, 22)

Intrada, Pastorale, Nr. 1, ('Per il S. Natale')
21-44, timpani, 2 organs
MS CH:E (Th.60, 24)

Intrada
20-44, timpani, 2 organs
MS CH:E (Th.60, 25) [missing horns 1, 2]

Intrada
-44, timpani, 4 organs
MS CH:E (Th.60, 27)

Intrada, Pastorale. Andantino, ('Per il Santo Natale')
20-44, timpani, 2 organs
MS CH:E (Th.60, 27a)

Intrada
Chorus 1: 21-32; chorus 2: 2000-12, timpani
MS CH:E (Th.60, 30)

Marche
21-02
MS CH:E (Th.62, 2)

(2) *Pas redoubles* and (1) *Marche Polonaise*
21-12, serpent
MS CH:Fcu (Ebaz 111-193)

(22) *kurze Stucke*
1020-12
MS CH:Fcu (Ebaz IV-39)

Albertin, Alphonso

Sonata (1787, 'per la Festa di Pasqua')
-44, timpani, 4 organs
MS CH:E (Th.55, 51)

Eichhorn, Johann

Variations pour le Basson
Bassoon, with 20-02
MS CH:Lz (Mus.311)

Frohlich, ?

(3) *Märsche*
21-12
MS CH:E (Th.54, 12)

Haering, Joseph

Deux Simphonies et un Rondau
'Plusieurs Instruments en vents'
MS CH:E (Th.185, 11)

(18) *Pièces pour la Musique militar* ('dedié a l'usage de l'Ecole de Notre Dames des Hermites')
2022-12
MS CH:E (Th.185, 2) [with two copies of each clarinet part]

Pièces d'Harmonie (40 short works)
2022-12, bass drum
MS CH:E (Th.185, 3)

Kaa, Franz Ignaz

Motetto Per la Processione della Madonna del Rosario
SATB, 2200-22, organ, basso
MS CH:E (Th.506, 4)

Mayer, Ambros

Stationes ('Pro Festo Corporis Christi'), 4 movements
SATB, 21-02
MS CH:Fcu (Ebaz 11-80)

Mayr, Placidus, O.S.B.

Kleine und leichte Walzer
31-03
MS CH:EN (MS.A.469)

Sinphonie
21-02
MS CH:EN (MS.A.468)

Sextetto
22-02
MS CH:EN (MS.A.461)

Meucci, Giuseppe

Messa
TTB, 1022-, cello, basso
MS CH:E (Th.548, 1)

Necchi, Francesco Antonio

Gloria
SATB, 200-02, basso
MS CH:E (Th.566, 2)

Credo
Three voices, 101-02, basso
MS CH:E (Th.285, 2/3)

Sarasin, Lukas (1730–1802)

Quintetto ('Marche de mon sieur')
21-02
MS (score) CH:Bu (kr.IV.302)

Schon, ?

Parthia, Nr. 5 in F (1778)
201-02
MS CH:E (Th.61, 32)

Serenata in E♭
22-02
MS CH:E (Th.91, 28)

Zech, Markus (1727–1770)

Lauda Sÿon
SATB, 2200-22, cello, organ
MS CH:E (Th.280, 15)

Lauda Sion
SATB, 2200-22, cello, organ
MS CH:E (Th.277, 8)

Lauda Syon Salvatorem
SSAATTBB, 2200-22, cello, organ, timpani
MS CH:E (Th.277, 16)

Te Deum
SATB, 2 violons or 2 oboes, -22, cello, organ
MS CH:E (Th.279, 4)

Index

Index of Names

A

Aber, Giovanni, Italian flautist, 1779, as composer, 362
Abingdon, 4th Earl of, 1740–1799, composer for Harmoniemusik, 251
Adam, unknown work arr. Starke for Harmoniemusik, 152ff
Adrien, l'aîné, 18th century France, *Hymne à la Victoire*, for band, 268
Ahl, C., as arranger of works for Harmoniemusik, 89, 137
Aiblinger, *Die Fee und der Ritter,* arr. Sedlak for Harmoniemusik, 150
Albertin, Alphonso, 18th century Swiss composer, 372
Alessandri, Felice, 1742–1798, composer for Harmoniemusik, 3, 362
Alessio, Francesco, composer for Harmoniemusik, 163, 171ff [56 Parthias]
Altenburg, Johann Ernst, b. 1734, German composer, treatise on Trumpet, 301
Amalie, Prinzessin von Preussen (sister to Frederick the Great), as composer, 301
Amantino, ?, (12) *Divertimenti* for Harmoniemusik, 173
Anddreozzi, unknown composition arranged for Harmoniemusik by Courtin, 154
Anfossi, Pasquale, 1727–1797, as composer, 3, 362
Anonymous, (88) opera arrangements for Harmoniemusik, 151
Anonymous, (89) opera arrangements for Harmoniemusik, 151
Anonymous, 15 original Italian works for Harmoniemusik, 362
Anonymous, 170 original English band compositions, 250
Anonymous, 18 original French works for band, 267
Anonymous, 194 Austrian-Bohemian original works for Harmoniemusik or band, 163
Anonymous, 257 original Swiss compositions for Harmoniemusik, 371ff
Anonymous, 454 original German works for Harmoniemusik or small band, 294
Anonymous, *Airs d'opera buffa, Fucheria e puntiglio,* arr. Fuchs for Harmoniemusik, 155
Anonymous, *Airs du Ballet de Vénus et Adonis*, arr. Vanderhagen for Harmoniemusik, 157
Anonymous, *Alexandre et Campase de Larisse*, ballet unknown arr. for Harmoniemusik, 154
Anonymous, *Ballo*, unknown arranger for Harmoniemusik, 158
Anonymous, *Beliebter Marsch*, unknown arranger for Harmoniemusik, 158
Anonymous, *Condrillon Romace*, unknown arranger for Harmoniemusik, 158
Anonymous, *dem bummen Gartner*, unknown arranger for Harmoniemusik, 155
Anonymous, *Der Quacksalber und die Zwerge*, arr. Triebensee for Harmoniemusik, 156
Anonymous, *Die Eingebildenden Philosophen*, opera, arr. Wendt for Harmoniemusik, 155
Anonymous, *Die Psyche*, arr. Ruzni for Harmoniemusik, 156
Anonymous, *Die Tage der Gefahr*, opera arr. Triebensee for Harmoniemusik, 157
Anonymous, *Die Zween Anton*, opera, arranged for Harmoniemuisk, 157
Anonymous, four marches for band from Belgium, 248
Anonymous, *König Lear*, arr. Blumenthal for Harmoniemusik, 156
Anonymous, *La Bianca e la Rolsa*, ballet, arr. Wendt for Harmoniemusik, 155
Anonymous, *La morte di Virginia*, unknown arranger for Harmoniemusik, 156
Anonymous, *La Sposa Persiana*, ballet, arr. Wendt for Harmoniemusik, 157
Anonymous, *Le Baal Angloise*, ballet, unknown arranger for Harmoniemusik, 155
Anonymous, *Le Festin de Piere*, ballet, unknown arranger for Harmoniemusik, 155
Anonymous, *Le fête flamende*, ballet, unknown arranger for Harmoniemuisk, 155
Anonymous, *Le Lavandajie de Cittera*, arr. Wendt for Harmoniemusik, 156
Anonymous, *Les Horaces*, ballet, unknown arranger for Harmoniemusik, 155
Anonymous, *Messellan*, arr. J. Wratni for Harmoniemusik, 156
Anonymous, *Rochus Pumpernickel*, unknown arranger for Harmoniemusik, 157
Anonymous, *Rundtanz aus Figaro*, ballet, unknown arranger for Harmoniemusik, 155
Anonymous, *Sposalizio Allegro*, unknown arranger for Harmoniemusik, 158
Anonymous, *Valses, 'Le bon gout,'* unknown arranger for Harmoniemusik, 155
Apell, Johann, 1754–1832, German, (12) *Notturni* for winds, 301
Arundall, Robert (Gallway, Lord Viscount), 18th century composer for Harmonie, 251
Ascherl, ?, *Marsch* for Harmoniemusik, 174

378 INDEX

Ashley, Josiah, *Royal Dorsetshire March*, 1797, for Harmoniemusik, 252

Aspelmayer, Franz, 1728–1786, composer for Harmoniemusik, 163, 174ff [76 Partittas]

Attwood, Thomas, b. 1765, English, (6) works for Harmoniemusik, 252

Auber, Daniel, 1782–1871, composer of works arranged for Harmoniemusik,
    La Maçon, opera, arr. Widder, 4
    La Bergère Châtelaine, unknown arranger, 3
    Der Klausner, unknown arranger, 5
    Emma, opera, unknown arranger, 4
    La Maçon, opera, [as *Der Maurer*], unknown arranger, 4
    La Muette de Portici, opera, arr. Sedlak and Weller, 4
    La Neige, opera, arr. Widder and one unknown arranger, 4
    Le Duc d'Olonne, opera, arr. Sedlak, 5
    Le Philtre, opera, unknown arranger, 5
    Le Serment, opera, arr. Berr, 5
    Unknown work arr. Poisel, 151
    Unknown work arr. Widder, 151

Avertal, ?, 18th century (Viennese), (6) *Parthias* for Harmoniemusik, 177

B

Bach, Johann Christian, 1735–1782, (10) *Symphonies*, (6) *Divertissements*, (9) *Marches* for Harmoniemusik, 302ff

Bach, Johann Christoph Friedrich, 1732–1795, *Septet* for Harmoniemusik, 302

Bach, Karl P.E., 1714–1788, (19) *Marches*, (6) *Sonatas* for Harmoniemusik, 303ff

Bachmann, Anton, 1716–1800, German, (9) *Marches*, *Allegro and Andante* for Harmoniemusik, 303ff

Backofen, Johann Georg, 1768–1830, works for Harmoniemusik, 304

Baer, F., arr., *Pièces d'Harmonie*, a collection for Harmoniemusik, 158

Baillie, R. Miss, *A Favorite March*, 1795, for Harmoniemusik, 252

Baldan, Angelo, 1747–1804, *Credos* for voices and winds, 1789, 362ff

Baronville, ?, French composer, (2) *Ordonnance des dragoons*, 1756, band, 268

Barra, political hero of the French Revolution, 270

Barth, Christian, 1735–1809, German, *Grand Sinfonie* for band, 304

Barth Christian, as arranger of works for Harmoniemusik, 59, 92, 94, 137

Barthelémon, François-Hippolyte, 1741–1808, *Prince of Wirttemberg March*, 252

Baudron, Antoine, 1743–1834, French, 5th *Suite du Concert Militaire*, Harmonie, 268

Baumgarten, C. Gotthilf, 1741–1813, works for military trumpet ensemble, 304

Bayer, ?, composer (in Prague?), *Ländler* for Harmoniemusik, 178

Beckford, Mons. De, 18th century French, *Marche* for Harmoniemusik, 253

Beckford, William, 1759–1844, student of Mozart, *March* for Harmoniemusik, 253

Bédard, Jean-Baptiste, 1765–1815, French, *Potpourri Connus* for Harmonie, 268

Beecke, Ignaz, 1733–1803, (2) *Partitas* for Harmonie with flutes, 304

Beecke, Ignaz, as arranger of works for Harmoniemusik, 22, 149

Beer, Joseph, 1744–1811 [here as Bärr], *Variatione* for Harmoniemusik, 178

Beethoven, 1770–1827, as composer of works arranged for Harmoniemusik,
    Egmont Music, op. 84, arr. Starke, 5
    Fidelio, opera, arr. Sedlak, 6
    Harmonie (orig. unknown), unknown arranger, 8
    Quintet, op. 16, arr. Triebensee, 6
    Septet, op. 20, three unknown arrangers, 6
    Septet, op. 20, arr. Bernhard Crusell (for band), 6
    Septet, op. 20, arr. Druschetzky, 6
    Sestetto, unknown arranger, 6
    Sonata pathétique, two unknown arrangers, 7
    Symphony Nr. 1, arr. Hutschenrieyter, Sr., 7
    Symphony Nr. 7, unknown arranger, 7
    Symphony Nr. 8, , unknown arranger, 7
    Trauer Marsch (orig. unknown), unknown arranger, 8
    Wellingtons Sieg, unknown arranger, 8

Beffroy de Regny, unidentified work arr. Vanderhagen, 153

Beinet, ?, 18th century French (3) *Suites* for Harmoniemusik, 268

Beinet, as arranger for Harmoniemusik, 153ff

Bellini, Vincenzo, 1801–1835 as composer of works arranged for Harmoniemusik,
    Breatrice di Tenda, opera, arr. Sedlak (mss by Perschl), 9
    I Capuleti e i Montecchi, opera, arr. Sedlak and two unknown arrangers, 8
    I Puritani di Scozia, opera, arr. Sedlak and one unknown arranger, 9
    La Sonnambula, opera, arr. Sedlak (mss by Perschl), 9
    La Straniera, opera, arr. Sedlak, or Perschl, 8
    Norma, opera, arr. Sedlak, 9
    Bianca e Gernando, opera, arr. Carulli for band, 8

Belloli, Agostino, *Vitelius Maximus*, arr. for Harmoniemusik, 157

Bém, Vaclav, composer in Prague, *Parthia* for Harmoniemusik, 178

Benda, ?, *Dragoner-Marsch* for Harmoniemusik, 305

Bender, H., 19th century German, (6) *Pièces für Kavalleriemusik*, 305

Bernardini, Marcello, (Marcello di Capua), *Furberia et Pontiglio*, opera?, arranged for Harmoniemusik, 13

Berr, as arranger of works for Harmoniemusik, 5, 47, 69
Berton, Henri, 1767–1844, *March militaire* and *Hymne pour la fête de l'Agriculture* for band, 268ff
Berton, Henri, 1767–1844, as composer of works arranged for Harmoniemusik,
    Aline, Reine de Golconde, opera, arr. Triebensee and five unknown arrangers, 10
    Féodor, opera?, unknown arranger, 10
    Françoise de Foix, opera, unknown arranger, 11
    Montano et Stéphanie, opera, arr. Fuchs, 9
    Le grand Deuil, opera, arr. Vanderhagen and two unknown arrangers, 9
Bertoni, Ferdinando, 1725–1813, church music for voices and winds, 363
Bertuzzi, A.M., 18th century Italian, church music for winds and voices, 363
Besozzi, Carlo, b. 1738, 5 *Parthias* for Harmoniemusik, 363
Bianchi, Francesco, 1752–1810, *La Villanella rapita*, unknown arranger for Harmonie, 11
Bianchi, unnamed opera arr. Fuchs, 155
Bianchi, unnamed opera by unknown arranger, 101
Bierey, Gottlob, 1772–1840, *Das Blumenmädchen*, unknown arranger for Harmonie, 11
Birch, Lt. Col., 18th century officer in British military, 252
Bisch, ?, 18th century French, *Recueil de marches* for Harmoniemusik, 269
Bisch, unnamed works in collections arr. Pleyel for Harmonie, 103, 178, 230
Blackwell, J.G., 18th century English, *Divertimento* for military band, 253
Blasius, Matthiew, 1758–1829, numerous works for military Harmonie, a *Messe* for male soli and Harmoniemusik, 269
Blasius, as composer of six unnamed works by unknown arranger for Harmoniemusik, 278
Blasius, as arranger of works for Harmoniemusik, 24, 106
Blumenthal, J. von, arr., *Grosser Marsch aus König Lear* for Harmoniemusik, 156
Bocchoroni, ?, *Hamlet* (original unknown), arr. Ruzni for Harmoniemusik, 11
Bochsa, Charles, 1789–1856, as arranger of Haydn Symphonies for Harmonie, 46ff
Boieldieu, François, 1775–1834, as composer of works arranged for Harmoniemusik,
    Jean de Paris, opera, arr. Sedlak, Triebensee and three unknown arrangers, 12
    La Dame blanche, opera, unknown arranger, 12
    Ma Tante Aurore, arr. Koslowsky, 11
    Unnamed work arr. Starke, 152
Bono, Giusepe, 1710–1788, (11) *Parthias* for Harmonie, 178ff
Bordorf, Jean Erneste, a march by 'a Lewin,' 305
Bordoux, Jean Ernest, 18th century *Nouveau Marche* for Harmoniemusik, 269ff

Bornstädt, 18th century German general, 297
Boser, ?, German, (7) *Partitas*, ca. 1768, for Harmoniemusik, 305
Braccini, Luigi, 18th century Italian, *Miserere* for voices and winds, 363
Braun, Johann, 1753–1795, German, works for Harmoniemusik, 306
Bresciani, Pietro, as composer of works arranged for Harmoniemusik, 12, 13
Bridgeman, Charles, 18th century, English, (8) *Marches* for Harmonie, fifes, 253
Briederike, Princess, wedding in Berlin, 1791, 342
Briscoli, Domenico, 18th c. Italian, 3 *Symphonies* for Harmonie with flutes, 364
Brixi, Frantisek, 1732–1771, (4) *Parthias* for Harmonie, 179
Brod, as arranger of Weber, *Der Freischütz*, opera, for Harmoniemusik, 132
Brooks, James, (36) *Select pieces for Military Band*, 1797, 253
Brösel, ?, German, (3) *Marches*, ca. 1780, for Harmoniemusik, 306
Brunett (Brunetti), Gaéton, 1740–1809, (2) volumes of dances for Harmonie, 269
Bruni, Antonio, 1751–1821, as composer of works arranged for Harmoniemusik,
    La Recontre en voyage, opera, arr. Fuchs, 13
    Spinette et Marini, opera?, arr. Fuchs, 13
    Toberne, opera, arr. M.J. Gebauer, 13
    Unnamed work arr. Fuchs, 153
    Unnamed work arr. Ruzni, 151
Brusek (Bruscheck), Joseph, composer for Harmonie and music for voices and winds, 179ff
Buchal, J., as arranger of works for Harmoniemusik, 63, 140, 141
Buchna, ?, *Todten-Marsch* for Harmoniemusik, 180
Buchnal, as arranger of works for Harmoniemusik, 91, 147
Bucholtz, Johann, d. 1800, German, (3) *Partie*, 1766, for Harmoniemusik, 306
Bühler, Franz, 1760–1824, German church work for voices and Harmoniemusik, 306
Bülow, General, German, 18th century, 301
Busby, Thomas, 1755–1838, English composer, (3) *Marches*, 2536ff
Buschmann, ?, German, (2) *Partitas*, ca. 1760, for Harmoniemusik, 306
Buttstett, Franz, 1735–1814, German, *Quintet*, 1793, for Harmoniemusik, 307

C

Calenberg [Gallenberg], ?, *Hamlet*, Overture, unknown arr. for Harmoniemusik, 13
Cambini, Giovanni, 1746–1825 (11) works, voices and Harmonie, & *Marche*, 269ff

Cannabich, Johann, 1731–1798, German, *March* for band, 307
Cantelo, ?, 18th century English collector, (24) *American country dances* ..., 254
Capua, Marcello, b. ca. 1740, *Furberia et Pontiglio*, unknown arr. for Harmonie, 13
Carafa, Michele, 1787–1872, as composer of works arranged for Harmoniemusik, 14
Cartellieri, Antonio, 1772–1807, (3) *Divertimenti* for Harmoniemusik, 180
Carulli, Benedetto, arranger of Bellini *Bianca e Gernando*, opera, for band, 8
Catel, Charles, 1773–1830, (9) works for voices and band, (2) *Overtures* (2) *Symphonies*, (6) *Marches* for Harmoniemusik, 269ff
Catel, Charles–Simon, as composer of works arranged for Harmoniemusik,
    l'Officier enlevé, opera?, unknown arranger, 14
    Sémiramis, three unknown arrangers, 14
    Wallace, opera, two unknown arrangers, 14
    Zirphile et Fleur de Myrte, opera?, arr. Schaffner, 15
Catrufo, Giuseppe, 1771–1851, *Félicie*, opera, two unknown arr. for Harmonie, 15
Cejka, Valentin, (3) *Divertimenti* for Harmoniemusik, 180
Celestino, Eligio, 1739–1812, German, untitled work for Harmoniemusik, 307
Cellesi, Luigi [dedication], quintets by Ghardeschi, 18th century, 365
Champein, Stanislas, 1753–1830, works arranged for Harmoniemusik, 15, 153
Chapelle, unnamed composition arr. Ozi for Harmoniemusik, 153
Chapman, Richard, 18th century English, *Royal Circus* music, 254
Chardiny, unnamed composition arr. Ozi for Harmoniemusik, 153
Cherubini, Luigi, 1760–1842, (9) original works for voices and band, 273ff
Cherubini, Luigi, 1760–1842, as composer of works arranged for Harmoniemusik,
    Anacréon, opera, arr. Triebensee and an unknown arranger, 17
    Élisa oder der Bernhardsberg, opera, arr. Triebensee, 16
    Faniska, opera, arr. Sedlak and four unknown arrangers, 18
    König Saul von Israel, opera, unknown arranger, 18
    L'Hôtellerie Portugaise, opera, two unknown arrangers, 16
    La Prisonniére, opera, arr. Triebensee and two unknown arrangers, 17
    Les deux Journées, opera, arr. Gopfert, Javault and an unknown arranger, 17
    Lodoiska, opera, arr. Havel and four unknown arrangers, 16
    Médée, opera, arr. Sedlak, 16
    Unnamed work, arr. Triebensee, 152
Christian von Hessen, 18th century Prince, 298
Cigler, ?, *Parthia* in F for Harmoniemusik, 181
Cimarosa, Domenico, 1749–1801, operas arranged for Harmoniemusik, 18ff
    1re Suite d'Airs d'l'Opéra arr. Fuchs, 21
    3e Suite d'Airs del'opéra buffa arr. Vanderhagen, 21
    Amor rende Sagace, opera?, four unknown arrangers, 21
    Bohémiens en foire, arr. Fuchs, 22
    Giannina e Bernardone, opera unknown arranger, 18
    Gli Orazi ed i Curiazi, opera, four unknown arrangers, 20
    I Nemici generosi, opera, unknown arranger, 21
    I Zingari in Fiera, opera, arr. Fuchs, 21
    Il Matrimonio segreto, opera, arr. Wendt, Fuchs and nine unknown arrangers, 19
    L'Impresario in Augustie, opera, arr. Fuchs, 18
    Le Astuzie femminili, opera, arr. Vanderhagen, 20
    Matrimonio per Raggiro, opera?, unknown arranger, 21
    Unnamed works arranged for Harmoniemusik, 11, 101, 155
Cisler, ?, *Parttia* for Harmoniemusik, 181
Ciuffolotti, Vincenzo, 18th century Italian, *Motetto*, 1796, for voices and winds, 364
Clerico, Francesco, composer in Venice, works arranged for Harmoniemusik, 22
Colman, John, English composer, (24) *Marches*, 1796, for band, 254
Comtesse de Wallerstein, 194
Condé, 18th century Prince de, 281
Courtin, arranger of a collection of Harmoniemusik, 154
Covalovsky, in an anonymous arrangement for Harmoniemusik, 151
Cramer, Johann, 1771–1858, *March from Divertimento*, arr. Triebensee, 22ff
Cramer, Wilhelm, 1746–1799, *Rondo* for Harmoniemusik, 307
Cremitasch, ?, *Parthia* for Harmoniemusik, 181
Croebelis, Domingo, composer in Denmark, *Quartet* for flutes, 249
Croes, Henri-Joseph, 1758–1842, (30) *Partitas* for Harmonie, 307ff
Crusell, Bernard, arranger of the Beethoven *Septet*, op. 20 for band, 5
Czar of Russia, 18th century, 352
Czeyka, Valentin, b. ca. 1769, Polish, works for band and Harmoniemusik, 181, 369

D

Dalayrac, Nicolas, 1753–1809, composer of works arranged for Harmoniemusik,
    d'une Heure de Marriage, opera, two unknown arrangers, 26

Corsaire, opera, arr. M. J. Gebauer, 25
Die Nacht in Walde, opera?, arr. Schmitt, 25
Gulistan, opera, arr. Vanderhagen and four unknwn arrangers, 24
Azemia, opera, arr. Fuchs and two unknown arrangers, 23
Camille, opera, arr. Fuchs?, 23
Gulnare, opera, arr. Fuchs and Blasius, 24
Jean et Genevieve, opera, unknown arranger, 26
La Boucle de Cheveux, opera, unknown arranger, 26
La jeune Prude, opera, arr. Vanderhagan, 24
La Tour de Neustadt, opera, arr. M. J. Gebauer, 25
Les deux petits Savoyards, opera, arr. Sedlak, 23
Nina, arr. Wendt, 154, and unknown arranger, 22ff
Picaros et Diègo, opera, two unknown arrangers, 26
Poëte et le Musicien, opera, arr. Sedlak, 25
Sargines, opera?, arr. M. J. Gebauer, 26
Suite (music unidentified), arr. Gebauer, 26
Unnamed movements arranged for Harmoniemusik, 13, 153ff
Danzi, Franz, 1763–1826, German, *Sestetto* and *Pot-pourri* for Harmoniemusik, 309
Danzi, Franz, 1763–1826, *Freudenfest*, arr. Sartorius for Harmoniemusik, 27
Daroudeau, ?, *Rosier*, arranged for Harmoniemusik, 27
De Maio, Gian Francesco, 18th century Italian, *Salve* for soprano and winds, 364
Deiselbach, ?, 18th Century German, *Parthia* for Harmoniemusik, 309
Delaborde, ?, Ouverture de *Cinquantine*, arr. Fuchs for Harmoniemusik, 27
Della Maria, Pierre-Antoine Dominique, 1769–1800, operas arr. for Harmonie, 27ff
  L'Oncle Valet, opera, two unknown arrangers, 27
  L'Opéra-comique, opera, arr. Nicolas Jörg and two unknown arrangers, 27
  Le Prisonnier, opera, two unknown arrangers, 27
  vieux Chateau, opera?, arr. Gebauer, 27
  Pièces d'harmoni, unknown arranger, 274
  Unnamed work arr. Ruzni, 151
Deshayes, Prosper-Diodier, d. 1815, composer of works arranged for Harmoniemusik,
  Le faux serment, opera, arr. Ozi, 29
  Zelia, opera overture, unknown arranger, 29
  Premiere suite d'harmonie, unknown arranger, 274
  Unnamed movement arr. Ozi, 153
Devasini, ?, 18th century Italian, *Sestetto*, for Harmoniemusik with flute, 364
Devienne, François, 1759–1803, *Overture* and (2) works for voices, Harmonie, 274
Devienne, as composer of works arranged for Harmoniemusik,
  L'Amour filial, opera, arr. Gaveaux, 35
  Les Visitandines, opera, unknown arranger, 29

Le valet de deux maîtres, opera, two unknown arrangers for Harmonie, 29
Dezède (Desaides), Nicolas, ca. 1740–1792, works arranged for Harmoniemusik,
  Blaise et Babet, opera, two unknown arrangers, 28
  La fête de la Cinquantaine, opera, two unknown arrangers, 28
  Unnamed work arr. Vanderhagen, 153
Diabeli, Antonio, 1781–1858, Tambourin solo, from *Madmoiselle Neuman* [arr. Triebensee for Harmoniemusik], 30
Diabelli, unnamed work arr. Triebensee, 152
Dibdin, Charles, 18th century English, (12) *Marches* for Harmoniemusik, 254ff
Diez, Johann, 1711–1793, German, *Lauda* for SATB, trumpets, 310
Discher, J., Bohemian composer, (5) *Partias* for Harmoniemusik, 181
Dittersdorf, Karl Ditters von, 1739–1799, (67) *Partitas* for Harmoniemusik, 310ff
Dittersdorf, Karl Ditters von, 1739–1799, operas arranged for Harmoniemusik,
  Betrug durch Aberglauben, opera, unknown arranger, 30
  Der Doctor und Apotheker, opera, three unknown arrangers, 30
  Hironimus Knicker, opera, two unknown arrangers, 30
  Unnamed work, unknown arranger, 154
Dittrichstein, Graf Moritz, 1775–1864, *Minuetto* for Harmoniemusik, 181
Dixon, William, b. 1760, English, Church music for voices and winds, 254
Dobihal, Josef, *Farso,* opera?, unknown arranger for Harmoniemusik. Dobihal was a clarinetist, military band conductor and mentioned in Beethoven's conversation book for 1813–1814, 31
Donizetti, Gaetano, 1797–1848, operas arranged for Harmoniemusik,
  Anna Bolena, opera, unknown arranger, 31
  L'Elisiar d'Amore, opera, arr. Sedlak, 31
  Lucia di Lammermoor, opera, arr. Sedlak, 31
  Marino Faliero, opera, arr. Sedlak, 31
  Torquato Tasso, opera, arr. Sedlak, 31
  Unnamed work arr. Poisel, 151
  Unnamed work arr. Starke, 152ff
Donninger, Ferdinand, 1716–1781, *Partita* in 10 movements, Harmoniemusik, 313
Döring, Johann Friedrich, 1766–1840, *New Year's Song*, voices and brass, 313
Dousa, Karl, *Missa in honoren St. Venceslai* for voices and winds, 182
Dramar, unnamed work arr. Ruzni, 151
Drechsler, Josef, 1782–1852, *Marcia Mor. di Nelson*, for Harmoniemusik, 182

Drobisch, ?, 18th century German, (6) *Angloises* for Harmoniemusik, 313

Drosler, ? (12) *Ländler* for Harmoniemusik, 182

Droste-Hülshoff de Vischering, Max, 18th century German, *Dances* and *Das Hallelujah* for voices and Harmoniemusik, 313

Druot, ?, 18th century German, *Partita* for Harmoniemusik, 314

Druschetzky, Georg, 1745–1819, Hungarian, (102) *Partitas* for Harmoniemusik, plus music for voices and winds, 182ff

Druschetzky as arranger for Harmoniemusik, 6, 44, 45, 182, 206

Duernoy, Frédéric, 1765–1838, *Pas de Manoeuvre* for band, 274

Duport, Jean Louis, 1749–1819, in Paris, ballets arr. for Harmoniemusik,
   Der blöde Ritter, ballet, arr. Triebensee, 32
   Figaro, ballet, arr. Triebensee, 32
   Zephir, ballet, arr. Triebensee and three unknown arrangers, 32

Düring, J. C., arr. Himmel *Fanchon* for Harmoniemusik, 48

Duscheck (Tuschek), ? (6) *Parthias* for Harmoniemusik, 192

Dusek, Frantisek, 1731–1799, Bohemian composer, (50) *Parthias* for Harmoniemusik, 188ff

Dussec, unnamed work arr. Rummel, 150ff

Duttilieu, Pierre, 1754–1797, *Die Macht des schönen Geshlechts*, arr. Wendt and two unknown arrangers for Harmoniemusik, 32ff

E

Eastland, Edwin, 18th century English, (12) *Marches* for 2 flutes, bassoon, 255

Ebdon, Thomas, 1738–1811, English, *March*, 1795, 255

Ebell, H., 18th century German, *Partita* for Harmoniemusik, 314

Eberwein, Christian, 1750–1810, German, (4) *Parthien*, Harmonie, flutes, 314

Ehmann, ?, 18th century German, *Marsch* for Harmoniemusik, 314

Ehrenfried, Henrico, as arranger for Harmoniemusik, 22, 40, 75, 105, 299

Eichhorn, Johann, 18th century Swiss composer of Harmoniemusic with solo bassoon, 372

Eichner, Ernest, 1740–1777, German, (8) *Divertissement* for Harmoniemusik, 314ff

Eisner, Carl, 18th century German, *Sextett* for winds, 315

Eler, André-Frédéric, 1764–1821, *Overture* (7) *Dances*, (3) *Quatuors*, op. 11 and one work for voice and Harmoniemusik, 275

Eley, C. F., English, (32) *Marches* and *Military Pieces* for Harmoniemusik, 255ff

Enke, H., as arranger of Mozart's *Gran Partita*, K.361, for 4-hand piano, 218

Ermitasch, ?, *Parthia* for Harmoniemusik, 192

Ernest, Mr., as arranger for Harmoniemusik, 117ff

Ernst, François, fl. 1786, German, *Harmoniemusik*, 315

Ernst, Franz, d. 1805?, *Tarrare*, opera, unknown arranger for Harmoniemusik, 33

Esch, Louis von, 18th century French composer, 275

Eschstruth, Hans von, 1756–1796, German (12) *Marches* for Harmoniemusk, 315

Esmeister, ?, (3) *Partitas* for Harmoniemusik, 192

Espinosa, Manuel, Spanish, collection of band music, 1761, 370

Essex, Timothy, English composer, (4) *Marches* for band, ca. 1795, 256

F

Federici, Francesco, d. 1830, composer of *Zaira*, opera, arr. for Harmonie, 33

Feldmayer, Georg, 1756–1818, German, (24) *Partitas*, for Harmoniemusik, 315ff, 336

Feldmayer, as arranger of Mozart's *Die Zauberflöte*, opera, for Harmoniemusik, 81

Feraud, 18th century French political figure, 284, 289

Feray, Abbé, fl. 1792, music for chorus and Harmoniemusik, 275

Fergus, John, English composer, *Grand March*, 1794, for Harmoniemusik, 256

Ferrari, Giacomo, 1759–1842, *La Villenella rapita*, two unknown arrangers for Harmoniemusik, 33

Fiala, Josef, 1754–1816, German, (29) *Divertimenti* for Harmoniemusik, 317ff

Fioravanti, Valentino, 1764–1837, works arranged for Harmoniemusik, 33, 34

Fiorillo, Ignazio, Ignazio, 1715–1787, *Il Venditore d'aceto*, arr. for Harmonie, 34

Fischer, ?, *Todten Marsch* in E minor for Harmoniemusik, 193

Fischer, ?, *Vincent*, opera, arr. Triebensee for Harmoniemusik, 34

Fischer, Anton, as arr. of Grétry's, *Raoul Barbe Bleue*, opera, for Harmoniemusik, 40

Fischer, Heinrich Wilhelm, German, *Trauer Marsch*, for Harmoniemusik, 319

Fischer, J., German composer (5) *Partitas* for Harmoniemusik, 319ff

Fischer, Johann Christian, 1733–1800, *Triumphmarsch* for Harmoniemusik, 319

Fischer, Thomas, *Il Couraggio* for Harmoniemusik (soli oboe, Eng. hn), 193

Fitzpatrick, Capt. Joseph, Isle of Wight Volunteers, 264

Flachs, as arranger of Weber's *Der Freischütz*, opera, for Harmoniemusik, 132

Flack, Casper, English comp., (36) *Military Divertimenti*, 1793, for Harmonie, 256

Flaska, Joseph, 1706–1772, *Musique d'harmonie* and *Marches* for Harmonie, 275

Flemming, Wilhelm, 18th century, Polish, *Partie*, for Harmoniemusik, 369

Foignet, Charles, 1750–1823, *Le mont Alphéa*, opera, arranged Fuchs for Harmonie, 34

Forstmeyer, Ehrenfried, 1730–1787, (4) *Partitas* for Harmoniemusik, 320

Framery, unnamed work arr. Beinet for Harmoniemusik, 153

Fränzl, Ignaz, 1736–1811, German, *Partia* for Harmoniemusik, 320

Frederick II, 'the Great' 1712–1786, 301, 320 [(3) *Marches* for band], 324

Freeman, Thomas Augustine, 18th century English composer, 266

Freundthalier, ? (4) *Divertimenti* for Harmoniemusik, 193

Fricke, Elias, 18th century German editor, *Collection of Dances* for Harmonie, 320

Friedem, ?, 18th century French, (2) *Sextets*, for Harmoniemusik, 275

Fröhlich, ?, 18th century Swiss, *Märche* for Harmoniemusik, 373

Frontzel, ?, 18th century, German, *Parthia* for Harmoniemusik, 320

Fuchs, Georg-Friedrich, 1752–1821, French, (22) *Harmonies*, (6) Harmonie collections, (6) *Fanfares* for brass ensemble, (19) *Marches*, (12) *Noctures* for Harmoniemusik, 275, copies of Mozart scores, 216ff

Fuchs, Georg Frederick, 1752–1821, as arranger for Harmoniemusik, 9, 11, 13, 18ff, 21,23ff, 27, 29, 34, 39, 53, 55, 57ff, 61, 64ff, 75, 77ff, 79, 89, 91, 93, 100ff, 106, 108ff, 110ff, 122ff, 126, 129ff, 153, 155, 158ff, 240,

Furlanetto, Bonaventura, 1730–1817, Italian, church music for voices and winds, 364

G

Gallenberg, Robert, 1783–1839, composer of works arranged for Harmoniemusik,
Alfred der Grosse, ballet, arr. Sedlak and one unknown arranger, 34
Jeanne d'Arc, ballet, unknown arranger, 35
Ottavio Pinelli, ballet, arr. Sedlak, 35

Gallignani, G., 18th century Italian, *Suonatina* for Harmoniemusik, flute, 365

Gambaro, ?, 18th century Italian, *Harmonie* for Harmoniemusik, 366

Gambaro, as arranger for Harmoniemusik, 13, 47, 67, 93, 107, 109ff, 121

Gambaro, V., 18th century French, (4) Suites, *Overture* for band, 278

Gandini, A., 18th century Italian, *Tantum Ergo* for tenor and winds, 365

Gardel, composer of unnamed work arr. Ozi for Harmoniemusik, 153

Gassmann, Florian, 1729–1774 (10) *Partitas* for Harmoniemusik, 193ff

Gaston, *Randgesang*, a wind work performed in a Weber opera, 195

Gaveaux, Pierre, 1761–1825, as composer of works arranged for Harmoniemusik,
L'Amour filial, arr. Devienne and one unknown arranger, 35
Le Diable Auteur, opera?, arr. M. J. Gebauer, 36
Le diable en vacances, opera, arr. three unknown arrangers, 35
Le petit Matelot, opera, unknown arranger, 35
Le traité nul, opera, unknown arranger, 36
Monsieur Deschalumeaux, opera, unknown arranger, 36
Sophie et Moncars, opera, unknown arranger, 36

Gazzaniga, Giuseppe, 1743–1818, Italian, *Quoniam* for Bass and seven winds, 365

Gebauer, Etienne, as arranger of Spontini, *La Vestale*, opera, for Harmoniemusik, 125

Gebauer, F. R., as arranger of a Haydn Symphony for Harmoniemusik, 47

Gébauer, François René, 1773–1844, (6) *Suites* for Harmoniemusik, (9) Marches, Collection of (35) Marches, (9) wind quintets, 279ff

Gebauer, J., arr., Mozart, *Cosi fan tutte*, opera, for Harmoniemusik, 77

Gebauer, M. J., as arranger for Harmoniemusik, 11, 13, 25ff, 28, 36, 45ff

Gebel, ?, (2) Harmonie, op. 11 for Harmoniemusik, 194

Gehot, Joseph, Belgium composer (24) *Military Pieces* for Harmoniemusik, 248

Gerl (Görl), Franz Xaver, 1764–1827, *Der dumme Gärtner aus dem Gebirge*, 36

Gherardeschi, Guiseppe, 1759–1815, Italian, 3 *Quintetti, Miserere*, for winds, 365

Gianella, Louis, 1778–1817, *Acis et Galathée*, ballet, arr. Triebensee and one unknown arranger, 36

Gianella, Luigi, as arranger of Paisiello's, *Nina*, opera, for Harmoniemusik, 100

Giarnovick, unnamed work arr. Beinet for Harmoniemusik, 153

Giroult, composer of unnamed work arr. Ozi for Harmoniemusik, 153

Gleissner, F., as arranger of Mozart's *Gran Partita*, K.361, for 9 winds, string quartet, 218

Gleissner, Franz, 1759–1818, German, works for Harmoniemusik, 320ff

Gloger, ?, 18th century German, *Exercises* for fifes and percussion, 321

Gluck, Christoph Willibald, 1714–1787, works arranged for Harmoniemusik,
Alceste, opera, unknown arranger, probably Wendt, 37
Armide, opera, unknown arranger, 38
das kleine Wasser, opera (original unknown), arr. Wendt, 38

Gesang (original unidentified), unknown arranger, 38
Iphigénie en Aulide, opera, unknown arranger, 37
Iphigénie en Tauride, opera, arr. Triebensee and three unknown arrangers, 38
La Rencontre imprevus, opera, arr. Wendt and four unknown arrangers, 37
'March and Echo Aria' from *Armide*, arr.Triebensee, 38
Mochomet, opera (original unknown), arr. Wendt, 38
Godfrey, W., English composer, *The Thrush*, ca. 1785, band, solo piccolo, 256
Golabek, ?, *Partita* for Harmoniemusik, 194
Golabek, Jakub, 1739–1789, Polish, *Partita* for Harmoniemusik, 369
Göller, ?, 18th century German, *Partita* for Harmoniemusik, 321
Göpfert, as arranger for Harmoniemusik, 7, 17, 81, 82ff
Goschelock, J. [see Kozeluch]
Gossec, François, 1734–1829, (23) Revolutionary works for chorus and band, (6) *Marches*, (3) *Symphonies*, one for Harmonie, two for band, (6) works for Harmoniemusik, 280ff
Gossec, as arranger of Rouget de Lisle's, *Marche des Marseillois* for band, 292
Gossec, *Le triomphe de la république*, arr. Fuchs, 39
Gosssec, composer of unnamed work arranged for Harmoniemusik, 151
Göttling, ?, 18th century German, (6) Harmoniemusik works, 321
Gow, Nathaniel, 1763–1831, English composer, 257
Gräfe, Johann Friedrich, 1711–1787, German composer, *March*, 340
Graff, C. E., 18th century German, *Die Schlacht bei Austerlitz*, for band, 321
Grazioli, Giovanni, 1746–1820, Italian, *Credo* for voices and 6 winds, 365
Grégoire, as arranger for Harmoniemusik, 107ff, 110ff.
Grenser, Johann, 1758–1794, (7) *Partitas* for Harmoniemusik, 321ff
Grétry, André, 1741–1813, as composer of works arranged for Harmoniemusik
    La Caravane du Caire, opera, arr. two unknown arrangers, 39
    Le rival confident, opera, unknown arranger, 41
    Panurge dans l'Isle des Lanternes, arr. Vanderhagen and one unknown arranger, 40
    Raoul Barbe Bleue, opera, arr. Anton Fischer, 40
    Richard Coeur-de-Lion, opera, unknown arranger, 40
    Silvain, opera, arr. Röser, 39
    Zémire et Azor, operaarr. four unknown arrangers, 39
    Twelve opera arias (original unidentified), unknown arranger, 41
    Two unnamed works arr. Beinet, 153
    Two unnamed works arr. Vanderhagen, 153, 154
    Unnamed work arr. Ozi, 153

Grétry, in an anonymous collection of Harmoniemusik, 154
Gretsch, Johann Konrad, 1710–1778, German (2) *Partitas* for Harmoniemusik, 322
Griesbach, Charles, English comp., (24) *Military Divertimenti*, for Harmonie, 257
Griessbacher, Reimund, Director of the Harmoniemusik for Prince Grassalkowitz in Vienna in 1796, 195
Gross, ?, German, ca. 1770, *Echo* for Harmoniemusik with solo oboe, 322
Grot, ?, *Parthia* for Harmoniemusik, 195
Gruner, Nathaniel, 1732–1792, German, music for chorus and Harmoniemusik, 322
Gudon, General, 182
Guglielmi, Pietro, 1728–1788, *La bella Pescatrice*, opera, arr. Wendt for Harmoniemusik, 42
Guglielmi, Pietro, *La Pastorella nobile*, arr. Wendt for Harmonie, 41
Guiliani, unnamed work arranged for Harmoniemusik by Starke, 152
Günther, Carl, 18th century, (32) *Marches* for the German army, 322
Gyrowetz, Adalbert, 1763–1850, (36) compositions for Harmoniemusik, 195ff
Gyrowetz (Girovetz, Jirovec), Adalbert, 1763–1806, his works arr. for Harmonie,
    Agnes Sorel, opera, arr. Sedlak and three unknown arrangers, 42
    Der Augenarzt, opera, arr. Starke and one unknown arranger, 43
    Die beiden Eremiten (original unknown), unknown arranger, 44
    Die Hochzeit der Thetis und des Peleus, arr. Sedlak for Harmonie 43
    Die Pagen des Herzoge von Vendome, ballet, unknown arranger, 43
    Der Zauberschlaf, unknown arranger, 154
    Die Zwey Tanten (original unknown), unknown arranger, 44
    Federica ed Adolfo, opera, arr. Triebensee, 43
    Miriam (original unknown), unknown arranger, 44

H

Habert, M., arr., Grétry, *Richard Coeur-de-Lion*, opera, for Harmoniemusik, 40
Haering, Joseph, 18th century Swiss, (60) works for winds, 373
Hammer, Carl, German ca. 1800, *Partita* for Harmoniemusik, 323
Hammerl, as arranger of Mozart operas for Harmoniemusik, 73, 78ff
Händel, Georg Friedrich, 1685–1759, *Saül*, unknown arranger for Harmonie, 44
Handke, Mauritius, composer in a Partita collection, 163

Handl, J., arr., Salieri, *Palmira, Regina di Persia*, opera, for Harmoniemusik, 118
Hanschke, ?, *Partia* for Harmoniemusik, 196
Harbordt, Gottfried, 1768–1837, German, *Trauer Marsch*, for Harmoniemusik, 323
Hargrave, Henry, 18th century English, (5) *Concerti*, bassoon ensemble, 257
Harke, Friedrich, (6) *Märchen* for Harmoniemusik, 197
Hartmann, ?, 18th century English, *A Set of Military Pieces*, 257
Hasse, ?, 18th century German, *Marches* for military band, 323
Hattasch (Hatas), Dismas Jan, 1724–1777, (9) *Parthias* for Harmoniemusik, 205ff
Hauff (Hanff), Wilhelm, German, ca. 1776, (6) *Sextuers* for winds, 323
Häusler, Ernst, 1761–1837, German, *Notturni* and church music with Harmonie, 323
Havel, as arranger for Harmoniemusik, 16, 141, 150
Haydenreich, as arranger of Mozart for Harmoniemusik, 80, 83
Haydn, Franz Josef, 1732–1809, 197ff, original works for Harmoniemusik, (24) *Partitas*, (21) *Divertimenti*, (10) *Marches*
Haydn, music arranged for Harmoniemusik,
  Harmonie tirée des ouvres d'Haydn, arr. Gambaro, 47
  Unnamed work arr. Beinet, 153
  Unnamed work arr. Ozi, 153
  Collection of several unnamed works, 152
  [see Mozart K. C. 19.09 and K. C. 17.10, 222ff
  'Gott erhalte den Kaiser,' arr. Haydn, 44
  Morceaux choisis du célèbre Haydn, arr. Vanderhagen, 47
  Symphony ('Oxford'), arr. Triebensee, 46
  Symphony (I, 51), arr. M. J. Gebauer, 45
  Symphony (I, 55), unknown arranger, 45
  Symphony (I, 70), unknown arranger, 45
  Symphony (I, 73), arr. M. J. Gebauer (mvts I, IV), 46
  Symphony (I, 75), unknown arranger, 46
  Unidentified symphony, arranged F. R. Gebauer, 47
  Unidentified symphony, arr. Triebensee, 46
  Unidentified *Symphony in Eb*, unknown arranger, 47
  Andante mit den Paukenschlag, unknown arranger, 46
  Die Schöpfung Oratorio [complete!], arr. Druschetzky, 44
  The Seasons (*Jahrszeiten*), [complete!], arr. Druschetzky, 45
  Symphonies arr. Stefan Kolb, 330
  Presto, unidentified symphony, arr. Triebensee, 46
Haydn, Franz Josef, 1732–1809, works for band,
  Overture, Part II, Seven Last Words for band (original composition), 202
  Symphony (I, 85 'La Reine'), arr. Charles Bochsa for band, 46
  Symphony (I, 91), arranged Bochsa for band, 46
  Symphony (I, 102), arranged Bochsa for band, 46
Haydn, Michael, 1737–1806, *Sinfonia par Hayden*, unknown arranger for Harmoniemusik, 47
Heidenreich, as arranger of Mozart *Gran Partita* for 8 winds, 218
Heinrich, Joseph, as arranger of an unidentified opera for Harmoniemusik, 158
Hennig, ?, 18th century, German, (3) *Marsche* for military Harmoniemusik, 324
Hérold, Louis Joseph Ferdinand, 1791–1833, works arr. for Harmoniemusik
  La Clochette, unknown arranger, 47
  Le dernier jour de Missolonghi, incidental music, arr. Berr, 47
  Le Pré aux Clercs, opera, unknown arranger, 47
  Zampa, opera arr. Sedlak, 47
  Zweikampf oder Schreiber Wiese bey Paris), arr. Sedlak, 48
Herschel, Friedrich Wilhelm, 1738–1822 [the famous astronomer/oboist], (3) works for Harmoniemusik, 257
Hertel, Johann, 1727–1789, German, (6) *Märche* for band, 324
Hewitt, James, 1770–1827 English, (4) Quick Marches for Harmoniemusik, 257
Hiebesch, Johann N., as arranger of Mozart, *Die Zauberflöte*, opera, for Harmoniemusik, 80
Hill, Frederic, English composer, (4) Marches ca. 1780, for Harmoniemusik, 258
Hill, John, 1724–1797, English, *Hill's Church music, with symphonies*, 258
Hiller, Johann, 1728–1804, German, *Hymn* for voices and brass, 1790, 324
Himmel, Friedrich, 1765–1814, *Marches, Trauer-Cantate* for Harmonie, 324
Himmel, Friedrich, *Fanchon, das Leiermädchen*, arr. J. C. Düring for Harmonie, 48
Hoberecht, J. L., *A Grand Military Piece*, ca. 1799 for Harmoniemusik, 258
Hoche, French General, 273, 290, 367
Hoffmeister, Franz, 1754–1812, German, (50) *Parthias* for Harmoniemusik, 325ff
Hoffmeister, Franz Anton, works arranged for Harmoniemusik, 48
Hoffmeister, as arranger, *Douze ariettes* (composers unidentified) for Harmoniemusik, 159
Holden, Smollet, 19th century, Irish, *A Collection of Quick & Slow Marches*, 258
Holler, Augustin, 1745–1814, German, (2) *Parthias* and *Dances* for band, 328
Holzbauer, Ignaz, 1711–1783, German, *Divertimento* for bassoons & horns, 329
Holzinger, ?, 18th century German, *Missa* for voices and winds, 329
Honauer, Leonz, fl. 1760–1778 in Paris, (3) *Suites* for Harmoniemusik, piano, 284

Horix, ?, *Marche*, 1798, for band, 285
Hoschna, Jacob Phil., *Parthia* in F for Harmoniemusik, 204
Hoven, J. (pseudonym for von Püttlingen), arr., *Johanna d'Arc*, for Harmonie, 130
Huber, Jakub, (2) *Messa choralis* for SATB and winds, 204
Hummel, arr. Sedlak for Harmoniemusik, 152
Hummel, *Helena und Paris*, ballet?, arr. Triebensee for Harmoniemusik, 49
Hummel, Johann Nepomuk, 1778–1837 *Die Eselshaut*, opera, arr. Sedlak, Starke for Harmoniemusik, 49
Hummel, unnamed work arr. Sedlak, 152
Hummel, Johann, 18th century, German, (2) military *Marsches* for Harmonie, 325
Hummel, Karl, military *Marsch*, ca. 1770, 258
Hutschenrieyter, Sr., as arranger of Beethoven *Symphony Nr. 1* for Harmoniemusik, 7

I

Inge, William Phillips, 18th century officer in the British military, 257
Inglis, Col., 18th century officer in the British military, 251
Isouard, Niccoló, 1775–1818, works arranged for Harmoniemusik,
   Aladin, opera, two unknown arrangers, 53
   Cendrillon, (*Aschenbrödel*) opera, arr. Triebensee and nine unknown arrangers, 51
   Jeannot et Colin, opera, two unknown arrangers, 52
   Joconde, opera, arr. Sedlak and two unknown arrangers, 52
   Josepf und der Kleinen Dieblin, arr. Sedlak, 53
   L'impromptu de campagne, opera, unknown arranger, 53
   L'Intrigue aux Fenêtres, opera, two unknown arrangers, 50
   Le Billet de Loterie, opera, two unknown arrangers, 51
   Le Magicien sans Magie, opera, two unknown arrangers, 52
   Le Médecin Turc, opera, arr. three unknown arrangers, 50
   Le Prince de Catane, opera, unknown arranger, 52
   Léonce, opera, two unknown arrangers, 53
   Les Confidences, opera, arr. Vanderhagen, 50
   Lully et Quinault, opera, two unknown arrangers, 52
   Michel-Ange, opera, arr. Sedlak, Vanderhagen and four unknown arrangers, 50
   Un Jour á Paris, opera, unknown arranger, 50

J

Jadin, Hyacinthe, 1769–1800, French composer, *Overture* and (2) works for voices and Harmoniemusik, 285
Jadin, Louis, 1768–1853, French, Overture, *Symphonie*, (2) *Marches* for band, (3) *Sextuors concertans* for Harmoniemusik, (3) *Quintets concertans* for winds and piano, (2) Revolutionary works for voices and band, 285ff

Jahn, August, 18th century German, *Military signals* for pfieffen & clarini, 329
Jahn, Otto, 1813–1869, German musicologist, 218
Javault, as arranger of Cherubini, *Les deux Journées*, opera, for Harmoniemusik, 17
Jetschmann, ?, 18th century German, *Parade Marsch & Fast Marsch*, 329
Jommelli, Nicolo, 1714–1774, Italian, church music, marches for winds, 366
Jörg, Nicolas, as arranger for Harmoniemusik, 27, 159ff

K

Kaa, Franz, 18th century Swiss, *Motetto* for chorus, Harmoniemusik, fls, 373
Kaffka, Wilhelm, 1751–1806, German, *Divertimento* for Harmonie (& violas?), 329
Kalckstein, 18th century German military leader, 334
Kalkbrenner, unnamed work arranged for Harmoniemusik by Starke, 152
Kalkbrenner, unnamed work arranged for Harmoniemusik by Rummel, 150ff
Kammel, ?, (2) *Serenata* for Harmoniemusik, 205
Kanne, ?, *Orpheus*, opera, arr. Triebensee (one movement) for Harmoniemusik, 53
Kauer, Ferdinand, 1751–1831 (2) *Parthias* and *Nelsons grosse Seeschlacht* for Harmoniemusik, 205ff
Kauer, Ferdinand, 1751–1831, *Das Donauweibchen*, opera, unknown arranger for Harmoniemusik, 54
Kauer, unnamed work arranged for Harmoniemusik by Ruzni, 151
Kauntze George, English, *The Downfall of Paris March*, c. 1800, 4 winds and pf, 258
Keil, Johann, 18th century German, *Parthia* for Harmonimusik, 329
King, Matthew, 1733–1823, (4) military marchs, for Harmoniemusik, 259ff
Kinsky, Josef, Prince of Bohemia, b. 1781, one of the three financial supporters of Beethoven, *Das Landliche Fest im Waldchen bei Kis-Bér*, opera, arr. Triebensee and one unknonwn arranger for Harmoniemusik, 54
Kirchner, Johann, 1765–1831 (4) *Cantatas* for voices and winds, 329
Kirsten, ?, (2) *Partitas* for Harmoniemusik, 205
Knezek, Vaclav, 1745–1806 (2) *Partitas* for Harmoniemusik, 205
Knorr, Bernhard, Freiherr von, 18th century, Vienna, *Quintet* for winds, 205
Koch, Heinrich, 1749–1816, *Chorale book* for Harmonie, *Marches*, 330
Köchel, Ludwig, Nachlass, 217
Köhler, Gottlieb, 1765–1833, German (3) *Parthien* for Harmoniemusik, 331
Kolb, Stefan, b. 1743, German, (9) *Partitas* for Harmoniemusik, 330

Kolbe, Oscar, arr., Leidersdorf, *Fest Overture bei Gelegenheit der Feyerlichen Krönung Ihrer Majestät Carolina Kaiserin von Osterreich zur Konigin von Ungarn* (1837) for Harmoniemusik, 56

Kollmann, August, 1756–1829, 18th century, *A New March*, 259

König, M., 18th century German, (7) *Marches* for Harmoniemusik, 331

Kopprasch, Wilhelm, 1750–1832, German composer for brass instruments, 331ff

Koschevitz, Josef, (6) *Hongroises* arr. Druschetzky for Harmoniemusik, 206

Koslowsky, J, 'amateur,' arranged Boieldieu, *Ma Tante Aurore*, opera for Harmonie, 11

Kospoth, Otto, 1753–1817, (2) *Parthias* for Harmoniemusik, 331

Kotterz, ?, *Parthia* for Harmoniemusik, 206ff

Kozeluch, Jan Antonin, 1738–1814, *Cassation* for Harmoniemusik, 206

Kozeluch, Leopold, 1752–1818, (17) *Partitas*, (2) *Marches* for Harmoniemusik, 206ff

Kozeluch, Leopold, 1752–1818, *La ritrovata Figlia d'Ottone II*, arr. Wendt, Satorus and one unknown arranger for Harmonie, 54

Kozeluch, *Die wieder gefundene Tochter Otto III*, arr. Krommer, Wendt and two unknown arrangers for Harmoniemusik, 54

Krasa, ?, (2) *Partitas* for Harmoniemusik, 208

Krechtler, arranger of Mozart, *La Clemenza di Tito*, opera, for Harmoniemusik, 78

Kreith, Karl, d. 1809 (32) *Partitas*, (23) *Marches* for Harmoniemusik, 208ff

Kreith, arranger of Paisiello, *Il Re Teodoro in Venezia*, opera, for Harmoniemusik, 97

Kreutzer, Rodolphe, 1766–1831, *Overture* for band, 286

Kreutzer, Rodolphe, 1766–1831, his operas arranged for Harmoniemusik, 55ff
    Antonius und Cleopatra, ballet, arr. Triebensee and one unknown arranger, 55
    Lodoïska, opera, arr. Richter, 55
    Paul et Virginia, opera, arr. Fuchs and one unknown arranger, 55
    Unnamed work arr. Wenusch, 150
    Unnamed work arr. Ozi, 153

Krommer, Franz, 1759–1831, *Symphony*, arr. Triebensee for Harmoniemusik, 56

Krommer, as arranger of Kozeluch, *Die wieder gefundene Tochter Otto III*, ballet, for Harmoniemusik, 54

Kucharz, Johann Baptist, 1751–1829, (Various) *Partitas* for Harmoniemusik, 210

Küffner, arr., Rossini, *Otello*, opera, for Harmoniemusik, 110

Küffner, as arranger of Weber, *Der Freischütz*, opera, for Harmoniemusik, 132

Kühnau, Johann, 1735–1805, German, *TeDeum* with brass insts., 331

Kuntzen, Adolph, 1720–1781, German (7) *Marches* for Harmoniemusik, 331

Kunzen, Friedrich, 1761–1817, *Chorale*, voice and Harmoniemusik, 332

Kunzen, Friedrich, 1761–1817, *Das Fest der Winzer*, opera, arr. Simoni for Harmoniemusik, 56

Kunzer, ?, 18th century German, (6) *German Dances*, for Harmoniemusik, 332

Kürzinger, Paul, ca. 1755–1820, *Robert und Caliste*, arr. Süssmayr for Harmonie], 56

Kurzweil, Franz, 18th century German, (7) *Parthia* for Harmoniemusik, 332ff

L

Lachner, unnamed work arr. Poisel for Harmoniemusik, 151

Lachnith, as arranger of Paer, *Agnesse di Fitz-Henry*, opera, for Harmoniemusik, 93

Lamberti, Louis, b. 1769, *Pièces en harmonie*, 286

Langlé, Honoré François, 1741–1807, (6) *Sinfonie* for Harmoniemusik and a *Hymn* for voice and Harmoniemusik, 286

Lanner, composer in a collection of Harmoniemusik by an unknown arranger, 152

Lasueur, *Paul et Virginia*, opera, arr. Fuchs and Vanderhagen for Harmonie, 58

Laube, Antonin, 1718–1784, (12) *Partitas* and a *Te Deum* for Harmoniemusik, 211ff

Lefèvre, Jean Xavier, 1763–1829, French, *Overture*, (14) *Marches*, (2) *Hymns* for band, 287

Legier, John Bernard, 18th century English, (13) *Sets of Military Pieces*, 259

Legrand, as arranger for Harmoniemusik, 76, 106, 108, 110

Legrand, historian, Army of the Rhine, 18th century, 274

Lehman, Frederick, 18th century German, (6) *Marches* for winds, 332

Leidersdorf, Franz, *Fest Overture bei Gelegenheit der Feyerlichen Krönung Ihrer Majestät Carolina Kaiserin von Osterreich zur Konigin von Ungarn* (1837), arr. Oscar Kolbe for Harmoniemusik, 56

Lemoyne, Jean Baptiste, 1751–1796, *Ouverture* arranged for Harmoniemusik, 56

Lemoyne, *Les Prétendus*, opera, arr. three unknown arrangers for Harmoniemusik, 56

Lesueur, Jean François, 1760–1837, (8) Revolutionary *Hymns* for voices and band, 287ff

Lesueur, Jean François, his operas arranged for Harmoniemusik, 57ff

Liber, Joseph, 1732–1809, *Divertimento*, Harnmonie with 2 violas (?), 332

Lindpainter, Peter, 1791–1856, *Joko*, ballet, arr. C. H. Mayer for Harmonie, 58

Linek, Jiri, *Fanfare*, 1785, 4 trumpets and timpani, 212

Liverati, Giovanni, 1772-?, *David, oder Goliaths Tod*, oratorio, arr. Sedlak and one unknown arranger for Harmonie, 58

Loewe, Johann, b. 1766, German *Notturno* for Harmonie and 2 Eng. hns, 333

Loibl, Benedikt, 1766–1833 German, OSB, *Parthia* for Harmoniemusik, 333

Lorentz, (13) *Parthias* for Harmoniemusik, 212ff

Lorenzini, Raimondo, 1730–1806, *6 Nocturnes* for Harmoniemusik, serpent, 366

Lorenziti, Bernardo, 18th century in Paris, *Canon ou divertissement* for 4 winds, 288

Lortzing, Gustav, 1801–1851, *Czaar und Zimmermann*, opera, arr. Wallentin for Harmonie, 59

Lottum, 18th century German Count, 301

Louis de Szechny, Count, of Hungray, 188

Louis XV, 281

Louis XVIII, 279

Ludwig IX, von Hessen-Darmstadt, 1719–1790, (54) *Märsche* for band, 333

Lutter, ?, *Parthia*, for Harmoniemusik, 212

M

Mackintosh, Robert, 1745–1807, Scottish, *Edinburgh March*, for Harmonie, 259

Madame D., *Airs pour le clavecin*, unknown arranger for Harmoniemusik, 157

Mahon, John, 1749–1834 English, (2) *Marches*, c. 1797, 259

Maier, L, German, fl. 1782, (2) *Parthias* for Harmoniemusik, 333

Main, ?, 18th century German, *Sextour* for Harmoniemusik, 333

Malherbe, l'ainé, *Trois marches don't la première est à grand orchestre exécutée à La Haye le vingt neuf février, 1788*, unknown arranger for Harmonie, 59

Malzat, Ignaz, 1757–1804, (6) *Parthias* for Harmoniemusik, 212

Mankell, 18th c. composer in a Dutch collection of marches, 360

Marcello di Capua, 1730–1799, Ouvert. to *Furberia et Pontiglio*, unknown arranger for Harmoniemusik, 59

Marie Esterházy, Prinzessin, *Ländler,* arr. Triebensee for Harmoniemusik, 59

Marschner, Heinrich, 1795–1861, *Stücke aus Der Templer und die Jüdin*, opera, arr. Barth for Harmoniemusik, 59

Martin y Soler, Vicente, 1754–1806, works arranged for Harmoniemusik,
    Andramaca, opera, unknown arranger, 62
    Die geberserte Eigensinnige, arr. Sartorus, 62
    L'Abore di Diana, opera, arr. Wendt, Sartorus and five unknown arrangers, 61
    La scola de'maritati, arr. Fuchs, Stumpf and one unknown arranger, 61
    Una Cosa rara, opera, arr. Sartorus, Wendt and five unknown arrangers, 59

Martini, Jean Paul, 1741–1816, works arranged for Harmoniemusik, 62, 153, 154, 301

Martini, Johann (Martini el Tedesco), 1741–1816 (2) Revolutionary *Hymns* for band, 288

Martinides, Carlo, 1731–1794, German, *Parthia* for Harmoniemusik, 333

Maschek, Paul, as arranger of Weigl, *Die Tänzerin*, ballet, for Harmoniemusik, 142

Matiegka, W., (12) *Aufzüge* for brass ensemble and timpani, 213ff

Maurer, ?, 18th c. German, *Variations on a Russian Melody* for Harmonie, 333

Maurer, unnamed work arranged for Harmoniemusik by Triebensee, 152

Maurer, Louis, 1789–1878, *Alznu*, ballet, arr. Triebensee for Harmoniemusik, 62

Mauser, ?, 18th century German, (2) *Parthia* for Harmoniemusik, 334

Mayer, Ambros, 18th century Swiss, *Stationes* for voices and Harmoniemusik, 373

Mayer, C. H., as arranger of Lindpainter, *Joko*, ballet for Harmoniemusik, 58

Maÿer, Franz, (5) *Parthias* for Harmoniemusik, 213

Mayr, arr. by Triebensee for Harmoniemusik, 150

Mayr, Johann Simon, 1763–1845, works arranged for Harmoniemusik,
    Adelasia e Aleramo, opera, arr. Triebensee and two unknown arrangers, 63
    Alonso e Cora, opera, arr. Sedlak and one unknown arranger, 63
    Ercole, opera?, unknown arranger, 64
    Ginevra di Scozia, opera, arr. J. Buchal and three unknown arrangers, 63
    Lodoiska, opera, arr. four unknown arrangers, 62
    Solitari, opera?, arr. Leo. Ratti, 64

Mayr, Placidus, OSB, 18th century Swiss, Harmoniemusik, 373

Mayseder, unnamed work arr. Starke for Harmoniemusik, 152

Mazzorin, ?, 18th century Italian, *Tantum Ergo* for voices and winds, 366

McLean, J. M., English, (4) *Marches,* 1795, for Harmoniemusik, 260

Meder, Johann, 18th century German, (6) *Marches* for Harmoniemusik, 334

Mederitsch, Johann, 1752–1835, *Chor der Tempelherrn*, for SATB, winds, 213

Méhul, Étienne, 1763–1817, *Overture* for band, 7 works for voices and band, 288ff

Méhul, Etienne Nicolas, 1763–1817, his operas arranged for Harmoniemusik,
- *Adrien*, opera, unknown arranger, 64
- *Ariodant*, opera, arr. Fuchs, 65
- *Beiden Füchse* (original unknown), unknown arranger, 68
- *Bion* (original unknown), unknown arranger, 67
- *Cora*, opera, unknown arranger, 64
- *Der Bauer*, opera, arr. Triebensee, 67
- *Der Temperamente*, opera, arr. Triebensee, 68
- *Euphrosine*, opera, arr. Fuchs, 64
- *Héléna*, opera, three unknown arrangers, 66
- *Joseph*, opera, arr. Sedlak, J. Weigl and three unknown arrangers, 66
- *L'Irato*, opera, arr. Ozi, 65
- *La Journée aux Aventures*, opera, arr. Gambaro and three unknown arrangers, 67
- *Le jeune Henry*, opera, three unknown arrangers, 64
- *Le Trésor supposé*, opera arr. Triebensee, 65
- *Les deux Aveugles de Tolède*, opera, two unknown arrangers, 66
- *Stratonice* (original unknown), two unknown arrangers, 67
- *Une Folie*, opera, arr. Sedlak and two unknown arrangers, 65
- Unnamed work arr. Vanderhagen, 153
- Unnamed work arr. Horix, 285

Mendelssohn, Felix, 1809–1847, *Overture zum Sommernachtstram*, arr. C. H. Meyer for Harmoniemusik, 68

Mercadante, Saverio, 1795–1870, works arranged for Harmoniemusik,
- *Anacreonte in Samo*, arr. Sedlak, 69
- *Elisa e Claudio*, opera, arr. Sedlak, Starke and one unknown arranger, 68
- *Donna Caritea*, unknown arranger, 69
- *Il Posto abbandonato*, opera, arr. Sedlak? and three unknown arrangers, 68
- Unnamed work arr. Sedlak, 150

Mering, ?, *Parthia* in C, for Harmoniemusik, 213

Meucci, Giuseppe, 18th century Swiss, *Messa* for male voices and winds, cello, 374

Meyer, ?, *Theresa et Claudio*, opera?, arr. Richter for Harmoniemusik, 69

Meyer, C. H., as arranger for Harmoniemusik, 68

Meyerbeer, Giacomo, 1791–1864, his opera arranged for Harmoniemusik, 69ff
- *Il Crociato in Egitto*, opera, unknown arranger, 69
- *Les Huguenots*, opera, arr. Sedlak and one unknown arranger, 69
- *Margherita d'Anjou*, opera, arr. Berr, 69
- *Robert-le-Diable*, opera, arr. Neithardt and one unknown arranger, 69
- Unnamed work arr. Widder, 151

Michel, F., works arr. Pleyel, for chamber winds, 103

Michl, Joseph, 1745–1815 *Polonaise* and church music for voices and winds, 214

Miller, M., 18th century, English, (12) *Military Marches*, for Harmoniemusik, 260

Milling, ?, (2) *Parthias* for Harmoniemusik, 214

Millingre, ?, French composer, *Suite pour la Harmonie*, 1794, 289

Minoja, Ambrogio, b. 1752, French, *March* and *Funeral symphony*, for band, 290

Misik, Frantisek, (19) *Partitas* for Harmoniemusik, 214ff

Mitscha, François Adam, 1746–1811, French, *Pièces d'harmonie*, 290

Moellendort, General, 297ff, 301

Molke, Graf von, *Grossen Kurfuraten Reitermarsch* for band, 334

Monckton, Robert, 1726–1782, English, (2) *Minuets*, for Harmoniemusik, 260

Moniuszko, Stanislaw, 1819–1872, *Halka*, opera, unknown arranger for Harmonie, 70

Monn, Giovanni, *Musica turchese*, 1799, for small band, 215

Monsigny, Pierre, 1729–1817, works arranged for Harmoniemusik, 70, 153, 154

Montferini, ?, 18th century Italian, (6) *Partien*, 1782, for Harmoniemusik, 366

Montorlo, Antonio, 18th c. Italian, *Che Fernando* for 2 soprani, Harmoniemusik, 366

Moravetz, ?, *Parthia*, 1799, for Harmoniemusik, 216

Morlacchi, Francesco, 1784–1841, *Tebaldo e Isolina*, opera [unknown arr for Harmonie], 70

Morris, Joseph, 18th century composer, 201, 222

Mortiz, 18th century German prince, 297

Möser, ?, *Die Berg-Schotten*, arr. Triebensee for Harmoniemusik, 70, 72

Mozart, Wolfgang Amadeus, 1756–1791, (28) original, spurious works and arrangements for Harmoniemusik, 216ff

Mozart, Wolfgang, 1756–1791 operas arranged for Harmoniemusik,
- *Cosi fan tutte*, opera, arr. Vojacek, Wendt, Legrand, Stumpf, J. Gebauer, and six unknown arrangers, 76ff
- *Der Schauspieldirektor*, opera, unknown arranger, 71
- *Die Entführung aus dem Serail*, opera, arr. Wendt and three unknown arrangers, 71
- *Die Zauberflöte*, opera, arr. Stumpf, Oswald, Wendt, Haydenreich, Hiebesch, Feldmayer, Sartorus, Rosiniack, Göpfert, and eleven unknown arrangers, 79ff
- *Don Giovanni*, opera, arr. Triebensee, Nowatny, Osswald, Wendt, Rosiniack, Stumpf, Schacht, Ehrenfried, Fuchs, Vanderhagen and ten unknown arrangers, 73ff

Idomeneo, opera, unknown arranger, 70, 83
La Clemenza di Tito, opera, arr. Fuchs, Seyfried, Triebensee, Krechtler, Sartorus, Schmitt, Stumpf, Hammerl and eleven unknown arrangers, 77ff, 83
Le Nozze di Figaro, opera, arr. Wendt, Rosiniack, Nowotny, Sartorus, Vogel, Vanderhagen, Hammerl, Purebl and seven unknown arrangers, 30, 72
Mozartscher Opern (unidentified), arr. Fleischmann, 82
Unnamed works arr. Triebensee, 150, 152
Unnamed work arr. Widder, 151
Unnamed work arr. Courtin, 154
Mozart, instrumental works arranged for Harmoniemusik,
  Sonate, K.300i/331, unknown arranger, 84
  Mozart, *Symphony,* K.425, arr. Triebensee, 84
  Mozart, *Symphony,* K.543, arr. Triebensee, 84
  Mozart, *Sinfonie en harmonie* (K.297/300a), arr. Göpfert, 84
  Mozart, *Quintet,* K.386c/407, unknown arranger, 83
  Harmoniemusik (3 Quartets), arr. Hermstedt for Harmoiemusik, 83
  VI Marches pour harmonie, arr. Göpfert, 83
  Grande Serenade tirées des oeuvres de Mozart, arr. Stumpf, 83
  Harmonie, Nr. 1, arr. Göpfert, 83
  Pièces d'harmonie, arr. Göpfert, 82, 83
  Douze nouvelles suites d'harmonie, arr. Gebauer, 83
Unidentified works attributed to Mozart, 70, 201, 222, 266
Müller, August, 1767–1817, *Cantatine zu Familienfesten*, voices, Harmonie, 334
Müller, Wenzel, 1767–1835, Bohemian composer, works arranged for Harmoniemusik,
  Betrüg durch Aberglänten, unknown arranger, 87
  Das Neusonntagsknd, opera, arr. Schmitt and five unknown arrangers, 85
  Der Alte Uiberall u. N., unknown arranger, 87
  Die Jungfrauen, opera, two unknown arrangers, 86
  Die Schwestern von Prag, opera, arr. Wanerzovsky and two unknown arrangers, 86
  Kaspar der Fagottist, opera, arr. Sartorus, Schmitt and six unknown arrangers, 85
  Das Sonnenfest der Braminen, arr. Triebensee and two unknown arrangers, 84
  Pizzichi, arr. Sartorius, 87
  Unnamed works, unknown arranger, 224
Müller, *Tiroller Vastell*, 6 movements arr. an unknown arranger for Harmonie, 86
Mülling, ?, *Parthia* in B♭ for Harmoniemusik, 224
Myslivecek, Josef, 1737–1781 (3) *Partitas* for Harmoniemusik, 224ff

N

Napoleon, 183, 276, 290, 298
Nasolini, Sebastiano, 1768–1806, *Sesostri*, unknown arranger for Harmonie, 87
Naumann, Johann, 1741–1801, (8) *Marches*, music for voices and band, 334
Naumann, Johann Gottlieb, 1741–1801, works arranged for Harmoniemusik, 87
Necchi, Francesco, 18th century Swiss, church music for voices and winds, 374
Neithardt, as arranger for Harmoniemusik, 69, 133
Neubuer, Franz Christoph, 1760–1795, (23) *Partitas* for Harmoniemusik, 224ff
Neuhauser, ?, *Marcia Turcica*, 1797, for small band, 225
Neumann, Anton, 1740–1776, (7) *Partitas* for Harmoniemusik, 225
Niccolini, Giuseppe, 1763–1842, works arranged for Harmoniemusik, 87, 88
Nopitsch, Christoph, 1758–1824, *Ariette*, 1790, voices and winds, 334
Nowatny, as arranger for Harmoniemusik, 72ff, 74
Nudera, Vojtech, *Parthia* for Harmoniemusik, 226

O

Oliver, J. A., 18th century French composer (14) *divertissements militaries*, 1792, 260
Ordonez, Carlo, 1734–1786, *Octet* for Harmonie and *Partitta Turc* for small band, 226
Osswald, as arranger for Harmoniemusik, 74, 80, 109, 157
Oswald, James, 1711–1768, English, (57) military marches, ca. 1765, 260
Ozi, Etienne, 1754–1813, French composer, (32) *Suites* for Harmoniemusik, 3 *Marches*, a *Hymn* for voices and Harmoniemusik, 290ff
Ozi, as arranger for Harmoniemusik, 29, 65, 153, 159

P

Pachta, ?, *Sinfonia*, ca. 1780 for Harmoniemusik, 335
Pachty, Jana, Prag, Collection. (35) *Partitas* from the estate of Jana Pachty, Prag, for Harmonie, 167ff
Pacini, Giovanni, 1796–1867, works arranged for Harmoniemusik, 88, 150
Paer, Ferdinando, 1771–1839, Italian, works arranged for Harmoniemmusik,
  Achille, opera, arr. Sedlak, Buchnal, Fuchs and six unknown arrangers, 91
  Agnesse di Fitz-Henry, opera, arr. Gambaro and Lachnith, 93
  Camilla, opera, arr. Wendt, Stumpf and three unknown arrangers, 90
  Cantate per Il Natale, unknown arranger, 94
  Der lustige Schuster, opera?, arr. Stumpf, 94
  Die Wanderuten Komedianten, unknown arranger, 94
  L'Intrigo amoroso, opera, arr. Sedlak and two unknown arrangers, 89
  Il Morto vivo, opera, arr. Triebensee, Stumpf, 90

Il Principe di Taranto, opera, arranged Sedlak and one unknown arranger, 89

La Virtù al Cimento, opera, arr. Fuchs, C. Ahl and two unknown arrangers, 89

Le Maître de Chapelle, opera, unknown arranger, 94

Léonora, opera, arr. Barth, 92

Numa Pompillo, opera, arr. Wendt and three unknown arrangers, 93

Oratorio del Passione, unknown arranger, 94

Sargino, opera, arr. Triebensee, Sedlak and two unknown arrangers, 92

Sofonisba, opera, arr. Triebensee, 92

Tarsino, (original unidentified), unknown arranger, 94

Una in bene et en male, opera, arr. Fuchs and two arrangers, 92

Pièces d'Harmonie, arr. Barth, 94

Unnamed works arr. Triebensee, 152

Unidentified *Duetto*, unknown arranger for Harmoniemusik, 94

6 *Pièces d'Harmonie*, unknown arranger for Harmoniemusik, 94

6 *Walser*, arr. Vanderhagen and one unknown arranger, 95

Paisiello, Giovanni, 1740–1816, (16) *Divertimenti*, 3 *Marches*, Harmonie, 367

Paisiello, Giovanni, 1740–1816, works arranged for Harmoniemusik,

Gli Astrologi immaginari, arr. Wendt and three unknown arrangers, 96

Il Barbiere di Siviglia, three unknown arrangers, 97

Il Re Teodoro in Venezia, opera, unknown arranger, 97

L'Amor contrastato (known as *La Molinara*), arr. Wendt, Stumpf and seven unknown arrangers, 99

Didone abbandonata, opera, unknown arranger, 100

L'Olimpiade, opera, arr. Witt, 98

La Cantadina di Spinto, opera, arr. Wendt, 100

La finta Amante, opera, arr. Wendt and two unknown arrangers, 96

La Frascatana, opera, arr. Wendt, Satorus and five unknown arrangers, 95

La Gare generosa, opera, arr. three unknown arrangers, 98

La Nitteti, opera, unknown arranger, 96

La Passione di Gesù Cristo, oratorio, unknown arranger, 97

La Serva Padrona, opera, unknown arranger, 97

Le due Contesse, opera, unknown arranger, 96

Le finte Contessa, unknown arranger, 95

Nina, opera, arr. Fuchs, Luigi Gianella, Wendt and one unknown arranger, 100, 154, 278

Noces de Dorine, arr. Fuchs, , 100

Proserpine, opera, arr. Fuchs, 100

Unnamed work arr. Beinet, 153

Unnamed work arr. Vanderhagen, 153

Unnamed work arr. Ozi, 153

Unnamed work, unknown arranger, 101

Unnamed work arr. Fuchs, 61

Palma, Silvestro, 1762–1834, works arranged for Harmoniemusik, 11, 101, 155

Paluselli, Stefan, 1748–1805, church music for voices and winds, *Partiten*, 367

Panizza, Giovanni, *Sextet* for Harmoniemusik and flute, 226

Panoitschka, ?, 18th century German, *Parthia* for Harmoniemusik, 355

Parzízek, Alexis, b. 1748, Polish, *Nocturne* for winds, 369

Pavesi, Stefano, 1779–1850, *Ser Mercantonio*, arr. Sedlak for Harmoniemusik, 101

Payer, unnamed work arr. Sedlak for Harmoniemusik, 150

Pensel, unnamed work arr. Sedlak for Harmoniemusik, 150

Percival, John, English, *Bristol Volunteer March*, 1799, for Harmoniemusik, 261

Perschl, as copyist, for Sedlak's Harmoniemusik arrangements, 5, 8, 9, 31, 34, 69, 104

Persuis, Louis, 1769–1819, his operas arranged for Harmoniemusik,

Estelle, opera, arr. Fuchs, 102

Nina, ballet, arr. Sedlak and one unknown arranger, 102

Der Zauberschlaf, [composer in question], arr. Starke and Sedlak, 154

Pfeilstücker, Nicolas, 18th century German, (3) *Walzer* for military band, 355

Philidor, *12e suite des amusements militaries contenant une choix d'ariettes …*, arr. Vanderhagen for Harmoniemusik, 102

Philidor, unnamed work arr. Ozi, 153

Philidor, François André Danican, 1726–1795, *Ernelinde Princesse de Norvège*, opera, arr. Röser for Harmoniemusik, 102

Philippine Charlotte (sister to Frederick the Great), *Marches* for Harmonie, 324

Piccinni, Nicola, 1728–1800 *Raffael Marcia, des löblich Ständischen Frenkorps*, 1799, for Harmoniemusik, 226

Piccinni, Nicola, 1728–1800, works arranged for Harmoniemusik,

Alessandro nell'Indie, unknown arranger for Harmoniemusik, 102

Amazilia, opera?, arr. Sedlak, 103

Didon, opera, two unknown arrangers, 102

Unnamed work arr. Vanderhagen, 154

Unnamed work arr. Ozi, 153

Unnamed work, unkown arranger, 103, 154

Pichl, Wenzel, 1741–1805, (38) *Partitas* for Harmoniemusik, 226ff

Pierre, Constant, 18th century collector of French Revolution music, 273, 281

Pirch, G., 18th century German, (7) *Märsche* for Harmoniemusik, 355
Piticchio, Francesco, (22) works for Harmoniemusik, 355, 367
Pizzini, ?, *Das Mädchen von Frascati* arr. Rosiniack for Harmoniemusik, 103
Pleyel, Ignaz, 1757–1831, (34) *Partitas* for Harmoniemusik and one work with voice, 222, 228ff, 252
Pleyel, works arranged for Harmoniemusik,
    Pièces d'harmonie, arr. Mr. Bisch, 103
    3 Quartets, arr. F. Michel for Harmonie, 103
    Quintet in Eb, arr. F. Michel, 103
    Sonata for clavier, arr. Triebensee, 103
    Suite de morceaux, arr. Bisch, 103
    Unnamed work arr. Vanderhagen, 153
    Unnamed work arr. Triebensee, 152
    Unnamed works arr. Ozi, 153
Poisel, arr., *Harmonie für die königliche Tafelmusik*, a collection of Harmonie, 151
Pokorny, F. X., 1729–1794, Czech composer, *Partita*, ca. 1760 and *Presto*, ca. 1770, for Harmoniemusik, 355
Posselt, Franz, *Partitta* for Harmoniemusik, 230
Powell, Thomas, b. 1776, *Grand March and Rondo*, military, Harmoniemusik, 261
Prachensky, Joaues, (2) *Parthias* for Harmoniemusik, (2) *Parthias* for small band, 230
Pujolas, ?, French composer, numerous military marches for small band, 290ff
Purebl as arranger of Mozart, *Le Nozze di Figaro*, opera, for Harmoniemusik, 73
Puschman, Joseph (7) *Parthias Turika*, c. 1800, for Harmoniemusik, 231ff
Puschmann, Giu., [see Mozart, K. C. 17.01], 221

R

Raimondi, Ignazio, 1737–1813, Italian, *Six grand marches*, for band, 261
Rajhrad, as arranger of Mozart, *Quintet*, K. 386c/407 for Harmoniemusik, 83
Rampini, Domenico, d. 1816, Italian, *Kyrie* for voices and 12 winds, 367
Rathgen, 'Siciliano,' unknown arranger for Harmoniemusik, 301
Rathgen, A., English, (7) *Sonatas*, (6) *Military Divertimentos* for Harmonie, 261
Ratti, Leo., as arranger for Harmoniemusik, 64
Rauscher, 18th c. composer in a Dutch collection of marches, 381
Rawlings, J. A., English, *Grand Military March*, 1780, for Harmoniemusik, 261
Reicha, Joseph, 1746–1795, (12) *Partitas* for Harmoniemusik, 355ff
Reichardt, Johann, 1752–1814, Der May, 1780, for voices and Harmoniemusik, 336

Reichelt, F. G., d. 1798, German, *Parthia* for Harmoniemusik, 337
Reid, John [General], 1721–1807, English, (12) *Marches*, (6) oboe *Solos* with Harmoniemusik, 261
Reinagle, Joseph, 1762–1825, English, (2) *Marches*, 1776, for Harmoniemusik, 262
Reissiger, Karl, 1798–1859, *Die Felsenmühle zu Estalières*, unknown arr. for Harmonie, 104ff
Rellstab, Johann, 1759–1813, German, (12) *Marches* for Harmoniemusik, 337
Relluzi, ?, *Parthia* for Harmoniemusik, 231
Ricci, Luigi, 1805–1859, works arr. Sedlak for Harmoniemusik, 104
Richter, Anton, 18th century German, (3) works for Harmonie and flute, 337
Richter, as arranger for Harmoniemusik, 55, 69
Riegel, Henri Joseph, 1741–1799, French composer, *Parthia*, for Harmonie, 291
Riegel, Henri-Jean, 1772–1852, *Les Deux Meuniers*, unknown arr. for Harmoniemusik, 104
Riepel, Josef, 1709–1782, German, *Divertimento* for Harmoniemusik, 337
Riess, 18th c. composer in a Dutch collection of marches, 360
Rigel, pére, 18th century French, *Hymn* for chorus and small band, 291
Righini, Vincenzo, 1756–1812, (7) *Partitas* and *Serenati* for Harmoniemusik, 231
Righini, Vincenzo, 1756–1812, works arranged for Harmoniemusik,
    Armida, opera, arr. Ehrenfried, 105
    Enes nel Lazio, opera, 'Trio' arr. Schmitt, 105
    Gerusalemme liberate, opera, unknown arranger, 105
    L'Incontro Inaspettato, arr. Sedlak, Triebensee and one unknown arranger, 104
    Pièces d'harmonie, arr. F. Tausch, 105
Rindl, Hermann, (2) *Prüfungslied*, 1799–1800, for SATB, Harmoniemusik, 232
Ritter, Geroge, 1748–1808, German, (4) *Parthien*, (12) *Kleine Stücke*, Harmonie, 337
Robertson, Col., 18th century officer in the British military, 256
Rode, unnamed work arr. Sedlak for Harmoniemusik, 152
Roeser, *Presto*, arr. Sedlak for Harmoniemusik, 301
Roetscher, Sen., 18th c. German, (4) *Marches* and *Lied* for Friedrick Wilhelm III, 337
Roger, ?, 18th century German, (20) *Divertissements* for Harmoniemusik, 338
Rogers, ?, 18th century English composer (24) *Divertissements* for Harmonie, 262
Rolle, Christian, ca. 1765, church music for brass ensemble, 338
Roller, ?, (13) *Partitas* for Harmoniemusik, 232

Romani, unnamed work arr. Sedlak, for Harmoniemusik, 150
Romberg, Andreas, 1767–1821, *Simphonie*, arr. Walch for Harmoniemusik, 105
Rong, Wilhelm, fl. 1720, German, (7) *Marches*, 338
Rose, J. H., 18th century Scottish, (2) *Marches* for Harmoniemusik, 262
Röser, as arranger of works for Harmoniemusik, 39, 102
Röser, Johann Georg, 1740–1797, *Tantum ergo*, SATB, Harmoniemusik, 233
Röser, Valentin, 1735–1782, French composer, (56) Sets of *Divertissements militaries* and (4) *Suites* of compositions for Harmoniemusik, 291ff
Rosetti, Franz, 1750–1792, German, (49) *Partitas* for Harmoniemusik, 338ff
Rosetti, unidentified works for Harmoniemusik, 151, 327, 347
Rosiniack, as arranger for Harmoniemusik, 72, 75, 81, 97, 103, 144, 148
Rossini, Gioacchino, 1792–1868, his works arranged for Harmoniemusik,
    Almavivas, or *Il Barbier von Sevilla*, opera, arr. Sedlak, Ruzni, Osswald, Fuchs, Gambaro and three unknown arrangers, 108
    Armida, opera, arr. Starke and Fuchs, 111
    Bianca e Falliero, opera, arr. Skace, 112
    Blaubart, ballet, arr. Sedlak and Starke, 114
    Ciro in Babilonia, opera, arr. Sedlak, 106
    L'Inganno felice, arr. Starke, Legrand, Blasius and Fuchs, 106
    Die diebische Elster (original unidentified), arr. Starke, 114
    Eduardo e Cristiana, opera, arr. Fuchs, 112
    Elisabetta, Regina d'Inghilterra, arr. Sedlak and one unknown arranger, 108
    Guillaume Tell, opera, arr. Sedlak and one unknown arranger, 114
    Il Turco in Italia, opera, arr. Starke and Grégoire, 108
    L'Italiana in Algeri, opera, arr. Sedlak, Legrand, Fuchs and three unknown arrangers, 108
    La Cenerentola, opera, arr. Fuchs, 110
    La Donna del Lago, opera, arr. Grégoire and one unknown arranger, 112
    La Gazza Ladra, opera, arr. Legrand, Grégoire, Gambaro, Fuchs and one unknown arranger, 110
    La Scala di Seta, opera, unknown arranger, 106
    Le Comte Ory, opera, unknown arranger, 113
    Le Siège de Corinthe, opera, arr. Sedlak and one unknown arranger, 113
    Mosè in Egitto, opera, arr. Grégoire and three unknown arrangers, 111
    Otello, opera, arr. Starke, Gambaro, Küffner, Grégoire and three unknown arrangers, 110
    Pietro il Grando, opera, two uniknown arrangers, 114
    Ricciardo e Zoraide, opera, arr. Sedlak and one unknown arranger, 112
    Semiramide, opera, arr. Widder, Sedlak and two unknown arrangers, 4, 113
    Tancredi, opera, arr. Legrand, Sedlak, Grégoire, Gambaro, Fuchs, Rummel and four unknown arrangers, 106
    Torvaldo e Dorliska, opera, arr. Fuchs, 108
    Zelmira, opera, arr. Sedlak, Starke, 112
    Unnamed works arr. Sedlak, 150, 152
    Unnamed work arr. Starke, 152
    Unnamed work arr. Widder, 151
    Unnamed works arr. Fuchs, 61
    Unnamed work, unknown arranger, 151
    Collection de 10 Ouvertures, arranger unknown, 114
Roth, Sinforiano, ca. 1750, military marches, 368
Rouget de Lissle, Claude-Joseph, 1760–1836, *Marche des Marseillois*, arr. Gossec, 293, and Ozi, 153
Rousseau, Jean Jacques, 1712–1778, as composer, *Air pour la Musique*, for winds and percussion, 292ff
Rousseau, Jean-Jacques, 284, 286
Rouwyzer, François, 1737–1827, church music for voices and winds, 361
Rudolph, Anton, b. 1742, German, (6) *Partitas* for Harmoniemusik, 342
Rugni, as arranger of Weber, *Lorzing*, for Harmoniemusik, 133
Ruloffs, Bartholomeus, b. 1740, *Musique militaire* for Harmoniemusik, 361
Rummel, as arranger of works for Harmoniemusik, 107, 133, 150ff
Russell, W., English, *Guilford Volunteers March*, 1795, for band, 262
Ruzni, as arranger of works for Harmoniemusik, 11, 109, 128, 151, 156

S

Sacchini, Antonio, 1730–1786, works arrasnged for Harmoniemusik, 114, 153, 154
Sacher, Josef, ca. 1770, German, *Feldpartie* for Harmoniemusik, 342
Saldern, General, 18th century German, 301
Salieri, Antonio, 1750–1825, (11) *Serenades* for Harmoniemusik, (13) *Marches* for Harmoniemusik, 233
Salieri, Antonio, 1750–1825, works arranged for Harmoniemusik,
    Arbore di Diana et Azur, unknown arranger, 61
    Cesare in Farmacusa, opera, arr. two unknown arrangers, 119
    La Fiera di Venezia, opera, unknown arranger, 115
    Der Rauchfangkehrer, opera, arr. two unknown arrangers, 115
    Falstaff, opera, unknown arranger, 119

Il ricco d'un giorno, opera, arr. Wendt, 115
Il Talismano, opera, arr. Wendt, Stumpf and four unknown arrangers, 117
König von England (original unidentified), unknown arranger, 119
La Dama Pastorella or *La Cifra*, opera, arr. Wendt and three unknown arrangers, 115
La Grotta di Trofonio, opera, arr. Wendt and five unknown arrangers, 116
Palmira, Regina di Persia, opera, arr. Wendt, J. Handl and five unknown arrangers, 118
Tarare, or *Axur re d'Ormus*, opera, arr. Wendt, Stumpf, Mr. Ernest and three unknown arrangers, 116
Unnamed work arr. Triebensee, 150
Unnamed work arr. Beinet, 153
Unnamed work arr. Ozi, 153
Unnamed work, unknown arranger, 61

Salisbury, 'Marquiss,' 18th century British noble, 253
Salner, G. P., 18th century English composer, *St. Helena March*, for band, 262
Sarasin, Lukas, 1730–1802, *Quintetto* for Harmoniemusik, 374
Sarsino, ?, Duet from *Nonon*, unknown arranger for Harmoniemusik, 119
Sarti, Giuseppe, 1729–1802, as arranger of works for Harmoniemusik, 119, 120, 154
Sartorius, as arranger of works for Harmoniemusik, 27, 48, 54, 61, 62, 72, 78, 81, 85, 87, 95, 130, 144, 145, 147
Schacht, Theodor, 1748–1823, German, (22) *Partitas* for Harmoniemusik, 342ff
Schacht, as arranger for Harmoniemusik, 3, 75
Schaffner, as arranger of Catel, *Zirphile et Fleur de Myrte*, opera?, for Harmonie, 15
Schaffner, N. A., Overture to *Chasse*, arr. Gambaro for Harmoniemusik, 121
Schall, Claus, Danish composer, *Carasel Musique*, 1791, for Harmoniemusik, 249
Scheinpflug, Christian, 1722–1770, German (16) *Partiten* for Harmoniemusik, 344
Schenk, Johann, 1753–1836, *Die Weinlese*, opera, arr. Wendt for Harmoniemusik, 121
Schetky, Johann, 1740–1820, Scottish, (24) *Airs & Strathspeys* for band, 262
Schmidbauer, ?, (2) *Partitas* for Harmoniemusik, 234
Schmidt, ?, 18th century German, *Parthia* for Harmoniemusik, 344
Schmitt, ?, 18th century German, *Scherzo* for Harmoniemusik and flute, 344
Schmitt, as arranger for Harmoniemusik, 25, 54, 85, 87, 105, 127, 131
Schmittbaur, Joseph, 1718–1809, (8) works for Harmonie or band, 344
Schneider, ?, 18th century German, (18) *Harmonien* with 2 flutes, 344ff

Schoeps, ?, 18th century German, *Partiten*, for Harmoniemusik, 345
Scholl, Nickolaus, as arranger of *L'Arbore di Diana*, overture for Harmonie, 12
Schön, ?, 18th century German, (2) *Parthias*, for Harmoniemusik, 345
Schön, ?, 18th century Swiss, *Parthias* for Harmoniemusik, 374
Schöringer, Carl, *Parthia* for Harmoniemusik, 234
Schroeder, H. B., English (7) *Marches*, c. 1795, for Harmoniemusik, 263ff
Schubert, Ferdinand, as arranger of Mozart *Alma dei*, K. 277, 223
Schubert, Joseph, 1757–1837, German, many works for Harmoniemusik, 345ff
Schuester, ?, (9) *Parthias* for Harmoniemusik, 234
Schulz, as arranger of works for Harmoniemusik, 124, 131
Schwartz, an *Adagio* in a Swiss manuscript, 371
Schwarz, ?, (11) *Märsche für die ganze Türkische Musik oder Harmonie*, 235
Schwarz, *Adagio*, unknown arranger for Harmoniemusik, 151
Schwegler, Johann, 18th century German, (4) *Quartuors* for flutes, horns, 345
Schwencke, C. F. G., as arranger of Mozart K.361, 219
Sedlak, Wenzel, 1767–1835, as arranger of works for Harmoniemusik, 4, 5, 6, 8, 9, 12, 16, 18, 23, 25, 31, 34, 35, 42, 43, 47, 48, 49, 52, 53, 58, 63, 65, 66, 68, 69, 88, 89, 91, 92, 101, 102, 103, 104, 106, 107, 108, 109, 112, 113, 114, 118, 128, 129, 132, 142, 146, 147, 148, 150, 152, 154
Seyfried, Ignaz Ritter von, 1776–1841, works arranged for Harmoniemusik,
    Marpissa, opera, arr. Triebensee, 122
    Mitternacht, opera, arr. Triebensee, 122
    Saul, Konig in Israel, unknown arranger, 121
    Alamar der Mare, arr. Triebensee, 122
    Richard Löwenherz (original unknown), unknown arranger, 122
    Unknown work, arr. Triebensee, 152
Seyfried, as arranger of Mozart, *La Clemenza di Tito*, opera, for Harmoniemusik, 77
Sigl, Georg, 18th century German, (11) *Partitas, Messe* with Harmoniemusik, 345ff
Simon, ?, (4) *Partitas* for Harmoniemusik, 235
Simonet, as arranger of Solié, *Le jockey*, opera, for Harmoniemusik, 123
Simonetti, ?, ca. 1767, *Dresdner Menuetten* for band, 346
Simoni, arr., Kunzen, *Das Fest der Winzer*, opera, for Harmoniemusik, 56
Sixt, Johann, 1757–1797 (6) *Allemandes* for Harmoniemusik, 346
Skacel, as arranger of Rossini, *Bianca e Falliero*, opera, for Harmoniemusik, 117
Smart, Timothy, 18th century English, (24) *Select military pieces for Harmonie*, 264

Sòlere, Etienne, 1753–1817, *Overture* for small band, 293
Seyfried, arr., Mozart, *La Clemenza di Tito*, opera, for Harmoniemusik, 77
Solié, Jean Pierre, 1755–1812, *March* for small band, 293
Solié, works arranged for Harmoniemusik, 123
Sommer, Johann, ca. 1780, *Pieze* for Harmonie, 2 violas (?), 347
Spencer, Capt. John, English, *Oxfordshire Militia March*, 1793, for band, 264
Spergen, ?, *Parthia*, 1799, for Harmoniemusik, 235
Sperger, Johann, 18th century German, (77) *Partitas* for Harmoniemusik, 347ff
Spiller, ?, 18th century German, *Partia* for Harmoniemusik, 352
Spohr, Ludwig, 1784–1859, works arranged for Harmoniemusik, 123, 124
Spontini, Gaspare, 1774–1851, works arranged for Harmoniemusik,
 Dieux Rivaux, unknown arranger, 125
 Fernand Cortez, opera, unknown arranger, 125
 Julie, opera, unknown arranger, 124
  Milton, opera, unknown arranger, 124
 La Vestale, opera, arr. Triebensee, Etienne Gebauer and nine unknown arrangers, 124
Stadler, Anton, 1753–1812, *Partitas* for Harmoniemusik, 235
Stadler, Josef de Wolfersgrun, (12) *Tadeschi pour Musique d'Harmonie*, 235
Stadler, Maximilian, 1748–1833, *Hoch du mein Vaterland*, chorus and Harmoniemusik, 236
Stamitz, Karl, 1745–1801 c. (77) works for Harmoniemusik, 352ff
Starke, as arranger for Harmoniemusik, 5, 43, 44, 49, 106, 108, 110, 111, 112, 114, 138, 152, 154, 159
Starzer, Josef, 1726–1787, (5) compositions for Harmoniemusik, 236
Starzer, Josef, 1726–1787, *Adelheid von Ponthieu*, ballet, two unknown arrangers for Harmoniemusik, 126
Stefani Jean l'aine, French, 1746–1829 (6) *Parties* for Harmoniemusik, 369
Steffani, ?, (6) *Parthien*, op. 1, for Harmoniemusik, 236
Steibelt, Daniel, 1765–1823, works arranged for Harmoniemusik,
 Bataille d'Austerlitz, arr. Fuchs, 126
 Cinquième pot-pourry, arr. Fuchs, 126
 Combat naval (originally for piano), arr. Göpfert, 126
 La Journée d'Ulm, unknown arranger, 126
 March and trio, arr. Triebensee, 126
Steinfeld, Albert, 18th century German, (6) *Quartets* for Harmoniemusik, 353
Stengel, F. von, 18th century German, untitled work for Harmoniemusik, 353
Stepan, Josef, 1726–1797, (9) works for Harmoniemusik, 236ff

Stevens, Richard, 1757–1837, English, (2) *Marches* for band, 264ff
Storace, Stephen, 1763–1796, English, music for voices and 10 winds, 264
Storace, Stephen, 1763–1796, works arranged for Harmoniemusik, 127, 252
Storace, collaborator in a *Divertimento* with Pleyel, Attwood, 252
Storaro, ?, 18th century Italian, *March* for 11 winds and organ, 368
Stranensky, ?, ca. 1800, German, (6) *Partitas* for Harmoniemusik, 353
Strauss, ?, *Krapfenwaldelwalzer*, unknown arranger for Harmoniemusik, 127
Strauss, composer in a collection of Harmoniemusik by an unknown arranger, 152
Strauss, Johann, arr. Widder for Harmoniemusik, 151
Strouhal, Padre Bernard, (18) *Parthias* for Harmoniemusik, 237ff
Stückel, as arranger of Weigl, *Richard Löwenherz*, ballet, for Harmoniemusik, 139
Stumpf, Johann Christian, d. 1801, (2) *Partitas* for Harmoniemusik, 353ff
Stumpf, as arranger for Harmoniemusik, 29, 61, 75, 76ff, 78ff, 80ff, 90, 91, 94, 99ff, 117, 118, 135, 144, 148, 159
Süssmayer, Franz Xaver, 1766–1803, (3) works for Harmoniemusik, 238
Süssmayr, Franz Xaver, 1766–1803, works arranged for Harmoniemusik,
 Der Retter in Gefahr, cantata, arr. Sedlak, 128
 Der Spiegel von Arkadien, arr. Triebensee, Wendt, Schmitt and four unknown arrangers, 127
 Soliman der Zweite, opera, arr. Triebensee for Harmoniemusik, 128
Sussmayr, as arranger of Kürzinger, *Robert und Caliste*, ballet, for Harmoniemusik, 56

T

Taaffe, Den., Capt., of regiment at St. Helena, 262
Tag, Christian, 1735–1811, German, church music for voices and winds, 353
Taglioni, Marie, 1804–1884, Swedish ballerina, 'Pas de Deux,' arr. Triebensee for Harmoniemusik, 128
Tarchi, Angelo, 1760–1814, works arranged for Harmoniemusik, 13, 128, 129, 152, 153
Tausch, F., as arranger of Righini, *Pièces d'harmonie*, for Harmoniemusik, 105
Tausch, Franz, 1762–1817, (17) *Marches*, (14) chamber works for Harmonie, 354
Tebay, J., English, *The Bath Volunteer's March*, ca. 1785, for Harmoniemusik, 264
Thern, Carl, *Wachtparade* for Harmoniemusik, 238
Tipsly, unnamed work arr. Triebensee for Harmoniemusik, 152

Titl, Anton, 1809–1882, *Der Zauberschleier*, arr. Wajacek, for Harmoniemusik, 129
Toeschi, Carlo, 1724–1788, *La Chasse royale* for Harmoniemusik, 354
Toja, Giovanni, 18th century Italian, *Serenata* for Harmonie and flute, 368
Touchemoulin, Joseph, 1727–1801, *Divertimento* for Harmonie, 2 violas (?), 354
Triebensee, as arranger for Harmoniemusik, 6, 10, 12, 16, 17, 22, 30, 32, 33, 34, 36, 38, 39, 43, 44, 46, 47, 48, 49, 51, 53, 54, 55, 56, 57, 59, 62, 63, 65, 67, 68, 70, 74, 77, 78, 84, 87, 88, 90, 92ff, 103, 104, 122, 124, 126, 127, 128, 129, 130, 131, 136, 137, 143, 144, 145, 146, 147, 148, 150, 151, 152, 156, 157
Trietto, unnamed work arr. Ozi for Hasrmoniemusik, 153
Troop, A., 18th century Scottish (3) *Scotch Marches* for band, 264
Trost, J. G. M., 18th century German, *Parthia* for Harmoniemusik, 354

U

Ulbrecht, Franz, 18th century German, (5) Sätze for Harmoniemusik, 354
Umlauf, Ignaz, 1746–1796 original Harmonie within an opera, 239
Umlauff, Ignaz, 1746–1796, *Die schöne Schusterin*, opera, 1799, unknown arranger for 2 horns, 3 basset horns, 129
Umlauff, Michael, 1781–1842, works arranged for Harmoniemusik,
    Aeneas in Carthago, ballet, arr. Wendt, 129
    Das eigensinnige Landmädchen, ballet, arr. Triebensee and one unknown arranger, 129
    Don Quixotte (original unknown), arr. Triebensee, 129
    Paul et Rosetta, ballet, arr. Sedlak, 129
Ungelenk, ?, 18th century German, (4) *Partitas* for Harmoniemusik, 354
Urbridge, Earl of, 18th century English noble, 258

V

Vandergahen, Armand, 1753–1822, as arranger for Harmoniemusik, 9, 20, 21, 24, 40, 47, 49, 50, 58, 70, 73, 75, 95, 102, 153, 157, 159, 160,
Vanerovsky, ?, (2) *Parthias* and (2) works for voices and Harmoniemusik, 239
Vanhal, Johann Baptist, 1739–1813, (18) works and a *Hymn* for voices and winds, 239ff
Vesque von Püttlingen, Johann, 1803–1883, *Johanna d'Arc*, for Harmnonie, 130
Viala, political hero of the French Revolution, 271
Vignali, Gabriele, 18th century Italian, church music with winds, canzoni, 368ff
Viotti, unnamed work arr. Ozi for Harmoniemusik, 153

Vogel, unnamed work arr. Beinet for Harmoniemusik, 153
Vogel, Johann Christoph, 1756–1788, *Démophon*, opera, arr. Fuchs, Triebensee and three unknown arrangers for Harmoniemusik, 130ff
Vogel, Kajetan, as arranger of Mozart, *Le Nozze di Figaro*, opera, for Harmoniemusik, 72
Vogel, Pater Cajetan, 1750–1794, *Démophon Overture* for Harmoniemusik, 240
Vogler, Georg Abbé, 1749–1814, church works for voices and winds, 355
Vogler, Georg Joseph, 1749–1814, *Castore e Polluca*, arr. Triebensee for Harmoniemusik, 130
Vojácek, as arranger of Mozart, *Cosi fan tutte*, opera, for Harmoniemusik, 76
Voltaire, 282

W

Wagner, Carl, 1772–1822, *March* for trumpets, c. 1790, 355
Wagner, Jakob Karl, 1772–1822, ‚Liebe und Freundschaft,' arr. Sartorius for Harmoniemusik, 130
Wajacek, as arranger of Titl, 1809–1882, *Der Zauberschleier*, for Harmoniemusik, 129
Walch, as arranger of Romberg, *Simphonie*, for Harmoniemusik, 105
Waldek, Prince, 152
Wallentin, as arranger of Lortzing, *Czaar und Zimmermann*, opera, for Harmoniemusik, 59
Wallerstein, Prince, 18th century German, 356ff
Wallis, 18th century Prince of England, 302
Wallner, Vinzenz, 1769–1799, a collection of Hamoniemusik, 240
Walter, G., ca. 1797, (7) *Partitas* for Harmoniemusik, 355
Wanerzovsky, as arranger of Müller, *Die Schwestern von Prag*, opera, for Harmonie, 86
Wanhall, composer in an anonymous collection for Harmoniemusic, 151
Webb, William, Isle of Wight Vol. march, 264
Weber, unnamed work arranged for Harmoniemusik, 133
Weber, ?, 18th century German, (11) *Partien* for Harmoniemusik, 355
Weber, 'Lützows wilde Jagd, und Schwerdtlied,' arr. Neithardt for brass, 133
Weber, Bernhard Anselm, 1766–1821, *Die Jungfrau v. Orleans*, arr. Triebensee, Schulz and one unknown arranger, 131
Weber, Bernhard Anselm, 1766–1842, works arr. Schulz for Harmoniemusik, 124
Weber, Carl Maria von, 1786–1826, works arranged for Harmoniemusik,
    Euryanthe, opera, three unknown arrangers, 132
    Der Freischütz, opera, arr. Flachs, Sedlak, Küffner, Brod and four unknown arrangers, 131
    Johanna, opera, arr. Schmitt, 131

Lorzing, arr. Rugni, 133
Jubilaire, overture, arr. Rummel, 133
Oberon, opera, arr. Weller (for band), 133
Preciosa, opera, unknown arranger for Harmoniemusik, 131
Unnamed work, unknown arranger for Harmoniemusik, 195
Unnamed work arr. Rummel for Harmoniemusik, 150ff
Unnamed work arr. Widder for Harmoniemusik, 151
Weideman, Charles, d. 1782, English, *Old Buffs March*, c. 1760, for Harmonie, 265
Weigart, Francesco, (8) *Partitas* for Harmoniemusik, 240ff
Weigh, John, 18th century, English (2) *Marches* for Harmoniemusik, 265
Weigl, Joseph, 1740–1820 (3) original works for Harmoniemusik, 241
Weigl, Joseph, 1766–1846, works arranged for Harmoniemusik,
   Adrian von Ostade, opera, unknown arranger, 136
   Alceste, ballet, arr. Wendt and two unknown arrangers, 142
   Alcina, ballet, arr. Wendt, Buchal and two unknown arrangers, 141
   Alonzo e Cora, ballet, two unknown arrangers, 141
   Clothilde, Prinzessin von Salerno, ballet, arr. Havel and one unknown arranger, 141
   Ginevra di Scozia (original unknown), unknown arranger, 144
   Giulietta e Pierotto, opera, arr. Wendt, 134
   Insel Christina, ballet, unknown arranger for Harmoniemusik, 140
   I solitari, opera, arr. Wendt, 134
   Il pazzo per forza, opera, arr. Wendt and two unknown arrangers, 134
   Das Sinnbild des menschlichen Lebens, ballet, arr. Wendt and three unknown arrangers, 138
   Das Waisenhus, opera, arr. four unknown arrangers, 136
   Der Raub der Helena, ballet arr. Wendt and four unknown arrangers, 140
   Die Atheniensische Tänzerin, ballet, arr. Paul Maschek, Sedlak and one unknown arranger, 142
   Die Reue des Pygmalion, ballet, arr. Wendt and four unknown arrangers, 138
   Die Schweizerfamilie, opera, arr. Triebensee, Ahl, Barth and ten unknown arrangers 136
   Die Spanier auf der Insel Christina, ballet, two unknown arrangers, 142
   Die Uniform, opera, unknown arranger, 135
   Das Petermännchen, opera, unknown arranger, 133
   Kaiser Hadrian, opera, arr. Triebensee and five unknown arrangers, 135
   L'Amor marinaro, opera, arr. Stumpf and 3 unknown arrangers for Harmoniemusik, 135
   La Principessa d'Amalfi, opera, arr. Wendt and one unknown arranger, 134
   Nachtigall und Rabe, opera, arr. Starke, 138
   Palmira (original unknown), unknown arranger, 143
   Piolla, ballet (with movements from other operas), unknown arranger, 143
   Richard Löwenherz, ballet, arr. Wendt, Stückel, Buchal and eight unknown arrangers, 139
   Die Verbrennung und Zestörung der Stadt Troja, arr. two unknown arrangers, 140ff
   Unnamed work arr. Triebensee, 152
   Unnamed work arr. Ruzni, 151
   10 *Arien* (original unidentified), unknown arranger, 144
Weigl, J., as arranger of Méhul, *Joseph*, opera, for Harmoniemusik, 66
Weigl, Thadeus, fl. 1797–1804, works arranged for Harmoniemusik,
   Bachus et Ariadne, ballet, arr. Triebensee, Wendt and one unknown arranger, 143
   Die Huldigung, ballet, arr. Wendt, 143
   Die Vermählung im Keller, ballet, arr. four unknown arrangers, 143
Weigl, ?, *Tiroler Jahrmarkt*, ballet, unknown arranger for Harmoniemusik, 143
Weigl, ?, *Vesta's Feuer*, opera, unknown arranger for Harmoniemusik, 135
Weilland, ?, ca. 1797, German, (3) *Harmonie* for Harmoniemusik, 355
Weiss, ?, *Amphion*, ballet, arr. Triebensee (one movement) for Harmoniemusik, 144
Weiss, composer in a collection of Harmoniemusik by an unknown arranger, 152
Weiss, Wenzel, 18th century German, *Marsch und Echo* for Harmoniemusik, 356
Weller, as arranger of works for Harmoniemusik or band, 5, 133ff
Wendt (Went, Vent), Johann, 1745–1809, (99) *Parthias* for Harmoniemusik, 241ff
Wendt, as arranger for Harmoniemusik, 19, 30, 32, 37, 38, 41, 42, 54, 61, 71, 72, 75, 76, 80, 90, 93, 95, 96, 97, 99, 101, 104, 115, 116, 117, 118, 120, 121, 127, 129, 134, 138, 139, 140, 141, 142, 143, 146, 155, 156, 157, 160
Wenusch, arr., *VIII Stücke aus opern und Ballets*, a collection for Harmonie, 150
Werckmeister, 18th century publisher in Orangeburg, 354
Werttig, Joseph, 18th century German, (30) *Märches*, (12) *Pièces*, Harmonie, 356
Wesley, Samuel, English, *March*, 1777, for Harmoniemusik, 265
Widder, as arranger for Harmoniemusik, 4, 113, 151
Widerkehr, J. C., 1759–1823, (10?) *Simphonie concertantes*, 6 winds & cello, 293
Wiedeman, 18th century composer, 264

Wilhelm, J., in an anonymous arrangement for Harmoniemusik, 151
Wilhelmus von Nassau, 18th century, 298
Willy, Jean, (7) *Parthias*, ca. 1766, for Harmoniemusik, 244
Wineberger, Paul, 1758–1821, German, (22) *Partitas* for Harmonie with flutes, 356ff
Winter, Peter von, 1754–1825, (6) *Parthias*, (3) works for voices and Harmoniemusik, 245
Winter, Peter von, 1754–1825, works arranged for Harmoniemusik,
    Babylone Pyramiden, opera, unknown arranger, 146
    Brüder von Stauffenberg, arr. Triebensee, 147
    Elise Graefin von Hilburg, arr. Sartorius and one unknown arranger, 147
    Helena und Paris, opera, arr.. Sartorius for Harmoniemusik, 144
    Henry IV, ballet, arr. Rosiniack, 144
    Das Labirint, opera, arr. Wendt, Triebensee, Sedlak and three unknown arrangers], 146
    Marie von Montalban, opera, arr. Sedlak, Buchnal and four unknown arrangers, 146
    Tamerlan, opera, arr. Triebensee, 147
    Das unterbrochene Opferfest, opera, arr. Stumpf, Sartorius, Triebensee and six unknown arrangers, 144ff
    Oboe Quartet, one movement, arr. Triebensee, 148
    Harmonie tirée des ses Opera, unknown arranger, 148
    Unknown work arr. Ruzni for Harmoniemusik, 151
Witt, Friedrich, 1770–1836, German, (5) *Partitas* for Harmonie with flutes, 358
Witt, as arranger of Paisiello, *L'Olimpiade*, opera, for Harmoniemusik, 98
Wivill, Zarubbabel, English, *Berkshire March*, 1793, for band, 265
Wolf, Franz, ca. 1799, German (4) works for Harmoniemusik, 358
Wölfl, Joseph, 1773–1812, (6) *Sonatas* for Harmoniemusik, 358
Worgan, James, Jr., (2) *Marches* and a *Song* with Harmoniemusik, 265
Wranitzky, Anton, 1761–1820, (12) *Marches* for Harmoniemusik, 245
Wranitzky, Paul, 1756–1808, works arranged for Harmoniemusik,
    Das Waldmädchen, ballet, arr. Sedlak, Beecke and five unknown arrangers, 148
    Oberon, König der Elfen,, arr. Rosiniack, Stumpf, 148
    Unnamed work arr. Triebensee, 150
    Unnamed work arr. Wenusch, 150
    Unnamed works, unknown arranger, 246
Wratni, J., as arranger of *Messano* (composer unidentified) for Harmoniemusik, 156
Wright, Thomas, 1763–1829, English, (5) *Marches* for Harmoniemusik, 265ff

Y

Yost, Michel, 1754–1786, German, *Suito* for Harmoniemusik, 359

Z

Zapf, Johann Nepomuk, *Parthia* for Harmoniemusik, 246
Zech, Markus, 1727–1770, church music for voices and winds, 374
Ziha, ?, (5) *Partittas* for Harmoniemusik, 246ff
Zimmermann, Anton, 1741–1781, (6) *Parthias* for Harmoniemusik, 247
Zingarelli, Nicola Antonio, 1752–1837, works arranged for Harmoniemusik, 149, 150, 154
Zobl, ?, 18th century German, *Partita* for Harmoniemusik, 359
Zoëdler, ?, *Parthia* for Harmoniemusik, 247
Zoncada, Giovanni, 18th century Italian, *Partita*, solo oboe, Harmoniemusik, 368
Zumsteeg, Johann, 1760–1802, German, (6) works for winds, 359
Zwing, M., 18th century German, (9) works for small band, 359

About the Author

Dr. David Whitwell is a graduate ('with distinction') of the University of Michigan and the Catholic University of America, Washington DC (PhD, Musicology, Distinguished Alumni Award, 2000) and has studied conducting with Eugene Ormandy and at the Akademie für Musik, Vienna. Prior to coming to Northridge, Dr. Whitwell participated in concerts throughout the United States and Asia as Associate First Horn in the USAF Band and Orchestra in Washington DC, and in recitals throughout South America in cooperation with the United States State Department.

At the California State University, Northridge, which is in Los Angeles, Dr. Whitwell developed the CSUN Wind Ensemble into an ensemble of international reputation, with international tours to Europe in 1981 and 1989 and to Japan in 1984. The CSUN Wind Ensemble has made professional studio recordings for BBC (London), the Köln Westdeutscher Rundfunk (Germany), NOS National Radio (The Netherlands), Zürich Radio (Switzerland), the Television Broadcasting System (Japan) as well as for the United States State Department for broadcast on its 'Voice of America' program. The CSUN Wind Ensemble's recording with the Mirecourt Trio in 1982 was named the 'Record of the Year' by The Village Voice. Composers who have guest conducted Whitwell's ensembles include Aaron Copland, Ernest Krenek, Alan Hovhaness, Morton Gould, Karel Husa, Frank Erickson and Vaclav Nelhybel.

Dr. Whitwell has been a guest professor in 100 different universities and conservatories throughout the United States and in 23 foreign countries (most recently in China, in an elite school housed in the Forbidden City). Guest conducting experiences have included the Philadelphia Orchestra, Seattle Symphony Orchestra, the Czech Radio Orchestras of Brno and Bratislava, The National Youth Orchestra of Israel, as well as resident wind ensembles in Russia, Israel, Austria, Switzerland, Germany, England, Wales, The Netherlands, Portugal, Peru, Korea, Japan, Taiwan, Canada and the United States.

He is a past president of the College Band Directors National Association, a member of the Prasidium of the International Society for the Promotion of Band Music, and was a member of the founding board of directors of the World Association for Symphonic Bands and Ensembles (WASBE). In 1964 he was made an honorary life member of Kappa Kappa Psi, a national professional music fraternity. In September, 2001, he was a delegate to the UNESCO Conference on Global Music in Tokyo. He has been knighted by sovereign organizations in France, Portugal and Scotland and has been awarded the gold medal of Kerkrade, The Netherlands, and the silver medal of Wangen, Germany, the highest honor given wind conductors in the United States, the medal of the Academy of Wind and Percussion Arts (National Band Association) and the highest honor given wind conductors in Austria, the gold medal of the Austrian Band Association. He is a member of the Hall of Fame of the California Music Educators Association.

Dr. Whitwell's publications include more than 127 articles on wind literature including publications in Music and Letters (London), the London Musical Times, the Mozart-Jahrbuch (Salzburg), and 39 books, among which is his 13-volume *History and Literature of the Wind Band and Wind Ensemble* and an 8-volume series on *Aesthetics in Music*. In addition to numerous modern editions of early wind band music his original compositions include 5 symphonies.

David Whitwell was named as one of six men who have determined the course of American bands during the second half of the 20th century, in the definitive history, *The Twentieth Century American Wind Band* (Meredith Music).

A doctoral dissertation by German Gonzales (2007, Arizona State University) is dedicated to the life and conducting career of David Whitwell through the year 1977. David Whitwell is one of nine men described by Paula A. Crider in *The Conductor's Legacy* (Chicago: GIA, 2010) as 'the legendary conductors' of the 20th century.

> 'I can't imagine the 2nd half of the 20th century—without David Whitwell and what he has given to all of the rest of us.' Frederick Fennell (1993)

www.ingramcontent.com/pod-product-compliance
Lightning Source LLC
Chambersburg PA
CBHW080533300426
44111CB00017B/2705